The Exploring Expedition to the Rocky Mountains, Oregon and California

Brevet Col. J.C. Fremont

Contents

PREFACE.	7
A REPORT OF THE EXPLORING EXPEDITION	113
TO OREGON AND NORTH CALIFORNIA, IN THE YEARS 1843-'44.	113
GOLD REGIONS OF CALIFORNIA.	376
PURITY OF CALIFORNIA GOLD DUST.	387
PHYSICAL GEOGRAPHY OF CALIFORNIA.	388
DIFFERENT ROUTES TO CALIFORNIA.	397
THE GOLD REGIONS--MISCELLANEOUS MATTER.	404

THE EXPLORING EXPEDITION TO THE ROCKY MOUNTAINS, OREGON

AND CALIFORNIA

BY

Brevet Col. J.C. Fremont

PREFACE.

No work has appeared from the American press within the past few years better calculated to interest the community at large than Colonel J.C. Fremont's Narrative of his Exploring Expedition to the Rocky Mountains, Oregon, and North California, undertaken by the orders of the United States government. Eminently qualified for the task assigned him, Colonel Fremont entered upon his duties with alacrity, and has embodied in the following pages the results of his observations. The country thus explored is daily making deeper and more abiding impressions upon the minds of the people, and information is eagerly sought in regard to its natural resources, its climate, inhabitants, productions, and adaptation for supplying the wants and providing the comforts for a dense population. The day is not far distant when that territory, hitherto so little known, will be intersected by railroads, its waters navigated, and its fertile portions peopled by an active and intelligent population. To all persons interested in the successful extension of our free institutions over this now wilderness portion of our land, this work of Fremont commends itself as a faithful and accurate statement of the present state of affairs in that country. Since the preparation of this report, Colonel Fremont has been engaged in still farther explorations by order of the government, the results of which will probably be presented to the country as soon as he shall be relieved from his present arduous and responsible station. He is now engaged in active military service in New Mexico, and has won imperishable renown by his rapid and successful subjugation of that country.

The map accompanying this edition is not the one prepared by the order of government, but it is one that can be relied upon for its accuracy.

July, 1847.

A REPORT ON AN EXPLORATION OF THE COUNTRY LYING BETWEEN THE MISSOURI RIVER AND THE ROCKY MOUNTAINS, ON THE LINE OF THE KANSAS AND GREAT PLATTE RIVERS.

* * * * *

Washington, March 1, 1843.
To Colonel J.J. Abert, **Chief of the Corps of Top. Eng.**

Sir: Agreeably to your orders to explore and report upon the country between the frontiers of Missouri and the South Pass in the Rocky Mountains, and on the line of the Kansas and Great Platte rivers, I set out from Washington city on the 2d day of May, 1842, and arrived at St. Louis by way of New York, the 22d of May, where the necessary preparations were completed, and the expedition commenced. I proceeded in a steamboat to Chouteau's landing, about four hundred miles by water from St. Louis, and near the mouth of the Kansas river, whence we proceeded twelve miles to Mr. Cyprian Chouteau's trading-house, where we completed our final arrangements for the expedition.

Bad weather, which interfered with astronomical observations, delayed us several days in the early part of June at this post, which is on the right bank of the Kansas river, about ten miles above the mouth, and six beyond the western boundary of Missouri. The sky cleared off at length and we were enabled to determine our position, in longitude 90 deg. 25' 46", and latitude 39 deg. 5' 57". The elevation above the sea is about 700 feet. Our camp, in the mean time, presented an animated and bustling scene. All were busily engaged in completing the necessary arrangements for our campaign in the wilderness, and profiting by this short stay on the verge of civilization, to provide ourselves with all the little essentials to comfort in the nomadic life we were to lead for the ensuing summer months. Gradually, however, every thing--the *materiel* of the camp--men, horses, and even mules--settled into its place; and by the 10th we were ready to depart; but, before we mount our horses, I will give a short description of the party with which I performed the service.

I had collected in the neighborhood of St. Louis twenty-one men, principally Creole and Canadian *voyageurs*, who had become familiar with prairie life in the service of the fur companies in the Indian country. Mr. Charles Preuss, native of Germany, was my assistant in the topographical part of the survey; L. Maxwell, of Kaskaskia, had been engaged as hunter, and Christopher Carson (more familiarly known, for his exploits in the mountains, as Kit Carson) was our guide. The persons engaged in St. Louis were:

Clement Lambert, J.B. L'Esperance, J.B. Lefevre, Benjamin Potra, Louis Gouin, J.B. Dumes, Basil Lajeunesse, Francois Tessier, Benjamin Cadotte, Joseph Clement, Daniel Simonds, Leonard Benoit, Michel Morly, Baptiste Bernier, Honore Ayot, Francois La Tulipe, Francis Badeau, Louis Menard, Joseph Ruelle, Moise Chardonnais, Auguste Janisse, Raphael Proue.

In addition to these, Henry Brant, son of Col. J.B. Brant, of St. Louis, a young man of nineteen years of age, and Randolph, a lively boy of twelve, son of the Hon. Thomas H. Benton, accompanied me, for the development of mind and body such an expedition would give. We were well armed and mounted, with the exception of eight men, who conducted as many carts, in which were packed our stores, with the baggage and instruments, and which were drawn by two mules. A few loose horses, and four oxen, which had been added to our stock of provisions, completed the train. We set out on the morning of the 10th, which happened to be Friday, a circumstance which our men did not fail to remember and recall during the hardships and vexations of the ensuing journey. Mr. Cyprian Chouteau, to whose kindness, during our stay at his house, we were much indebted, accompanied us several miles on our way, until we met an Indian, whom he had engaged to conduct us on the first thirty or forty miles, where he was to consign us to the ocean of prairie, which, we were told, stretched without interruption almost to the base of the Rocky Mountains.

From the belt of wood which borders the Kansas, in which we had passed several good-looking Indian farms, we suddenly emerged on the prairies, which received us at the outset with some of their striking characteristics; for here and there rode an Indian, and but a few miles distant heavy clouds of smoke were rolling before the fire. In about ten miles we reached the Santa Fe road, along which we continued for a short time, and encamped early on a small stream--having traveled about eleven miles. During our journey, it was the customary practice to encamp an hour or two before sunset, when the carts were disposed so as to form a sort of barricade around a circle some eighty yards in diameter. The tents were pitched, and the horses hobbled and turned loose to graze; and but a few minutes elapsed before the cooks of the messes, of which there were four, were busily engaged in preparing the evening meal. At nightfall, the horses, mules, and oxen were driven in and picketed,--that is, secured by a halter, of which one end was tied to a small steel-shod picket, and driven into the ground; the halter being twenty or thirty feet long, which enabled them to obtain a little food during the night. When we had reached a part of the country where such a precaution became necessary, the carts being regularly arranged for defending the camp, guard was mounted at eight o'clock, consisting of three men, who were relieved every two hours --the morning-watch being horse-guard for the day. At daybreak the camp was roused, the animals turned loose to graze, and breakfast generally over between six and seven o'clock, when we resumed our march, making regularly a halt at noon for one or two hours. Such was usually the order of the day, except when accident of country forced a variation; which, however, happened but rarely. We traveled the next day along the Santa Fe road, which we left in the afternoon, and encamped late in the evening on a small creek, called by the Indians, Mishmagwi. Just as we arrived at camp, one of the horses set off at full speed on his return, and was followed by others. Several men were sent in pursuit, and returned with the fugitives about midnight, with the exception of one man, who did not make his appearance until morning. He had lost his way in the darkness of the night, and slept on the prairie. Shortly after midnight it began to rain heavily, and, as our tents were of light and thin cloth, they offered but little obstruction to the rain: we were all well soaked, and glad when morning came. We had a rainy march on the 12th, but the weather grew fine as the day advanced. We encamped in a remarkably beautiful situation on the Kansas bluffs, which commanded a fine view of the river valley, here from four to five miles wide. The central portion was occupied by a broad belt of heavy timber, and nearer the hills the prairies were of the richest verdure. One of the oxen was killed here for food.

We reached the ford of the Kansas late in the afternoon of the 14th, where the river was two hundred and thirty yards wide, and commenced, immediately, preparations for crossing. I had expected to find the river fordable; but it had swollen by the late rains, and was sweeping by with an angry current, yellow and turbid as the Missouri. Up to this point the road we had traveled was a remarkably fine one, well beaten, and level-- the usual road of a prairie country. By our route, the ford was one hundred miles from the mouth of the Kansas river. Several mounted men led the way into the stream to swim across. The animals were driven in after them, and in a few minutes all had reached the opposite bank in safety, with the exception of the oxen, which swam some distance down the river, and, returning to the right bank, were not got over till the next morning. In the mean time, the carts had been unloaded and dismantled, and an India-rubber boat, which I had brought with me for the survey of the Platte river, placed in the water. The boat was twenty feet long and five broad, and on it were placed the body and wheels of a cart, with the load belonging to it, and three men with paddles.

The velocity of the current, and the inconvenient freight, rendering it difficult to be managed, Basil Lajeunesse, one of our best swimmers, took in his teeth a line attached to the boat, and swam ahead in order to reach a footing as soon as possible, and assist in drawing her over. In this manner six passages had been successfully made, and as many carts with their contents, and a greater portion of the party, deposited on the left bank; but night was drawing near, and, in our anxiety to have all over before the darkness closed in, I put upon the boat the remaining two carts, with their accompanying load. The man at the helm was timid on water, and in his alarm capsized the boat. Carts, barrels, boxes, and bales, were in a moment floating down the current; but all the men who were on the shore jumped into the water, without stopping to think if they could swim, and almost every thing--even heavy articles, such as guns and lead--was recovered.

Two of the men who could not swim came nigh being drowned, and all the sugar belonging to one of the messes wasted its sweets on the muddy waters; but our heaviest loss was a large bag of coffee, which contained nearly all our provision. It was a loss which none but a traveler in a strange and inhospitable country can appreciate; and often afterward, when excessive toil and long marching had overcome us with fatigue and weariness, we remembered and mourned over our loss in the Kansas. Carson and Maxwell had been much in the water yesterday, and both, in consequence, were taken ill. The former continuing so, I remained in camp. A number of Kansas Indians visited us to-day. Going up to one of the groups who were scattered among the trees, I found one sitting on the ground, among some of the men, gravely and fluently speaking French, with as much facility and as little embarrassment as any of my own party, who were nearly all of French origin.

On all sides was heard the strange language of his own people, wild, and harmonizing well with their appearance. I listened to him for some time with feelings of strange curiosity and interest. He was now apparently thirty-five years of age; and, on inquiry, I learned that he had been at St. Louis when a boy, and there had learned the French language. From one of the Indian women I obtained a fine cow and calf in exchange for a yoke of oxen. Several of them brought us vegetables, pumpkins, onions, beans, and lettuce. One of them brought butter, and from a half-breed near the river, I had the good fortune to obtain some twenty or thirty pounds of coffee. The dense timber in which we had encamped interfered with astronomical observations, and our wet and damaged stores required exposure to the sun. Accordingly, the tents were struck early the next morning, and, leaving camp at six o'clock, we moved about seven miles up the river, to a handsome, open prairie, some twenty feet above the water, where the fine grass afforded a luxurious repast to our horses.

During the day we occupied ourselves in making astronomical observations, in order to lay down the country to this place; it being our custom to keep up our map regularly in the field, which we found attended with many advantages. The men were kept busy in drying the provisions, painting the cart covers, and otherwise completing our equipage, until the afternoon, when powder was distributed to them, and they spent some hours in firing at a mark. We were now fairly in the Indian country, and it began to be time to prepare for the chances of the wilderness.

17th.--The weather yesterday had not permitted us to make the observations I was desirous to obtain here, and I therefore did not move to-day. The people continued their target firing. In the steep bank of the river here, were nests of innumerable swallows, into one of which a large prairie snake had got about half his body, and was occupied in eating the young birds. The old ones were flying about in great distress, darting at him, and vainly endeavoring to drive him off. A shot wounded him, and, being killed, he was cut open, and eighteen young swallows were found in his body. A sudden storm, that burst upon us in the afternoon, cleared away in a brilliant sunset, followed by a clear night, which enabled us to determine our position in longitude 95 deg. 38' 05", and in latitude 39 deg. 06' 40".

A party of emigrants to the Columbia river, under the charge of Dr. White, an agent of the government in Oregon Territory, were about three weeks in advance of us. They consisted of men, women, and children. There were sixty-four men, and sixteen or seventeen families. They had a considerable number of cattle, and were transporting their household furniture in large, heavy wagons. I understood that there had been much sickness among them, and that they had lost several children. One of the party who had lost his child, and whose wife was very ill, had left them about one hundred miles hence on the prairies; and as a hunter, who had accompanied them, visited our camp this evening, we availed ourselves of his return to the States to write to our friends.

The morning of the 18th was very unpleasant. A fine rain was falling, with cold wind from the north, and mists made the river hills look dark and gloomy. We left our camp at seven, journeying along the foot of the hills which border the Kansas valley, generally about three miles wide, and extremely rich. We halted for dinner, after a march of about thirteen miles, on the banks of one of the many little tributaries to the Kansas, which look like trenches in the prairie, and are usually well timbered. After crossing this stream, I rode off some miles to the left, attracted by the appearance of a cluster of huts near the mouth of the Vermilion. It was a large but deserted Kansas village, scattered in an open wood, along the margin of the stream, chosen with the customary Indian fondness for beauty of scenery. The Pawnees had attacked it in the early spring. Some of the houses were burnt, and others blackened with smoke, and weeds were already getting possession of the cleared places. Riding up the Vermilion river, I reached the ford in time to meet the carts, and, crossing, encamped on its western side. The weather continued cold, the thermometer being this evening as low as 49 deg.; but the night was sufficiently clear for astronomical observations, which placed us in longitude 96 deg. 04' 07", and latitude 39 deg. 15' 19". At sunset, the barometer was at 28.845, thermometer 64 deg..

We breakfasted the next morning at half-past five, and left our encampment early. The morning was cool, the thermometer being at 45 deg.. Quitting the river bottom, the road ran along the uplands, over a rolling country, generally in view of the Kansas from eight to twelve miles distant. Many large boulders, of a very compact sandstone, of various shades of red, some of them of four or five tons in weight, were scattered along the hills; and many beautiful plants in flower, among which the ***amorpha canescens*** was a characteristic, enlivened the green of the prairie. At the heads of the ravines I remarked, occasionally, thickets of ***saix longifolia***, the most common willow of the country. We traveled nineteen miles and pitched our tents at evening on the head-waters of a small creek, now nearly dry, but having in its bed several fine springs. The barometer indicated a considerable rise in the country--here about fourteen hundred feet above the sea--and the increased elevation appeared already to have some slight influence upon vegetation. The night was cold, with a heavy dew; the thermometer at 10 P.M. standing at 46 deg., barometer 28.483. Our position was in longitude 96 deg. 14' 49", and latitude 39 deg. 30' 40".

The morning of the 20th was fine, with a southerly breeze and a bright sky; and at seven o'clock we were on the march. The country to-day was rather more broken, rising still, and covered everywhere with fragments of silicious limestone, particularly on the summits, where they were small, and thickly strewed as pebbles on the shore of the sea. In these exposed situations grew but few plants; though, whenever the soil was good and protected from the winds, in the creek bottoms and ravines, and on the slopes, they flourished abundantly; among them the ***amorpha***, still retaining its characteristic place. We crossed, at 10 A.M. the Big Vermilion, which has a rich bottom of about one mile in breadth, one-third of which is occupied by timber. Making our usual halt at noon, after a day's march of twenty-four miles, we reached the Big Blue, and encamped on the uplands of the western side, near a small creek, where was a fine large spring of very cold water. This is a clear and handsome stream, about one hundred and twenty feet wide, running with a rapid current, through a well-timbered valley. To-day antelope were seen running over the hills, and at evening Carson brought us a fine deer. Longitude of the camp 96 deg. 32' 35", latitude 39 deg. 45' 08". Thermometer at sunset 75 deg.. A pleasant southerly breeze and fine morning had given place to a gale, with indications of bad weather; when, after a march of ten miles, we halted to noon on a small creek, where the water stood in deep pools. In the bank of the creek limestone made its appearance in a stratum about one foot thick. In the afternoon, the people seemed to suffer for want of water. The road led along a high dry ridge; dark lines of timber indicated the heads of streams in the plains below; but there was no water near, and the day was oppressive, with a hot wind, and the thermometer at 90 deg.. Along our route the *amorpha* has been in very abundant but variable bloom--in some places bending beneath the weight of purple clusters; in others without a flower. It seemed to love best the sunny slopes, with a dark soil and southern exposure. Everywhere the rose is met with, and reminds us of cultivated gardens and civilization. It is scattered over the prairies in small bouquets, and, when glittering in the dews and waving in the pleasant breeze of the early morning, is the most beautiful of the prairie flowers. The *artemisia*, absinthe, or prairie sage, as it is variously called, is increasing in size, and glittering like silver, as the southern breeze turns up its leaves to the sun. All these plants have their insect inhabitants, variously colored--taking generally the hue of the flower on which they live. The *artemisia* has its small fly accompanying it through every change of elevation and latitude; and wherever I have seen the *asclepias tuberosa*, I have always remarked, too, on the flower a large butterfly, so nearly resembling it in color as to be distinguishable at a little distance only by the motion of its wings. Traveling on, the fresh traces of the Oregon emigrants relieve a little the loneliness of the road; and to-night, after a march of twenty-two miles, we halted on a small creek which had been one of their encampments. As we advanced westward, the soil appears to be getting more sandy; and the surface rock, an erratic deposite of sand and gravel, rests here on a bed of coarse yellow and gray and very friable sandstone. Evening closed over with rain and its usual attendant hordes of mosquitoes, with which we were annoyed for the first time.

22d.--We enjoyed at breakfast this morning a luxury, very unusual in this country, in a cup of excellent coffee, with cream, from our cow. Being milked at night, cream was thus had in the morning. Our mid-day halt was at Wyeth's creek, in the bed of which were numerous boulders of dark, ferruginous sandstone, mingled with others of the red sandstone already mentioned. Here a pack of cards, lying loose on the grass, marked an encampment of our Oregon emigrants; and it was at the close of the day when we made our bivouac in the midst of some well-timbered ravines near the Little Blue, twenty-four miles from our camp of the preceding night. Crossing the next morning a number of handsome creeks, with water clear and sandy beds we reached, at 10 A.M., a very beautiful wooded stream, about thirty-five feet wide, called Sandy creek, and sometimes, as the Ottoes frequently winter there, the Otto fork. The country has become very sandy, and the plants less varied and abundant, with the exception of the *amorpha*, which rivals the grass in quantity, though not so forward as it has been found to the eastward.

At the Big Trees, where we had intended to noon, no water was to be found. The bed of the little creek was perfectly dry, and, on the adjacent sandy bottom, *cacti*, for the first time made their appearance. We made here a short delay in search of water; and, after a hard day's march of twenty-eight miles, encamped, at 5 o'clock, on the Little Blue, where our arrival made a scene of the Arabian desert. As fast as they arrived men and horses rushed into the stream, where they bathed and drank together in common enjoyment. We were now in the range of the Pawnees, who were accustomed to infest this part of the country, stealing horses from companies on their way to the mountains; and, when in sufficient force, openly attacking and plundering them, and subjecting them to various kinds of insult. For the first time, therefore, guard was mounted to-night. Our route the next morning lay up the valley, which, bordered by hills with graceful slopes, looked uncommonly green and beautiful. The stream was about fifty feet wide, and three or four deep, fringed by cotton-wood and willow, with frequent groves of oak, tenanted by flocks of turkeys. Game here, too, made its appearance in greater plenty. Elk were frequently seen on the hills, and now and then an antelope bounded across our path, or a deer broke from the groves. The road in the afternoon was over the upper prairies, several miles from the river, and we encamped at sunset on one of its small tributaries, where an abundance of prele (*equisetum*) afforded fine forage to our tired animals. We had traveled thirty-one miles. A heavy bank of black clouds in the west came on us in a storm between nine and ten, preceded by a violent wind. The rain fell in such torrents that it was difficult to breathe facing the wind; the thunder rolled incessantly, and the whole sky was tremulous with lightning--now and then illuminated by a blinding flash, succeeded by pitchy darkness. Carson had the watch from ten to midnight, and to him had been assigned our young **compagnons de voyage**, Messrs. Brant and R. Benton. This was their first night on guard, and such an introduction did not augur very auspiciously of the pleasures of the expedition. Many things conspired to render their situation uncomfortable; stories of desperate and bloody Indian fights were rife in the camp; our position was badly chosen, surrounded on all sides by timbered hollows, and occupying an area of several hundred feet, so that necessarily the guards were far apart; and now and then I could hear Randolph, as if relieved by the sound of a voice in the darkness, calling out to the sergeant of the guard, to direct his attention to some imaginary alarm; but they stood it out, and took their turn regularly afterwards.

The next morning we had a specimen of the false alarms to which all parties in these wild regions are subject. Proceeding up the valley, objects were seen on the opposite hills, which disappeared before a glass could be brought to bear upon them. A man who was a short distance in the rear, came springing up in great haste, shouting "Indians! Indians!" He had been near enough to see and count them, according to his report, and had made out twenty-seven. I immediately halted; arms were examined and put in order; the usual preparations made; and Kit Carson, springing upon one of the hunting horses, crossed the river, and galloped off into the opposite prairies, to obtain some certain intelligence of their movements.

Mounted on a fine horse, without a saddle, and scouring bare-headed over the prairies, Kit was one of the finest pictures of a horseman I have ever seen. A short time enabled him to discover that the Indian war-party of twenty-seven consisted of six elk, who had been gazing curiously at our caravan as it passed by, and were now scampering off at full speed. This was our first alarm, and its excitement broke agreeably on the monotony of the day. At our noon halt, the men were exercised at a target; and in the evening we pitched our tents at a Pawnee encampment of last July. They had apparently killed buffalo here, as many bones were lying about, and the frames where the hides had been stretched were yet standing. The road of the day had kept the valley, which is sometimes rich and well timbered, though the country generally is sandy. Mingled with the usual plants, a thistle (**carduus leucographus**) had for the last day or two made its appearance; and along the river bottom, *tradescantia* (virginica) and milk plant (***asclepias syriaca***) [Footnote: This plant is very odoriferous, and in Canada charms the traveler, especially when passing through woods in the evening. The French there eat the tender shoots in the spring, as we do asparagus. The natives make a sugar of the flowers, gathering them in the morning when they are covered with dew, and collect the cotton from their pods to fill their beds. On account of the silkiness of this cotton, Parkinson calls the plant Virginian silk.-- **Loudon's Encyclopaedia of Plants**.

The Sioux Indians of the Upper Platte eat the young pods of this plant, boiling them with the meat of the buffalo.] in considerable quantities.

Our march to-day had been twenty-one miles, and the astronomical observations gave us a chronometric longitude of 98 deg. 22' 12", and latitude 40 deg. 26' 50". We were moving forward at seven in the morning, and in about five miles reached a fork of the Blue, where the road leaves that river, and crosses over to the Platte. No water was to be found on the dividing ridge, and the casks were filled, and the animals here allowed a short repose. The road led across a high and level prairie ridge, where were but few plants, and those principally thistle, (***carduus leucographus***,) and a kind of dwarf artemisia. Antelope were seen frequently during the morning, which was very stormy. Squalls of rain, with thunder and lightning, were around us in every direction; and while we were enveloped in one of them, a flash, which seemed to scorch our eyes as it passed, struck in the prairie within a few hundred feet, sending up a column of dust.

Crossing on the way several Pawnee roads to the Arkansas, we reached, in about twenty-one miles from our halt on the Blue, what is called the coast of the Nebraska, or Platte river. This had seemed in the distance a range of high and broken hills; but on a nearer approach was found to be elevations of forty to sixty feet into which the wind had worked the sand. They were covered with the usual fine grasses of the country, and bordered the eastern side of the ridge on a breadth of about two miles. Change of soil and country appeared here to have produced some change in the vegetation. ***Cacti*** were numerous, and all the plants of the region appeared to flourish among the warm hills. Among them the ***amorpha***, in full bloom, was remarkable for its large and luxuriant purple clusters. From the foot of the coast, a distance of two miles across the level bottom brought us to our encampment on the shore of the river, about twenty miles below the head of Grand Island, which lay extended before us, covered with dense and heavy woods. From the mouth of the Kansas, according to our reckoning, we had traveled three hundred and twenty-eight miles; and the geological formation of the country we had passed over consisted of lime and sand stone, covered by the same erratic deposits of sand and gravel which forms the surface rock of the prairies between the Missouri and Mississippi rivers. Except in some occasional limestone boulders, I had met with no fossils. The elevation of the Platte valley above the sea is here about two thousand feet. The astronomical observations of the night placed us in longitude 98 deg. 45' 49", latitude 40 deg. 41' 06".

27th.--The animals were somewhat fatigued by their march of yesterday, and, after a short journey of eighteen miles along the river bottom, I encamped near the head of Grand Island, in longitude, by observation, 99 deg. 05' 24", latitude 40 deg. 39' 32". The soil was here light but rich, though in some places rather sandy; and, with the exception of scattered fringe along the bank, the timber, consisting principally of poplar, (*populus moniliefera*,) elm, and hackberry, (*celtis crassifolia*,) is confined almost entirely to the islands.

28th.--We halted to noon at an open reach of the river, which occupies rather more than a fourth of the valley, here only about four miles broad. The camp had been disposed with the usual precaution, the horses grazing at a little distance, attended by the guard, and we were all sitting quietly at our dinner on the grass, when suddenly we heard the startling cry, "Du monde!" In an instant, every man's weapon was in his hand, the horses were driven in, hobbled and picketed, and horsemen were galloping at full speed in the direction of the newcomers, screaming and yelling with the wildest excitement. "Get ready, my lads!" said the leader of the approaching party to his men, when our wild looking horsemen were discovered bearing down upon them--"nous allons attraper des coups de baguette." They proved to be a small party of fourteen, under the charge of a man named John Lee, and, with their baggage and provisions strapped to their backs, were making their way on foot to the frontier. A brief account of their fortunes will give some idea of navigation in the Nebraska. Sixty days since, they had left the mouth of Laramie's fork, some three hundred miles above, in barges laden with the furs of the American Fur Company. They started with the annual flood, and, drawing but nine inches water, hoped to make a speedy and prosperous voyage to St. Louis; but, after a lapse of forty days, found themselves only one hundred and thirty miles from their point of departure. They came down rapidly as far as Scott's bluffs, where their difficulties began. Sometimes they came upon places where the water was spread over a great extent, and here they toiled from morning until night, endeavoring to drag their boat through the sands, making only two or three miles in as many days. Sometimes they would enter an arm of the river, where there appeared a fine channel, and, after descending prosperously for eight or ten miles, would come suddenly upon dry sands, and be compelled to return, dragging their boat for days against the rapid current; and at others, they came upon places where the water lay in holes, and, getting out to float off their boat, would fall into water up to their necks, and the next moment tumble over against a sandbar. Discouraged at length, and finding the Platte growing every day more shallow, they discharged the principal part of their cargoes one hundred and thirty miles below Fort Laramie, which they secured as well as possible, and, leaving a few men to guard them, attempted to continue their voyage, laden with some light furs and their personal baggage. After fifteen or twenty days more struggling in the sands, during which they made but one hundred and forty miles, they sunk their barges, made a *cache* of their remaining furs and property in trees on the bank, and, packing on his back what each man could carry, had commenced, the day before we encountered them, their journey on foot to St. Louis. We laughed then at their forlorn and vagabond appearance, and, in our turn, a month or two afterwards, furnished the same occasion for merriment to others. Even their stock of tobacco, that *sine qua non* of a voyageur, without which the night fire is gloomy, was entirely exhausted. However, we shortened their homeward journey by a small supply from our own provision. They gave us the welcome intelligence that the buffalo were abundant some two days' march in advance, and made us a present of some choice pieces, which were a very acceptable change from our salt pork. In the interchange of news, and the renewal of old acquaintanceships, we found wherewithal to fill a busy hour; then we mounted our horses and they shouldered their packs, and we shook hands and parted. Among them, I had found an old companion on the northern prairie, a hardened and hardly served veteran of the mountains, who had been as much hacked and scarred as an old moustache of Napoleon's "old guard." He flourished in the sobriquet of La Tulipe, and his real name I never knew. Finding that he was going to the States only because his company was bound in that direction, and that he was rather more willing to return with me, I took him again into my service. We traveled this day but seventeen miles.

At our evening camp, about sunset, three figures were discovered approaching, which our glasses made out to be Indians. They proved to be Cheyennes--two men, and a boy of thirteen. About a month since, they had left their people on the south fork of the river, some three hundred miles to the westward, and a party of only four in number had been to the Pawnee villages on a horse-stealing excursion, from which they were returning unsuccessful. They were miserably mounted on wild horses from the Arkansas plains, and had no other weapons than bows and long spears; and had they been discovered by the Pawnees, could not, by any possibility, have escaped. They were mortified by their ill-success, and said the Pawnees were cowards, who shut up their horses in their lodges at night. I invited them to supper with me, and Randolph and the young Cheyenne, who had been eyeing each other suspiciously and curiously, soon became intimate friends. After supper we sat down on the grass, and I placed a sheet of paper between us, on which they traced, rudely, but with a certain degree of relative truth, the water-courses of the country which lay between us and their villages, and of which I desired to have some information. Their companions, they told us, had taken a nearer route over the hills; but they had mounted one of the summits to spy out the country, whence they had caught a glimpse of our party, and, confident of good treatment at the hands of the whites, hastened to join company. Latitude of the camp 40 deg. 39' 51".

We made the next morning sixteen miles. I remarked that the ground was covered in many places with an efflorescence of salt, and the plants were not numerous. In the bottoms were frequently seen tradescantia, and on the dry lenches were carduus, cactus, and amorpha. A high wind during the morning had increased to a violent gale from the northwest, which made our afternoon ride cold and unpleasant. We had the welcome sight of two buffaloes on one of the large islands, and encamped at a clump of timber about seven miles from our noon halt, after a day's march of twenty-two miles.

The air was keen the next morning at sunrise, the thermometer standing at 44 deg., and it was sufficiently cold to make overcoats very comfortable. A few miles brought us into the midst of the buffalo, swarming in immense numbers over the plains, where they had left scarcely a blade of grass standing. Mr. Preuss, who was sketching at a little distance in the rear, had at first noted them as large groves of timber. In the sight of such a mass of life, the traveler feels a strange emotion of grandeur. We had heard from a distance a dull and confused murmuring, and, when we came in view of their dark masses, there was not one among us who did not feel his heart beat quicker. It was the early part of the day, when the herds are feeding; and everywhere they were in motion. Here and there a huge old bull was rolling in the grass, and clouds of dust rose in the air from various parts of the bands, each the scene of some obstinate fight. Indians and buffalo make the poetry and life of the prairie, and our camp was full of their exhilaration. In place of the quiet monotony of the march, relieved only by the cracking of the whip, and an "avance donc! enfant de garce!" shouts and songs resounded from every part of the line, and our evening camp was always the commencement of a feast, which terminated only with our departure on the following morning. At any time of the night might be seen pieces of the most delicate and choicest meat, roasting ***en appolas***, on sticks around the fire, and the guard were never without company. With pleasant weather and no enemy to fear, an abundance of the most excellent meat, and no scarcity of bread or tobacco, they were enjoying the oasis of a voyageur's life. Three cows were killed to-day. Kit Carson had shot one, and was continuing the chase in the midst of another herd, when his horse fell headlong, but sprang up and joined the flying band. Though considerably hurt, he had the good fortune to break no bones; and Maxwell, who was mounted on a fleet hunter, captured the runaway after a hard chase. He was on the point of shooting him, to avoid the loss of his bridle, (a handsomely mounted Spanish one,) when he found that his horse was able to come up with him. Animals are frequently lost in this way; and it is necessary to keep close watch over them, in the vicinity of the buffalo, in the midst of which they scour off to the plains, and are rarely retaken. One of our mules took a sudden freak into his head, and joined a neighboring band to-day. As we were not in a condition to lose horses, I sent several men in pursuit, and remained in camp, in the hope of recovering him; but lost the afternoon to no purpose, as we did not see him again. Astronomical observations placed us in longitude 100 deg. 05' 47", latitude 40 deg. 49' 55"

JULY.

1st.--Along our road to-day the prairie bottom was more elevated and dry, and the river hills which border the right side of the river higher, and more broken and picturesque in the outline. The country, too, was better timbered. As we were riding quietly along the bank, a grand herd of buffalo, some seven or eight hundred in number, came crowding up from the river, where they had been to drink, and commenced crossing the plain slowly, eating as they went. The wind was favorable; the coolness of the morning invited to exercise; the ground was apparently good, and the distance across the prairie (two or three miles) gave us a fine opportunity to charge them before they could get among the river hills. It was too fine a prospect for a chase to be lost; and, halting for a few moments, the hunters were brought up and saddled, and Kit Carson, Maxwell, and I, started together. They were now somewhat less than half a mile distant, and we rode easily along until within about three hundred yards, when a sudden agitation, a wavering in the band, and a galloping to and fro of some which were scattered along the skirts, gave us the intimation that we were discovered. We started together at a hand gallop, riding steadily abreast of each other; and here the interest of the chase became so engrossingly intense, that we were sensible to nothing else. We were now closing upon them rapidly, and the front of the mass was already in rapid motion for the hills, and in a few seconds the movement had communicated itself to the whole herd.

A crowd of bulls, as usual, brought up the rear, and every now and then some of them faced about, and then dashed on after the band a short distance, and turned and looked again, as if more than half inclined to fight. In a few moments, however, during which we had been quickening our pace, the rout was universal, and we were going over the ground like a hurricane. When at about thirty yards, we gave the usual shout, (the hunter's ***pas de charge***,) and broke into the herd. We entered on the side, the mass giving way in every direction in their heedless course. Many of the bulls, less active and fleet than the cows, paying no attention to the ground, and occupied solely with the hunter, were precipitated to the earth with great force, rolling over and over with the violence of the shock, and hardly distinguishable in the dust. We separated on entering, each singling out his game.

My horse was a trained hunter, famous in the West under the name of Proveau; and, with his eyes flashing and the foam flying from his mouth, sprang on after the cow like a tiger. In a few moments he brought me alongside of her, and rising in the stirrups, I fired at the distance of a yard, the ball entering at the termination of the long hair, and passing near the heart. She fell headlong at the report of the gun; and, checking my horse, I looked around for my companions. At a little distance, Kit was on the ground, engaged in tying his horse to the horns of a cow he was preparing to cut up. Among the scattered bands, at some distance below, I caught a glimpse of Maxwell; and while I was looking, a light wreath of smoke curled away from his gun, from which I was too far to hear the report. Nearer, and between me and the hills, towards which they were directing their course, was the body of the herd; and, giving my horse the rein, we dashed after them. A thick cloud of dust hung upon their rear, which filled my mouth and eyes, and nearly smothered me. In the midst of this I could see nothing, and the buffalo were not distinguishable until within thirty feet. They crowded together more densely still as I came upon them, and rushed along in such a compact body, that I could not obtain an entrance--the horse almost leaping upon them. In a few moments the mass divided to the right and left, the horns clattering with a noise heard above every thing else, and my horse darted into the opening. Five or six bulls charged on us as we dashed along the line, but were left far behind; and, singling out a cow, I gave her my fire, but struck too high. She gave a tremendous leap, and scoured on swifter than before. I reined up my horse, and the band swept on like a torrent, and left the place quiet and clear. Our chase had led us into dangerous ground. A prairie-dog village, so thickly settled that there were three or four holes in every twenty yards square, occupied the whole bottom for nearly two miles in length. Looking around, I saw only one of the hunters, nearly out of sight, and the long, dark line of our caravan crawling along, three or four miles distant. After a march of twenty-four miles, we encamped at nightfall, one mile and a half above the lower end of Brady's Island. The breadth of this arm of the river was eight hundred and eighty yards, and the water nowhere two feet in depth. The island bears the name of a man killed on this spot some years ago. His party had encamped here, three in company, and one of the number went off to hunt, leaving Brady and his companion together. These two had frequently quarreled, and on the hunter's return he found Brady dead, and was told that he had shot himself accidentally. He was buried here on the bank; but, as usual, the wolves tore him out, and some human bones that were lying on the ground we supposed were his. Troops of wolves that were hanging on the skirts of the buffalo, kept up an uninterrupted howling during the night, venturing almost into camp. In the morning, they were sitting at a short distance, barking, and impatiently waiting our departure, to fall upon the bones.

2d.--The morning was cool and smoky. Our road led closer to the hills, which here increased in elevation, presenting an outline of conical peaks three hundred to five hundred feet high. Some timber, apparently pine, grows in the ravines, and streaks of clay or sand whiten their slopes. We crossed, during the morning, a number of hollows, timbered principally with box, elder, (*acer negundo*,) poplar, and elm. Brady's Island is well wooded, and all the river along which our road led to-day, may, in general, be called tolerably well timbered. We passed near the encampment of the Oregon emigrants, where they appeared to have reposed several days. A variety of household articles were scattered about, and they had probably disburdened themselves here of many things not absolutely necessary. I had left the usual road before the mid-day halt, and in the afternoon, having sent several men in advance to reconnoitre, marched directly for the mouth of the South fork. On our arrival, the horsemen were sent in and scattered about the river to search for the best fording- places, and the carts followed immediately. The stream is here divided by an island into two channels. The southern is four hundred and fifty feet wide, having eighteen or twenty inches water in the deepest places. With the exception of a few dry bars, the bed of the river is generally quicksands, in which the carts began to sink rapidly so soon as the mules halted, so that it was necessary to keep them constantly in motion.

The northern channel, two thousand two hundred and fifty feet wide, was somewhat deeper, having frequently three feet water in the numerous small channels, with a bed of coarse gravel. The whole breadth of the Nebraska, immediately below the junction, is five thousand three hundred and fifty feet. All our equipage had reached the left bank safely at six o'clock, having to-day made twenty miles. We encamped at the point of land immediately at the junction of the North and South forks. Between the streams is a low rich prairie extending from their confluence eighteen miles westwardly to the bordering hills, where it is five and a half miles wide. It is covered with a luxuriant growth of grass, and along the banks is a slight and scattered fringe of cottonwood and willow. In the buffalo- trails and wallows, I remarked saline efflorescences, to which a rapid evaporation in the great heat of the sun probably contributes, as the soil is entirely unprotected by timber. In the vicinity of these places there was a bluish grass, which the cattle refuse to eat, called by the voyageurs "herbe salee," (salt grass.) The latitude of the junction is 41 deg. 04' 47", and longitude, by chronometer and lunar distances, 100 deg. 49' 43". The elevation above the sea is about two thousand seven hundred feet. The hunters came in with a fat cow; and, as we had labored hard, we enjoyed well a supper of roasted ribs and boudins, the chef d'oeuvre of a prairie cook. Mosquitoes thronged about us this evening; but, by ten o'clock, when the thermometer had fallen to 47 deg., they had all disappeared.

3d.--As this was to be a point in our homeward journey, I made a cache (a term used in all this country for what is hidden in the ground) of a barrel of pork. It was impossible to conceal such a proceeding from the sharp eyes of our Cheyenne companions, and I therefore told them to go and see what it was they were burying. They would otherwise have not failed to return and destroy our cache in expectation of some rich booty; but pork they dislike and never eat. We left our camp at nine, continuing up the South fork, the prairie-bottom affording us a fair road; but in the long grass we roused myriads of mosquitoes and flies, from which our horses suffered severely. The day was smoky, with a pleasant breeze from the south, and the plains on the opposite side were covered with buffalo. Having traveled twenty-five miles, we encamped at six in the evening; and the men were sent across the river for wood, as there is none here on the left bank. Our fires were partially made of the **bois de vache**, the dry excrement of the buffalo, which, like that of the camel in the Arabian deserts, furnishes to the traveler a very good substitute for wood, burning like turf. Wolves in great numbers surrounded us during the night, crossing and recrossing from the opposite herds to our camp, and howling and trotting about in the river until morning.

4th.--The morning was very smoky, the sun shining dimly and red, as in thick fog. The camp was roused by a salute at daybreak, and from our scanty store a portion of what our Indian friends called the "red fire- water" served out to the men. While we were at breakfast, a buffalo-calf broke through the camp, followed by a couple of wolves. In its fright, it had probably mistaken us for a band of buffalo. The wolves were obliged to make a circuit round the camp, so that the calf got a little the start, and strained every nerve to reach a large herd at the foot of the hills, about two miles distant; but first one and then another, and another wolf joined in the chase, until his pursuers amounted to twenty or thirty, and they ran him down before he could reach his friends. There were a few bulls near the place, and one of them attacked the wolves and tried to rescue him; but was driven off immediately, and the little animal fell an easy prey, half devoured before he was dead. We watched the chase with the interest always felt for the weak; and had there been a saddled horse at hand, he would have fared better. Leaving camp, our road soon approached the hills, in which strata of a marl like that of the Chimney rock, hereafter described, made their appearance. It is probably of this rock that the hills on the right bank of the Platte, a little below the junction, are composed, and which are worked by the winds and rains into sharp peaks and cones, giving them, in contrast to the surrounding level region, something of a picturesque appearance. We crossed, this morning, numerous beds of the small creeks which, in the time of rains and melting snow, pour down from the ridge, bringing down with them, always, great quantities of sand and gravel, which have gradually raised their beds four to ten feet above the level of the prairie, which they cross, making each one of them a miniature Po. Raised in this way above the surrounding prairie, without any bank, the long yellow and winding line of their beds resembles a causeway from the hills to the river. Many spots on the prairie are yellow with sunflower, (*helianthus*.)

As we were riding slowly along this afternoon, clouds of dust in the ravines, among the hills to the right, suddenly attracted our attention, and in a few minutes column after column of buffalo came galloping down, making directly to the river. By the time the leading herds had reached the water, the prairie was darkened with the dense masses. Immediately before us, when the bands first came down into the valley, stretched an unbroken line, the head of which was lost among the river hills on the opposite side; and still they poured down from the ridge on our right. From hill to hill, the prairie bottom was certainly not less than two miles wide; and, allowing the animals to be ten feet apart, and only ten in a line, there were already eleven thousand in view. Some idea may thus be formed of their number when they had occupied the whole plain. In a short time they surrounded us on every side, extending for several miles in the rear, and forward as far as the eye could reach; leaving around us, as we advanced, an open space of only two or three hundred yards. This movement of the buffalo indicated to us the presence of Indians on the North fork.

I halted earlier than usual, about forty miles from the junction, and all hands were soon busily engaged in preparing a feast to celebrate the day. The kindness of our friends at St. Louis had provided us with a large supply of excellent preserves and rich fruit-cake; and when these were added to a macaroni soup, and variously prepared dishes of the choicest buffalo-meat, crowned with a cup of coffee, and enjoyed with prairie appetite, we felt, as we sat in barbaric luxury around our smoking supper on the grass, a greater sensation of enjoyment than the Roman epicure at his perfumed feast. But most of all it seemed to please our Indian friends, who, in the unrestrained enjoyment of the moment, demanded to know if our "medicine-days came often." No restraint was exercised at the hospitable board, and, to the great delight of his elders, our young Indian lad made himself extremely drunk.

Our encampment was within a few miles of the place where the road crosses to the North fork, and various reasons led me to divide my party at this point. The North fork was the principal object of my survey; but I was desirous to ascend the South branch, with a view of obtaining some astronomical positions, and determining the mouths of its tributaries as far as St. Vrain's fort, estimated to be some two hundred miles farther up the river, and near to Long's Peak. There I hoped to obtain some mules, which I found would be necessary to relieve my horses. In a military point of view, I was desirous to form some opinion of the country relative to the establishment of posts on a line connecting the settlements with the south pass of the Rocky Mountains, by way of the Arkansas and the South and Laramie forks of the Platte. Crossing the country northwestwardly from St. Vrain's fort, to the American Company's fort at the mouth of the Laramie, would give me some acquaintance with the affluents which head-in the mountain between the two; I therefore determined to set out the next morning, accompanied by four men--Maxwell, Bernier, Ayot, and Basil Lajeunesse. Our Cheyennes, whose village lay up this river, also decided to accompany us. The party I left in charge of Clement Lambert, with orders to cross to the North fork; and at some convenient place, near to the **Coulee des Frenes**, make a cache of every thing not absolutely necessary to the further progress of our expedition. From this point, using the most guarded precaution in his march through the country, he was to proceed to the American Company's fort at the mouth of the Laramie's fork, and await my arrival, which would be prior to the 16th, as on that and the following night would occur some occultations which I was desirous to obtain at that place.

5th.--Before breakfast all was ready. We had one led horse in addition to those we rode, and a pack-mule, destined to carry our instruments, provisions, and baggage; the last two articles not being of great weight. The instruments consisted of a sextant, artificial horizon, &c., a barometer, spy-glass, and compass. The chronometer I of course kept on my person. I had ordered the cook to put up for us some flour, coffee, and sugar, and our rifles were to furnish the rest. One blanket, in addition to his saddle and saddle blanket, furnished the materials for each man's bed, and every one was provided with a change of linen. All were armed with rifles or double-barrelled guns; and, in addition to these, Maxwell and myself were furnished with excellent pistols. Thus accoutred, we took a parting breakfast with our friends; and set forth.

Our journey the first day afforded nothing of any interest. We shot a buffalo towards sunset, and having obtained some meat for our evening meal, encamped where a little timber afforded us the means of making a fire. Having disposed our meat on roasting-sticks, we proceeded to unpack our bales in search of coffee and sugar, and flour for bread. With the exception of a little parched coffee, unground, we found nothing. Our cook had neglected to put it up, or it had been somehow forgotten. Tired and hungry, with tough bull-meat without salt, (for we had not been able to kill a cow,) and a little bitter coffee, we sat down in silence to our miserable fare, a very disconsolate party; for yesterday's feast was yet fresh in our memories, and this was our first brush with misfortune. Each man took his blanket, and laid himself down silently; for the worst part of these mishaps is, that they make people ill-humored. To-day we had traveled about thirty-six miles.

6th.--Finding that our present excursion would be attended with considerable hardship, and unwilling to expose more persons than necessary, I determined to send Mr. Preuss back to the party. His horse, too, appeared in no condition to support the journey; and accordingly, after breakfast, he took the road across the hills, attended by one of my most trusty men, Bernier. The ridge between the rivers is here about fifteen miles broad, and I expected he would probably strike the fork near their evening camp. At all events he would not fail to find their trail, and rejoin them the next day.

We continued our journey, seven in number, including the three Cheyennes. Our general course was southwest, up the valley of the river, which was sandy, bordered on the northern side of the valley by a low ridge; and on the south, after seven or eight miles, the river hills became higher. Six miles from our resting-place we crossed the bed of a considerable stream, now entirely dry--a bed of sand. In a grove of willows, near the mouth, were the remains of a considerable fort, constructed of trunks of large trees. It was apparently very old, and had probably been the scene of some hostile encounter among the roving tribes. Its solitude formed an impressive contrast to the picture which our imaginations involuntarily drew of the busy scene which had been enacted here. The timber appeared to have been much more extensive formerly than now. There were but few trees, a kind of long-leaved willow, standing; and numerous trunks of large trees were scattered about on the ground. In many similar places I had occasion to remark an apparent progressive decay in the timber. Ten miles farther we reached the mouth of Lodge Pole creek, a clear and handsome stream, running through a broad valley. In its course through the bottom it has a uniform breadth of twenty-two feet and six inches in depth. A few willows on the banks strike pleasantly on the eye, by their greenness, in the midst of hot and barren sands.

The *amorpha* was frequent among the ravines, but the sunflower (**helianthus**) was the characteristic; and flowers of deep warm colors seem most to love the sandy soil. The impression of the country traveled over to-day was one of dry and barren sands. We turned in towards the river at noon, and gave our horses two hours for food and rest. I had no other thermometer than the one attached to the barometer, which stood at 89 deg., the height of the column in the barometer being 26.235 at meridian. The sky was clear, with a high wind from the south. At 2 we continued our journey; the wind had moderated, and it became almost unendurably hot, and our animals suffered severely. In the course of the afternoon, the wind rose suddenly, and blew hard from the southwest, with thunder and lightning, and squalls of rain; these were blown against us with violence by the wind; and, halting, we turned our backs to the storm until it blew over. Antelope were tolerably frequent, with a large gray hare; but the former were shy, and the latter hardly worth the delay of stopping to shoot them; so, as the evening drew near, we again had recourse to an old bull, and encamped at sunset on an island in the Platte.

    We ate our meat with a good relish this evening, for we were all in fine health, and had ridden nearly all of a long summer's day, with a burning sun reflected from the sands. My companions slept rolled up in their blankets, and the Indians lay in the grass near the fire; but my sleeping- place generally had an air of more pretension. Our rifles were tied together near the muzzle, the butts resting on the ground, and a knife laid on the rope, to cut away in case of an alarm. Over this, which made a kind of frame, was thrown a large India-rubber cloth, which we used to cover our packs. This made a tent sufficiently large to receive about half of my bed, and was a place of shelter for my instruments; and as I was careful always to put this part against the wind, I could lie here with a sensation of satisfied enjoyment, and hear the wind blow, and the rain patter close to my head, and know that I should be at least half dry. Certainly I never slept more soundly. The barometer at sunset was 26.010, thermometer at 81 deg., and cloudy; but a gale from the west sprang up with the setting sun, and in a few minutes swept away every cloud from the sky. The evening was very fine, and I remained up to take astronomical observations, which made our position in latitude 40 deg. 51' 17", and longitude 103 deg. 07' 00".

    7th.--At our camp this morning, at six o'clock, the barometer was at 26.183, thermometer 69 deg., and clear, with a light wind from the southwest. The past night had been squally, with high winds, and occasionally a few drops of rain. Our cooking did not occupy much time, and we left camp early. Nothing of interest occurred during the morning. The same dreary barrenness, except that a hard marly clay had replaced the sandy soil. Buffalo absolutely covered the plain, on both sides of the river, and whenever we ascended the hills, scattered herds gave life to the view in every direction. A small drove of wild horses made their appearance on the low river bottoms, a mile or two to the left, and I sent off one of the Indians (who seemed very eager to catch one) on my led horse, a spirited and fleet animal. The savage manoeuvred a little to get the wind of the horses, in which he succeeded--approaching within a hundred yards without being discovered. The chase for a few minutes was interesting. My hunter easily overtook and passed the hindmost of the wild drove, which the did not attempt to *lasso*; all his efforts being directed to capture the leader. But the strength of the horse, weakened by insufficient nourishment of grass, failed in a race, and all the drove escaped. We halted at noon on the bank of the river, the barometer at that time being 26.192, and thermometer 103 deg., with a light air from the south and clear weather.

In the course of the afternoon, dust rising among the hills, at a particular place, attracted our attention; and, riding up, we found a band of eighteen or twenty buffalo bulls engaged in a desperate fight. Though butting and goring were bestowed liberally, and without distinction, yet their efforts were evidently directed against one--a huge, gaunt old bull, very lean, while his adversaries were all fat and in good order. He appeared very weak, and had already received some wounds; and, while we were looking on, was several times knocked down and badly hurt, and a very few moments would have put an end to him. Of course, we took the side of the weaker party, and attacked the herd; but they were so blind with rage, that they fought on, utterly regardless of our presence although on foot and on horseback we were firing, in open view, within twenty yards of them. But this did not last long. In a very few seconds, we created a commotion among them. One or two, which were knocked over by the balls, jumped up and ran off into the hills; and they began to retreat slowly along a broad ravine to the river, fighting furiously as they went. By the time they had reached the bottom, we had pretty well dispersed them, and the old bull hobbled off to lie down somewhere. One of his enemies remained on the ground where we had first fired upon them, and we stopped there for a short time to cut from him some meat for our supper. We had neglected to secure our horses, thinking it an unnecessary precaution in their fatigued condition; but our mule took it into his head to start, and away he went, followed at full speed by the pack-horse, with all the baggage and instruments on his back. They were recovered and brought back, after a chase of a mile. Fortunately, everything was well secured, so that nothing, not even the barometer, was in the least injured.

The sun was getting low, and some narrow lines of timber, four or five miles distant, promised us a pleasant camp, where, with plenty of wood for fire, and comfortable shelter, and rich grass for our animals, we should find clear cool springs, instead of the warm water of the Platte. On our arrival, we found the bed of a stream fifty to one hundred feet wide, sunk some thirty feet below the level of the prairie, with perpendicular banks, bordered by a fringe of green cottonwood, but not a drop of water. There were several small forks to the stream, all in the same condition. With the exception of the Platte bottom, the country seemed to be of a clay formation, dry, and perfectly devoid of any moisture, and baked hard by the sun. Turning off towards the river, we reached the bank in about a mile, and were delighted to find an old tree, with thick foliage and spreading branches, where we encamped. At sunset, the barometer was at 25.950, thermometer 81 deg., with a strong wind from S. 20 deg. E., and the sky partially covered with heavy masses of cloud, which settled a little towards the horizon by ten o'clock, leaving it sufficiently clear for astronomical observations, which placed us in latitude 40 deg. 33' 26", and longitude 103 deg. 30' 37".

8th.--The morning was very pleasant. The breeze was fresh from S. 50 deg. E., with few clouds; the barometer at six o'clock standing at 25.970, and the thermometer at 70 deg.. Since leaving the forks our route had passed over a country alternately clay and sand, each presenting the same naked waste. On leaving camp this morning, we struck again a sandy region, in which the vegetation appeared somewhat more vigorous than that which we had observed for the last few days; and on the opposite side of the river were some tolerably large groves of timber.

Journeying along, we came suddenly upon a place where the ground was covered with horses' tracks, which had been made since the rain, and indicated the immediate presence of Indians in our neighborhood. The buffalo, too, which the day before had been so numerous were nowhere in sight--another sure indication that there were people near. Riding on, we discovered the carcass of a buffalo recently killed--perhaps the day before. We scanned the horizon carefully with the glass, but no living object was to be seen. For the next mile or two, the ground was dotted with buffalo carcasses, which showed that the Indians had made a surround here, and were in considerable force. We went on quickly and cautiously, keeping the river bottom, and carefully avoiding the hills; but we met with no interruption, and began to grow careless again. We had already lost one of our horses, and here Basil's mule showed symptoms of giving out, and finally refused to advance, being what the Canadians call *reste*. He therefore dismounted, and drove her along before him; but this was a very slow way of traveling. We had inadvertently got about half a mile in advance, but our Cheyennes, who were generally a mile or two in the rear, remained with him. There were some dark-looking objects among the hills, about two miles to the left, here low and undulating, which we had seen for a little time, and supposed to be buffalo coming in to water; but, happening to look behind,

Maxwell saw the Cheyennes whipping up furiously, and another glance at the dark objects showed them at once to be Indians coming up at speed.

Had we been well mounted and disencumbered of instruments, we might have set them at defiance; but as it was, we were fairly caught. It was too late to rejoin our friends, and we endeavored to gain a clump of timber about half a mile ahead; but the instruments and tired state of our horses did not allow us to go faster than a steady canter, and they were gaining on us fast. At first, they did not appear to be more than fifteen or twenty in number, but group after group darted into view at the top of the hills, until all the little eminences seemed in motion; and, in a few minutes from the time they were first discovered, two or three hundred, naked to the breechcloth, were sweeping across the prairie. In a few hundred yards we discovered that the timber we were endeavoring to make was on the opposite side of the river; and before we reach the bank, down came the Indians upon us.

I am inclined to think that in a few seconds more the leading man, and perhaps some of his companions, would have rolled in the dust; for we had jerked the covers from our guns, and our fingers were on the triggers. Men in such cases generally act from instinct, and a charge from three hundred naked savages is a circumstance not well calculated to promote a cool exercise of judgment. Just as he was about to fire, Maxwell recognised the leading Indian, and shouted to him in the Indian language, "You're a fool, G---- damn you--don't you know me?" The sound of his own language seemed to shock the savage; and, swerving his horse a little, he passed us like an arrow. He wheeled, as I rode out towards him, and gave me his hand, striking his breast and exclaiming "Arapaho!" They proved to be a village of that nation, among whom Maxwell had resided as a trader a year or two previously, and recognised him accordingly. We were soon in the midst of the band, answering as well as we could a multitude of questions; of which the very first was, of what tribe were our Indian companions who were coming in the rear? They seemed disappointed to know that they were Cheyennes, for they had fully anticipated a grand dance around a Pawnee scalp that night.

The chief showed us his village at a grove on the river six miles ahead, and pointed out a band of buffalo on the other side of the Platte, immediately opposite us, which he said they were going to surround. They had seen the band early in the morning from their village, and had been making a large circuit, to avoid giving them the wind, when they discovered us. In a few minutes the women came galloping up, astride on their horses, and naked from their knees down and the hips up. They followed the men, to assist in cutting up and carrying off the meat.

The wind was blowing directly across the river, and the chief requested us to halt where we were for awhile, in order to avoid raising the herd. We therefore unsaddled our horses, and sat down on the bank to view the scene; and our new acquaintances rode a few hundred yards lower down, and began crossing the river. Scores of wild-looking dogs followed, looking like troops of wolves, and having, in fact, but very little of the dog in their composition. Some of them remained with us, and I checked one of the men, whom I found aiming at one, which he was about to kill for a wolf. The day had become very hot. The air was clear, with a very slight breeze; and now, at 12 o'clock, while the barometer stood at 25.920, the attached thermometer was at 108 deg.. Our Cheyennes had learned that with the Arapaho village were about twenty lodges of their own, including their own families; they therefore immediately commenced making their toilette. After bathing in the river, they invested themselves in some handsome calico shirts, which I afterwards learned they had stolen from my own men, and spent some time in arranging their hair and painting themselves with some vermilion I had given them. While they were engaged in this satisfactory manner, one of their half-wild horses, to which the crowd of prancing animals which had just passed had recalled the freedom of her existence among the wild droves on the prairie, suddenly dashed into the hills at the top of her speed. She was their pack-horse, and had on her back all the worldly wealth of our poor Cheyennes, all their accoutrements, and all the little articles which they had picked up among us, with some few presents I had given them. The loss which they seemed to regret most were their spears and shields, and some tobacco which they had received from me. However, they bore it all with the philosophy of an Indian, and laughingly continued their toilette. They appeared, however, to be a little mortified at the thought of returning to the village in such a sorry plight. "Our people will laugh at us," said one of them, "returning to the village on foot, instead of driving back a drove of Pawnee horses." He demanded to know if I loved my sorrel hunter very much; to which I replied, he was the object of my most intense affection. Far from being able to give, I was myself in want of horses; and any suggestion of parting with the few I had valuable, was met with a peremptory refusal. In the mean time, the slaughter was about to commence on the other side. So soon as they reached it, Indians separated into two bodies. One party proceeded across the prairie, towards the hills, in an extended line, while the other went up the river; and instantly as they had given the wind to the herd, the chase commenced. The buffalo started for the hills, but were intercepted and driven back towards the river, broken and running in every direction. The clouds of dust soon covered the whole scene, preventing us from having any but an occasional view. It had a very singular appearance to us at a distance, especially when looking with the glass. We were too far to hear the report of the guns, or any sound; and at every instant, through the clouds of dust, which the sun made luminous, we could see for a moment two or three buffalo dashing along, and close behind them an Indian with his long spear, or other weapon, and instantly again they disappeared. The apparent silence, and the dimly seen figures flitting by with such rapidity, gave it a kind of dreamy effect, and seemed more like a picture than a scene of real life. It had been a large herd when the ***cerne*** commenced, probably three or four hundred in number; but, though I watched them closely, I did not see one emerge from the fatal cloud where the work of destruction was going on. After remaining here about an hour, we resumed our journey in the direction of the village.

Gradually, as we rode on, Indian after Indian came dropping along, laden with meat; and by the time we had neared the lodges, the backward road was covered with the returning horsemen. It was a pleasant contrast with the desert road we had been traveling. Several had joined company with us, and one of the chiefs invited us to his lodge. The village consisted of about one hundred and twenty-five lodges, of which twenty were Cheyennes; the latter pitched a little apart from the Arapahoes. They were disposed in a scattering manner on both sides of a broad, irregular street, about one hundred and fifty feet wide, and running along the river. As we rode along, I remarked near some of the lodges a kind of tripod frame, formed of three slender poles of birch, scraped very clean, to which were affixed the shield and spear, with some other weapons of a chief. All were scrupulously clean, the spear-head was burnished bright; and the shield white and stainless. It reminded me of the days of feudal chivalry; and when, as I rode by, I yielded to the passing impulse, and touched one of the spotless shields with the muzzle of my gun, I almost expected a grim warrior to start from the lodge and resent my challenge. The master of the lodge spread out a robe for me to sit upon, and the squaws set before us a large wooden dish of buffalo meat. He had lit his pipe in the mean while, and when it had been passed around, we commenced our dinner while he continued to smoke. Gradually, however, five or six other chiefs came in, and took their seats in silence. When we had finished, our host asked a number of questions relative to the object of our journey, of which I made no concealment; telling him simply that I had made a visit to see the country, preparatory to the establishment of military posts on the way to the mountains. Although this was information of the highest interest to them, and by no means calculated to please them, it excited no expression of surprise, and in no way altered the grave courtesy of their demeanor. The others listened and smoked. I remarked, that in taking the pipe for the first time, each had turned the stem upward, with a rapid glance, as in offering to the Great Spirit, before he put it in his mouth. A storm had been gathering for the past hour, and some pattering drops in the lodge warned us that we had some miles to our camp. An Indian had given Maxwell a bundle of dried meat, which was very acceptable, as we had nothing; and, springing upon our horses, we rode off at dusk in the face of a cold shower and driving wind. We found our companions under some densely foliaged old trees, about three miles up the river. Under one of them lay the trunk of a large cottonwood, to leeward of which the men had kindled a fire, and we sat here and roasted our meat in tolerable shelter. Nearly opposite was the mouth of one of the most considerable affluents of the South fork, **la Fourche aux Castors**, (Beaver fork,) heading off in the ridge to the southeast.

9th.--This morning we caught the first faint glimpse of the Rocky mountains, about sixty miles distant. Though a tolerably bright day, there was a slight mist, and we were just able to discern the snowy summit of "Long's peak," ("**les deux oreilles**" of the Canadians,) showing like a cloud near the horizon. I found it easily distinguishable, there being a perceptible difference in its appearance from the white clouds that were floating about the sky. I was pleased to find that among the traders the name of "Long's peak" had been adopted and become familiar in the country. In the ravines near this place, a light brown sandstone made its first appearance. About 8, we discerned several persons on horseback a mile or two ahead, on the opposite side of the river. They turned in towards the river, and we rode down to meet them. We found them to be two white men, and a mulatto named

Jim Beckwith, who had left St. Louis when a boy, and gone to live with the Crow Indians. He had distinguished himself among them by some acts of daring bravery, and had risen to the rank of chief, but had now, for some years, left them. They were in search of a band of horses that had gone off from a camp some miles above, in charge of Mr. Chabonard. Two of them continued down the river, in search of the horses, and the American turned back with us, and we rode on towards the camp. About eight miles from our sleeping-place, we reached Bijou's fork, an affluent of the right bank. Where we crossed it, a short distance from the Platte, it has a sandy bed about four hundred yards broad; the water in various small streams, a few inches deep. Seven miles further brought us to the camp of some four or five whites, (New Englanders, I believe,) who had accompanied Captain Wyeth to the Columbia river, and were independent trappers. All had their squaws with them, and I was really surprised at the number of little fat, buffalo-fed boys that were tumbling about the camp, all apparently of the same age, about three or four years old. They were encamped on a rich bottom, covered with a profusion of rich grass, and had a large number of fine-looking horses and mules. We rested with them a few minutes, and in about two miles arrived at Chabonard's camp, on an island in the Platte. On the heights above, we met the first Spaniard I had seen in the country. Mr. Chabonard was in the service of Bent and St. Vrain's company, and had left their fort some forty or fifty miles above, in the spring, with boats laden with the furs of the last year's trade. He had met the same fortune as the voyageurs on the North fork; and, finding it impossible to proceed, had taken up his summer's residence on this island, which he had named St. Helena. The river hills appeared to be composed entirely of sand, and the Platte had lost the muddy character of its waters, and here was tolerably clear. From the mouth of the South fork, I had found it occasionally broken up by small islands; and at the time of our journey, which was at a season of the year when the waters were at a favorable stage, it was not navigable for any thing drawing six inches water. The current was very swift--the bed of the stream a coarse gravel. From the place at which we had encountered the Arapahoes, the Platte had been tolerably well fringed with timber, and the island here had a fine grove of very large cottonwoods, under whose broad shade the tents were pitched. There was a large drove of horses in the opposite prairie bottom; smoke was rising from the scattered fires, and the encampment had quite a patriarchal air. Mr. C.

received us hospitably. One of the people was sent to gather mint, with the aid of which he concocted very good julep; and some boiled buffalo tongue, and coffee with the luxury of sugar, were soon set before us. The people in his employ were generally Spaniards, and among them I saw a young Spanish woman from Taos, whom I found to be Beckwith's wife.

10th.--We parted with our hospitable host after breakfast the next morning, and reached St. Vrain's fort, about forty-five miles from St. Helena, late in the evening. This post is situated on the South fork of the Platte, immediately under the mountains, about seventeen miles east of Long's peak. It is on the right bank, on the verge of the upland prairie, about forty feet above the river, of which the immediate valley is about six hundred yards wide. The stream is divided into various branches by small islands, among which it runs with a swift current. The bed of the river is sand and gravel, the water very clear, and here may be called a mountain-stream. This region appears to be entirely free from the limestones and marls which give to the Lower Platte its yellow and dirty color. The Black hills lie between the stream and the mountains, whose snowy peaks glitter a few miles beyond. At the fort we found Mr. St. Vrain, who received us with much kindness and hospitality. Maxwell had spent the last two or three years between this post and the village of Taos; and here he was at home, and among his friends. Spaniards frequently came over in search of employment; and several came in shortly after our arrival. They usually obtain about six dollars a month, generally paid to them in goods. They are very useful in a camp, in taking care of horses and mules; and I engaged one, who proved to be an active, laborious man, and was of very considerable service to me. The elevation of the Platte here is five thousand four hundred feet above the sea. The neighboring mountains did not appear to enter far the region of perpetual snow, which was generally confined to the northern side of the peaks. On the southern, I remarked very little. Here it appeared, so far as I could judge in the distance, to descend but a few hundred feet below the summits.

I regretted that time did not permit me to visit them; but the proper object of my survey lay among the mountains farther north; and I looked forward to an exploration of their snowy recesses with great pleasure. The piney region of the mountains to the south was enveloped in smoke, and I was informed had been on fire for several months. Pike's peak is said to be visible from this place, about one hundred miles to the southward; but the smoky state of the atmosphere prevented my seeing it. The weather continued overcast during my stay here, so that I failed in determining the latitude, but obtained good observations for the time on the mornings of the 11th and 12th. An assumed latitude of 40 deg. 22' 30" from the evening position of the 12th, enabled me to obtain for a tolerably correct longitude, 105 deg. 12' 12".

12th.--The kindness of Mr. St. Vrain enabled me to obtain a couple of horses and three good mules; and, with a further addition to our party of the Spaniard whom I had hired, and two others, who were going to obtain service at Laramie's fork, we resumed our journey at ten, on the morning of the 12th. We had been able to procure nothing at the post in the way of provision. An expected supply from Taos had not yet arrived, and a few pounds of coffee was all that could be spared to us. In addition to this we had dried meat enough for the first day; on the next, we expected to find buffalo. From this post, according to the estimate of the country, the fort at the mouth of Laramie's fork, which was our next point of destination, was nearly due north, distant about one hundred and twenty-five miles.

For a short distance our road lay down the valley of the Platte, which resembled a garden in the splendor of fields of varied flowers, which filled the air with fragrance. The only timber I noticed consisted of poplar, birch, cottonwood, and willow. In something less than three miles we crossed Thompson's creek, one of the affluents to the left bank of the South fork--a fine stream about sixty-five feet wide, and three feet deep. Journeying on, the low dark line of the Black hills lying between us and the mountains to the left, in about ten miles from the fort, we reached *Cache a la Poudre*, where we halted to noon. This is a very beautiful mountain-stream, about one hundred feet wide, flowing with a full swift current over a rocky bed. We halted under the shade of some cottonwoods, with which the stream is wooded scatteringly. In the upper part of its course, it runs amid the wildest mountain scenery, and, breaking through the Black hills, falls into the Platte about ten miles below this place. In the course of our late journey, I had managed to become the possessor of a very untractable mule--a perfect vixen--and her I had turned over to my Spaniard. It occupied us about half an hour to-day to get saddle upon her; but, once on her back, Jose could not be dismounted, realizing the accounts given of Mexican horses and horsemanship; and we continued our route in the afternoon.

At evening, we encamped on Crow creek, having traveled about twenty-eight miles. None of the party were well acquainted with the country, and I had great difficulty in ascertaining what were the names of the streams we crossed between the North and South forks of the Platte. This I supposed to be Cow creek. It is what is called a salt stream, and the water stands in pools, having no continuous course. A fine-grained sandstone made its appearance in the banks. The observations of the night placed us in latitude 40 deg. 42', longitude 104 deg. 57' 49". The barometer at sunset was 25.231; attached thermometer at 66 deg.. Sky clear, except in the east, with a light wind from the north.

13th.--There being no wood here, we used last night the **_bois de vache_**, which is very plentiful. At our camp this morning, the barometer was at 25.235; the attached thermometer 60 deg.. A few clouds were moving through a deep-blue sky, with a light wind from the west. After a ride of twelve miles, in a northerly direction, over a plain covered with innumerable quantities of **_cacti_**, we reached a small creek in which there was water, and where several herds of buffalo were scattered about among the ravines, which always afford good pasturage. We seem now to be passing along the base of a plateau of the Black hills, in which the formation consists of marls, some of them white and laminated; the country to the left rising suddenly, and falling off gradually and uniformly to the right. In five or six miles of a northeasterly course, we struck a high ridge, broken into conical peaks, on whose summits large boulders were gathered in heaps. The magnetic direction of the ridge is northwest and southeast, the glittering white of its precipitous sides making it visible for many miles to the south. It is composed of a soft earthy limestone and marls, resembling that hereafter described in the neighborhood of the Chimney rock, on the North fork of the Platte, easily worked by the winds and rains, and sometimes moulded into very fantastic shapes. At the foot of the northern slope was the bed of a creek, some forty feet wide, coming, by frequent falls, from the bench above. It was shut in by high, perpendicular banks, in which were strata of white laminated marl. Its bed was perfectly dry, and the leading feature of the whole region is one of remarkable aridity, and perfect freedom from moisture. In about six miles we crossed the bed of another dry creek; and, continuing our ride over high level prairie, a little before sundown we came suddenly upon a beautiful creek, which revived us with a feeling of delighted surprise by the pleasant contrast of the deep verdure of its banks with the parched desert we had passed. We had suffered much to-day, both men and horses, for want of water; having met with it but once in our uninterrupted march of forty miles; and an exclusive meat diet creates much thirst.

"***Les bestias tienen mucha hambre***," said the young Spaniard, inquiringly: "***y la gente tambien***," said I, "***amiago***, we'll camp here." A stream of good and clear water ran winding about through the little valley, and a herd of buffalo were quietly feeding a little distance below. It was quite a hunter's paradise; and while some ran down towards the band to kill one for supper, others collected **bois de vache** for a fire, there being no wood; and I amused myself with hunting for plants among the grass.

It will be seen, by occasional remarks on the geological formation, that the constituents of the soil in these regions are good, and every day served to strengthen the impression in my mind, confirmed by subsequent observation, that the barren appearance of the country is due almost entirely to the extreme dryness of the climate. Along our route, the country had seemed to increase constantly in elevation. According to the indication of the barometer, we were at our encampment 5,440 feet above the sea.

The evening was very clear, with a fresh breeze from the south, 50 deg. east. The barometer at sunset was 24.862, the thermometer attached showing 68 deg.. I supposed this to be a fork of Lodge Pole creek, so far as I could determine from our uncertain means of information. Astronomical observations gave for the camp a longitude of 104 deg. 39' 37", and latitude 41 deg. 08' 31".

14th.--The wind continued fresh from the same quarter in the morning; the day being clear, with the exception of a few clouds in the horizon. At our camp, at six o'clock, the height of the barometer was 24.830, the attached thermometer 61 deg.. Our course this morning was directly north by compass, the variation being 15 deg. or 16 deg. easterly. A ride of four miles brought us to Lodge Pole creek, which we had seen at the mouth of the South fork; crossing on the way two dry streams, in eighteen miles from our encampment of the past night, we reached a high bleak ridge, composed entirely of the same earthy limestone and marl previously described. I had never seen any thing which impressed so strongly on my mind a feeling of desolation. The valley, through which ran the waters of Horse creek, lay in view to the north, but too far to have any influence on the immediate view. On the peak of the ridge where I was standing, some seven hundred feet above the river, the wind was high and bleak; the barren and arid country seemed as if it had been swept by fires, and in every direction the same dull ash- colored hue, derived from the formation, met the eye. On the summits were some stunted pines, many of them dead, all wearing the same ashen hue of desolation. We left the place with pleasure; and, after we had descended several hundred feet, halted in one of the ravines, which, at the distance of every mile or two, cut the flanks of the ridge with little rushing streams, wearing something of a mountain character. We had already begun to exchange the comparatively barren lands for those of a more fertile character. Though the sandstone formed the broken banks of the creek, yet they were covered with a thin grass; and the fifty or sixty feet which formed the bottom land of the little stream were clothed with very luxuriant grass, among which I remarked willow and cherry, (*cerasus virginiana*,) and a quantity of gooseberry and currant bushes occupied the greater part.

The creek was three or four feet broad, and about six inches deep, with a swift current of clear water, and tolerably cool. We had struck it too low down to find the cold water, which we should have enjoyed nearer to its sources. At two, P.M., the barometer was at 25.050, and the attached thermometer 104 deg.. A day of hot sunshine, with clouds, and moderate breeze from the south. Continuing down the stream, in about four miles we reached its mouth, at one of the main branches of Horse creek. Looking back upon the ridge, whose direction appeared to be a little to the north of east, we saw it seamed at frequent intervals with the dark lines of wooded streams, affluents of the river that flowed so far as we could see along its base. We crossed, in the space of twelve miles from our noon halt, three or four forks of Horse creek, and encamped at sunset on the most easterly.

The fork on which we encamped appeared to have followed an easterly direction up to this place; but here it makes a very sudden bend to the north, passing between two ranges of precipitous hills, called, as I was informed, Goshen's hole. There is somewhere in or near this locality a place so called, but I am not certain that it was the place of our encampment. Looking back upon the spot, at the distance of a few miles to the northward, the hills appear to shut in the prairie, through which runs the creek, with a semicircular sweep, which might very naturally be called a hole in the bills. The geological composition of the ridge is the same which constitutes the rock of the Court-house and Chimney, on the North fork, which appeared to me a continuation of this ridge. The winds and rains work this formation into a variety of singular forms. The pass into Goshen's hole is about two miles wide, and the hill on the western side imitates, in an extraordinary manner, a massive fortified place, with a remarkable fulness of detail. The rock is marl and earthy limestone, white, without the least appearance of vegetation, and much resembles masonry at a little distance; and here it sweeps around a level area two or three hundred yards in diameter, and in the form of a half moon, terminating on either extremity in enormous bastions. Along the whole line of the parapets appear domes and slender minarets, forty or fifty feet high, giving it every appearance of an old fortified town. On the waters of White river, where this formation exists in great extent, it presents appearances which excite the admiration of the solitary voyageur, and form a frequent theme of their conversation when speaking of the wonders of the country. Sometimes it offers the perfectly illusive appearance of a large city, with numerous streets and magnificent buildings, among which the Canadians never fail to see their *cabaret*--and sometimes it takes the form of a solitary house, with many large chambers, into which they drive their horses at night, and sleep in these natural defences perfectly secure from any attack of prowling savages. Before reaching our camp at Goshen's hole, in crossing the immense detritus at the foot of the Castle rock, we were involved amidst winding passages cut by the waters of the hill; and where, with a breadth scarcely large enough for the passage of a horse, the walls rise thirty and forty feet perpendicularly. This formation supplies the discoloration of the Platte. At sunset, the height of the mercurial column was 25.500, the attached thermometer 80 deg., and wind moderate from S. 38 deg. E. Clouds covered the sky with the rise of the moon, but I succeeded in obtaining the usual astronomical observations, which placed us in latitude 41 deg. 40' 13", and longitude 104 deg. 24' 36".

15th.--At six this morning, the barometer was at 25.515 the thermometer 72 deg.; the day was fine, with some clouds looking dark on the south, with a fresh breeze from the same quarter. We found that in our journey across the country we had kept too much to the eastward. This morning, accordingly, we traveled by compass some 15 or 20 to the west of north, and struck the Platte some thirteen miles below Fort Laramie. The day was extremely hot, and among the hills the wind seemed to have just issued from an oven. Our horses were much distressed, as we had traveled hard; and it was with some difficulty that they were all brought to the Platte, which we reached at one o'clock. In riding in towards the river, we found the trail of our carts, which appeared to have passed a day or two since.

After having allowed our animals two hours for food and repose, we resumed our journey, and towards the close of the day came in sight of Laramie's fork. Issuing from the river hills, we came first in view of Fort Platte, a post belonging to Messrs. Sybille, Adams & Co., situated immediately in the point of land at the junction of Laramie with the Platte. Like the post we had visited on the South fork, it was built of earth, and still unfinished, being enclosed with walls (or rather houses) on three of the sides, and open on the fourth to the river. A few hundred yards brought us in view of the post of the American Fur Company, called Fort John, or Laramie. This was a large post having more the air of military construction than the fort at the mouth of the river. It is on the left bank, on a rising ground some twenty-five feet above the water; and its lofty walls, whitewashed and picketed, with the large bastions at the angles, gave it quite an imposing appearance in the uncertain light of evening. A cluster of lodges, which the language told us belonged to Sioux Indians, was pitched under the walls; and, with the fine background of the Black hills and the prominent peak of Laramie mountain, strongly drawn in the clear light of the western sky, where the sun had already set, the whole formed at the moment a strikingly beautiful picture. From the company at St. Louis I had letters for Mr. Boudeau, the gentleman in charge of the post, by whom I was received with great hospitality and an efficient kindness, which was invaluable to me during my stay in the country. I found our people encamped on the bank, a short distance above the fort. All were well; and, in the enjoyment of a bountiful supper, which coffee and bread made luxurious to us, we soon forgot the fatigues of the last ten days.

16th.--I found that, during my absence, the situation of affairs had undergone some change; and the usual quiet and somewhat monotonous regularity of the camp had given place to excitement and alarm. The circumstances which occasioned this change will be found narrated in the following extract from the journal of Mr. Preuss, which commences with the day of our separation on the South fork of the

Platte:

"6th.--We crossed the plateau or highland between the two forks in about six hours. I let my horse go as slow as he liked, to indemnify us both for the previous hardship; and about noon we reached the North fork. There was no sign that our party had passed; we rode, therefore, to some pine trees, unsaddled the hoses, and stretched our limbs on the grass, awaiting the arrival of our company. After remaining here two hours, my companion became impatient, mounted his horse again, and rode off down the river to see if he could discover our people. I felt so marode yet, that it was a horrible idea to me to bestride that saddle again; so I lay still. I knew they could not come any other way, and then my companion, one of the best men of the company, would not abandon me. The sun went down--he did not come. Uneasy I did not feel, but very hungry. I had no provisions, but I could make a fire; and as I espied two doves in a tree, I tried to kill one. But it needs a better marksman than myself to kill a little bird with a rifle. I made a fire, however, lighted my pipe--this true friend of mine in every emergency--lay down, and let my thoughts wander to the far east. It was not many minutes after when I heard the tramp of a horse, and my faithful companion was by my side. He had found the party, who had been delayed by making their *cache*, about seven miles below. To the good supper which he brought with him I did ample justice. He had forgotten salt, and I tried the soldier's substitute in time of war, and used gunpowder; but it answered badly--bitter enough, but no flavor of kitchen salt. I slept well; and was only disturbed by two owls, which were attracted by the fire, and took their place in the tree under which we slept. Their music seemed as disagreeable to my companion as to myself; he fired his rifle twice, and then they let us alone.

"7th.--At about 10 o'clock, the party arrived; and we continued our journey through a country which offered but little to interest the traveler. The soil was much more sandy than in the valley below the confluence of the forks, and the face of the country no longer presented the refreshing green which had hitherto characterized it. The rich grass was now found only in dispersed spots, on low grounds, and on the bottom land of the streams. A long drought, joined to extreme heat, had so parched up the upper prairies, that they were in many places bald, or covered only with a thin growth of yellow and poor grass. The nature of the soil renders it extremely susceptible to the vicissitudes of the climate. Between the forks, and from their junction to the Black hills, the formation consists of marl and a soft earthy limestone, with granitic sandstone. Such a formation cannot give rise to a sterile soil; and, on our return in September, when the country had been watered by frequent rains, the valley of the Platte looked like a garden; so rich was the verdure of the grasses, and so luxuriant the bloom of abundant flowers. The wild sage begins to make its appearance, and timber is so scarce that we generally made our fires of the ***bois de vache***. With the exception of now and then an isolated tree or two, standing like a lighthouse on the river bank, there is none to be seen.

"8th.--Our road to-day was a solitary one. No game made its appearance-- not even a buffalo or a stray antelope; and nothing occurred to break the monotony until about 5 o'clock, when the caravan made a sudden halt. There was a galloping in of scouts and horsemen from every side--a hurrying to and fro in noisy confusion; rifles were taken from their covers; bullet pouches examined: in short, there was the cry of 'Indians,' heard again. I had become so much accustomed to these alarms, that they now made but little impression on me; and before I had time to become excited, the newcomers were ascertained to be whites. It was a large party of traders and trappers, conducted by Mr. Bridger, a man well known in the history of the country. As the sun was low, and there was a fine grass patch not far ahead, they turned back and encamped for the night with us. Mr. Bridger was invited to supper; and, after the ***table-cloth*** was removed, we listened with eager interest to an account of their adventures. What they had met, we would be likely to encounter; the chances which had befallen them, would probably happen to us; and we looked upon their life as a picture of our own. He informed us that the condition of the country had become exceedingly dangerous. The Sioux, who had been badly disposed, had broken out into open hostility, and in the preceding autumn his party had encountered them in a severe engagement, in which a number of lives had been lost on both sides. United with the Cheyenne and Gros Ventre Indians, they were scouring the upper country in war parties of great force, and were at this time in the neighborhood of the ***Red Buttes***, a famous landmark, which was directly in our path. They had declared war upon every living thing that should be found westward of that point; though their main object was to attack a large camp of whites and Snake Indians, who had a rendezvous in the Sweet Water valley. Availing himself of his intimate knowledge of the country, he had reached Laramie by an unusual route through the Black hills, and avoided coming into contact with any of the scattered parties. This gentleman offered his services to accompany us as far as the head of the Sweet Water; but the absence of our leader, which was deeply regretted by us all, rendered it impossible for us to enter upon such arrangements. In a camp consisting of men whose lives had been spent in this country, I expected to find every one prepared for occurrences of this nature; but, to my great surprise, I found, on the contrary, that this news had thrown them all into the greatest consternation; and, on every side, I heard only one exclamation, '***Il n'y aura pas de vie pour nous***.' All the night, scattered groups were assembled around the fires, smoking their pipes, and listening with the greatest eagerness to exaggerated details of Indian hostilities; and in the morning I found the camp dispirited, and agitated by a variety of conflicting opinions. A majority of the people were strongly disposed to return; but Clement Lambert, with some five or six others, professed their determination to follow Mr. Fremont to the uttermost limit of his journey. The others yielded to their remonstrances, and somewhat ashamed of their cowardice, concluded to advance at least as far as Laramie fork, eastward of which they were aware no danger was to be apprehended. Notwithstanding the confusion and excitement, we were very early on the road, as the days were extremely hot, and we were anxious to profit by the freshness of the morning. The soft marly formation, over which we were now journeying, frequently offers to the traveler views of remarkable and picturesque beauty. To several of these localities, where the winds and the rain have worked the bluffs into curious shapes, the voyageurs have given names according to some fancied resemblance. One of these, called the **Court-house**, we passed about six miles from our encampment of last night, and towards noon came in sight of the celebrated **Chimney rock**. It looks, at this distance of about thirty miles, like what it is called--the long chimney of a steam factory establishment, or a shot tower in Baltimore. Nothing occurred to interrupt the quiet of the day, and we encamped on the river, after a march of twenty-four miles. Buffalo had become very scarce, and but one cow had been killed, of which the meat had been cut into thin slices, and hung around the carts to dry.

"10th.--We continued along the same fine plainly beaten road, which the smooth surface of the country afforded us, for a distance of six hundred and thirty miles, from the frontiers of Missouri to the Laramie fork. In the course of the day we met some whites, who were following along in the train of Mr. Bridger; and, after a day's journey of twenty-four miles, encamped about sunset at the Chimney rock. It consists of marl and earthy limestone, and the weather is rapidly diminishing its height, which is not more than two hundred feet above the river. Travelers who visited it some years since, placed its height at upwards of **500 feet**.

"11th.--The valley of the North fork is of a variable breadth, from one to four, and sometimes six miles. Fifteen miles from the Chimney rock we reached one of those places where the river strikes the bluffs, and forces the road to make a considerable circuit over the uplands. This presented an escarpment on the river of about nine hundred yards in length, and is familiarly known as Scott's bluffs. We had made a journey of thirty miles before we again struck the river, at a place where some scanty grass afforded an insufficient pasturage to our animals. About twenty miles from the Chimney rock we had found a very beautiful spring of excellent and cold water; but it was in such a deep ravine, and so small, that the animals could not profit by it, and we therefore halted only a few minutes, and found a resting-place ten miles further on. The plain between Scott's bluffs and Chimney rock was almost entirely covered with drift- wood, consisting principally of cedar, which, we were informed, had been supplied from the Black hills, in a flood five or six years since.

"12th.--Nine miles from our encampment of yesterday we crossed Horse creek, a shallow stream of clear water, about seventy yards wide, falling into the Platte on the right bank. It was lightly timbered, and great quantities of drift-wood were piled up on the banks, appearing to be supplied by the creek from above. After a journey of twenty-six miles, we encamped on a rich bottom, which afforded fine grass to our animals. Buffalo have entirely disappeared, and we live now upon the dried meat, which is exceedingly poor food. The marl and earthy limestone, which constituted the formation for several days past, had changed, during the day, into a compact white or grayish-white limestone, sometimes containing hornstone; and at the place of our encampment this evening, some strata in the river hills cropped out to the height of thirty or forty feet, consisting of fine-grained granitic sandstone; one of the strata closely resembling gneiss.

"13th.--To-day, about four o'clock, we reached Fort Laramie, where we were cordially received. We pitched our camp a little above the fort, on the bank of the Laramie river, in which the pure and clear water of the mountain stream looked refreshingly cool, and made a pleasant contrast to the muddy, yellow waters of the Platte."

I walked up to visit our friends at the fort, which is a quadrangular structure, built of clay, after the fashion of the Mexicans, who are generally employed in building them. The walls are about fifteen feet high, surmounted with a wooden palisade, and form a portion of ranges of houses, which entirely surround a yard of about one hundred and thirty feet square. Every apartment has its door and window,--all, of course, opening on the inside. There are two entrances, opposite each other, and midway the wall, one of which is a large and public entrance; the other smaller and more private--a sort of postern gate. Over the great entrance is a square tower with loopholes, and, like the rest of the work, built of earth. At two of the angles, and diagonally opposite each other, are large square bastions, so arranged as to sweep the four faces of the walls.

This post belongs to the American Fur Company, and, at the time of our visit, was in charge of Mr. Boudeau. Two of the company's clerks, Messrs. Galpin and Kellogg, were with him, and he had in the fort about sixteen men. As usual, these had found wives among the Indian squaws; and, with the usual accompaniment of children, the place had quite a populous appearance. It is hardly necessary to say, that the object of the establishment is trade with the neighboring tribes, who, in the course of the year, generally make two or three visits to the fort. In addition to this, traders, with a small outfit, are constantly kept amongst them. The articles of trade consist, on the one side, almost entirely of buffalo robes; and, on the other, of blankets, calicoes, guns, powder and lead, with such cheap ornaments as glass beads, looking-glasses, rings, vermilion for painting, tobacco, and principally, and in spite of the prohibition, of spirits, brought into the country in the form of alcohol, and diluted with water before sold. While mentioning this fact, it is but justice to the American Fur Company to state, that, throughout the country, I have always found them strenuously opposed to the introduction of spirituous liquors. But in the present state of things, when the country is supplied with alcohol--when a keg of it will purchase from an Indian every thing he possesses--his furs, his lodge, his horses, and even his wife and children--and when any vagabond who has money enough to purchase a mule can go into a village and trade against them successfully, without withdrawing entirely from the trade, it is impossible for them to discontinue its use.

In their opposition to this practice, the company is sustained, not only by their obligation to the laws of the country and the welfare of the Indians, but clearly, also, on grounds of policy; for, with heavy and expensive outfits, they contend at manifestly great disadvantage against the numerous independent and unlicensed traders, who enter the country from various avenues, from the United States and from Mexico, having no other stock in trade than some kegs of liquor, which they sell at the modest price of thirty-six dollars per gallon. The difference between the regular trader and the ***coureur des bois***, (as the French call the itinerant or peddling traders,) with respect to the sale of spirits, is here, as it always has been, fixed and permanent, and growing out of the nature of their trade. The regular trader looks ahead, and has an interest in the preservation of the Indians, and in the regular pursuit of their business, and the preservation of their arms, horses, and every thing necessary to their future and permanent success in hunting: the ***coureur des bois*** has no permanent interest, and gets what he can, and for what he can, from every Indian he meets, even at the risk of disabling him from doing any thing more at hunting.

The fort had a very cool and clean appearance. The great entrance, in which I found the gentlemen assembled, and which was floored, and about fifteen feet long, made a pleasant, shaded seat, through which the breeze swept constantly; for this country is famous for high winds. In the course of the conversation, I learned the following particulars, which will explain the condition of the country. For several years the Cheyennes and Sioux had gradually become more and more hostile to the whites, and in the latter part of August, 1841, had had a rather severe engagement with a party of sixty men, under the command of Mr. Frapp of St. Louis. The Indians lost eight or ten warriors, and the whites had their leader and four men killed. This fight took place on the waters of Snake river; and it was this party, on their return under Mr. Bridger, which had spread so much alarm among my people. In the course of the spring, two other small parties had been cut off by the Sioux--one on their return from the Crow nation, and the other among the Black hills. The emigrants to Oregon and Mr. Bridger's party met here, a few days before our arrival. Divisions and misunderstandings had grown up among them; they were already somewhat disheartened by the fatigue of their long and wearisome journey, and the feet of their cattle had become so much worn as to be scarcely able to travel. In this situation, they were not likely to find encouragement in the hostile attitude of the Indians, and the new and unexpected difficulties which sprang up before them. They were told that the country was entirely swept of grass, and that few or no buffalo were to be found on their line of route; and, with their weakened animals, it would be impossible for them to transport their heavy wagons over the mountains. Under these circumstances, they disposed of their wagons and cattle at the forts; selling them at the prices they had paid in the States, and taking in exchange coffee and sugar at one dollar a pound, and miserable worn-out horses, which died before they reached the mountains. Mr. Boudeau informed me that he had purchased thirty, and the lower fort eighty head of fine cattle, some of them of the Durham breed. Mr. Fitzpatrick, whose name and high reputation are familiar to all who interest themselves in the history of this country, had reached Laramie in company with Mr. Bridger; and the emigrants were fortunate enough to obtain his services to guide them as far as the British post of Fort Hall, about two hundred and fifty miles beyond the South Pass of the mountains. They had started for this post on the 4th of July, and immediately after their departure, a war party of three hundred and fifty braves set out upon their trail. As their principal chief or partisan had lost some relations in the recent fight, and had sworn to kill the first whites on his path, it was supposed that their intention was to attack the party, should a favorable opportunity offer; or, if they were foiled in their principal object by the vigilance of Mr. Fitzpatrick, content themselves with stealing horses and cutting off stragglers. These had been gone but a few days previous to our arrival.

The effect of the engagement with Mr. Frapp had been greatly to irritate the hostile spirit of the savages; and immediately subsequent to that event, the Gross Ventre Indians had united with the Oglallahs and Cheyennes, and taken the field in great force--so far as I could ascertain, to the amount of eight hundred lodges. Their object was to make an attack on a camp of Snake and Crow Indians, and a body of about one hundred whites, who had made a rendezvous somewhere in the Green river valley, or on the Sweet Water. After spending some time in buffalo hunting in the neighborhood of the Medicine Bow mountain, they were to cross over to the Green river waters, and return to Laramie by way of the South Pass and the Sweet Water valley. According to the calculation of the Indians, Mr. Boudeau informed me they were somewhere near the head of the Sweet Water. I subsequently learned that the party led by Mr. Fitzpatrick were overtaken by their pursuers near Rock

Independence, in the valley of the Sweet Water; but his skill and resolution saved them from surprise; and, small as his force was; they did not venture to attack him openly. Here they lost one of their party by an accident, and, continuing up the valley, they came suddenly upon the large village. From these they met with a doubtful reception. Long residence and familiar acquaintance had given to Mr. Fitzpatrick great personal influence among them, and a portion of them were disposed to let him pass quietly; but by far the greater number were inclined to hostile measures; and the chiefs spent the whole of one night, during which they kept the little party in the midst of them, in council, debating the question of attacking them the next day; but the influence of "the Broken Hand," as they called Mr. Fitzpatrick, (one of his hands having been shattered by the bursting of a gun,) at length prevailed, and obtained for them an unmolested passage; but they sternly assured him that this path was no longer open, and that any party of the whites which should hereafter be found upon it would meet with certain destruction. From all that I have been able to learn, I have no doubt that the emigrants owe their lives to Mr. Fitzpatrick.

Thus it would appear that the country was swarming with scattered war parties; and when I heard, during the day, the various contradictory and exaggerated rumors which were incessantly repeated to them, I was not surprised that so much alarm prevailed among my men. Carson, one of the best and most experienced mountaineers, fully supported the opinion given by Bridger of the dangerous state of the country, and openly expressed his conviction that we could not escape without some sharp encounters with the Indians. In addition to this, he made his will; and among the circumstances which were constantly occurring to increase their alarm, this was the most unfortunate; and I found that a number of my party had become so much intimidated, that they had requested to be discharged at this place. I dined to-day at Fort Platte, which has been mentioned as situated at the junction of Laramie river with the Nebraska. Here I heard a confirmation of the statements given above. The party of warriors, which had started a few days since on the trail of the emigrants, was expected back in fourteen days, to join the village with which their families and the old men had remained. The arrival of the latter was hourly expected; and some Indians have just come in who had left them on the Laramie fork, about twenty miles above. Mr. Bissonette, one of the traders belonging to Fort Platte, urged the propriety of taking with me an interpreter and two or three old men of the village; in which case, he thought there would be little or no hazard in encountering any of the war parties The principal danger was in being attacked before they should know who we were.

They had a confused idea of the numbers and power of our people, and dreaded to bring upon themselves the military force of the United States. This gentleman, who spoke the language fluently, offered his services to accompany me so far as the Red Buttes. He was desirous to join the large party on its return, for purposes of trade, and it would suit his views, as well as my own, to go with us to the Buttes; beyond which point it would be impossible to prevail on a Sioux to venture, on account of their fear of the Crows. From Fort Laramie to the Red Buttes, by the ordinary road, is one hundred and thirty-five miles; and, though only on the threshold of danger, it seemed better to secure the services of an interpreter for the partial distance, than to have none at all.

So far as frequent interruption from the Indians would allow, we occupied ourselves in making some astronomical calculations, and bringing the general map to this stage of our journey; but the tent was generally occupied by a succession of our ceremonious visitors. Some came for presents, and others for information of our object in coming to the country; now and then, one would dart up to the tent on horseback, jerk off his trappings, and stand silently at the door, holding his horse by the halter, signifying his desire to trade. Occasionally a savage would stalk in with an invitation to a feast of honor, a dog feast, and deliberately sit down and wait quietly until I was ready to accompany him. I went to one; the women and children were sitting outside the lodge, and we took our seats on buffalo robes spread around. The dog was in a large pot over the fire, in the middle of the lodge, and immediately on our arrival was dished up in large wooden bowls, one of which was handed to each. The flesh appeared very glutinous, with something of the flavor and appearance of mutton. Feeling something move behind me, I looked round and found that I had taken my seat among a litter of fat young puppies. Had I been nice in such matters, the prejudices of civilization might have interfered with my tranquillity; but, fortunately, I am not of delicate nerves, and continued quietly to empty my platter.

The weather was cloudy at evening, with a moderate south wind, and the thermometer at six o'clock 85 deg.. I was disappointed in my hope of obtaining an observation of an occultation, which took place about midnight. The moon brought with her heavy banks of clouds, through which she scarcely made her appearance during the night.

The morning of the 18th was cloudy and calm, the thermometer at six o'clock at 64 deg.. About nine, with a moderate wind from the west, a storm of rain came on, accompanied by sharp thunder and lightning, which lasted about an hour. During the day the expected village arrived, consisting principally of old men, women, and children. They had a considerable number of horses, and large troops of dogs. Their lodges were pitched near the fort, and our camp was constantly crowded with Indians of all sizes, from morning until night, at which time some of the soldiers generally came to drive them all off to the village. My tent was the only place which they respected. Here only came the chiefs and men of distinction, and generally one of them remained to drive away the women and children. The numerous strange instruments, applied to still stranger uses, excited awe and admiration among them; and those which I used in talking with the sun and stars they looked upon with especial reverence, as mysterious things of "great medicine."

Of the three barometers which I had brought with me thus far successfully, I found that two were out of order, and spent the greater part of the 19th in repairing them--an operation of no small difficulty in the midst of the incessant interruptions to which I was subjected. We had the misfortune to break here a large thermometer, graduated to show fifths of a degree, which I used to ascertain the temperature of boiling water, and with which I had promised myself some interesting experiments in the mountains. We had but one remaining, on which the graduation extended sufficiently high; and this was too small for exact observations. During our stay here, the men had been engaged in making numerous repairs, arranging pack-saddles, and otherwise preparing for the chance of a rough road and mountain travel. All things of this nature being ready, I gathered them around me in the evening, and told them that "I had determined to proceed the next day. They were all well armed. I had engaged the services of Mr. Bissonette as interpreter, and had taken, in the circumstances, every possible means to ensure our safety. In the rumors we had heard, I believed there was much exaggeration; that they were men accustomed to this kind of life and to the country; and that these were the dangers of every-day occurrence, and to be expected in the ordinary course of their service.

They had heard of the unsettled condition of the country before leaving St. Louis, and therefore could not make it a reason for breaking their engagements. Still, I was unwilling to take with me, on a service of some certain danger, men on whom I could not rely; and I had understood that there were among them some who were disposed to cowardice, and anxious to return; they had but to come forward at once, and state their desire, and they would be discharged, with the amount due to them for the time they had served." To their honor be it said, there was but one among them who had the face to come forward and avail himself of the permission. I asked him some few questions, in order to expose him to the ridicule of the men, and let him go. The day after our departure, he engaged himself to one of the forts, and set off with a party to the Upper Missouri. I did not think that the situation of the country justified me in taking our young companions, Messrs. Brant and Benton, along with us. In case of misfortune, it would have been thought, at the least, an act of great imprudence; and therefore, though reluctantly, I determined to leave them. Randolph had been the life of the camp, and the "***petit garcon***" was much regretted by the men, to whom his buoyant spirits had afforded great amusement. They all, however, agreed in the propriety of leaving him at the fort, because, as they said, he might cost the lives of some of the men in a fight with the Indians.

21st.--A portion of our baggage, with our field-notes and observations, and several instruments, were left at the fort. One of the gentlemen, Mr. Galpin, took charge of a barometer, which he engaged to observe during my absence; and I in trusted to Randolph, by way of occupation, the regular winding up of two of my chronometers, which were among the instruments left. Our observations showed that the chronometer which I retained for the continuation of our voyage had preserved its rate in a most satisfactory manner. As deduced from it, the longitude of Fort Laramie is 7h 01' 21", and from Lunar distance 7h 01' 29"; giving for the adopted longitude 104 deg. 47' 43". Comparing the barometrical observations made during our stay here, with those of Dr. G. Engleman at St. Louis, we find for the elevation of the fort above the Gulf of Mexico 4,470 feet. The winter climate here is remarkably mild for the latitude; but rainy weather is frequent, and the place is celebrated for winds, of which the prevailing one is the west. An east wind in summer, and a south wind in winter, are said to be always accompanied with rain.

We were ready to depart; the tents were struck, the mules geared up, and our horses saddled, and we walked up to the fort to take the **stirrup cup** with our friends in an excellent home-brewed preparation. While thus pleasantly engaged, seated in one of the little cool chambers, at the door of which a man had been stationed to prevent all intrusion from the Indians, a number of chiefs, several of them powerful, fine-looking men, forced their way into the room in spite of all opposition. Handing me the following letter, they took their seats in silence:--

"FORT PLATTE, Juillet 21, 1842.

"Mr. Fremont:--Les chefs s'etant assembles presentement me disent de vous avertir de ne point vous mettre en route, avant que le parti de jeunes gens, qui est en dehors, soient de retour. De plus, ils me disent qu'ils sont tres-certains qu'ils feront feu a la premiere rencontre. Ils doivent etre de retour dans sept a huit jours. Excusez si je vous fais ces observations, mais il me semble qu'il est mon devoir de vous avertir du danger. Meme de plus, les chefs sont les porteurs de ce billet, qui vous defendent de partir avant le retour des guerriers.

"Je suis votre obeissant serviteur, "JOSEPH BISSONETTE, "Par L.B. CHARTRAIN.

"***Les noms de quelques chefs***.--Le Chapeau de Loutre, le Casseur de Fleches, la Nuit Noir, la Queue de Boeuf."

"FORT PLATTE, July 21, 1842.

"MR. FREMONT:--The chiefs having assembled in council, have just told me to warn you not to set out before the party of young men which is now out shall have returned. Furthermore, they tell me that they are very sure they will fire upon you as soon as they meet you. They are expected back in seven or eight days. Excuse me for making these observations, but it seems my duty to warn you of danger. Moreover, the chiefs who prohibit your setting out before the return of the warriors are the bearers of this note.

"I am your obedient servant, "JOSEPH BISSONETTE, "By L.B. CHARTRAIN.

"***Names of some of the chiefs***.--The Otter Hat, the Breaker of Arrows, the Black Night, the Bull's Tail."

After reading this, I mentioned its purport to my companions; and, seeing that all were fully possessed of its contents, one of the Indians rose up, and, having first shaken hands with me, spoke as follows:

"You have come among us at a bad time. Some of our people have been killed, and our young men, who are gone to the mountains, are eager to avenge the blood of their relations, which has been shed by the whites. Our young men are bad, and, if they meet you, they will believe that you are carrying goods and ammunition to their enemies, and will fire upon you. You have told us that this will make war. We know that our great father has many soldiers and big guns, and we are anxious to have our lives. We love the whites, and are desirous of peace. Thinking of all these things, we have determined to keep you here until our warriors return. We are glad to see you among us. Our father is rich, and we expected that you would have brought presents to us--horses, guns, and blankets. But we are glad to see you. We look upon your coming as the light which goes before the sun; for you will tell our great father that you have seen us, and that we are naked and poor, and have nothing to eat; and he will send us all these things." He was followed by others to the same effect.

The observations of the savage appeared reasonable; but I was aware that they had in view only the present object of detaining me, and were unwilling I should go further into the country. In reply, I asked them, through the interpretation of Mr. Boudeau, to select two or three of their number to accompany us until we should meet their people--they should spread their robes in my tent, and eat at my table, and on their return I would give them presents in reward of their services. They declined, saying, that there were no young men left in the village, and that they were too old to travel so many days on horseback, and preferred now to smoke their pipes in the lodge, and let the warriors go on the war-path. Besides, they had no power over the young men, and were afraid to interfere with them. In my turn I addressed them.

"You say that you love the whites; why have you killed so many already this spring? You say that you love the whites, and are full of many expressions of friendship to us; but you are not willing to undergo the fatigue of a few days' ride to save our lives. We do not believe what you have said, and will not listen to you. Whatever a chief among us, tells his soldiers to do, is done. We are the soldiers of the great chief, your father. He has told us to come here and see this country, and all the Indians, his children. Why should we not go? Before we came, we heard that you had killed his people, and ceased to be his children; but we came among you peaceably, holding out our hands. Now we find that the stories we heard are not lies, and that you are no longer his friends and children. We have thrown away our bodies, and will not turn back. When you told us that your young men would kill us, you did not know that our hearts were strong, and you did not see the rifles which my young men carry in their hands. We are few, and you are many, and may kill us all; but there will be much crying in your villages, for many of your young men will stay behind, and forget to return with your warriors from the mountains. Do you think that our great chief will let his soldiers die, and forget to cover their graves? Before the snows melt again, his warriors will sweep away your villages as the fire does the prairie in the autumn. See! I have pulled down my ***white houses***, and my people are ready: when the sun is ten paces higher, we shall be on the march. If you have any thing to tell us, you will say it soon."

I broke up the conference, as I could do nothing with these people; and, being resolved to proceed, nothing was to be gained by delay. Accompanied by our hospitable friends, we returned to the camp. We had mounted our horses, and our parting salutations had been exchanged, when one of the chiefs (the Bull's Tail) arrived to tell me that they had determined to send a young man with us; and if I would point out the place of our evening camp, he should join us there. "The young man is poor," said he; "he has no horse, and expects you to give him one." I described to him the place where I intended to encamp, and, shaking hands, in a few minutes we were among the hills, and this last habitation of whites shut out from our view.

The road led over an interesting plateau between the North fork of the Platte on the right, and Laramie river on the left. At the distance of ten miles from the fort, we entered the sandy bed of a creek, a kind of defile, shaded by precipitous rocks, down which we wound our way for several hundred yards, to a place where, on the left bank, a very large spring gushes with considerable noise and force out of the limestone rock. It is called the "Warm Spring," and furnishes to the hitherto dry bed of the creek a considerable rivulet. On the opposite side, a little below the spring, is a lofty limestone escarpment, partially shaded by a grove of large trees, whose green foliage, in contrast with the whiteness of the rock, renders this a picturesque locality. The rock is fossiliferous, and, so far as I was able to determine the character of the fossils, belongs to the carboniferous limestone of the Missouri river, and is probably the western limit of that formation. Beyond this point I met with no fossils of any description.

I was desirous to visit the Platte near the point where it leaves the Black hills, and therefore followed this stream, for two or three miles, to its mouth, where I encamped on a spot which afforded good grass and prele (equisetum) for our animals. Our tents having been found too thin to protect ourselves and the instruments from the rains, which in this elevated country are attended with cold and unpleasant weather, I had procured from the Indians at Laramie a tolerably large lodge, about eighteen feet in diameter, and twenty feet in height. Such a lodge, when properly pitched, is, from its conical form, almost perfectly secure against the violent winds which are frequent in this region, and, with a fire in the centre, is a dry and warm shelter in bad weather. By raising the lower part, so as to permit the breeze to pass freely, it is converted into a pleasant summer residence, with the extraordinary advantage of being entirely free from musquitoes, one of which I never saw in an Indian lodge. While we were engaged very unskilfully in erecting this, the interpreter, Mr. Bissonette, arrived, accompanied by the Indian and his wife. She laughed at our awkwardness, and offered her assistance, of which we were frequently afterwards obliged to avail our selves, before the men acquired sufficient expertness to pitch it without difficulty. From this place we had a fine view of the gorge where the Platte issues from the Black hills, changing its character abruptly from a mountain stream into a river of the plains. Immediately around us the valley of the stream was tolerably open; and at the distance of a few miles, where the river had cut its way through the hills, was the narrow cleft, on one side of which a lofty precipice of bright red rock rose vertically above the low hills which lay between us.

22d.--In the morning, while breakfast was being prepared, I visited this place with my favorite man, Basil Lajeunesse. Entering so far as there was footing for the mules, we dismounted, and, tying our animals, continued our way on foot. Like the whole country, the scenery of the river had undergone an entire change, and was in this place the most beautiful I have ever seen. The breadth of the stream, generally near that of its valley, was from two to three hundred feet, with a swift current, occasionally broken by rapids, and the water perfectly clear. On either side rose the red precipices, and sometimes overhanging, two and four hundred feet in height, crowned with green summits, on which were scattered a few pines. At the foot of the rocks was the usual detritus, formed of masses fallen from above. Among the pines that grew here, and on the occasional banks, were the cherry, (***cerasus virginiana***,) currants, and grains de boeuf, (***shepherdia argentea***.) Viewed in the sunshine of a pleasant morning, the scenery was of a most striking and romantic beauty, which arose from the picturesque disposition of the objects, and the vivid contrast of colors. I thought with much pleasure of our approaching descent in the canoe through such interesting places; and, in the expectation of being able at that time to give to them a full examination, did not now dwell so much as might have been desirable upon the geological formations along the line of the river, where they are developed with great clearness. The upper portion of the red strata consists of very compact clay, in which are occasionally seen imbedded large pebbles. Below was a stratum of compact red sandstone, changing a little above the river into a very hard silicious limestone. There is a small but handsome open prairie immediately below this place, on the left bank of the river, which would be a good locality for a military post. There are some open groves of cottonwood on the Platte. The small stream which comes in at this place is well timbered with pine, and good building rock is abundant.

If it is in contemplation to keep open the communication with Oregon territory, a show of military force in this country is absolutely necessary; and a combination of advantages renders the neighborhood of Fort Laramie the most suitable place, on the line of the Platte, for the establishment of a military post. It is connected with the mouth of the Platte and the Upper Missouri by excellent roads, which are in frequent use, and would not in any way interfere with the range of the buffalo, on which the neighboring Indians mainly depend for support. It would render any posts on the Lower Platte unnecessary; the ordinary communication between it and the Missouri being sufficient to control the intermediate Indians. It would operate effectually to prevent any such coalitions as are now formed among the Gros Ventres, Sioux, Cheyennes, and other Indians, and would keep the Oregon road through the valley of the Sweet Water and the South Pass of the mountains constantly open. It lies at the foot of a broken and mountainous region, along which, by the establishment of small posts in the neighborhood of St. Vrain's fort, on the South fork of the Platte, and Bent's fort, on the Arkansas, a line of communication would be formed, by good wagon-roads, with our southern military posts, which would entirely command the mountain passes, hold some of the most troublesome tribes in check, and protect and facilitate our intercourse with the neighboring Spanish settlements. The valleys of the rivers on which they would be situated are fertile; the country, which supports immense herds of buffalo, is admirably adapted to grazing; and herds of cattle might be maintained by the posts, or obtained from the Spanish country, which already supplies a portion of their provisions to the trading posts mentioned above.

Just as we were leaving the camp this morning, our Indian came up, and stated his intention of not proceeding any further until he had seen the horse which I intended to give him. I felt strongly tempted to drive him out of the camp; but his presence appeared to give confidence to my men, and the interpreter thought it absolutely necessary. I was therefore obliged to do what he requested, and pointed out the animal, with which he seemed satisfied, and we continued our journey. I had imagined that Mr. Bissonette's long residence had made him acquainted with the country; and, according to his advice, proceeded directly forward, without attempting to gain the usual road. He afterwards informed me that he had rarely ever lost sight of the fort; but the effect of the mistake was to involve us for a day or two among the hills, where, although we lost no time, we encountered an exceedingly rough road.

To the south, along our line of march to-day, the main chain of the Black or Laramie hills rises precipitously. Time did not permit me to visit them; but, from comparative information, the ridge is composed of the coarse sandstone or conglomerate hereafter described. It appears to enter the region of clouds, which are arrested in their course, and lie in masses along the summits. An inverted cone of black cloud (cumulus) rested during all the forenoon on the lofty peak of Laramie mountain, which I estimated to be about two thousand feet above the fort, or six thousand five hundred above the sea. We halted to noon on the **Fourche Amere**, so called from being timbered principally with the *liard amere*, (a species of poplar,) with which the valley of the little stream is tolerably well wooded, and which, with large expansive summits, grows to the height of sixty or seventy feet.

The bed of the creek is sand and gravel, the water dispersed over the broad bed in several shallow streams. We found here, on the right bank, in the shade of the trees, a fine spring of very cold water. It will be remarked that I do not mention, in this portion of the journey, the temperature of the air, sand, springs, &c.--an omission which will be explained in the course of the narrative. In my search for plants, I was well rewarded at this place.

With the change in the geological formation on leaving Fort Laramie, the whole face of the country has entirely altered its appearance. Eastward of that meridian, the principal objects which strike the eye of a traveler are the absence of timber, and the immense expanse of prairie, covered with the verdure of rich grasses, and highly adapted for pasturage. Wherever they are not disturbed by the vicinity of man, large herds of buffalo give animation to this country. Westward of Laramie river, the region is sandy, and apparently sterile; and the place of the grass is usurped by the *artemisia* and other odoriferous plants, to whose growth the sandy soil and dry air of this elevated region seem highly favorable.

One of the prominent characteristics in the face of the country is the extraordinary abundance of the *artemisias*. They grow everywhere--on the hills, and over the river bottoms, in tough, twisted, wiry clumps; and, wherever the beaten track was left, they rendered the progress of the carts rough and slow. As the country increased in elevation on our advance to the west, they increased in size; and the whole air is strongly impregnated and saturated with the odor of camphor and spirits of turpentine which belongs to this plant. This climate has been found very favorable to the restoration of health, particularly in cases of consumption; and possibly the respiration of air so highly impregnated with aromatic plants may have some influence.

Our dried meat had given out, and we began to be in want of food; but one of the hunters killed an antelope this evening, which afforded some relief, although it did not go far among so many hungry men. At eight o'clock at night, after a march of twenty-seven miles, we reached our proposed encampment on the *Fer-a-Cheval*, or Horse-shoe creek. Here we found good grass, with a great quantity of *prele*, which furnished good food for our tired animals. This creek is well timbered, principally with *liard amere*, and, with the exception of Deer creek, which we had not yet reached, is the largest affluent of the right bank between Laramie and the mouth of the Sweet Water.

23d.--The present year had been one of unparalleled drought, and throughout the country the water had been almost dried up. By availing themselves of the annual rise, the traders had invariably succeeded in carrying their furs to the Missouri; but this season, as has already been mentioned, on both forks of the Platte they had entirely failed. The greater number of the springs, and many of the streams, which made halting places for the **voyageurs**, had been dried up. Everywhere the soil looked parched and burnt, the scanty yellow grass crisped under the foot, and even the hardest plants were destroyed by want of moisture. I think it necessary to mention this fact, because to the rapid evaporation in such an elevated region, nearly five thousand feet above the sea, almost wholly unprotected by timber, should be attributed much of the sterile appearance of the country, in the destruction of vegetation, and the numerous saline efflorescences which covered the ground. Such I afterwards found to be the case.

 I was informed that the roving villages of Indians and travelers had never met with difficulty in finding abundance of grass for their horses; and now it was after great search that we were able to find a scanty patch of grass sufficient to keep them from sinking; and in the course of a day or two they began to suffer very much. We found none to-day at noon; and, in the course of our search on the Platte, came to a grove of cottonwood, where some Indian village had recently encamped. Boughs of the cottonwood yet green covered the ground, which the Indians had cut down to feed their horses upon. It is only in the winter that recourse is had to this means of sustaining them; and their resort to it at this time was a striking evidence of the state of the country. We followed their example, and turned our horses into a grove of young poplars. This began to present itself as a very serious evil, for on our animals depended altogether the further prosecution of our journey.

 Shortly after we had left this place, the scouts came galloping in with the alarm of Indians. We turned in immediately towards the river, which here had a steep, high bank, where we formed with the carts a very close barricade, resting on the river, within which the animals were strongly hobbled and picketed. The guns were discharged and reloaded, and men thrown forward under cover of the bank, in the direction by which the Indians were expected. Our interpreter, who, with the Indian, had gone to meet them, came in, in about ten minutes, accompanied by two Sioux. They looked sulky, and we could obtain from them only some confused information. We learned that they belonged to the party which had been on the trail of the emigrants, whom they had overtaken at Rock Independence, on the Sweet Water. Here the party had disagreed, and came nigh fighting among themselves. One portion were desirous of attacking the whites, but the others were opposed to it; and finally they had broken up into small bands, and dispersed over the country. The greatest portion of them had gone over into the territory of the Crows, and intended to return by way of the Wind River valley, in the hope of being able to fall upon some small parties of Crow Indians. The remainder were returning down the Platte, in scattered parties of ten and twenty; and those whom we had encountered belonged to those who had advocated an attack on the emigrants. Several of the men suggested shooting them on the spot; but I promptly discountenanced any such proceeding. They further informed me that buffalo were very scarce, and little or no grass to be found. There had been no rain, and innumerable quantities of grasshoppers had destroyed the grass. The insects had been so numerous since leaving Fort Laramie, that the ground seemed alive with them; and in walking, a little moving cloud preceded our footsteps. This was bad news. No grass, no buffalo--food for neither horse nor man. I gave them some plugs of tobacco, and they went off, apparently well satisfied to be clear of us; for my men did not look upon them very lovingly, and they glanced suspiciously at our warlike preparations, and the little ring of rifles which surrounded them. They were evidently in a bad humor, and shot one of their horses when they had left us a short distance.

    We continued our march; and after a journey of about twenty-one miles, encamped on the Platte. During the day, I had occasionally remarked among the hills the ***psoralea esculenta***, the bread root of the Indians. The Sioux use this root very extensively, and I have frequently met with it among them, cut into thin slices and dried. In the course of the evening we were visited by six Indians, who told us that a large party was encamped a few miles above. Astronomical observations placed us in longitude 104 deg. 59' 59", and latitude 42 deg. 29' 25".

    We made the next day twenty-two miles, and encamped on the right bank of the Platte, where a handsome meadow afforded tolerably good grass. There were the remains of an old fort here, thrown up in some sudden emergency, and on the opposite side was a picturesque bluff of ferruginous sandstone. There was a handsome grove a little above, and scattered groups of trees bordered the river. Buffalo made their appearance this afternoon, and the hunters came in, shortly after we had encamped, with three fine cows. The night was fine, and observations gave for the latitude of the camp, 42 deg. 47' 40".

25th.--We made but thirteen miles this day, and encamped about noon in a pleasant grove on the right bank. Low scaffolds were erected, upon which the meat was laid, cut up into thin strips, and small fires kindled below. Our object was to profit by the vicinity of the buffalo, to lay in a stock of provisions for ten or fifteen days. In the course of the afternoon the hunters brought in five or six cows, and all hands were kept busily employed in preparing the meat, to the drying of which the guard attended during the night. Our people had recovered their gayety, and the busy figures around the blazing fires gave a picturesque air to the camp. A very serious accident occurred this morning, in the breaking of one of the barometers. These had been the object of my constant solicitude, and, as I had intended them principally for mountain service, I had used them as seldom as possible, taking them always down at night, and on the occurrence of storms, in order to lessen the chances of being broken. I was reduced to one, a standard barometer of Troughton's construction. This I determined to preserve, if possible. The latitude is 42 deg. 51' 35", and by a mean of the results from chronometer and lunar distances, the adopted longitude of this camp is 105 deg. 50' 45".

26th.--Early this morning we were again in motion. We had a stock of provisions for fifteen days carefully stored away in the carts, and this I resolved should only be encroached upon when our rifles should fail to procure us present support. I determined to reach the mountains, if it were in any way possible. In the mean time, buffalo were plenty. In six miles from our encampment (which, by way of distinction, we shall call Dried Meat camp) we crossed a handsome stream, called *La Fourche Boisce*. It is well timbered, and, among the flowers in bloom on its banks, I remarked several *asters*.

Five miles further, we made our noon halt on the banks of the Platte, in the shade of some cottonwoods. There were here, as generally now along the river, thickets of *hippophae*, the *grains de boeuf* of the country. They were of two kinds--one bearing a red berry, (the *shepherdia argentea* of Nuttall;) the other a yellow berry, of which the Tartars are said to make a kind of rob.

By a meridian observation, the latitude of the place was 42 deg. 50' 08". It was my daily practice to take observations of the sun's meridian altitude; and why they are not given, will appear in the sequel. Eight miles further we reached the mouth of Deer creek, where we encamped. Here was abundance of rich grass, and our animals were compensated for past privations. This stream was at this time twenty feet broad, and well timbered with cottonwood of an uncommon size. It is the largest tributary of the Platte, between the mouth of the Sweet Water and the Laramie. Our astronomical observations gave for the mouth of the stream a longitude of 106 deg. 08' 24", and latitude 42 deg. 52' 24".

27th.--Nothing worthy of mention occurred on this day; we traveled later than usual, having spent some time searching for grass, crossing and recrossing the river before we could find a sufficient quantity for our animals. Towards dusk we encamped among some artemisia bushes, two and three feet in height, where some scattered patches of short tough grass afforded a scanty supply. In crossing, we had occasion to observe that the river was frequently too deep to be forded, though we always succeeded in finding a place where the water did not enter the carts. The stream continued very clear, with two or three hundred feet breadth of water, and the sandy bed and banks were frequently covered with large round pebbles. We had traveled this day twenty-seven miles. The main chain of the Black hills was here only about seven miles to the south, on the right bank of the river, rising abruptly to the height of eight and twelve hundred feet. Patches of green grass in the ravines on the steep sides marked the presence of springs, and the summits were clad with pines.

28th.--In two miles from our encampment, we reached the place where the regular road crosses the Platte. There was two hundred feet breadth of water at this time in the bed, which has a variable width of eight to fifteen hundred feet. The channels were generally three feet deep, and there were large angular rocks on the bottom, which made the ford in some places a little difficult. Even at its low stages, this river cannot be crossed at random, and this has always been used as the best ford. The low stage of the water the present year had made it fordable in almost any part of its course, where access could be had to its bed.

For the satisfaction of travelers, I will endeavor to give some description of the nature of the road from Laramie to this point. The nature of the soil may be inferred from its geological formation. The limestone at the eastern limit of this section is succeeded by limestone without fossils, a great variety of sandstone, consisting principally of red sandstone and fine conglomerates. The red sandstone is argillaceous, with compact white gypsum or alabaster, very beautiful. The other sandstones are gray, yellow, and ferruginous, sometimes very coarse. The apparent sterility of the country must therefore be sought for in other causes than the nature of the soil. The face of the country cannot with propriety be called hilly. It is a succession of long ridges, made by the numerous streams which come down from the neighboring mountain range. The ridges have an undulating surface, with some such appearance as the ocean presents in an ordinary breeze.

The road which is now generally followed through this region is therefore a very good one, without any difficult ascents to overcome. The principal obstructions are near the river, where the transient waters of heavy rains have made deep ravines with steep banks, which renders frequent circuits necessary. It will be remembered that wagons pass this road only once or twice a year, which is by no means sufficient to break down the stubborn roots of the innumerable artemisia bushes. A partial absence of these is often the only indication of the track; and the roughness produced by their roots in many places gives the road the character of one newly opened in a wooded country. This is usually considered the worst part of the road east of the mountains; and, as it passes through an open prairie region, may be much improved, so as to avoid the greater part of the inequalities it now presents.

From the mouth of the Kansas to the Green River valley west of the mountains, there is no such thing as a mountain road on the line of communication.

We continued our way, and four miles beyond the ford Indians were discovered again; and I halted while a party were sent forward to ascertain who they were. In a short time they returned, accompanied by a number of Indians of the Oglallah band of Sioux. From them we received some interesting information. They had formed part of the great village, which they informed us had broken up, and was on its way home. The greater part of the village, including the Arapahoes, Cheyennes, and Oglallahs, had crossed the Platte eight or ten miles below the mouth of the Sweet Water, and were now behind the mountains to the south of us, intending to regain the Platte by way of Deer creek. They had taken this unusual route in search of grass and game. They gave us a very discouraging picture of the country. The great drought, and the plague of grasshoppers, had swept it so that scarce a blade of grass was to be seen, and there was not a buffalo to be found in the whole region. Their people, they further said, had been nearly starved to death, and we would find their road marked by lodges, which they had thrown away in order to move more rapidly, and by the carcasses of the horses which they had eaten, or which had perished by starvation. Such was the prospect before us.

When he had finished the interpretation of these things, Mr. Bissonette immediately rode up to me, and urgently advised that I should entirely abandon the further prosecution of my exploration. "***Le meilleure avis que je pourrais vous donner c'est de virer de suite***." "The best advice I can give you, is to turn back at once." It was his own intention to return, as we had now reached the point to which he had engaged to attend me. In reply, I called up my men, and communicated to them fully the information I had just received. I then expressed to them my fixed determination to proceed to the end of the enterprise on which I had been sent; but as the situation of the country gave me some reason to apprehend that it might be attended with an unfortunate result to some of us, I would leave it optional with them to continue with me or to return.

Among them were some five or six who I knew would remain. We had still ten days' provisions; and should no game be found, when this stock was expended, we had our horses and mules, which we could eat when other means of subsistence failed. But not a man flinched from the undertaking. "We'll eat the mules," said Basil Lajeunesse; and thereupon we shook hands with our interpreter and his Indians, and parted. With them I sent back one of my men, Dumes, whom the effects of an old wound in the leg rendered incapable of continuing the journey on foot, and his horse seemed on the point of giving out. Having resolved to disencumber ourselves immediately of every thing not absolutely necessary to our future operations, I turned directly in towards the river, and encamped on the left bank, a little above the place where our council had been held, and where a thick grove of willows offered a suitable spot for the object I had in view.

The carts having been discharged, the covers and wheels were taken off, and, with the frames, carried into some low places, among the willows, and concealed in the dense foliage in such a manner that the glitter of the iron-work might not attract the observation of some straggling Indian. In the sand, which had been blown up into waves among the willows, a large hole was then dug, ten feet square and six feet deep. In the mean time, all our effects had been spread out upon the ground, and whatever was designed to be carried along with us separated and laid aside, and the remaining part carried to the hole and carefully covered up. As much as possible, all traces of our proceedings were obliterated, and it wanted but a rain to render our *cache* safe beyond discovery. All the men were now set at work to arrange the pack-saddles and make up the packs.

The day was very warm and calm, and the sky entirely clear, except where, as usual along the summits of the mountainous ridge opposite, the clouds had congregated in masses. Our lodge had been planted, and, on account of the heat, the ground-pins had been taken out, and the lower part slightly raised. Near to it was standing the barometer, which swung in a tripod frame; and within the lodge, where a small fire had been built, Mr. Preuss was occupied in observing temperature of boiling water. At this instant, and without any warning until it was within fifty yards, a violent gust of wind dashed down the lodge, burying under it Mr. Preuss and about a dozen men, who had attempted to keep it from being carried away. I succeeded in saving the barometer, which the lodge was carrying off with itself, but the thermometer was broken. We had no others of a high graduation, none of those which remained going higher than 135 deg. Fahrenheit. Our astronomical observations gave to this place, which we named *Cache* camp, a longitude of 106 deg. 38' 26", latitude 42 deg. 50' 53".

29th.--All our arrangements having been completed, we left the encampment at 7 o'clock this morning. In this vicinity the ordinary road leaves the Platte, and crosses over to the Sweet Water river, which it strikes near Rock Independence. Instead of following this road, I had determined to keep the immediate valley of the Platte so far as the mouth of the Sweet Water, in the expectation of finding better grass. To this I was further prompted by the nature of my instructions. To Mr. Carson was assigned the office of guide, as we had now reached a part of the country with which, or a great part of which, long residence had made him familiar. In a few miles we reached the Red Buttes, a famous landmark in this country, whose geological composition is red sandstone, limestone, and calcareous sandstone and pudding-stone.

The river here cuts its way through a ridge; on the eastern side of it are the lofty escarpments of red argillaceous sandstone, which are called the Red Buttes.

In this passage the stream is not much compressed or pent up, there being a bank of considerable though variable breadth on either side. Immediately on entering, we discovered a band of buffalo. The hunters failed to kill any of them; the leading hunter being thrown into a ravine, which occasioned some delay, and in the mean time the herd clambered up the steep face of the ridge. It is sometimes wonderful to see these apparently clumsy animals make their way up and down the most broken precipices. We halted to noon before we had cleared this passage, at a spot twelve miles distant from **Cache** camp, where we found an abundance of grass. So far, the account of the Indians was found to be false. On the banks were willow and cherry trees. The cherries were not yet ripe, but in the thickets were numerous fresh tracks of the grizzly bear, which are very fond of this fruit. The soil here is red, the composition being derived from the red sandstone. About seven miles brought us through the ridge, in which the course of the river is north and south. Here the valley opens out broadly, and high walls of the red formation present themselves among the hills to the east. We crossed here a pretty little creek, an affluent of the right bank. It is well timbered with cottonwood in this vicinity, and the absinthe has lost its shrub-like character, and becomes small trees six and eight feet in height, and sometimes eight inches in diameter. Two or three miles above this creek we made our encampment, having traveled to-day twenty-five miles. Our animals fared well here, as there is an abundance of grass. The river bed is made up of pebbles, and in the bank, at the level of the water, is a conglomerate of coarse pebbles, about the size of ostrich eggs, and which I remarked in the banks of the Laramie fork. It is overlaid by a soil of mixed clay and sand, six feet thick. By astronomical observations, our position is in longitude 106 deg. 54' 32", and latitude 42 deg. 38'.

30th.--After traveling about twelve miles this morning, we reached a place where the Indian village had crossed the river. Here were the poles of discarded lodges and skeletons of horses lying about. Mr. Carson, who had never been higher up than this point on the river, which has the character of being exceedingly rugged, and walled in by precipices above, thought it advisable to encamp near this place, where we were certain of obtaining grass, and to-morrow make our crossing among the rugged hills to the Sweet Water river. Accordingly we turned back and descended the river to an island near by, which was about twenty acres in size, covered with a luxuriant growth of grass. The formation here I found highly interesting. Immediately at this island the river is again shut up in the rugged hills, which come down to it from the main ridge in a succession of spurs three or four hundred feet high, and alternated with green level *prairillons* or meadows, bordered on the river banks with thickets of willow, and having many plants to interest the traveler. The island lies between two of these ridges, three or four hundred yards apart, of which that on the right bank is composed entirely of red argillaceous sandstone, with thin layers of fibrous gypsum. On the left bank, the ridge is composed entirely of silicious pudding-stone, the pebbles in the numerous strata increasing in size from the top to the bottom, where they are as large as a man's head. So far as I was able to determine, these strata incline to the northeast, with a dip of about 15 deg.. This pudding- stone, or conglomerate formation, I was enabled to trace through an extended range of country, from a few miles east of the meridian of Fort Laramie to where I found it superposed on the granite of the Rocky mountains, in longitude 109 deg. 00'. From its appearance, the main chain of the Laramie mountain is composed of this rock; and in a number of places I found isolated hills, which served to mark a former level which had been probably swept away.

These conglomerates are very friable, and easily decomposed; and I am inclined to think this formation is the source from which was derived the great deposite of sand and gravel which forms the surface rock of the prairie country west of the Mississippi.

Crossing the ridge of red sandstone, and traversing the little prairie which lies to the southward of it, we made in the afternoon an excursion to a place which we called the Hot Spring Gate. This place has much the appearance of a gate, by which the Platte passes through a ridge composed of a white and calcareous sandstone. The length of the passage is about four hundred yards, with a smooth green prairie on either side. Through this place, the stream flows with a quiet current, unbroken by any rapid, and is about seventy yards wide between the walls, which rise perpendicularly from the water. To that on the right bank, which is the lower, the barometer gave a height of three hundred and sixty feet. This place will be more particularly described hereafter, as we passed through it on our return.

We saw here numerous herds of mountain sheep, and frequently heard the volley of rattling stones which accompanied their rapid descent down the steep hills. This was the first place at which we had killed any of these animals; and, in consequence of this circumstance, and of the abundance of these sheep or goats, (for they are called by each name,) we gave our encampment the name of Goat Island. Their flesh is much esteemed by the hunters, and has very much the flavor of Alleghany mountain sheep. I have frequently seen the horns of this animal three feet long and seventeen inches in circumference at the base, weighing eleven pounds. But two or three of these were killed by our party at this place, and of these the horns were small. The use of these horns seems to be to protect the animal's head in pitching down precipices to avoid pursuing wolves--their only safety being in places where they cannot be followed. The bones are very strong and solid, the marrow occupying but a very small portion of the bone in the leg, about the thickness of a rye straw. The hair is short, resembling the winter color of our common deer, which it nearly approaches in size and appearance. Except in the horns, it has no resemblance whatever to the goat. The longitude of this place, resulting from chronometer and lunar distances, and an occultation of Arietis, is 107 deg. 13' 29", and the latitude 42 deg. 33' 27". One of our horses, which had given out, we left to receive strength on the island, intending to take her, perhaps, on our return.

31st.--This morning we left the course of the Platte, to cross over to the Sweet Water. Our way, for a few miles, lay up the sandy bed of a dry creek, in which I found several interesting plants. Leaving this, we wended our way to the summit of the hills, of which the peaks are here eight hundred feet above the Platte, bare and rocky. A long and gradual slope led from these hills to the Sweet Water, which we reached in fifteen miles from Goat Island. I made an early encampment here, in order to give the hunters an opportunity to procure a supply from several bands of buffalo, which made their appearance in the valley near by. The stream is about sixty feet wide, and at this time twelve to eighteen inches deep, with a very moderate current.

The adjoining prairies are sandy, but the immediate river bottom is a good soil, which afforded an abundance of soft green grass to our horses, and where I found a variety of interesting plants, which made their appearance for the first time. A rain to-night made it unpleasantly cold; and there was no tree here, to enable us to pitch our single tent, the poles of which had been left at our **Cache camp**. We had, therefore, no shelter except what was to be found under cover of the ***absinthe*** bushes, which grew in many thick patches, one or two and sometimes three feet high.

AUGUST.

1st.--The hunters went ahead this morning, as buffalo appeared tolerably abundant, and I was desirous to secure a small stock of provisions; and we moved about seven mules up the valley, and encamped one mile below Rock Independence. This is an isolated granite rock, about six hundred and fifty yards long, and forty in height. Except in a depression of the summit, where a little soil supports a scanty growth of shrubs, with a solitary dwarf pine, it is entirely bare. Everywhere within six or eight feet of the ground, where the surface is sufficiently smooth, and in some places sixty or eighty feet above, the rock is inscribed with the names of travelers. Many a name famous in the history of this country, and some well known to science, are to be found mixed among those of the traders and travelers for pleasure and curiosity, and of missionaries among the savages. Some of these have been washed away by the rain, but the greater number are still very legible. The position of this rock is in longitude 107 deg. 56', latitude 42 deg. 29' 36". We remained at our camp of August 1st until noon of the next day, occupied in drying meat. By observation, the longitude of the place is 107 deg. 25' 23", latitude 42 deg. 29' 56".

2d.--Five miles above Rock Independence we came to a place called the Devil's Gate, where the Sweet Water cuts through the point of a granite ridge. The length of the passage is about three hundred yards, and the width thirty-five yards. The walls of rock are vertical, and about four hundred feet in height; and the stream in the gate is almost entirely choked up by masses which have fallen from above. In the wall, on the right bank, is a dike of trap-rock, cutting through a fine-grained gray granite. Near the point of this ridge crop out some strata of the valley formation, consisting of a grayish micaceous sandstone, and fine-grained conglomerate, and marl. We encamped eight miles above the Devil's Gate. There was no timber of any kind on the river, but good fires were made of drift wood, aided by the ***bois de vache***.

We had to-night no shelter from the rain, which commenced with squalls of wind about sunset. The country here is exceedingly picturesque. On either side of the valley, which is five miles broad, the mountains rise to the height of twelve and fifteen hundred or two thousand feet. On the south side, the range appears to be timbered, and to-night is luminous with fires--probably the work of the Indians, who have just passed through the valley. On the north, broken and granite masses rise abruptly from the green sward of the river, terminating in a line of broken summits. Except in the crevices of the rock, and here and there on a ledge or bench of the mountain, where a few hardy pines have clustered together, these are perfectly bare and destitute of vegetation.

Among these masses, where there are sometimes isolated hills and ridges, green valleys open in upon the river, which sweeps the base of these mountains for thirty-six miles. Everywhere its deep verdure and profusion of beautiful flowers is in pleasing contrast with the sterile grandeur of the rock and the barrenness of the sandy plain, which, from the right bank of the river, sweeps up to the mountain range that forms its southern boundary. The great evaporation on the sandy soil of this elevated plain, and the saline efflorescences which whiten the ground, and shine like lakes reflecting in the sun, make a soil wholly unfit for cultivation.

3d.--We were early on the road the next morning, traveling along the upper part of the valley, which is overgrown with ***artemisia***. Scattered about on the plain are occasional small isolated hills. One of these which I have examined, about fifty feet high, consisted of white clay and marl, in nearly horizontal strata. Several bands of buffalo made their appearance to-day, with herds of antelope; and a grizzly bear--the only one we encountered during the journey--was seen scrambling up among the rocks. As we passed over a slight rise near the river, we caught the first view of the Wind River mountains, appearing, at this distance of about seventy miles, to be a low and dark mountainous ridge. The view dissipated in a moment the pictures which had been created in our minds, by many descriptions of travelers, who have compared these mountains to the Alps in Switzerland, and speak of the glittering peaks which rise in icy majesty amidst the eternal glaciers nine or ten thousand feet into the region of eternal snows. The nakedness of the river was relieved by groves of willows, where we encamped at night, after a march of twenty-six miles; and numerous bright-colored flowers had made the river bottom look gay as a garden. We found here a horse, which had been abandoned by the Indians, because his hoofs had been so much worn that he was unable to travel; and during the night a dog came into the camp.

4th.--Our camp was at the foot of the granite mountains, which we climbed this morning to take some barometrical heights; and here among the rocks was seen the first magpie. On our return, we saw one at the mouth of the Platte river. We left here one of our horses, which was unable to proceed farther. A few miles from the encampment we left the river, which makes a bend to the south, and traversing an undulating country, consisting of a grayish micaceous sandstone and fine-grained conglomerates, struck it again, and encamped after a journey of twenty-five miles. Astronomical observations placed us in latitude 42 deg. 32' 30", and longitude 108 deg. 30' 13".

5th.--The morning was dark, with a driving rain, and disagreeably cold. We continued our route as usual and the weather became so bad, that we were glad to avail ourselves of the shelter offered by a small island, about ten miles above our last encampment, which was covered with a dense growth of willows. There was fine grass for our animals, and the timber afforded us comfortable protection and good fires. In the afternoon, the sun broke through the clouds for a short time, and the barometer at 5 P.M. was 23.713, the thermometer 60 deg., with the wind strong from the northwest. We availed ourselves of the fine weather to make excursions in the neighborhood. The river, at this place, is bordered by hills of the valley formation. They are of moderate height; one of the highest peaks on the right bank being, according to the barometer, one hundred and eighty feet above the river. On the left bank they are higher. They consist of a fine white clayey sandstone, a white calcareous sandstone, and coarse sandstone or pudding-stone.

6th.--It continued steadily raining all day; but, notwithstanding, we left our encampment in the afternoon. Our animals had been much refreshed by their repose, and an abundance of rich, soft grass, which had been much improved by the rains. In about three miles, we reached the entrance of a ***kanyon***, where the Sweet Water issues upon the more open valley we had passed over. Immediately at the entrance, and superimposed directly upon the granite, are strata of compact calcareous sandstone and chert, alternating with fine white and reddish-white, and fine gray and red sandstones. These strata dip to the eastward at an angle of about 18 deg., and form the western limit of the sandstone and limestone formations on the line of our route. Here we entered among the primitive rocks. The usual road passes to the right of this place; but we wound, or rather scrambled, our way up the narrow valley for several hours. Wildness and disorder were the character of this scenery. The river had been swollen by the late rains, and came rushing through with an impetuous current, three or four feet deep, and generally twenty yards broad. The valley was sometimes the breadth of the stream, and sometimes opened into little green meadows, sixty yards wide, with open groves of aspen. The stream was bordered throughout with aspen, beech, and willow; and tall pines grow on the sides and summits of the crags. On both sides the granite rocks rose precipitously to the height of three hundred and five hundred feet, terminating in jagged and broken pointed peaks; and fragments of fallen rock lay piled up at the foot of the precipices. Gneiss, mica slate, and a white granite, were among the varieties I noticed. Here were many old traces of beaver on the stream; remnants of dams, near which were lying trees, which they had cut down, one and two feet in diameter. The hills entirely shut up the river at the end of about five miles, and we turned up a ravine that led to a high prairie, which seemed to be the general level of the country. Hence, to the summit of the ridge, there is a regular and very gradual rise. Blocks of granite were piled up at the heads of the ravines, and small bare knolls of mica slate and milky quartz protruded at frequent intervals on the prairie, which was whitened in occasional spots with small salt lakes, where the water had evaporated, and left the bed covered with a shining incrustation of salt. The evening was very cold, a northwest wind driving a fine rain in our faces; and at nightfall we descended to a little stream, on which we encamped, about two miles from the Sweet Water. Here had recently been a very large camp of the Snake and Crow Indians; and some large poles lying about afforded the means of pitching a tent, and making other places of shelter. Our fires to-night were made principally of the dry branches of the artemisia, which covered the slopes. It burns quickly, and with a clear oily flame, and makes a hot fire. The hills here are composed of hard, compact mica slate, with veins of quartz.

    7th.--We left our encampment with the rising sun. As we rose from the bed of the creek, the *snow* line of the mountains stretched gradually before us, the white peaks glittering in the sun. They had been hidden in the dark weather of the last few days, and it had been *snowing* on them, while it *rained* in the plains. We crossed a ridge, and again struck the Sweet Water--here a beautiful, swift stream, with a more open valley, timbered with beech and cottonwood. It now began to lose itself in the many small forks which make its head; and we continued up the main stream until near noon, when we left it a few miles, to make our noon halt on a small creek among the hills, from which the stream issues by a small opening. Within was a beautiful grassy spot, covered with an open grove of large beech-trees, among which I found several plants that I had not previously seen.

The afternoon was cloudy, with squalls of rain; but the weather became fine at sunset, when we again encamped on the Sweet Water, within a few miles of the SOUTH PASS. The country over which we have passed to-day consists principally of the compact mica slate, which crops out on all ridges, making the uplands very rocky and slaty. In the escarpments which border the creeks, it is seen alternating with a light-colored granite, at an inclination of 45 deg.; the beds varying in thickness from two or three feet to six or eight hundred. At a distance, the granite frequently has the appearance of irregular lumps of clay, hardened by exposure. A variety of *asters* may how be numbered among the characteristic plants, and the artemisia continues in full glory; but *cacti* have become rare, and mosses begin to dispute the hills with them. The evening was damp and unpleasant--the thermometer, at ten o'clock, being at 36 deg., and the grass wet with a heavy dew. Our astronomical observations placed this encampment in longitude 109 deg. 21' 32", and latitude 42 deg. 27' 15".

Early in the morning we resumed our journey, the weather, still cloudy, with occasional rain. Our general course was west, as I had determined to cross the dividing ridge by a bridle-path among the country more immediately at the foot of the mountains, and return by the wagon road, two and a half miles to the south of the point where the trail crosses.

About six miles from our encampment brought us to the summit. The ascent had been so gradual, that, with all the intimate knowledge possessed by Carson, who had made the country his home for seventeen years, we were obliged to watch very closely to find the place at which we had reached the culminating point. This was between two low hills, rising on either hand fifty or sixty feet. When I looked back at them, from the foot of the immediate slope on the western plain, their summits appeared to be about one hundred and twenty feet above. From the impression on my mind at this time, and subsequently on our return, I should compare the elevation which we surmounted immediately at the Pass, to the ascent of the Capitol hill from the avenue, at Washington. It is difficult for me to fix positively the breadth of this Pass. From the broken ground where it commences, at the foot of the Wind River chain, the view to the southeast is over a champaign country, broken, at the distance of nineteen miles, by the Table rock; which, with the other isolated hills in its vicinity, seem to stand on a comparative plain. This I judged to be its termination, the ridge recovering its rugged character with the Table rock. It will be seen that it in no manner resembles the places to which the term is commonly applied--nothing of the gorge-like character and winding ascents of the Alleghany passes in America; nothing of the Great St. Bernard and Simplon passes in Europe. Approaching it from the mouth of the Sweet Water, a sandy plain, one hundred and twenty miles long, conducts, by a gradual and regular ascent, to the summit, about seven thousand feet above the sea; and the traveler, without being reminded of any change by toilsome ascents, suddenly finds himself on the waters which flow to the Pacific ocean. By the route we had traveled, the distance from Fort Laramie is three hundred and twenty miles, or nine hundred and fifty from the mouth of the Kansas.

Continuing our march, we reached, in eight miles from the Pass, the Little Sandy, one of the tributaries of the Colorado, or Green river of the Gulf of California. The weather had grown fine during the morning, and we remained here the rest of the day, to dry our baggage and take some astronomical observations. The stream was about forty feet wide, and two or three deep, with clear water and a full swift current, over a sandy bed. It was timbered with a growth of low bushy and dense willows, among which were little verdant spots, which gave our animals fine grass, and where I found a number of interesting plants. Among the neighboring hills I noticed fragments of granite containing magnetic iron. Longitude of the camp was 109 deg. 37' 59", and latitude 42 deg. 27' 34".

9th.--We made our noon halt on Big Sandy, another tributary of Green river. The face of the country traversed was of a brown sand of granite materials, the ***detritus*** of the neighboring mountain. Strata of the milky quartz cropped out, and blocks of granite were scattered about, containing magnetic iron. On Sandy creek the formation was of parti- colored sand, exhibited in escarpments fifty to eighty feet high. In the afternoon we had a severe storm of hail, and encamped at sunset on the first New Fork. Within the space of a few miles, the Wind mountains supply a number of tributaries to Green river, which are called the New Forks. Near our camp were two remarkable isolated hills, one of them sufficiently large to merit the name of mountain. They are called the Two Buttes, and will serve to identify the place of our encampment, which the observations of the evening placed in longitude 109 deg. 58' 11", and latitude 42 deg. 42' 46". On the right bank of the stream, opposite to the large hill, the strata which are displayed consist of decomposing granite, which supplies the brown sand of which the face of the country is composed to a considerable depth.

10th.--The air at sunrise is clear and pure, and the morning extremely cold, but beautiful. A lofty snowy peak of the mountain is glittering in the first rays of the sun, which have not yet reached us. The long mountain wall to the east, rising two thousand feet abruptly from the plain, behind which we see the peaks, is still dark, and cuts clear against the glowing sky. A fog, just risen from the river, lies along the base of the mountain. A little before sunrise, the thermometer was at 35 deg., and at sunrise 33 deg.. Water froze last night, and fires are very comfortable. The scenery becomes hourly more interesting and grand, and the view here is truly magnificent; but, indeed, it needs something to repay the long prairie journey of a thousand miles. The sun has shot above the wall, and makes a magical change. The whole valley is glowing and bright, and all the mountain peaks are gleaming like silver. Though these snow mountains are not the Alps, they have their own character of grandeur and magnificence, and doubtless will find pens and pencils to do them justice. In the scene before us, we feel how much wood improves a view. The pines on the mountain seemed to give it much additional beauty. I was agreeably disappointed in the character of the streams on this side of the ridge. Instead of the creeks, which description had led me to expect, I find bold, broad streams, with three or four feet water, and a rapid current. The fork on which we are encamped is upwards of a hundred feet wide, timbered with groves or thickets of the low willow. We were now approaching the loftiest part of the Wind River chain; and I left the valley a few miles from our encampment, intending to penetrate the mountains as far as possible with the whole party. We were soon involved in very broken ground, among long ridges covered with fragments of granite. Winding our way up a long ravine, we came unexpectedly in view of a most beautiful lake, set like a gem in the mountains. The sheet of water lay transversely across the direction we had been pursuing; and, descending the steep, rocky ridge, where it was necessary to lead our horses, we followed its banks to the southern extremity. Here a view of the utmost magnificence and grandeur burst upon our eyes. With nothing between us and their feet to lessen the effect of the whole height, a grand bed of snow-capped mountains rose before us, pile upon pile, glowing in the bright light of an August day. Immediately below them lay the lake, between two ridges, covered with dark pines, which swept down from the main chain to the spot where we stood. Here, where the lake glittered in the open sunlight, its banks of yellow sand and the light foliage of aspen groves contrasted well with the gloomy pines. "Never before," said Mr. Preuss, "in this country or in Europe, have I seen such grand, magnificent rocks." I was so much pleased with the beauty of the place, that I determined to make the main camp here, where our animals would find good pasturage, and explore the mountains with a small party of men. Proceeding a little further, we came suddenly upon the outlet of the lake, where it found its way through a narrow passage between low hills. Dark pines which overhung the stream, and masses of rock, where the water foamed along, gave it much romantic beauty. Where we crossed, which was immediately at the outlet, it is two hundred and fifty feet wide, and so deep that with difficulty we were able to ford it. Its bed was an accumulation of rocks, boulders, and broad slabs, and large angular fragments, among which the animals fell repeatedly.

The current was very swift, and the water cold, and of a crystal purity. In crossing this stream, I met with a great misfortune in having my barometer broken. It was the only one. A great part of the interest of the journey for me was in the exploration of these mountains, of which so much had been said that was doubtful and contradictory; and now their snowy peaks rose majestically before me, and the only means of giving them authentically to science, the object of my anxious solicitude by night and day, was destroyed. We had brought this barometer in safety a thousand miles, and broke it almost among the snow of the mountains. The loss was felt by the whole camp--all had seen my anxiety, and aided me in preserving it. The height of these mountains, considered by many hunters and traders the highest in the whole range, had been a theme of constant discussion among them; and all had looked forward with pleasure to the moment when the instrument, which they believed to be as true as the sun, should stand upon the summits, and decide their disputes. Their grief was only inferior to my own.

The lake is about three miles long, and of very irregular width, and apparently great depth, and is the head-water of the third New Fork, a tributary to Green river, the Colorado of the west. In the narrative I have called it Mountain lake. I encamped on the north side, about three hundred and fifty yards from the outlet. This was the most western point at which I obtained astronomical observations, by which this place, called Bernier's encampment, is made in 110 deg. 08' 03" west longitude from Greenwich, and latitude 43 deg. 49' 49". The mountain peaks, as laid down, were fixed by bearings from this and other astronomical points. We had no other compass than the small ones used in sketching the country; but from an azimuth, in which one of them was used, the variation of the compass is 18 deg. east. The correction made in our field-work by the astronomical observations indicates that this is a very correct observation.

As soon as the camp was formed, I set about endeavoring to repair my barometer. As I have already said, this was a standard cistern barometer, of Troughton's construction. The glass cistern had been broken about midway; but as the instrument had been kept in a proper position, no air had found its way into the tube, the end of which had always remained covered. I had with me a number of vials of tolerably thick glass, some of which were of the same diameter as the cistern, end I spent the day in slowly working on these, endeavoring to cut them of the requisite length; but, as my instrument was a very rough file, I invariably broke them. A groove was cut in one of the trees, where the barometer was placed during the night, to be out of the way of any possible danger, and in the morning I commenced again. Among the powder-horns in the camp, I found one which was very transparent, so that its contents could be almost as plainly seen as through glass. This I boiled and stretched on a piece of wood to the requisite diameter, and scraped it very thin, in order to increase to the utmost its transparency. I then secured it firmly in its place on the instrument, with strong glue made from a buffalo, and filled it with mercury, properly heated. A piece of skin, which had covered one of the vials, furnished a good pocket, which was well secured with strong thread and glue, and then the brass cover was screwed to its place. The instrument was left some time to dry; and when I reversed it, a few hours after, I had the satisfaction to find it in perfect order; its indications being about the same as on the other side of the lake before it had been broken. Our success in this little incident diffused pleasure throughout the camp; and we immediately set about our preparations for ascending the mountains.

As will be seen on reference to a map, on this short mountain chain are the head-waters of four great rivers on the continent, namely: the Colorado, Columbia, Missouri, and Platte rivers. It had been my design, after ascending the mountains, to continue our route on the western side of the range, and crossing through a pass at the northwestern end of the chain, about thirty miles from our present camp, return along the eastern slope, across the heads of the Yellowstone river, and join on the line to our station of August 7, immediately at the foot of the ridge. In this way, I should be enabled to include the whole chain, and its numerous waters, in my survey; but various considerations induced me, very reluctantly, to abandon this plan.

I was desirous to keep strictly within the scope of my instructions, and it would have required ten or fifteen additional days for the accomplishment of this object; our animals had become very much worn out with the length of the journey; game was very scarce; and, though it does not appear in the course of the narrative, (as I have avoided dwelling upon trifling incidents not connected with the objects of the expedition,) the spirits of the men had been much exhausted by the hardships and privations to which they had been subjected. Our provisions had wellnigh all disappeared. Bread had been long out of the question; and of all our stock, we had remaining two or three pounds of coffee, and a small quantity of macaroni, which had been husbanded with great care for the mountain expedition we were about to undertake. Our daily meal consisted of dry buffalo meat, cooked in tallow; and, as we had not dried this with Indian skill, part of it was spoiled; and what remained of good, was as hard as wood, having much the taste and appearance of so many pieces of bark. Even of this, our stock was rapidly diminishing in a camp which was capable of consuming two buffaloes in every twenty-four hours. These animals had entirely disappeared; and it was not probable that we should fall in with them again until we returned to the Sweet Water.

Our arrangements for the ascent were rapidly completed. We were in a hostile country, which rendered the greatest vigilance and circumspection necessary. The pass at the north end of the mountain was greatly infested by Blackfeet, and immediately opposite was one of their forts, on the edge of a little thicket, two or three hundred feet from our encampment. We were posted in a grove of beech, on the margin of the lake, and a few hundred feet long, with a narrow *prairillon* on the inner side, bordered by the rocky ridge. In the upper end of this grove we cleared a circular space about forty feet in diameter, and, with the felled timber, and interwoven branches, surrounded it with a breastwork five feet in height. A gap was left for a gate on the inner side, by which the animals were to be driven in and secured, while the men slept around the little work. It was half hidden by the foliage, and garrisoned by twelve resolute men, would have set at defiance any band of savages which might chance to discover them in the interval of our absence. Fifteen of the best mules, with fourteen men, were selected for the mountain party. Our provisions consisted of dried meat for two days, with our little stock of coffee and some macaroni. In addition to the barometer and thermometer, I took with me a sextant and spyglass, and we had of course our compasses. In charge of the camp I left Bernier, one of my most trustworthy men, who possessed the most determined courage.

12th.--Early in the morning we left the camp, fifteen in number, well armed, of course, and mounted on our best mules. A pack-animal carried our provisions, with a coffeepot and kettle, and three or four tin cups. Every man had a blanket strapped over his saddle, to serve for his bed, and the instruments were carried by turns on their backs. We entered directly on rough and rocky ground; and, just after crossing the ridge, had the good fortune to shoot an antelope. We heard the roar, and had a glimpse of a waterfall as we rode along, and, crossing in our way two fine streams, tributary to the Colorado, in about two hours' ride we reached the top of the first row or range of the mountains. Here, again, a view of the most romantic beauty met our eyes. It seemed as if, from the vast expanse of uninteresting prairie we had passed over, Nature had collected all her beauties together in one chosen place. We were overlooking a deep valley, which was entirely occupied by three lakes, and from the brink to the surrounding ridges rose precipitously five hundred and a thousand feet, covered with the dark green of the balsam pine, relieved on the border of the lake with the light foliage of the aspen. They all communicated with each other, and the green of the waters, common to mountain lakes of great depth, showed that it would be impossible to cross them. The surprise manifested by our guides when these impassable obstacles suddenly barred our progress, proved that they were among the hidden treasures of the place, unknown even to the wandering trappers of the region. Descending the hill, we proceeded to make our way along the margin to the southern extremity. A narrow strip of angular fragments of rock sometimes afforded a rough pathway for our mules, but generally we rode along the shelving side, occasionally scrambling up, at a considerable risk of tumbling back into the lake.

The slope was frequently 60 deg.; the pines grew densely together and the ground was covered with the branches and trunks of trees. The air was fragrant with the odor of the pines; and I realized this delightful morning the pleasure of breathing that mountain air which makes a constant theme of the hunter's praise, and which now made us feel as if we had all been drinking some exhilarating gas. The depths of this unexplored forest were a place to delight the heart of a botanist. There was a rich undergrowth of plants, and numerous gay-colored flowers in brilliant bloom. We reached the outlet at length, where some freshly-barked willows that lay in the water showed that beaver had been recently at work.

There were some small brown squirrels jumping about in the pines, and a couple of large mallard ducks swimming about in the stream.

The hills on this southern end were low, and the lake looked like a mimic sea, as the waves broke on the sandy beach in the force of a strong breeze. There was a pretty open spot, with fine grass for our mules; and we made our noon halt on the beach, under the shade of some large hemlocks. We resumed our journey after a halt of about an hour, making our way up the ridge on the western side of the lake. In search of smoother ground, we rode a little inland; and, passing through groves of aspen, soon found ourselves again among the pines. Emerging from these, we struck the summit of the ridge above the upper end of the lake.

We had reached a very elevated point, and in the valley below, and among the hills, were a number of lakes of different levels; some two or three hundred feet above others, with which they communicated by foaming torrents. Even to our great height the roar of the cataracts came up, and we could see them leaping down in lines of snowy foam. From this scene of busy waters, we turned abruptly into the stillness of a forest, where we rode among the open bolls of the pines, over a lawn of verdant grass, having strikingly the air of cultivated grounds. This led us, after a time, among masses of rock which had no vegetable earth but in hollows and crevices though still the pine forest continued. Towards evening we reached a defile, or rather a hole in the mountains, entirely shut in by dark pine-covered rocks.

A small stream, with scarcely perceptible current, flowed through a level bottom of perhaps eighty yards width, where the grass was saturated with water. Into this the mules were turned, and were neither hobbled nor picketed during the night, as the fine pasturage took away all temptation to stray; and we made our bivouac in the pines. The surrounding masses were all of granite. While supper was being prepared, I set out on an excursion in the neighborhood, accompanied by one of my men. We wandered about among the crags and ravines until dark, richly repaid for our walk by a fine collection of plants, many of them in full bloom. Ascending a peak to find the place of our camp, we saw that the little defile in which we lay communicated with the long green valley of some stream, which, here locked up in the mountains, far away to the south, found its way in a dense forest to the plains.

Looking along its upward course, it seemed to conduct, by a smooth gradual slope, directly towards the peak, which, from long consultation as we approached the mountain, we had decided to be the highest of the range. Pleased with the discovery of so fine a road for the next day, we hastened down to the camp, where we arrived just in time for supper. Our table-service was rather scant; and we held the meat in our hands, and clean rocks made good plates, on which we spread our macaroni. Among all the strange places on which we had occasion to encamp during our long journey, none have left so vivid an impression on my mind as the camp of this evening. The disorder of the masses which surrounded us--the little hole through which we saw the stars over head--the dark pines where we slept-- and the rocks lit up with the glow of our fires, made a night-picture of very wild beauty.

13th.--The morning was bright and pleasant, just cool enough to make exercise agreeable, and we soon entered the defile I had seen the preceding day. It was smoothly carpeted with soft grass, and scattered over with groups of flowers, of which yellow was the predominant color. Sometimes we were forced, by an occasional difficult pass, to pick our way on a narrow ledge along the side of the defile, and the mules were frequently on their knees; but these obstructions were rare, and we journeyed on in the sweet morning air, delighted at our good fortune in having found such a beautiful entrance to the mountains. This road continued for about three miles, when we suddenly reached its termination in one of the grand views which, at every turn, meet the traveler in this magnificent region. Here the defile up which we had traveled opened out into a small lawn, where, in a little lake, the stream had its source.

There were some fine *asters* in bloom, but all the flowering plants appeared to seek the shelter of the rocks, and to be of lower growth than below, as if they loved the warmth of the soil, and kept out of the way of the winds. Immediately at our feet, a precipitous descent led to a confusion of defiles, and before us rose the mountains, as we have represented them in the annexed view. It is not by the splendor of far-off views, which have lent such a glory to the Alps, that these impress the mind; but by a gigantic disorder of enormous masses, and a savage sublimity of naked rock, in wonderful contrast with innumerable green spots of a rich floral beauty, shut up in their stern recesses. Their wildness seems well suited to the character of the people who inhabit the country.

I determined to leave our animals here, and make the rest of our way on foot. The peak appeared so near, that there was no doubt of our returning before night; and a few men were left in charge of the mules, with our provisions and blankets. We took with us nothing but our arms and instruments, and, as the day had become warm, the greater part left our coats. Having made an early dinner, we started again. We were soon involved in the most ragged precipices, nearing the central chain very slowly, and rising but little. The first ridge hid a succession of others; and when, with great fatigue and difficulty, we had climbed up five hundred feet, it was but to make an equal descent on the other side; all these intervening places were filled with small deep lakes, which met the eye in every direction, descending from one level to another, sometimes under bridges formed by huge fragments of granite, beneath which was heard the roar of the water. These constantly obstructed our path, forcing us to make long *detours*; frequently obliged to retrace our steps, and frequently falling among the rocks. Maxwell was precipitated towards the face of a precipice, and saved himself from going over by throwing himself flat on the ground. We clambered on, always expecting, with every ridge that we crossed, to reach the foot of the peaks, and always disappointed, until about four o'clock, when, pretty well worn out, we reached the shore of a little lake, in which was a rocky island. We remained here a short time to rest, and continued on around the lake, which had in some places a beach of white sand, and in others was bound with rocks, over which the way was difficult and dangerous, as the water from innumerable springs made them very slippery.

By the time we had reached the further side of the lake, we found ourselves all exceedingly fatigued, and, much to the satisfaction of the whole party, we encamped. The spot we had chosen was a broad flat rock, in some measure protected from the winds by the surrounding crags, and the trunks of fallen pines afforded us bright fires. Near by was a foaming torrent, which tumbled into the little lake about one hundred and fifty feet below us, and which, by way of distinction, we have called Island lake. We had reached the upper limit of the piney region; as, above this point, no tree was to be seen, and patches of snow lay everywhere around us, on the cold sides of the rocks. The flora of the region we had traversed since leaving our mules was extremely rich, and, among the characteristic plants, the scarlet flowers of the **_dodecatheon dentatum_** everywhere met the eye, in great abundance. A small green ravine, on the edge of which we were encamped, was filled with a profusion of alpine plants, in brilliant bloom. From barometrical observations, made during our three days' sojourn at this place, its elevation above the Gulf of Mexico is 10,000 feet. During the day, we had seen no sign of animal life; but among the rocks here, we heard what was supposed to be the bleat of a young goat, which we searched for with hungry activity, and found to proceed from a small animal of a gray color, with short ears and no tail-- probably the Siberian squirrel. We saw a considerable number of them, and, with the exception of a small bird like a sparrow, it is the only inhabitant of this elevated part of the mountains. On our return, we saw, below this lake, large flocks of the mountain-goat. We had nothing to eat to-night. Lajeunesse, with several others, took their guns, and sallied out in search of a goat; but returned unsuccessful. At sunset, the barometer stood at 20.522; the attached thermometer 50 deg.. Here we had the misfortune to break our thermometer, having now only that attached to the barometer. I was taken ill shortly after we had encamped, and continued so until late in the night, with violent headache and vomiting. This was probably caused by the excessive fatigue I had undergone, and want of food, and perhaps, also, in some measure, by the rarity of the air. The night was cold, as a violent gale from the north had sprung up at sunset, which entirely blew away the heat of the fires. The cold, and our granite beds, had not been favorable to sleep, and we were glad to see the face of the sun in the morning. Not being delayed by any preparation for breakfast, we set out immediately.

On every side, as we advanced, was heard the roar of waters, and of a torrent, which we followed up a short distance, until it expanded into a lake about one mile in length. On the northern side of the lake was a bank of ice, or rather of snow covered with a crust of ice. Carson had been our guide into the mountains, and, agreeably to his advice, we left this little valley, and took to the ridges again, which we found extremely broken, and where we were again involved among precipices. Here were ice- fields; among which we were all dispersed, seeking each the best path to ascend the peak. Mr. Preuss attempted to walk along the upper edge of one of these fields, which sloped away at an angle of about twenty degrees; but his feet slipped from under him, and he went plunging down the plain. A few hundred feet below, at the bottom, were some fragments of sharp rock, on which he landed; and, though he turned a couple of somersets, fortunately received no injury beyond a few bruises. Two of the men, Clement Lambert and Descoteaux, had been taken ill, and lay down on the rocks, a short distance below; and at this point I was attacked with headache and giddiness, accompanied by vomiting, as on the day before. Finding myself unable to proceed, I sent the barometer over to Mr. Preuss, who was in a gap two or three hundred yards distant, desiring him to reach the peak if possible, and take an observation there. He found himself unable to proceed further in that direction, and took an observation, where the barometer stood at 19.401; attached thermometer 50 deg., in the gap. Carson, who had gone over to him, succeeded in reaching one of the snowy summits of the main ridge, whence he saw the peak towards which all our efforts had been directed, towering eight or ten hundred feet into the air above him. In the mean time, finding myself grow rather worse than better, and doubtful how far my strength would carry me, I sent Basil Lajeunesse, with four men, back to the place where the mules had been left.

We were now better acquainted with the topography of the country, and I directed him to bring back with him, if it were in any way possible, four or five mules, with provisions and blankets. With me were Maxwell and Ayer; and after we had remained nearly an hour on the rock, it became so unpleasantly cold, though the day was bright, that we set out on our return to the camp, at which we all arrived safely, straggling in one after the other. I continued ill during the afternoon, but became better towards sundown, when my recovery was completed by the appearance of Basil and four men, all mounted. The men who had gone with him had been too much fatigued to return, and were relieved by those in charge of the horses; but in his powers of endurance Basil resembled more a mountain-goat than a man. They brought blankets and provisions, and we enjoyed well our dried meat and a cup of good coffee. We rolled ourselves up in our blankets, and, with our feet turned to a blazing fire, slept soundly until morning.

15th.--It had been supposed that we had finished with the mountains; and the evening before it had been arranged that Carson should set out at daylight, and return to breakfast at the Camp of the Mules, taking with him all but four or five men, who were to stay with me and bring back the mules and instruments. Accordingly, at the break of day they set out. With Mr. Preuss and myself remained Basil Lajeunesse, Clement Lambert, Janisse, and Descoteaux. When we had secured strength for the day by a hearty breakfast, we covered what remained, which was enough for one meal, with rocks, in order that it might be safe from any marauding bird, and, saddling our mules, turned our faces once more towards the peaks. This time we determined to proceed quietly and cautiously, deliberately resolved to accomplish our object if it were within the compass of human means. We were of opinion that a long defile which lay to the left of yesterday's route would lead us to the foot of the main peak. Our mules had been refreshed by the fine grass in the little ravine at the Island camp, and we intended to ride up the defile as far as possible, in order to husband our strength for the main ascent. Though this was a fine passage, still it was a defile of the most rugged mountains known, and we had many a rough and steep slippery place to cross before reaching the end. In this place the sun rarely shone; snow lay along the border of the small stream which flowed through it, and occasional icy passages made the footing of the mules very insecure, and the rocks and ground were moist with the trickling waters in this spring of mighty rivers. We soon had the satisfaction to find ourselves riding along the huge wall which forms the central summits of the chain. There at last it rose by our sides, a nearly perpendicular wall of granite, terminating 2,000 to 3,000 feet above our heads in a serrated line of broken, jagged cones. We rode on until we came almost immediately below the main peak, which I denominated the Snow peak, as it exhibited more snow to the eye than any of the neighboring summits. Here were three small lakes of a green color, each, perhaps, of a thousand yards in diameter, and apparently very deep. These lay in a kind of chasm; and, according to the barometer, we had attained but a few hundred feet above the Island lake. The barometer here stood at 20.450, attached thermometer 70 deg..

We managed to get our mules up to a little bench about a hundred feet above the lakes, where there was a patch of good grass, and turned them loose to graze. During our rough ride to this place, they had exhibited a wonderful surefootedness. Parts of the defile were filled with angular, sharp fragments of rock, three or four and eight or ten feet cube; and among these they had worked their way, leaping from one narrow point to another, rarely making a false step, and giving us no occasion to dismount. Having divested ourselves of every unnecessary encumbrance, we commenced the ascent. This time, like experienced travelers, we did not press ourselves, but climbed leisurely, sitting down so soon as we found breath beginning to fail. At intervals we reached places where a number of springs gushed from the rocks, and about 1800 feet above the lakes came to the snow line. From this point our progress was uninterrupted climbing. Hitherto I had worn a pair of thick moccasins, with soles of ***parfleche***, but here I put on a light, thin pair, which I had brought for the purpose, as now the use of our toes became necessary to a further advance. I availed myself of a sort of comb of the mountain, which stood against the wall like a buttress, and which the wind and the solar radiation, joined to the steepness of the smooth rock, had kept almost entirely free from snow. Up this I made my way rapidly. Our cautious method of advancing at the outset had spared my strength; and, with the exception of a slight disposition to headache, I felt no remains of yesterday's illness. In a few minutes we reached a point where the buttress was overhanging, and there was no other way of surmounting the difficulty than by passing around one side of it, which was the face of a vertical precipice of several hundred feet.

Putting hands and feet in the crevices between the blocks, I succeeded in getting over it, and, when I reached the top, found my companions in a small valley below. Descending to them, we continued climbing, and in a short time reached the crest. I sprang upon the summit, and another step would have precipitated me into an immense snow-field five hundred feet below. To the edge of this field was a sheer icy precipice; and then, with a gradual fall, the field sloped off for about a mile, until it struck the foot of another lower ridge. I stood on a narrow crest, about three feet in width, with an inclination of about 20 deg.N. 51 deg.E. As soon as I had gratified the first feelings of curiosity, I descended, and each man ascended in his turn; for I would only allow one at a time to mount the unstable and precarious slab, which it seemed a breath would hurl into the abyss below. We mounted the barometer in the snow of the summit, and, fixing a ramrod in a crevice, unfurled the national flag to wave in the breeze where never flag waved before. During our morning's ascent, we had met no sign of animal life, except the small sparrow-like bird already mentioned. A stillness the most profound and a terrible solitude forced themselves constantly on the mind as the great features of the place. Here, on the summit, where the stillness was absolute, unbroken by any sound, and solitude complete, we thought ourselves beyond the region of animated life; but while we were sitting on the rock, a solitary bee (*bromus, the humble-bee*) came winging his flight from the eastern valley, and lit on the knee of one of the men.

It was a strange place, the icy rock and the highest peak of the Rocky mountains, for a lover of warm sunshine and flowers; and we pleased ourselves with the idea that he was the first of his species to cross the mountain barrier--a solitary pioneer to foretell the advance of civilization. I believe that a moment's thought would have made us let him continue his way unharmed; but we carried out the law of this country, where all animated nature seems at war; and, seizing him immediately, put him in at least a fit place--in the leaves of a large book, among the flowers we had collected on our way. The barometer stood at 18.293, the attached thermometer at 44 deg.; giving for the elevation of this summit 13,570 feet above the Gulf of Mexico, which may be called the highest flight of the bee. It is certainly the highest known flight of that insect. From the description given by Mackenzie of the mountains where he crossed them, with that of a French officer still farther to the north, and Colonel Long's measurements to the south, joined to the opinion of the oldest traders of the country, it is presumed that this is the highest peak of the Rocky mountains. The day was sunny and bright, but a slight shining mist hung over the lower plains, which interfered with our view of the surrounding country. On one side we overlooked innumerable lakes and streams, the spring of the Colorado of the Gulf of California; and on the other was the Wind River valley, where were the heads of the Yellowstone branch of the Missouri; far to the north, we could just discover the snowy heads of the *Trois Tetons*, where were the sources of the Missouri and Columbia rivers; and at the southern extremity of the ridge, the peaks were plainly visible, among which were some of the springs of the Nebraska or Platte river. Around us, the whole scene had one main, striking feature, which was that of terrible convulsion. Parallel to its length, the ridge was split into chasms and fissures; between which rose the thin lofty walls, terminated with slender minarets and columns. According to the barometer, the little crest of the wall on which we stood was three thousand five hundred and seventy feet above that place, and two thousand seven hundred and eighty above the little lakes at the bottom, immediately at our feet. Our camp at the Two Hills (an astronomical station) bore south 3 deg. east, which, with a bearing afterwards obtained from a fixed position, enabled us to locate the peak. The bearing of the *Trois Tetons* was north 50 deg. west, and the direction of the central ridge of the Wind River mountains south 39 deg. east. The summit rock was gneiss, succeeded by sienitic gneiss. Sienite and feldspar succeeded in our descent to the snow line, where we found a feldspathic granite. I had remarked that the noise produced by the explosion of our pistols had the usual degree of loudness, but was not in the least prolonged, expiring almost instantaneously.

Having now made what observations our means afforded, we proceeded to descend. We had accomplished an object of laudable ambition, and beyond the strict order of our instructions. We had climbed the loftiest peak of the Rocky mountains, and looked down upon the snow a thousand feet below; and, standing where never human foot had stood before, felt the exultation of first explorers. It was about two o'clock when we left the summit, and when we reached the bottom, the sun had already sunk behind the wall, and the day was drawing to a close. It would have been pleasant to have lingered here and on the summit longer; but we hurried away as rapidly as the ground would permit, for it was an object to regain our party as soon as possible, not knowing what accident the next hour might bring forth.

We reached our deposite of provisions at nightfall. Here was not the inn which awaits the tired traveler on his return from Mont Blanc, or the orange groves of South America, with their refreshing juices and soft fragrant air; but we found our little *cache* of dried meat and coffee undisturbed. Though the moon was bright, the road was full of precipices, and the fatigue of the day had been great. We therefore abandoned the idea of rejoining our friends, and lay down on the rock, and, in spite of the cold, slept soundly.

16th.--We left our encampment with the daylight. We saw on our way large flocks of the mountain-goat looking down on us from the cliffs. At the crack of the rifle, they would bound off among the rocks, and in a few minutes make their appearance on some lofty peak, some hundred or a thousand feet above. It is needless to attempt any further description of the country; the portion over which we traveled this morning was rough as imagination could picture it, and to us seemed equally beautiful. A concourse of lakes and rushing waters--mountains of rocks naked and destitute of vegetable earth--dells and ravines of the most exquisite beauty, all kept green and fresh by the great moisture in the air, and sown with brilliant flowers, and everywhere thrown around all the glory of most magnificent scenes,--these constitute the features of the place, and impress themselves vividly on the mind of the traveler. It was not until 11 o'clock that we reached the place where our animals had been left, when we first attempted the mountains on foot. Near one of the still burning fires we found a piece of meat, which our friends had thrown away, and which furnished us a mouthful--a very scanty breakfast. We continued directly on, and reached our camp on the mountain lake at dusk. We found all well. Nothing had occurred to interrupt the quiet since our departure, and the fine grass and good cool water had done much to re-establish our animals. All heard with great delight the order to turn our faces homeward; and towards sundown of the 17th, we encamped again at the Two Buttes.

In the course of this afternoon's march, the barometer was broken past remedy. I regretted it, as I was desirous to compare it again with Dr. Engleman's barometers at St. Louis, to which mine were referred; but it had done its part well, and my objects were mainly fulfilled.

19th.--We left our camp on Little Sandy river about seven in the morning, and traversed the same sandy, undulating country. The air was filled with the turpentine scent of the various *artemisias*, which are now in bloom, and, numerous as they are, give much gayety to the landscape of the plains. At ten o'clock, we stood exactly on the divide in the pass, where the wagon-road crosses; and, descending immediately upon the Sweet Water, halted to take a meridian observation of the sun. The latitude was 42 deg. 24' 32".

In the course of the afternoon we saw buffalo again, and at our evening halt on the Sweet Water the roasted ribs again made their appearance around the fires;

and, with them, good humor, and laughter and song, were restored to the camp. Our coffee had been expended, but we now made a kind of tea from the roots of the wild-cherry tree.

23d.--Yesterday evening we reached our encampment at Rock Independence, where I took some astronomical observations. Here, not unmindful of the custom of early travelers and explorers in our country, I engraved on this rock of the Far West a symbol of the Christian faith. Among the thickly inscribed names, I made on the hard granite the impression of a large cross, which I covered with a black preparation of India-rubber, well calculated to resist the influence of wind and rain. It stands amidst the names of many who have long since found their way to the grave, and for whom the huge rock is a giant gravestone.

One George Weymouth was sent out to Maine by the Earl of Southampton, Lord Arundel, and others; and in the narrative of their discoveries, he says: "The next day we ascended in our pinnace that part of the river which lies more to the westward, carrying with us a cross--a thing never omitted by any Christian traveler--which we erected at the ultimate end of our route." This was in the year 1605; and in 1842 I obeyed the feeling of early travelers, and left the impression of the cross deeply engraved on the vast rock one thousand miles beyond the Mississippi, to which discoverers have given the national name of **Rock Independence**.

In obedience to my instructions to survey the river Platte, if possible, I had determined to make an attempt at this place. The India-rubber boat was filled with air, placed in the water, and loaded with what was necessary for our operations; and I embarked with Mr. Preuss and a party of men. When we had dragged our boat a mile or two over the sands, I abandoned the impossible undertaking, and waited for the arrival of the party, when we packed up our boat and equipage, and at nine o'clock were again moving along on our land journey. We continued along the valley on the right bank of the Sweet Water, where the formation, as already described, consists of a grayish micaceous sandstone, and fine-grained conglomerate, and marl. We passed over a ridge which borders or constitutes the river hills of the Platte, consisting of huge blocks, sixty or eighty feet cube, of decomposing granite. The cement which united them was probably of easier decomposition, and has disappeared and left them isolate, and separated by small spaces. Numerous horns of the mountain-goat were lying among the rocks; and in the ravines were cedars, whose trunks were of extraordinary size. From this ridge we descended to a small open plain, at the mouth of the Sweet Water, which rushed with a rapid current into the Platte, here flowing along in a broad and apparently deep stream, which seemed, from its turbid appearance, to be considerably swollen. I obtained here some astronomical observations, and the afternoon was spent in getting our boat ready for navigation the next day.

24th.--We started before sunrise, intending to breakfast at Goat island. I had directed the land party, in charge of Bernier, to proceed to this place, where they were to remain, should they find no note to apprize them of our having passed. In the event of receiving this information, they were to continue their route, passing by certain places which had been designated. Mr. Preuss accompanied me, and with us were five of my best men, viz.: C. Lambert, Basil Lajeunesse, Honore Ayot, Benoist, and Descoteaux. Here appeared no scarcity of water, and we took on board, with various instruments and baggage, provisions for ten or twelve days. We paddled down the river rapidly, for our little craft was light as a duck on the water; and the sun had been some time risen, when we heard before us a hollow roar, which we supposed to be that of a fall, of which we had heard a vague rumor, but whose exact locality no one had been able to describe to us. We were approaching a ridge, through which the river passes by a place called "canon," (pronounced *kanyon*,)--a Spanish word, signifying a piece of artillery, the barrel of a gun, or any kind of tube; and which, in this country, has been adopted to describe the passage of a river between perpendicular rocks of great height, which frequently approach each other so closely overhead as to form a kind of tunnel over the stream, which foams along below, half choked up by fallen fragments. Between the mouth of the Sweet Water and Goat island, there is probably a fall of three hundred feet, and that was principally made in the canons before us; as, without them, the water was comparatively smooth. As we neared the ridge, the river made a sudden turn, and swept squarely down against one of the walls of the canon, with great velocity, and so steep a descent that it had, to the eye, the appearance of an inclined plane. When we launched into this, the men jumped overboard, to check the velocity of the boat; but were soon in water up to their necks, and our boat ran on. But we succeeded in bringing her to a small point of rocks on the right, at the mouth of the canon. Here was a kind of elevated sand-beach, not many yards square, backed by the rocks; and around the point the river swept at a right angle. Trunks of trees deposited on jutting points, twenty or thirty feet above, and other marks, showed that the water here frequently rose to a considerable height. The ridge was of the same decomposing granite already mentioned, and the water had worked the surface, in many places, into a wavy surface of ridges and holes. We ascended the rocks to reconnoitre the ground, and from the summit the passage appeared to be a continued cataract, foaming over many obstructions, and broken by a number of small falls. We saw nowhere a fall answering to that which had been described to us as having twenty or twenty-five feet; but still concluded this to be the place in question, as, in the season of floods, the rush of the river against the wall would produce a great rise; and the waters, reflected squarely off, would descend through the passage in a sheet of foam, having every appearance of a large fall. Eighteen years previous to this time, as I have subsequently learned from himself, Mr. Fitzpatrick, somewhere above on this river, had embarked with a valuable cargo of beaver. Unacquainted with the stream, which he believed would conduct him safely to the Missouri, he came unexpectedly into this canon, where he was wrecked, with the total loss of his furs. It would have been a work of great time and labor to pack our baggage across the ridge, and I determined to run the canon. We all again embarked, and at first attempted to check the way of the boat; but the water swept through with so much violence that we narrowly escaped being swamped, and were obliged to let her go in the full force of the current, and trust to the skill of the boatmen. The dangerous places in this canon were where huge rocks had fallen from above, and hemmed in the already narrow pass of the river to an open space of three or four and five feet. These obstructions raised the water considerably above, which was sometimes precipitated over in a fall; and at other places, where this dam was too high, rushed through the contracted opening with tremendous violence. Had our boat been made of wood, in passing the narrows she would have been staved; but her elasticity preserved her unhurt from every shock, and she seemed fairly to leap over the falls.

In this way we passed three cataracts in succession, where perhaps 100 feet of smooth water intervened; and, finally, with a shout of pleasure at our success, issued from our tunnel into the open day beyond. We were so delighted with the performance of our boat, and so confident in her powers, that we would not have hesitated to leap a fall of ten feet with her. We put to shore for breakfast at some willows on the right bank, immediately below the mouth of the canon; for it was now eight o'clock, and we had been working since daylight, and were all wet, fatigued, and hungry. While the men were preparing breakfast, I went out to reconnoitre. The view was very limited. The course of the river was smooth, so far as I could see; on both sides were broken hills; and but a mile or two below was another high ridge. The rock at the mouth of the canon was still the decomposing granite, with great quantities of mica, which made a very glittering sand.

We re-embarked at nine o'clock, and in about twenty minutes reached the next canon. Landing on a rocky shore at its commencement, we ascended the ridge to reconnoitre. Portage was out of the question. So far as we could see, the jagged rocks pointed out the course of the canon, on a winding line of seven or eight miles. It was simply a narrow, dark chasm in the rock; and here the perpendicular faces were much higher than in the previous pass, being at this end two to three hundred, and further down, as we afterwards ascertained, five hundred feet in vertical height. Our previous success had made us bold, and we determined again to run the canon. Every thing was secured as firmly as possible; and having divested ourselves of the greater part of our clothing, we pushed into the stream. To save our chronometer from accident, Mr. Preuss took it, and attempted to proceed along the shore on the masses of rock, which in places were piled up on either side; but, after he had walked about five minutes, every thing like shore disappeared, and the vertical wall came squarely down into the water. He therefore waited until we came up. An ugly pass lay before us. We had made fast to the stern of the boat a strong rope about fifty feet long; and three of the men clambered along among the rocks, and with this rope let her slowly through the pass. In several places high rocks lay scattered about in the channel; and in the narrows it required all our strength and skill to avoid staving the boat on the sharp points. In one of these, the boat proved a little too broad, and stuck fast for an instant, while the water flew over us; fortunately, it was but for an instant, as our united strength forced her immediately through. The water swept overboard only a sextant and a pair of saddle- bags. I caught the sextant as it passed by me; but the saddle-bags became the prey of the whirlpools. We reached the place where Mr. Preuss was standing, took him on board, and, with the aid of the boat, put the men with the rope on the succeeding pile of rocks. We found this passage much worse than the previous one, and our position was rather a bad one. To go back was impossible; before us, the cataract was a sheet of foam; and shut up in the chasm by the rocks, which, in some places, seemed almost to meet overhead, the roar of the water was deafening. We pushed off again; but, after making a little distance, the force of the current became too great for the men on shore, and two of them let go the rope. Lajeunesse, the third man, hung on, and was jerked headforemost into the river from a rock about twelve feet high; and down the boat shot like an arrow, Basil following us in the rapid current, and exerting all his strength to keep in mid channel--his head only seen occasionally like a black spot in the white foam. How far we went, I do not exactly know; but we succeeded in turning the boat into an eddy below. "*Cre Dieu*," said Basil Lajeunesse, as he arrived immediately after us, "*Je crois bien que j'ai nage un demi mile*." He had owed his life to his skill as a swimmer, and I determined to take him and the two others on board, and trust to skill and fortune to reach the other end in safety. We placed ourselves on our knees with the short paddles in our hands, the most skilful boatman being at the bow; and again we commenced our rapid descent. We cleared rock after rock, and shot past fall after fall, our little boat seeming to play with the cataract. We became flushed with success, and familiar with the danger; and, yielding to the excitement of the occasion, broke forth into a Canadian boat-song. Singing, or rather shouting; we dashed along, and were, I believe, in the midst of the chorus, when the boat struck a concealed rock immediately at the foot of a fall, which whirled her over in an instant. Three of my men could not swim, and my first feeling was to assist them, and save some of our effects; but a sharp concussion or two convinced me that I had not yet saved myself. A few strokes brought me into an eddy, and I landed on a pile of rocks on the left side. Looking around, I saw that Mr. Preuss had gained the shore on the same side, about twenty yards below; and a little climbing and swimming soon brought him to my side. On the opposite side, against the wall, lay the boat bottom up; and Lambert was in the act of saving Descoteaux, whom he had grasped by the hair, and who could not swim; "*Lache pas*," said he, as I afterwards learned, "*lache pas, cher frere*." "*Crains pas*," was the reply: "*je m'en vais mourir avant que de te lacher*." Such was the reply of courage and generosity in this danger. For a hundred yards below the current was covered with floating books and boxes, bales and blankets, and scattered articles of clothing; and so strong and boiling was the stream, that even our heavy instruments, which were all in cases, kept on the surface, and the sextant, circle, and the long black box of the telescope, were in view at once. For a moment, I felt somewhat disheartened. All our books--almost every record of the journey--our journals and registers of astronomical and barometrical observations--had been lost in a moment. But it was no time to indulge in regrets; and I immediately set about endeavoring to save something from the wreck. Making ourselves understood as well as possible by signs, (for nothing could be heard in the roar of the waters,) we commenced our operations. Of every thing on board, the only article that had been saved was my double- barreled gun, which Descoteaux had caught and clung to with drowning tenacity. The men continued down the river on the left bank. Mr. Preuss and myself descended on the side we were on; and Lajeunesse, with a paddle in his hand, jumped on the boat alone, and continued down the canon. She was now light, and cleared every bad place with much less difficulty. In a short time he was joined by Lambert, and the search was continued for about a mile and a half, which was as far as the boat could proceed in the pass.

Here the walls were about five hundred feet high, and the fragments of rocks from above had choked the river into a hollow pass, but one or two feet above the surface. Through this and the interstices of the rock, the water found its way. Favored beyond our expectations, all of our registers had been recovered, with the exception of one of my journals, which contained the notes and incidents of travel, and topographical descriptions, a number of scattered astronomical observations, principally meridian altitudes of the sun, and our barometrical register west of Laramie. Fortunately, our other journals contained duplicates of the most important barometrical observations which had been taken in the mountains. These, with a few scattered notes, were all that had been preserved of our meteorological observations. In addition to these, we saved the circle; and these, with a few blankets, constituted every thing that had been rescued from the waters.

The day was running rapidly away, and it was necessary to reach Goat island, whither the party had preceded us, before night. In this uncertain country, the traveler is so much in the power of chance, that we became somewhat uneasy in regard to them. Should any thing have occurred, in the brief interval of our separation, to prevent our rejoining them, our situation would be rather a desperate one.

We had not a morsel of provisions--our arms and ammunition were gone--and we were entirely at the mercy of any straggling party of savages, and not a little in danger of starvation. We therefore set out at once in two parties, Mr. Preuss and myself on the left, and the men on the opposite side of the river. Climbing out of the canon, we found ourselves in a very broken country, where we were not yet able to recognise any locality. In the course of our descent through the canon, the rocks, which at the upper end was of the decomposing granite, changed into a varied sandstone formation. The hills and points of the ridges were covered with fragments of a yellow sandstone, of which the strata were sometimes displayed in the broken ravines which interrupted our course, and made our walk extremely fatiguing. At one point of the canon the red argillaceous sandstone rose in a wall of five hundred feet, surmounted by a stratum of white sandstone; and in an opposite ravine a column of red sandstone rose, in form like a steeple, about one hundred and fifty feet high. The scenery was extremely picturesque, and notwithstanding our forlorn condition, we were frequently obliged to stop and admire it. Our progress was not very rapid. We had emerged from the water half naked, and, on arriving at the top of the precipice, I found myself with only one moccasin. The fragments of rock made walking painful, and I was frequently obliged to stop and pull out the thorns of the *cactus*, here the prevailing plant, and with which a few minutes' walk covered the bottoms of my feet. From this ridge the river emerged into a smiling prairie, and, descending to the bank for water, we were joined by Benoist. The rest of the party were out of sight, having taken a more inland route. We crossed the river repeatedly--sometimes able to ford it, and sometimes swimming--climbed over the ridges of two more canons, and towards evening reached the cut, which we here named the Hot Spring gate. On our previous visit in July, we had not entered this pass, reserving it for our descent in the boat; and when we entered it this evening, Mr. Preuss was a few hundred feet in advance. Heated with the long march, he came suddenly upon a fine bold spring gushing from the rock, about ten feet above the river. Eager to enjoy the crystal water, he threw himself down for a hasty draught, and took a mouthful of water almost boiling hot. He said nothing to Benoist, who laid himself down to drink; but the steam from the water arrested his eagerness, and he escaped the hot draught. We had no thermometer to ascertain the temperature, but I could hold my hand in the water just long enough to count two seconds. There are eight or ten of these springs discharging themselves by streams large enough to be called runs. A loud hollow noise was heard from the rock, which I supposed to be produced by the fall of water. The strata immediately where they issue is a fine white and calcareous sandstone, covered with an incrustation of common salt. Leaving this Thermopylae of the west, in a short walk we reached the red ridge which has been described as lying just above Goat island. Ascending this, we found some fresh tracks and a button, which showed that the other men had already arrived. A shout from the man who first reached the top of the ridge, responded to from below, informed us that our friends were all on the island; and we were soon among them. We found some pieces of buffalo standing around the fire for us, and managed to get some dry clothes among the people. A sudden storm of rain drove us into the best shelter we could find, where we slept soundly, after one of the most fatiguing days I have ever experienced.

25th.--Early this morning Lajeunesse was sent to the wreck for the articles which had been saved, and about noon we left the island. The mare which we had left here in July had much improved in condition, and she served us well again for some time, but was finally abandoned at a subsequent part of the journey. At 10 in the morning of the 26th we reached Cache camp, where we found every thing undisturbed. We disinterred our deposite, arranged our carts which had been left here on the way out; and, traveling a few miles in the afternoon, encamped for the night at the ford of the Platte.

27th.--At mid-day we halted at the place where we had taken dinner on the 27th of July. The country which, when we passed up, looked as if the hard winter frosts had passed over it, had now assumed a new face, so much of vernal freshness had been given to it by the rains. The Platte was exceedingly low--a mere line of water among the sandbars. We reached Laramie fort on the last day of August, after an absence of forty-two days, and had the pleasure to find our friends all well. The fortieth day had been fixed for our return; and the quick eyes of the Indians, who were on the lookout for us, discovered our flag as we wound among the hills. The fort saluted us with repeated discharges of its single piece, which we returned with scattered volleys of our small-arms, and felt the joy of a home reception in getting back to this remote station, which seemed so far off as we went out.

SEPTEMBER.

On the morning of the 3d September we bade adieu to our kind friends at the fort, and continued our homeward journey down the Platte, which was glorious with the autumnal splendor of innumerable flowers in full and brilliant bloom. On the warm sands, among the **helianthi**, one of the characteristic plants, we saw great numbers of rattlesnakes, of which five or six were killed in the morning's ride. We occupied ourselves in improving our previous survey of the river; and, as the weather was fine, astronomical observations were generally made at night and at noon.

We halted for a short time on the afternoon of the 5th with a village of Sioux Indians, some of whose chiefs we had met at Laramie. The water in the Platte was exceedingly low; in many places, the large expanse of sands, with some occasional stunted tree on its banks, gave it the air of the seacoast; the bed of the river being merely a succession of sandbars, among which the channel was divided into rivulets of a few inches deep. We crossed and recrossed with our carts repeatedly and at our pleasure; and, whenever an obstruction barred our way in the shape of precipitous bluffs that came down upon the river, we turned directly into it, and made our way along the sandy bed, with no other inconvenience than the frequent quicksands, which greatly fatigued our animals. Disinterring on the way the **cache** which had been made by our party when they ascended the river, we reached without accident, on the evening of the 12th of September, our old encampment of the 2d of July, at the junction of the forks. Our **cache** of the barrel of pork was found undisturbed, and proved a seasonable addition to our stock of provisions. At this place I had determined to make another attempt to descend the Platte by water, and accordingly spent two days in the construction of a bull boat. Men were sent out on the evening of our arrival, the necessary number of bulls killed, and their skins brought to the camp. Four of the best of them were strongly sewed together with buffalo sinew, and stretched over a basket frame of willow. The seams were then covered with ashes and tallow, and the boat left exposed to the sun for the greater part of one day, which was sufficient to dry and contract the skin, and make the whole work solid and strong. It had a rounded bow, was eight feet long and five broad, and drew with four men about four inches water. On the morning of the 15th we embarked in our hide boat, Mr. Preuss and myself, with two men. We dragged her over the sands for three or four miles, and then left her on a bar, and abandoned entirely all further attempts to navigate this river. The names given by the Indians are always remarkably appropriate; and certainly none was ever more so than that which they have given to this stream--"The Nebraska, or Shallow river." Walking steadily the remainder of the day, a little before dark we overtook our people at their remaining camp, about twenty-one miles below the junction. The next morning we crossed the Platte, and continued our way down the river bottom on the left bank, where we found an excellent, plainly-beaten road.

On the 18th we reached Grand Island, which is fifty-two miles long, with an average breadth of one mile and three-quarters. It has on it some small eminences, and is sufficiently elevated to be secure from the annual floods of the river. As has been already remarked, it is well timbered; with an excellent soil, and recommends itself to notice as the best point for a military position on the Lower Platte.

On the 22d we arrived at the village of the Grand Pawnees, on the right bank of the river, about thirty miles above the mouth of the Loup fork. They were gathering in their corn, and we obtained from them a very welcome supply of vegetables.

The morning of the 24th we reached the Loup fork of the Platte. At the place where we forded it, this stream was four hundred and thirty yards broad, with a swift current of ***clear*** water; in this respect, differing from the Platte, which has a yellow muddy color, derived from the limestone and marl formation, of which we have previously spoken. The ford was difficult, as the water was so deep that it came into the body of the carts, and we reached the opposite bank after repeated attempts, ascending and descending the bed of the river, in order to avail ourselves of the bars. We encamped on the left bank of the fork, in the point of land at its junction with the Platte. During the two days that we remained here for astronomical observations, the bad weather permitted us to obtain but one good observation for the latitude--a meridian altitude of the sun, which gave for the latitude of the mouth of the Loup fork, 41 deg. 22' 11".

Five or six days previously, I had sent forward C. Lambert, with two men, to Bellevue, with directions to ask from Mr. P. Sarpy, the gentleman in charge of the American Company's establishment at that place, the aid of his carpenters in constructing a boat, in which I proposed to descend the Missouri. On the afternoon of the 27th we met one of the men, who had been dispatched by Mr. Sarpy with a welcome supply of provisions and a very kind note, which gave us the very gratifying intelligence that our boat was in rapid progress. On the evening of the 30th we encamped in an almost impenetrable undergrowth on the left bank of the Platte, in the point of land at its confluence with the Missouri--315 miles, according to our reckoning, from the junction of the forks, and 520 from Fort Laramie. From the junction we had found the bed of the Platte occupied with numerous islands, many of them very large, and all well timbered; possessing, as well as the bottom lands of the river, a very excellent soil. With the exception of some scattered groves on the banks, the bottoms are generally without timber. A portion of these consist of low grounds, covered with a profusion of fine grasses, and are probably inundated in the spring; the remaining part is high river prairie, entirely beyond the influence of the floods. The breadth of the river is usually three-quarters of a mile, except where it is enlarged by islands. That portion of its course which is occupied by Grand island has an average breadth, from shore to shore, of two and a half miles.

OCTOBER.

1st.--I rose this morning long before daylight, and heard with a feeling of pleasure the tinkling of cow-bells at the settlements on the opposite side of the Missouri. Early in the day we reached Mr. Sarpy's residence; and, in the security and comfort of his hospitable mansion, felt the pleasure of being within the pale of civilization. We found our boat on the stocks; a few days sufficed to complete her; and, in the afternoon of the 4th, we embarked on the Missouri. All our equipage-- horses, carts, and the ***materiel*** of the camp--had been sold at public auction at Bellevue. The strength of my party enabled me to man the boat with ten oars, relieved every hour; and we descended rapidly. Early on the morning of the 10th, we halted to make some astronomical observations at the mouth of the Kansas, exactly four months since we had left the trading-post of Mr. Cyprian Chouteau, on the same river, ten miles above. On our descent to this place, we had employed ourselves in surveying and sketching the Missouri, making astronomical observations regularly at night and at mid- day, whenever the weather permitted. These operations on the river were continued until our arrival at the city of St. Louis, Missouri, on the 17th. At St. Louis, the sale of our remaining effects was made; and, leaving that city by steamboat on the 18th, I had the honor to report to you at the city of Washington on the 29th of October.

Very respectfully, sir, Your obedient servant, J. C. FREMONT, **2d Lieutenant Corps of Topographical Engineers.**

* * * * *

ASTRONOMICAL OBSERVATIONS

The Longitudes given in the subjoined Table are referred to the meridian of Greenwich.

For the determination of astronomical positions, we were provided with the following instruments:

One telescope, magnifying power 120. One circle, by Gambey, Paris. One sextant, by Gambey, Paris. One sextant, by Troughton. One box chronometer, No.7,810, by French. One Brockbank pocket chronometer. One small watch with a light chronometer balance, No. 4,632, by Arnold and Dent.

The rate of the chronometer, 7,810, is exhibited in the following statement:

"NEW YORK, May 5, 1842 "Chronometer No. 7,810, by French, is this day at noon-- " *Slow* of Greenwich mean time,

11' 4" "*Fast* of New York mean time,
4 *h.* 45' 1" "Loses per day
2".7 "ARTHUR STEWART, 74 Merchants' Exchange."

An accident among some rough ground in the neighborhood of the Kansas river, strained the balance of this chronometer, (No. 7,810) and rendered it useless during the remainder of the campaign. From the 9th of June to the 24th of August, inclusively, the longitudes depend upon the Brockbank pocket chronometer; the rate of which, on leaving St. Louis, was fourteen seconds. The rate obtained by observations at Fort Laramie, 14".05, has been used in calculation.

From the 24th of August until the termination of the journey, No. 4,632 (of which the rate was 35".79) was used for the same purposes. The rate of this watch was irregular, and I place little confidence in the few longitudes which depend upon it, though, so far as we have any means of judging, they appear tolerably correct.

Table of Latitudes and Longitudes, deduced from Observations made dur-

ing the Journey.

Date	Station	Latitude. Deg. min. sec.	Longitude. Deg. min. sec.
1842			
May 27	St. Louis, residence of Colonel Brunt,	38 37 34	
June 8	Chouteau's lower trading-post; Kansas river,	39 05 57	94 25 46
16	Left bank of Kansas river. 7 miles above the ford,	39 06 40	95 38 05
18	Vermilion creek	39 15 19	96 04 07
19	Cold springs, near the road to Laramie,	39 30 40	96 14 49
20	Big Blue river,	39 45 08	96 32 35
25	Little Blue river,	40 26 50	98 22 12
26	Right bank of Platte river,	40 41 06	98 45 49
27	Right bank of Platte river	40 39 32	99 05 24
28	Right bank of Platte river,	40 39 51	
30	Right bank of Platte river	40 39 55	100 05 47
July 2	Junction of north and south forks of the Nebraska or Platte river,	41 05 05	100 49 43
4	South fork of Platte river, left bank,		

6 South fork of Platte river, island............40 51 17 103 07
7 South fork of Platte river, left bank........40 53 26 103 30 37
11 South fork of Platte river, St. Vrain's fort ,...................40 22 35 105 12 12
12 Crow creek,.............40 41 59 104 57 49
13 On a stream, name unknown 41 08 30 104 39 37
14 Horse creek. Goshen's hole? 41 40 13 104 24 36
16 Fort Laramie, near the mouth of Laramie's fork, ...42 12 10 104 47 43
23 North fork of Platte river..................42 39 25 104 59 59
24 North fork of Platte river..................42 47 40
25 North fork of Platte river, Dried Meat camp..42 51 35 105 50 15
26 North fork of Platte river, noon halt........42 50 08
26 North fork of Platte river, mouth of Deer creek,..................42 52 24 106 08 24
28 North fork of Platte river, Cache camp,......42 50 53 106 38 26
29 North fork of Platte river, left bank........42 38 01 106 54 32
30 North fork of Platte river, Goat island......42 33 27 107 13 29
Aug. 1 Sweet Water river,

one mile below Rock
Independence,............42 29 56   107 25 23
4 Sweet Water river.......42 32 31   108 30 13
7 Sweet Water river.......42 27 15   109 21 32
8 Little Sandy creek,
tributary to the
Colorado of the West,...42 27 34   109 37 59
9 New fork, tributary to
the Colorado,............42 42 46   109 58 11
10 Mountain lake,... ......42 49 49   110 08 03
15 Highest peak of the
Wind River mountains,
19 Sweet Water, noon
halt,....................42 24 32
19 Sweet Water river,......42 22 22
20 Sweet Water river,......42 31 46
22 Sweet Water river,
noon halt,..............42 26 10
22 Sweet Water river,
Rock Independence,......42 29 36
23 North fork of Platte
river, mouth of Sweet
Water, ...42 27 18
30 Horse-shoe creek,
noon halt,..............42 24 24
Sept 3 North fork of Platte
river, right bank,......42 01 40
4 North fork of Platte
river, near Scott's
bluffs..................41 54 38
5 North fork of Platte
river, right bank,
six miles above

Chimney rock,	41	43	36
8 North fork of Platte river, mouth of Ash creek,	41	17	19
9 North fork of Platte river, right bank	41	14	30
10 North fork of Platte river, Cedar bluff,	41	10	16
16 Platte river, noon halt	40	54	31
16 Platte river, left bank,	40	52	74
17 Platte river, left bank,	40	42	38
18 Platte river, left bank,	40	40	21
19 Platte river, left bank	40	39	44
20 Platte river, noon halt, left bank,	40	48	19
20 Platte river, left bank,	40	54	02
21 Platte river, left bank	41	05	37
23 Platte river, noon halt, left bank	41	20	20
23 Platte river, left bank	41	22	52
25 Platte river, mouth of Loup fork,	41	22	11
28 Platte river, mouth of Elk Horn river	41	09	34
29 Platte river, left			

    bank,...................41 02 15
Oct. 2 Bellevue, at the post
  of the American Fur
  Company, right bank of
  the Missouri river......41 08 24 95 20
 4 Left bank of the
  Missouri, opposite to
  the right bank of the
  mouth of the Platte.....41 02 11
 5 Missouri river,.........40 34 08
 6 Bertholet's island,
  noon halt,..............40 27 08
 6 Missouri river, mouth
  of Nishnabatona river, .40 16 40
 8 Missouri river, left
  bank 39 36 02
 10 Missouri river, mouth
  of the Kansas river.....39 06 03

*   *   *   *   *

A REPORT OF THE EXPLORING EXPEDITION TO OREGON AND NORTH CALIFORNIA, IN THE YEARS 1843-'44.

Washington City, March 1, 1845
To Colonel J.J. ABERT, *Chief of the Corps of Top. Engineers:*

SIR:--In pursuance of your instructions, to connect the reconnoisance of 1842, which I had the honor to conduct, with the surveys of Commander Wilkes on the coast of the Pacific ocean, so as to give a connected survey of the interior of our continent, I proceeded to the Great West early in the spring of 1843, and arrived, on the 17th of May, at the little town of Kansas, on the Missouri frontier, near the junction of the Kansas river with the Missouri river, where I was detained near two weeks in completing the necessary preparations for the extended explorations which my instructions contemplated.

My party consisted principally of Creole and Canadian French, and Americans, amounting in all to thirty-nine men; among whom you will recognise several of those who were with me in my first expedition, and who have been favorably brought to your notice in a former report. Mr. Thomas Fitzpatrick, whom many years of hardship and exposure, in the western territories, had rendered familiar with a portion of the country it was designed to explore, had been selected as our guide; and Mr. Charles Preuss, who had been my assistant in a previous journey, was again associated with me in the same capacity on the present expedition. Agreeably to your directions, Mr. Theodore Talbot, of Washington city, had been attached to the party, with a view to advancement in his profession; and at St. Louis had been joined by Mr. Frederick Dwight, a gentleman of Springfield, Massachusetts, who availed himself of our overland journey to visit the Sandwich Islands and China, by way of Fort Vancouver.

The men engaged for the service were: Alexis Ayot, Francis Badeau, Oliver Beaulieu, Baptiste Bernier, John A. Campbell, John G. Campbell, Manuel Chapman, Ransom Clark, Philibert Courteau, Michel Crelis, William Creuss, Clinton Deforest, Baptiste Derosier, Basil Lajeunesse, Francois Lajeunesse, Henry Lee, Louis Menard, Louis Montreuil, Samuel Neal, Alexis Pera, Francois Pera, James Power, Raphael Proue, Oscar Sarpy, Baptiste Tabeau, Charles Taplin, Baptiste Tesson, Auguste Vasquez, Joseph Verrot, Patrick White, Tiery Wright, Louis Zindel, and Jacob Dodson, a free young colored man of Washington city, who volunteered to accompany the expedition, and performed his duty manfully throughout the voyage. Two Delaware Indians--a fine-looking old man and his son--were engaged to accompany the expedition as hunters, through the kindness of Major Cummins, the excellent Indian agent. L. Maxwell, who had accompanied the expedition as one of the hunters in 1842, being on his way to Taos, in New Mexico, also joined us at this place.

The party was generally armed with Hall's carbines, which with a brass twelve-pound howitzer, had been furnished to me from the United States arsenal at St. Louis, agreeably to the orders of Colonel S.W. Kearney, commanding the third military division. Three men were especially detailed for the management of this piece, under the charge of Louis Zindel, a native of Germany, who had been nineteen years a non-commissioned officer of artillery in the Prussian army, and regularly instructed in the duties of his profession. The camp equipage and provisions were transported in twelve carts, drawn each by two mules; and a light covered wagon, mounted on good springs, had been provided for the safer carriage of instruments. These were:

One refracting telescope, by Frauenhofer. One reflecting circle, by Gambey. Two sextants, by Troughton. One pocket chronometer, No. 837, by Goffe, Falmouth. One pocket chronometer, No. 739, by Brockbank. One syphon barometer, by Bunten, Paris. One cistern barometer, by Frye and Shaw, New York. Six thermometers, and a number of small compasses.

To make the exploration as useful as possible, I determined, in conformity to your general instructions, to vary the route to the Rocky mountains from that followed in 1842. The route was then up the valley of the Great Platte river to the

South Pass, in north latitude 42 deg.; the route now determined on was up the valley of the Kansas river, and to the head of the Arkansas river, and to some pass in the mountains, if any could be found, at the sources of that river.

By making this deviation from the former route, the problem of a new road to Oregon and California, in a climate more genial, might be solved; and a better knowledge obtained of an important river, and the country it drained, while the great object of the expedition would find its point of commencement at the termination of the former, which was at that great gate in the ridge of the Rocky mountains called the South Pass, and on the lofty peak of the mountain which overlooks it, deemed the highest peak in the ridge, and from the opposite side of which four great rivers take their rise, and flow to the Pacific or the Mississippi.

Various obstacles delayed our departure until the morning of the 29th, when we commenced our long voyage; and at the close of a day, rendered disagreeably cold by incessant rain, encamped about four miles beyond the frontier, on the verge of the great prairies.

Resuming our journey on the 31st, after the delay of a day to complete our equipment and furnish ourselves with some of the comforts of civilized life, we encamped in the evening at Elm Grove, in company with several emigrant wagons, constituting a party which was proceeding to Upper California, under the direction of Mr. J.B. Childs, of Missouri. The wagons were variously freighted with goods, furniture, and farming utensils, containing among other things an entire set of machinery for a mill which Mr. Childs designed erecting on the waters of the Sacramento river, emptying into the bay of San Francisco.

We were joined here by Mr. Wm. Gilpin of Mo., who, intending this year to visit the settlements in Oregon, had been invited to accompany us, and proved a useful and agreeable addition to the party.

JUNE.

From Elm Grove, our route until the third of June was nearly the same as that described to you in 1842. Trains of wagons were almost constantly in sight; giving to the road a populous and animated appearance, although the greater portion of the emigrants were collected at the crossing, or already on their march beyond the Kansas river. Leaving at the ford the usual emigrant road to the mountains, we continued our route along the southern side of the Kansas, where we found the country much more broken than on the northern side of the river, and where our progress was much delayed by the numerous small streams, which obliged us to make frequent bridges. On the morning of the 4th we crossed a handsome stream, called by the Indians Otter creek, about 130 feet wide, where a flat stratum of limestone, which forms the bed, made an excellent ford. We met here a small party of Kansas and Delaware Indians, the latter returning from a hunting and trapping expedition on the upper waters of the river; and on the heights above were five or six Kansas women, engaged in digging prairie potatoes, (*psoralea esculenta*.) On the afternoon of the 6th, whilst busily engaged in crossing a wooded stream, we were thrown into a little confusion by the sudden arrival of Maxwell, who entered the camp at full speed at the head of a war party of Osage Indians, with gay red blankets, and heads shaved to the scalp lock. They had run him a distance of about nine miles, from a creek on which we had encamped the day previous, and to which he had returned in search of a runaway horse belonging to Mr. Dwight, which had taken the homeward road, carrying with him saddle, bridle, and holster-pistols. The Osages were probably ignorant of our strength, and, when they charged into the camp, drove off a number of our best horses; but we were fortunately well mounted, and, after a hard chase of seven or eight miles, succeeded in recovering them all. This accident, which occasioned delay and trouble, and threatened danger and loss, and broke down some good horses at the start, and actually endangered the expedition, was a first fruit of having gentlemen in company--very estimable, to be sure, but who are not trained to the care and vigilance and self-dependence which such an expedition required, and who are not subject to the orders which enforce attention and exertion. We arrived on the 8th at the mouth of the Smoky-hill fork, which is the principal southern branch of the Kansas; forming here, by its junction with the Republican, or northern branch, the main Kansas river. Neither stream was fordable, and the necessity of making a raft, together with bad weather, detained us here until the morning of the 11th; when we resumed our journey along the Republican fork. By our observations, the junction of the streams is in lat. 39 deg. 30' 38", long. 96 deg. 24' 36", and at an elevation of 926 feet above the Gulf of Mexico. For several days we continued to travel along the Republican, through a country beautifully watered with numerous streams, and handsomely timbered; and rarely an incident occurred to vary the monotonous resemblance which one day on the prairies here bears to another, and which scarcely require a particular description. Now and then, we caught a glimpse of a small herd of elk; and occasionally a band of antelopes, whose curiosity sometimes brought them within rifle range, would circle round us and then scour off into the prairies. As we advanced on our road, these became more frequent; but as we journeyed on the line usually followed by the trapping and hunting parties of the Kansas and Delaware Indians, game of every kind continued very shy and wild. The bottoms which form the immediate valley of the main river were generally about three miles wide; having a rich soil of black vegetable mould, and, for a prairie country, well interspersed with wood. The country was everywhere covered with a considerable variety of grasses, occasionally poor and thin, but far more frequently luxuriant and rich. We had been gradually and regularly ascending in our progress westward, and on the evening of the 14th, when we encamped on a little creek in the valley of the Republican, 265 miles by our traveling road from the mouth of the Kansas, we were at an elevation of 1,520 feet. That part of the river where we were now encamped is called by the Indians the **Big Timber**. Hitherto our route had been laborious and extremely slow, the unusually wet spring and constant rain having so saturated the whole country that it was necessary to bridge every water-course, and, for days together, our usual march averaged only five or six miles. Finding that at such a rate of travel it would be impossible to comply with your instructions, I determined at this place to divide the party, and, leaving Mr. Fitzpatrick with twenty-five men in charge of the provisions and heavier baggage of the camp, to proceed myself in advance, with a light party of fifteen men, taking with me the howitzer and the light wagon which carried the instruments.

Accordingly, on the morning of the 16th, the parties separated; and, bearing a little out from the river, with a view of heading some of the numerous affluents, after a few hours' travel over somewhat broken ground, we entered upon an extensive and high level prairie, on which we encamped towards evening at a little stream, where a single dry cottonwood afforded the necessary fuel for preparing supper. Among a variety of grasses which to-day made their first appearance, I noticed bunch-grass, (*festuca*,) and buffalo-grass, (*sesleria dactlyloides*.) Amorpha canescens (**lead plant**) continued the characteristic plant of the country, and a narrow-leaved *lathyrus* occurred during the morning, in beautiful patches. **Sida** *coccinea* occurred frequently, with a *psoralea* near *psoralea floribunda*, and a number of plants not hitherto met, just verging into bloom. The water on which we had encamped belonged to Solomon's fort of the Smoky-hill river, along whose tributaries we continued to travel for several days.

The country afforded us an excellent road, the route being generally over high and very level prairies; and we met with no other delay than being frequently obliged to bridge one of the numerous streams, which were well timbered with ash, elm, cottonwood, and a very large oak--the latter being occasionally five and six feet in diameter, with a spreading summit. *Sida coccinea* is very frequent in vermilion-colored patches on the high and low prairie; and I remarked that it has a very pleasant perfume.

The wild sensitive plant (*schrankia angustata*) occurs frequently, generally on the dry prairies, in valleys of streams, and frequently on the broken prairie bank. I remark that the leaflets close instantly to a very light touch. *Amorpha*, with the same *psoralea*, and a dwarf species of *lupinus*, are the characteristic plants.

On the 19th, in the afternoon, we crossed the Pawnee road to the Arkansas, and traveling a few miles onward, the monotony of the prairies was suddenly dispelled by the appearance of five or six buffalo bulls, forming a vanguard of immense herds, among which we were traveling a few days afterwards. Prairie dogs were seen for the first time during the day; and we had the good fortune to obtain an antelope for supper. Our elevation had now increased to 1,900 feet. *Sida coccinea* was the characteristic on the creek bottoms, and buffalo grass is becoming abundant on the higher parts of the ridges.

21st.--During the forenoon we traveled up a branch of the creek on which we had encamped, in a broken country, where, however, the dividing ridges always afforded a good road. Plants were few; and with the short sward of the buffalo-grass, which now prevailed everywhere, giving to the prairies a smooth and mossy appearance, were mingled frequent patches of a beautiful red grass, (*aristida pallens*,) which had made its appearance only within the last few days.

We halted to noon at a solitary cottonwood in a hollow, near which was killed the first buffalo, a large old bull.

Antelope appeared in bands during the day. Crossing here to the affluents of the Republican, we encamped on a fork, about forty feet wide and one foot deep, flowing with a swift current over a sandy bed, and well wooded with ash-leaved maple, (***negundo fraxinifolium***,) elm, cottonwood, and a few white oaks. We were visited in the evening by a very violent storm, accompanied by wind, lightning, and thunder; a cold rain falling in torrents. According to the barometer, our elevation was 2,130 feet above the gulf.

At noon, on the 23d, we descended into the valley of a principal fork of the Republican, a beautiful stream with a dense border of wood, consisting principally of varieties of ash, forty feet wide and four deep. It was musical with the notes of many birds, which, from the vast expanse of silent prairie around, seemed all to have collected here. We continued during the afternoon our route along the river, which was populous with prairie dogs, (the bottoms being entirely occupied with their villages,) and late in the evening encamped on its banks. The prevailing timber is a blue-foliaged ash, (***fraxinus***, near ***F. Americana***,) and ash- leaved maple. With these were ***fraxinus Americana***, cottonwood, and long-leaved willow. We gave to this stream the name of Prairie Dog river. Elevation 2,350 feet. Our road on the 25th lay over high smooth ridges, 3,100 feet above the sea; buffalo in great numbers, absolutely covering the face of the country. At evening we encamped within a few miles of the main Republican, on a little creek, where the air was fragrant with the perfume of ***artemisia filifolia***, which we here saw for the first time, and which was now in bloom. Shortly after leaving our encampment on the 26th, we found suddenly that the nature of the country had entirely changed. Bare sand-hills everywhere surrounded us in the undulating ground along which we were moving, and the plants peculiar to a sandy soil made their appearance in abundance. A few miles further we entered the valley of a large stream, afterwards known to be the Republican fork of the Kansas, whose shallow waters, with a depth of only a few inches, were spread out over a bed of yellowish white sand 600 yards wide. With the exception of one or two distant and detached groves, no timber of any kind was to be seen; and the features of the country assumed a desert character, with which the broad river, struggling for existence among the quicksands along the treeless banks, was strikingly in keeping. On the opposite side, the broken ridges assumed almost a mountainous appearance; and fording the stream, we continued on our course among these ridges, and encamped late in the evening at a little pond of very bad water, from which we drove away a herd of buffalo that were standing in and about it. Our encampment this evening was 3,500 feet above the sea. We traveled now for several days through a broken and dry sandy region, about 4,000 feet above the sea, where there were no running streams; and some anxiety was constantly felt on account of the uncertainty of water, which was only to be found in small lakes that occurred occasionally among the hills. The discovery of these always brought pleasure to the camp, as around them were generally green flats, which afforded abundant pasturage for our animals; and here we usually collected herds of the buffalo, which now were scattered over all the country in countless numbers.

The soil of bare and hot sands supported a varied and exuberant growth of plants, which were much farther advanced than we had previously found them, and whose showy bloom somewhat relieved the appearance of general sterility. Crossing the summit of an elevated and continuous range of rolling hills, on the afternoon of the 30th of June, we found ourselves overlooking a broad and misty valley, where, about ten miles distant, and 1,000 feet below us, the South fork of the Platte was rolling magnificently along, swollen with the waters of the melting snows. It was in strong and refreshing contrast with the parched country from which we had just issued; and when, at night, the broad expanse of water grew indistinct, it almost seemed that we had pitched our tents on the shore of the sea.

JULY.

Traveling along up the valley of the river, here 4,000 feet above the sea, in the afternoon of July 1, we caught a far and uncertain view of a faint blue mass in the west, as the sun sank behind it; and from our camp in the morning, at the mouth of Bijou, Long's peak and the neighboring mountains stood out into the sky, grand and luminously white, covered to their bases with glittering snow.

On the evening of the 3d, as we were journeying along the partially overflowed bottoms of the Platte, where our passage stirred up swarms of musquitoes, we came unexpectedly on an Indian, who was perched upon a bluff, curiously watching the movements of our caravan. He belonged to a village of Oglallah Sioux, who had lost all their animals in the severity of the preceding winter, and were now on their way up the Bijou fork to beg horses from the Arapahoes, who were hunting buffalo at the head of that river. Several came into our camp at noon; and, as they were hungry, as usual, they were provided with buffalo-meat, of which the hunters had brought in an abundant supply.

About noon, on the 4th of July, we arrived at the fort, where Mr. St. Vrain received us with his customary kindness, and invited us to join him in a feast which had been prepared in honor of the day.

Our animals were very much worn out, and our stock of provisions entirely exhausted, when we arrived at the fort; but I was disappointed in my hope of obtaining relief, as I found it in a very impoverished condition; and we were able to procure only a little unbolted Mexican flour, and some salt, with a few pounds of powder and lead.

As regarded provisions, it did not much matter in a country where rarely the day passed without seeing some kind of game, and where it was frequently abundant. It was a rare thing to lie down hungry, and we had already learned to think bread a luxury; but we could not proceed without animals, and our own were not capable of prosecuting the journey beyond the mountains without relief.

I had been informed that a large number of mules had recently arrived at Taos, from Upper California; and as our friend, Mr. Maxwell, was about to continue his journey to that place, where a portion of his family resided, I engaged him to purchase for me ten or twelve mules, with the understanding that he should pack them with provisions and other necessaries, and meet me at the mouth of the **Fontaine-qui-bouit**, on the Arkansas river, to which point I would be led in the course of the survey.

Agreeably to his own request, and in the conviction that his habits of life and education had not qualified him to endure the hard life of a voyageur, I discharged here one of my party, Mr. Oscar Sarpy, having furnished him with arms and means of transportation to Fort Laramie, where he would be in the line of caravans returning to the States.

At daybreak, on the 6th of July, Maxwell was on his way to Taos; and a few hours after we also had recommenced our journey up the Platte, which was continuously timbered with cottonwood and willow, on a generally sandy soil. Passing on the way the remains of two abandoned forts, (one of which, however, was still in good condition,) we reached, in ten miles, Fort Lancaster, the trading establishment of Mr. Lupton.

His post was beginning to assume the appearance of a comfortable farm: stock, hogs, and cattle, were ranging about on the prairie--there were different kinds of poultry; and there was a wreck of a promising garden, in which a considerable variety of vegetables had been in a flourishing condition; but it had been almost entirely ruined by the recent high waters. I remained to spend with him an agreeable hour, and set off in a cold storm of rain, which was accompanied with violent thunder and lightning. We encamped immediately on the river, sixteen miles from St. Vrain's. Several Arapahoes, on their way to the village which was encamped a few miles above us, passed by the camp in the course of the afternoon. Night set in stormy and cold, with heavy and continuous rain, which lasted until morning.

7th.--We made this morning an early start, continuing to travel up the Platte; and in a few miles frequent bands of horses and mules, scattered for several miles round about, indicated our approach to the Arapaho village, which we found encamped in a beautiful bottom, and consisting of about one hundred and sixty lodges. It appeared extremely populous, with a great number of children--a circumstance which indicated a regular supply of the means of subsistence. The chiefs, who were gathered together at the farther end of the village, received us (as probably strangers are always received to whom they desire to show respect or regard) by throwing their arms around our necks and embracing us.

It required some skill in horsemanship to keep the saddle during the performance of this ceremony, as our American horses exhibited for them the same fear they have for a bear, or any other wild animal. Having very few goods with me, I was only able to make them a meager present, accounting for the poverty of the gift by explaining that my goods had been left with the wagons in charge of Mr. Fitzpatrick, who was well known to them as the White Head, or the Broken Hand. I saw here, as I had remarked in an Arapaho village the preceding year, near the lodges of the chiefs; tall tripods of white poles supporting their spears and shields, which showed it to be a regular custom.

Though disappointed in obtaining the presents which had been evidently expected, they behaved very courteously; and, after a little conversation, I left them, and, continuing on up the river, halted to noon on the bluff, as the bottoms are almost inundated; continuing in the afternoon our route along the mountains, which were dark, misty, and shrouded--threatening a storm; the snow peaks sometimes glittering through the clouds beyond the first ridge.

We surprised a grizzly bear sauntering along the river, which, raising himself upon his hind legs, took a deliberate survey of us, that did not appear very satisfactory to him, and he scrambled into the river and swam to the opposite side. We halted for the night a little above Cherry creek; the evening cloudy, with many musquitoes. Some indifferent observations placed the camp in lat. 39 deg. 43' 53", and chronometric long. 105 deg. 24' 34".

8th.--We continued to-day to travel up the Platte: the morning pleasant, with a prospect of fairer weather. During the forenoon our way lay over a more broken country, with a gravelly and sandy surface; although the immediate bottom of the river was a good soil, of a dark and sandy mould, resting upon a stratum of large pebbles, or rolled stones, as at Laramie fork. On our right, and apparently very near, but probably 8 or 10 miles distant, and two or three thousand feet above us, ran the first range of the mountains, like a dark corniced line, in clear contrast with the great snowy chain which, immediately beyond, rose glittering five thousand feet above them. We caught this morning a view of Pike's peak; but it appeared for a moment only, as clouds rose early over the mountains, and shrouded them in mist and rain all the day. In the first range were visible, as at the Red Buttes on the North fork, very lofty escarpments of red rock. While traveling through this region, I remarked that always in the morning the lofty peaks were visible and bright, but very soon small white clouds began to settle around them--brewing thicker and thicker as the day advanced, until the afternoon, when the thunder began to roll; and invariably at evening we had more or less of a thunder storm. At 11 o'clock, and 21 miles from St. Vrain's fort, we reached a point in this southern fork of the Platte, where the stream is divided into three forks; two of these (one of them being much the largest) issuing directly from the mountains on the west, and forming, with the eastern-most branch, a river of the plains. The elevation of this point is about 5,500 feet above the sea; this river falling 2,800 feet in a distance of 316 miles, to its junction with the North fork of the Platte. In this estimate, the elevation of the junction is assumed as given by our barometrical observations in 1842. On the easternmost branch, up which we took our way, we first came among the pines growing on the top of a very high bank, and where we halted on it to noon; quaking asp (***populus tremuloides***) was mixed with the cottonwood, and there were excellent grass and rushes for the animals.

During the morning there occurred many beautiful flowers, which we had not hitherto met. Among them, the common blue flowering flax made its first appearance; and a tall and handsome species of **_gilia_**, with slender scarlet flowers, which appeared yesterday for the first time, was very frequent to-day.

We had found very little game since leaving the fort, and provisions began to get unpleasantly scant, as we had had no meat for several days; but towards sundown, when we had already made up our minds to sleep another night without supper, Lajeunesse had the good fortune to kill a fine deer, which he found feeding in a hollow near by; and as the rain began to fall, threatening an unpleasant night, we hurried to secure a comfortable camp in the timber.

To-night the camp fires, girdled with **_appolas_** of fine venison, looked cheerful in spite of the stormy weather.

9th.--On account of the low state of our provisions and the scarcity of game, I determined to vary our route, and proceed several camps to the eastward, in the hope of falling in with the buffalo. This route along the dividing grounds between the South fork of the Platte and the Arkansas, would also afford some additional geographical information. This morning, therefore, we turned to the eastward, along the upper waters of the stream on which we had encamped, entering a country of picturesque and varied scenery; broken into rocky hills of singular shapes; little valleys, with pure crystal water, here leaping swiftly along, and there losing itself in the sands; green spots of luxuriant grass, flowers of all colors, and timber of different kinds--every thing to give it a varied beauty, except game. To one of these remarkably shaped hills, having on the summit a circular flat rock two or three hundred yards in circumference, some one gave the name of Poundcake, which it has been permitted to retain, as our hungry people seemed to think it a very agreeable comparison. In the afternoon a buffalo bull was killed, and we encamped on a small stream, near the road which runs from St. Vrain's fort to the Arkansas.

10th:--Snow fell heavily on the mountains during the night, and Pike's peak this morning is luminous and grand, covered from the summit, as low down as we can see, with glittering white. Leaving the encampment at 6 o'clock, we continued our easterly course over a rolling country, near to the high ridges, which are generally rough and rocky, with a coarse conglomerate displayed in masses, and covered with pines. The rock is very friable, and it is undoubtedly from its decomposition that the prairies derive their sandy and gravelly formation. In six miles we crossed a head-water of the Kioway river, on which we found a strong fort and **coral** that had been built in the spring, and halted to noon on the principal branch of the river. During the morning our route led over a dark and vegetable mould, mixed with sand and gravel, the characteristic plant being ***esparcette***, (***onobrychis sativa***,) a species of clover which is much used in certain parts of Germany for pasturage of stock--principally hogs. It is sown on rocky waste ground, which would otherwise be useless, and grows very luxuriantly, requiring only a renewal of the seed about once in fifteen years. Its abundance here greatly adds to the pastoral value of this region. A species of antennaria in flower was very common along the line of road, and the creeks were timbered with willow and pine. We encamped on Bijou's fork, the water of which, unlike the clear streams we had previously crossed, is of a whitish color, and the soil of the bottom a very hard, tough clay. There was a prairie dog village on the bottom, and, in the endeavor to unearth one of the little animals, we labored ineffectually in the tough clay until dark. After descending, with a slight inclination, until it had gone the depth of two feet, the hole suddenly turned at a sharp angle in another direction for one more foot in depth, when it again turned, taking an ascending direction to the next nearest hole. I have no doubt that all their little habitations communicate with each other. The greater part of the people were sick to-day, and I was inclined to attribute their indisposition to the meat of the bull which had been killed the previous day.

11th.--There were no indications of buffalo having been recently in the neighborhood; and, unwilling to travel farther eastward, I turned this morning to the southward, up the valley of Bijou. ***Esparcette*** occurred universally, and among the plants on the river I noticed, for the first time during this journey, a few small bushes of the ***absinthe*** of the voyageurs, which is commonly used for firewood, (***artemesia tridentata***.) Yesterday and to-day the road has been ornamented with the showy bloom of a beautiful lupinus, a characteristic in many parts of the mountain region, on which were generally great numbers of an insect with very bright colors, (***litta vesicatoria***.)

As we were riding quietly along, eagerly searching every hollow in search of game, we discovered, at a little distance in the prairie, a large grizzly bear, so busily engaged in digging roots that he did not perceive us until we were galloping down a little hill fifty yards from him, when he charged upon us with such sudden energy that several of us came near losing our saddles. Being wounded, he commenced retreating to a rocky piny ridge near by, from which we were not able to cut him off, and we entered the timber with him. The way was very much blocked up with fallen timber; and we kept up a running fight for some time, animated by the bear charging among the horses. He did not fall until after he had received six rifle balls. He was miserably poor, and added nothing to our stock of provisions.

We followed the stream to its head in a broken ridge, which, according to the barometer, was about 7,500 feet above the sea. This is a piny elevation, into which the prairies are gathered, and from which the waters flow, in almost every direction, to the Arkansas, Platte, and Kansas rivers; the latter stream having here its remotest sources. Although somewhat rocky and broken, and covered with pines, in comparison with the neighboring mountains, it scarcely forms an interruption to the great prairie plains which sweep up to their bases.

We had an excellent view of Pike's peak from this camp, at the distance of forty miles. This mountain barrier presents itself to travelers on the plains, which sweep almost directly to its bases--an immense and comparatively smooth and grassy prairie, in very strong contrast with the black masses of timber, and the glittering snow above them. With occasional exceptions, comparatively so very small as not to require mention, these prairies are everywhere covered with a close and vigorous growth of a great variety of grasses, among which the most abundant is the buffalo grass, (*sesleria dactyloides*.) Between the Platte and Arkansas rivers, that part of this region which forms the basin drained by the waters of the Kansas, with which our operations made us more particularly acquainted, is based upon a formation of calcareous rocks. The soil of all this country is excellent, admirably adapted to agricultural purposes, and would support a large agricultural and pastoral population. A glance at the map, along our several lines of travel, will show you that this plain is watered by many streams. Throughout the western half of the plain, these are shallow, with sandy beds, becoming deeper as they reach the richer lands approaching the Missouri river; they generally have bottom lands, bordered by bluffs varying from fifty to five hundred feet in height. In all this region the timber is entirely confined to the streams. In the eastern half, where the soil is a deep, rich, vegetable mould, retentive of rain and moisture, it is of vigorous growth, and of many different kinds; and throughout the western half it consists entirely of various species of cottonwood, which deserves to be called the tree of the desert--growing in sandy soils, where no other tree will grow --pointing out the existence of water, and furnishing to the traveler fuel, and food for his animals. Add to this that the western border of the plain is occupied by the Sioux, Arapaho, and Cheyenne nations, with the Pawnees and other half-civilized tribes in its eastern limits, for whom the intermediate country is a war-ground, and you will have a tolerably correct idea of the appearance and condition of the country. Descending a somewhat precipitous and rocky hillside among the pines, which rarely appear elsewhere than on the ridge, we encamped at its foot, where there were several springs, which you will find laid down upon the map as one of the extreme sources of the Smoky Hill fork of the Kansas. From this place the view extended over the Arkansas valley, and the Spanish peaks in the south beyond. As the greater part of the men continued sick, I encamped here for the day, and ascertained conclusively, from experiments on myself, that their illness was caused by the meat of the buffalo bull.

On the summit of the ridge, near the camp, were several rock-built forts, which in front were very difficult of approach, and in the rear were protected by a precipice entirely beyond the reach of a rifle-ball. The evening was tolerably clear, with a temperature at sunset of 63 deg.. Elevation of the camp seven thousand and three hundred feet.

Turning the next day to the southwest, we reached, in the course of the morning, the wagon-road to the settlements on the Arkansas river, and encamped in the afternoon on the **Fontaine-qui-bouit** (or Boiling Spring) river, where it was fifty feet wide, with a swift current. I afterwards found that the spring and river owe their names to the bubbling of the effervescing gas in the former, and not to the temperature of the water, which is cold. During the morning a tall species of **gilia**, with a slender white flower, was characteristic; and, in the latter part of the day, another variety of **esparcette**, (wild clover,) having the flower white, was equally so. We had a fine sunset of golden brown; and in the evening, a very bright moon, with the near mountains, made a beautiful scene. Thermometer, at sunset, was 69 deg., and our elevation above the sea 5,800 feet.

13th.--The morning was clear, with a northwesterly breeze, and the thermometer at sunrise at 46 deg.. There were no clouds along the mountains, and the morning sun showed very clearly their rugged character.

We resumed our journey very early down the river, following an extremely good lodge-trail, which issues by the head of this stream from the bayou Salade, a high mountain valley behind Pike's peak. The soil along the road was sandy and gravelly, and the river well timbered. We halted to noon under the shade of some fine large cottonwoods, our animals luxuriating on rushes, (*equisetum hyemale*,) which, along this river, were remarkably abundant. A variety of cactus made its appearance, and among several strange plants were numerous and beautiful clusters of a plant resembling *mirabilis jalapa*, with a handsome convolvulus I had not hitherto seen, (*calystegia*.) In the afternoon we passed near the encampment of a hunter named Maurice, who had been out into the plains in pursuit of buffalo calves, a number of which I saw among some domestic cattle near his lodge. Shortly afterwards, a party of mountaineers galloped up to us--fine-looking and hardy men, dressed in skins, and mounted on good fat horses; among them were several Connecticut men, a portion of Wyeth's party, whom I had seen the year before, and others were men from the western states.

Continuing down the river, we encamped at noon on the 14th, at its mouth, on the Arkansas river. A short distance above our encampment, on the left bank of the Arkansas, is a *pueblo*, (as the Mexicans call their civilized Indian villages,) where a number of mountaineers, who had married Spanish women in the valley of Taos, had collected together and occupied themselves in farming, carrying on at the same time a desultory Indian trade. They were principally Americans, and treated us with all the rude hospitality their situation admitted; but as all commercial intercourse with New Mexico was now interrupted, in consequence of Mexican decrees to that effect, there was nothing to be had in the way of provisions. They had, however, a fine stock of cattle, and furnished us an abundance of excellent milk. I learned here that Maxwell, in company with two other men, had started for Taos on the morning of the 9th, but that he would probably fall into the hands of the Utah Indians, commonly called the *Spanish Yutes*. As Maxwell had no knowledge of their being in the vicinity when he crossed the Arkansas, his chance of escape was very doubtful; but I did not entertain much apprehension for his life, having great confidence in his prudence and courage. I was further informed that there had been a popular tumult among the *pueblos*, or civilized Indians, residing near Taos, against the "*foreigners*" of that place; in which they had plundered their houses and ill-treated their families. Among those whose property had been destroyed, was Mr. Beaubien, father-in-law of Maxwell, from whom I had expected to obtain supplies, and who had been obliged to make his escape to Santa Fe.

By this position of affairs, our expectation of obtaining supplies from Taos was cut off. I had here the satisfaction to meet our good buffalo- hunter of 1842, Christopher Carson, whose services I considered myself fortunate to secure again; and as a reinforcement of mules was absolutely necessary, I dispatched him immediately, with an account of our necessities, to Mr. Charles Bent, whose principal post is on the Arkansas river, about seventy-five miles below **Fontaine-qui-bouit**. He was directed to proceed from that post by the nearest route across the country, and meet me, with what animals he should be able to obtain, at St. Vrain's fort. I also admitted into the party Charles Towns, a native of St. Louis, a serviceable man, with many of the qualities of a good voyageur. According to our observations, the latitude of the mouth of the river is 38 deg. 15' 23", its longitude 104 deg. 58' 30", and its elevation above the sea 4,880 feet.

On the morning of the 16th, the time for Maxwell's arrival having expired, we resumed our journey, leaving for him a note, in which it was stated that I would wait for him at St. Vrain's fort, until the morning of the 26th, in the event that he should succeed in his commission. Our direction was up the Boiling Spring river, it being my intention to visit the celebrated springs from which the river takes its name, and which are on its upper waters, at the foot of Pike's peak. Our animals fared well while we were on this stream, there being everywhere a great abundance of **prele**. *Ipomea leptophylla* in bloom, was a characteristic plant along the river, generally in large bunches, with two to five flowers on each. Beautiful clusters of the plant resembling *mirabilis jalapa* were numerous, and *glycyrrhiza lepidota* was a characteristic of the bottoms. Currants nearly ripe were abundant, and among the shrubs which covered the bottom was a very luxuriant growth of chenopodiaceous shrubs, four to six feet high. On the afternoon of the 17th we entered among the broken ridges at the foot of the mountains, where the river made several forks. Leaving the camp to follow slowly, I rode ahead in the afternoon in search of the springs. In the meantime, the clouds, which had been gathered all the afternoon over the mountains, began to roll down their sides; and a storm so violent burst upon me, that it appeared I had entered the storehouse of the thunder-storms. I continued, however, to ride along up the river until about sunset, and was beginning to be doubtful of finding the springs before the next day, when I came suddenly upon a large smooth rock, about twenty yards in diameter, where the water from several springs was bubbling and boiling up in the midst of a white incrustation, with which it had covered a portion of the rock. As this did not correspond with the description given the by the hunters, I did not stop to taste the water, but dismounting, walked a little way up the river, and, passing through a narrow thicket of shrubbery bordering the stream, stepped directly upon a huge white rock, at the foot of which the river, already become a torrent, foamed along, broken by a small fall. A deer which had been drinking at the spring was startled by my approach, and, springing across the river, bounded off up the mountain. In the upper part of the rock, which had apparently been formed by deposition, was a beautiful white basin, overhung by currant bushes, in which the cold clear water bubbled up, kept in constant motion by the escaping gas, and overflowing the rock, which it had almost entirely covered with a smooth crust of glistening white. I had all day refrained from drinking, reserving myself for the spring; and as I could not well be more wet than the rain had already made me, I lay down by the side of the basin, and drank heartily of the delightful water. The spring is situated immediately at the foot of lofty mountains, beautifully timbered, which sweep closely round, shutting up the little valley in a kind of cove. As it was beginning to grow dark, I rode quickly down the river, on which I found the camp a few miles below.

The morning of the 18th was beautiful and clear; and, all the people being anxious to drink of these famous waters, we encamped immediately at the springs, and spent there a very pleasant day. On the opposite side of the river is another locality of springs, which are entirely of same nature. The water has a very agreeable taste, which Mr. Preuss found very much to resemble that of the famous Selter springs in the grand duchy of Nassau, a country famous for wine and mineral waters; and it is almost entirely of the same character, though still more agreeable than that of the famous Bear springs, near Bear river of the Great Salt lake. The following is an analysis of an incrustation with which the water had covered a piece of wood lying on the rock:

Carbonate of lime, ----------------92.25
Carbonate of magnesia, ---------- 1.21

Sulphate of lime,----------------}
Chloride of calcium,   } .23
Chloride of magnesia,-----------}

Silica, ---------------------------- 1.50
Vegetable matter, ----------------- .20
Moisture and loss, ---------------- 4.61

                                  100.00

At eleven o'clock, when the temperature of the air was 73 deg., that of the water in this was 60.5 deg.; and that of the upper spring, which issued from the flat rock, more exposed to the sun, was 69 deg.. At sunset, when the temperature of the air was 66 deg., that of the lower springs was 58 deg., and that of the upper 61 deg..

19th.--A beautiful and clear morning, with a slight breeze from the northwest; the temperature of the air at sunrise being 57.5 deg.. At this time the temperature of the lower spring was 57.8 deg., springs was 58 deg., and that of the upper 54.3 deg..

The trees in the neighborhood were birch, willow, pine, and an oak resembling *quercus alba*. In the shrubbery along the river are currant bushes, (*ribes*,) of which the fruit has a singular piny flavor; and on the mountain side, in a red gravelly soil, is a remarkable coniferous tree, (perhaps an *abies*,) having the leaves singularly long, broad and scattered, with bushes of *spiraea ariaefolia*. By our observations, this place is 6,350 feet above the sea, in latitude 38 deg. 52' 10", and longitude 105 deg. 22' 45".

Resuming our journey on this morning, we descended the river, in order to reach the mouth of the eastern fork, which I proposed to ascend. The left bank of the river here is very much broken. There is a handsome little bottom on the right, and both banks are exceedingly picturesque--strata of red rock, in nearly perpendicular walls, crossing the valley from north to south. About three miles below the springs, on the right bank of the river, is a nearly perpendicular limestone rock, presenting a uniformly unbroken surface, twenty to forty feet high, containing very great numbers of a large univalve shell; which appears to belong to the genus *inoceramus*.

In contact with this, to the westward, was another, stratum of limestone, containing fossil shells of a different character; and still higher up on the stream were parallel strata, consisting of a compact somewhat crystalline limestone, and argillaceous bituminous limestone in thin layers. During the morning, we traveled up the eastern fork of the **Fontaine-qui-bouit** river, our road being roughened by frequent deep gullies timbered with pine, and halted to noon on a small branch of the stream, timbered principally with the narrow-leaved cottonwood, (***populus angustifolia***,) called by the Canadians ***liard amere***. On a hill near by, were two remarkable columns of a grayish-white conglomerate rock, one of which was about twenty feet high, and two feet in diameter. They are surmounted by slabs of a dark ferruginous conglomerate, forming black caps, and adding very much to their columnar effect at a distance. This rock is very destructible by the action of the weather, and the hill, of which they formerly constituted a part, is entirely abraded.

A shaft of the gun-carriage was broken in the afternoon; and we made an early halt, the stream being from twelve to twenty feet wide, with clear water. As usual, the clouds had gathered to a storm over the mountains, and we had a showery evening. At sunset, the thermometer stood at 62 deg., and our elevation above the sea was. 6,530 feet.

20th.--This morning (as we generally found the mornings under these mountains) was very clear and beautiful, and the air cool and pleasant, with the thermometer at 44 deg.. We continued our march up the stream, along a green sloping bottom; between pine hills on the one hand; and the main Black hills on the other; towards the ridge which separates the waters of the Platte from those of the Arkansas. As we approached the diving ridge, the whole valley was radiant with flowers; blue, yellow, pink, white, scarlet; and purple, vie with each other in splendor. Esparcette was one of the highly characteristic plants, and a bright-looking flower (***gaillardia aristata***) was very frequent; but the most abundant plant along our road today, was ***geranium maculatum***, which is the characteristic plant on this portion of the diving grounds. Crossing to the waters of the Platte, fields of blue flax added to the magnificence of this mountain garden; this was occasionally four feet in height, which was a luxuriance of growth that I rarely saw this almost universal plant attain throughout the journey. Continuing down a branch of the Platte, among high and very steep timbered hills, covered with fragments of sock, towards evening we issued from the piny region, and made a late encampment near Poundcake rock, on that fork of the river which we had ascended on the 8th of July. Our animals enjoyed the abundant rushes this evening, as the flies were so bad among the pines that they had been much harassed. A deer was killed here this evening; and again the evening was overcast, and a collection of brilliant red clouds in the west was followed by the customary squall of rain.

Achillea millefolium (milfoil) was among the characteristic plants of the river bottoms to-day. This was one of the most common plants during the whole of our journey, occurring in almost every variety of situation. I noticed it on the lowlands of the rivers, near the coast of the Pacific, and near to the snow among the mountains of the ***Sierra Nevada***.

During this excursion, we had surveyed to its head one of the two principal branches of the upper Arkansas, 75 miles in length, and entirely completed our survey of the South fork of the Platte, to the extreme sources of that portion of the river which belongs to the plains, and heads in the broken hills of the Arkansas dividing ridge, at the foot of the mountains. That portion of its waters which were collected among these mountains, it was hoped to explore on our homeward voyage.

Reaching St. Vrain's fort on the morning of the 23d, we found Mr. Fitzpatrick and his party in good order and excellent health, and my true and reliable friend, Kit Carson, who had brought with him ten good mules, with the necessary pack-saddles. Mr. Fitzpatrick, who had often endured every extremity of want during the course of his mountain life, and knew well the value of provisions in this country, had watched over our stock with jealous vigilance, and there was an abundance of flour, rice, sugar, and coffee, in the camp; and again we fared luxuriously. Meat was, however, very scarce; and two very small pigs, which we obtained at the fort, did not go far among forty men. Mr. Fitzpatrick had been here a week, during which time his men had been occupied in refitting the camp; and the repose had been very beneficial to his animals, which were now in tolerably good condition.

I had been able to obtain no certain information in regard to the character of the passes in this portion of the Rocky Mountain range, which had always been represented as impracticable for carriages, but the exploration of which was incidentally contemplated by my instructions, with the view of finding some convenient point of passage for the road of emigration, which would enable it to reach, on a more direct line, the usual ford of the Great Colorado--a place considered as determined by the nature of the country beyond that river. It is singular, that immediately at the foot of the mountains, I could find no one sufficiently acquainted with them to guide us to the plains at their western base; but the race of trappers, who formerly lived in their recesses, has almost entirely disappeared--dwindled to a few scattered individuals--some one or two of whom are regularly killed in the course of each year by the Indians. You will remember, that in the previous year I brought with me to their village near this post, and hospitably treated on the way, several Cheyenne Indians, whom I met on the Lower Platte. Shortly after their arrival here, these were out with a party of Indians, (themselves the principal men,) which discovered a few trappers in the neighboring mountains, whom they immediately murdered, although one of them had been nearly thirty years in the country, and was perfectly well known, as he had grown gray among them.

Through this portion of the mountains, also, are the customary roads of the war parties going out against the Utah and Shoshonee Indians; and occasionally parties from the Crow nation make their way down to the southward along this chain, in the expectation of surprising some straggling lodges of their enemies. Shortly before our arrival, one of their parties had attacked an Arapaho village in the vicinity, which they had found unexpectedly strong; and their assault was turned into a rapid flight and a hot pursuit, in which they had been compelled to abandon the animals they had rode and escape on their war-horses.

Into this uncertain and dangerous region, small parties of three or four trappers, who now could collect together, rarely ventured; and consequently it was seldom visited and little known. Having determined to try the passage by a pass through a spur of the mountains made by the ***Cache-a-la-Poudre*** river, which rises in the high bed of mountains around Long's peak, I thought it advisable to avoid any encumbrance which would occasion detention, and accordingly again separated the party into two divisions--one of which, under the command of Mr. Fitzpatrick, was directed to cross the plains to the mouth of Laramie river, and, continuing thence its route along the usual emigrant road, meet me at Fort Hall, a post belonging to the Hudson Bay Company, and situated on Snake river, as it is commonly called in the Oregon Territory, although better known to us as Lewis's fork of the Columbia. The latter name is there restricted to one of the upper forks of the river.

Our Delaware Indians having determined to return to their homes, it became necessary to provide this party with a good hunter; and I accordingly engaged in that capacity Alexander Godey, a young man about 25 years of age, who had been in this country six or seven years, all of which time had been actively employed in hunting for the support of the posts, or in solitary trading expeditions among the Indians. In courage and professional skill he was a formidable rival to Carson, and constantly afterwards was among the best and most efficient of the party, and in difficult situations was of incalculable value. Hiram Powers, one of the men belonging to Mr. Fitzpatrick's party, was discharged at this place.

A French *engage*, at Lupton's fort, had been shot in the back on the 4th of July, and died during our absence to the Arkansas. The wife of the murdered man, an Indian woman of the Snake nation, desirous, like Naomi of old, to return to her people, requested and obtained permission to travel with my party to the neighborhood of Bear river, where she expected to meet with some of their villages. Happier than the Jewish widow, she carried with her two children, pretty little half-breeds, who added much to the liveliness of the camp. Her baggage was carried on five or six pack-horses; and I gave her a small tent, for which I no longer had any use, as I had procured a lodge at the fort.

For my own party I selected the following men, a number of whom old associations had rendered agreeable to me:

Charles Preuss, Christopher Carson, Basil Lajeunesse, Francois Badeau, J.B. Bernier, Louis Menard, Raphael Proue, Jacob Dodson, Louis Zindel, Henry Lee, J.B. Derosier, Francois Lajeunesse, and Auguste Vasquez.

By observation, the latitude of the post is 40 deg. 16' 33", and its longitude 105 deg. 12' 23", depending, with all the other longitudes along this portion of the line, upon a subsequent occultation of September 13, 1843, to which they are referred by the chronometer. Its distance from Kansas landing, by the road we traveled, (which, it will be remembered, was very winding along the lower Kansas river,) was 750 miles. The rate of the chronometer, determined by observations at this place for the interval of our absence, during this month, was 33.72"; which you will hereafter see did not sensibly change during the ensuing month, and remained nearly constant during the remainder of our journey across the continent. This was the rate used in referring to St. Vrain's fort, the longitude between that place and the mouth of the ***Fontaine-qui-bouit***.

Our various barometrical observations, which are better worthy of confidence than the isolated determination of 1842, give, for the elevation of the fort above the sea, 4,930 feet. The barometer here used was also a better one, and less liable to derangement.

At the end of two days, which was allowed to my animals for necessary repose, all the arrangements had been completed, and on the afternoon of the 26th we resumed our respective routes. Some little trouble was experienced in crossing the Platte, the waters of which were still kept up by rains and melting snow; and having traveled only about four miles, we encamped in the evening on Thompson's creek, where we were very much disturbed by musquitoes.

The following days we continued our march westward over comparative plains, and, fording the Cache-a-la-Poudre on the morning of the 28th, entered the Black hills, and nooned on this stream in the mountains beyond them. Passing over a fine large bottom in the afternoon, we reached a place where the river was shut up in the hills; and, ascending a ravine, made a laborious and very difficult passage around by a gap, striking the river again about dusk. A little labor, however, would remove this difficulty, and render the road to this point a very excellent one. The evening closed in dark with rain, and the mountains looked gloomy.

29th.--Leaving our encampment about seven in the morning, we traveled until three in the afternoon along the river, which, for the distance of about six miles, runs directly through a spur of the main mountains.

We were compelled by the nature of the ground to cross the river eight or nine times, at difficult, deep, and rocky fords, the stream running with great force, swollen by the rains--a true mountain torrent, only forty or fifty feet wide. It was a mountain valley of the narrowest kind--almost a chasm--and the scenery very wild and beautiful. Towering mountains rose round about; their sides sometimes dark with forests of pine, and sometimes with lofty precipices, washed by the river; while below, as if they indemnified themselves in luxuriance for the scanty space, the green river-bottom was covered with a wilderness of flowers, their tall spikes sometimes rising above our heads as we rode among them. A profusion of blossoms on a white flowering vine, (*clematis lasianthi*) which was abundant along the river, contrasted handsomely with the green foliage of the trees. The mountains appeared to be composed of a greenish-gray and red granite, which in some places appeared to be in a state of decomposition, making a red soil.

The stream was wooded with cottonwood, box-elder, and cherry, with currant and serviceberry bushes. After a somewhat laborious day, during which it had rained incessantly, we encamped near the end of the pass at the mouth of a small creek, in sight of the great Laramie plains. It continued to rain heavily, and at evening the mountains were hid in mists; but there was no lack of wood, and the large fires we made to dry our clothes were very comfortable; and at night the hunters came in with a fine deer. Rough and difficult as we found the pass to-day, an excellent road may be made with a little labor. Elevation of the camp 5,540 feet, and distance from St. Vrain's fort 56 miles.

30th.--The day was bright again; the thermometer at sunrise 52 deg.; and leaving our encampment at eight o'clock, in about half a mile we crossed the **Cache-a-la-Poudre** river for the last time; and, entering a smoother country, we traveled along a kind of **vallon**, bounded on the right by red buttes and precipices; while to the left a high rolling country extended to a range of the Black hills, beyond which rose the great mountains around Long's peak.

By the great quantity of snow visible among them, it had probably snowed heavily there the previous day, while it had rained on us in the valley.

We halted at noon on a small branch; and in the afternoon traveled over a high country, gradually ascending towards a range of **buttes**, or high hills covered with pines, which forms the dividing ridge between the waters we had left and those of Laramie river.

Late in the evening we encamped at a spring of cold water, near the summit of the ridge, having increased our elevation to 7,520 feet. During the day we had traveled 24 miles. By some indifferent observations, our latitude is 41 deg. 02' 19". A species of **hedeome** was characteristic along the whole day's route.

Emerging from the mountains, we entered a region of bright, fair weather. In my experience in this country, I was forcibly impressed with the different character of the climate on opposite sides of the Rocky Mountain range. The vast prairie plain on the east is like the ocean; the rain and clouds from the constantly evaporating snow of the mountains rushing down into the heated air of the plains, on which you will have occasion to remark the frequent storms of rain we encountered during our journey.

31st.--The morning was clear; temperature 48 deg.. A fine rolling road, among piny and grassy hills, brought us this morning into a large trail where an Indian village had recently passed. The weather was pleasant and cool; we were disturbed by neither musquitoes nor flies; and the country was certainly extremely beautiful. The slopes and broad ravines were absolutely covered with fields of flowers of the most exquisitely beautiful colors. Among those which had not hitherto made their appearance, and which here were characteristic, was a new **_delphinium_**, of a green and lustrous metallic blue color, mingled with compact fields of several bright-colored varieties of **_astragalus_**, which were crowded together in splendid profusion. This trail conducted us, through a remarkable defile, to a little timbered creek, up which we wound our way, passing by a singular and massive wall of dark-red granite. The formation of the country is a red feldspathic granite, overlaying a decomposing mass of the same rock, forming the soil of all this region, which everywhere is red and gravelly, and appears to be of a great floral fertility.

As we emerged on a small tributary of the Laramie river, coming in sight of its principal stream, the flora became perfectly magnificent; and we congratulated ourselves, as we rode along our pleasant road; that we had substituted this for the uninteresting country between Laramie hills and the Sweet Water valley. We had no meat for supper last night or breakfast this morning, and were glad to see Carson come in at noon with a good antelope.

A meridian observation of the sun placed us in latitude 41 deg. 04' 06". In the evening we encamped on the Laramie river, which is here very thinly timbered with scattered groups of cottonwood at considerable intervals. From our camp, we are able to distinguish the gorges, in which are the sources of Cache-a-la-Poudre and Laramie rivers; and the Medicine Bow mountain, towards the point of which we are directing our course this afternoon, has been in sight the greater part of the day. By observation the latitude was 41 deg. 15' 02", and longitude 106 deg. 16' 54". The same beautiful flora continued till about four in the afternoon, when it suddenly disappeared, with the red soil, which became sandy, and of a whitish-gray color. The evening was tolerably clear; temperature at sunset 64 deg.. The day's journey was 30 miles.

AUGUST.

1st.--The morning was calm and clear, with sunrise temperature at 42 deg.. We traveled to-day over a plain, or open rolling country, at the foot of the Medicine Bow mountain; the soil in the morning being sandy, with fragments of rock abundant, and in the afternoon, when we approached closer to the mountain, so stony that we made but little way. The beautiful plants of yesterday reappeared occasionally; flax in bloom occurred during the morning, and esparcette in luxuriant abundance was a characteristic of the stony ground in the afternoon. The camp was roused into a little excitement by a chase after a buffalo bull, and an encounter with a war party of Sioux and Cheyenne Indians about 30 strong. Hares and antelope were seen during the day, and one of the latter was killed. The Laramie peak was in sight this afternoon. The evening was clear, with scattered clouds; temperature 62 deg.. The day's journey was 26 miles.

2d.--Temperature at sunrise 52 deg., and scenery and weather made our road to- day delightful. The neighboring mountain is thickly studded with pines, intermingled with the brighter foliage of aspens, and occasional spots like lawns between the patches of snow among the pines, and here and there on the heights. Our route below lay over a comparative plain, covered with the same brilliant vegetation, and the day was clear and pleasantly cool. During the morning, we crossed many streams, clear and rocky, and broad grassy valleys, of a strong black soil, washed down from the mountains, and producing excellent pasturage. These were timbered with the red willow and long-leaved cottonwood, mingled with aspen, as we approached the mountain more nearly towards noon. ***Esparcette*** was a characteristic, and flax occurred frequently in bloom. We halted at noon on the most western fork of Laramie river--a handsome stream about sixty feet wide and two feet deep, with clear water and a swift current, over a bed composed entirely of boulders or roll-stones. There was a large open bottom here, on which were many lodge poles lying about: and in the edge of the surrounding timber were three strong forts, that appeared to have been recently occupied. At this place I became first acquainted with the ***yampah***, (***anethum graveolens***,) which I found our Snake woman engaged in digging in the low timbered bottom of the creek. Among the Indians along the Rocky Mountains, and more particularly among the Shoshonee or Snake Indians, in whose territory it is very abundant, this is considered the best among the roots used for food. To us it was an interesting plant--a little link between the savage and civilized life. Here, among the Indians, its root is a common article of food, which they take pleasure in offering to strangers; while with us, in a considerable portion of America and Europe, the seeds are used to flavor soup. It grows more abundantly, and in greater luxuriance, on one of the neighboring tributaries of the Colorado, than in any other part of this region; and on that stream, to which the Snakes are accustomed to resort every year to procure a supply of their favorite plant, they have bestowed the name of ***Yampah*** river. Among the trappers it is generally known as Little Snake river; but in this and other instances, where it illustrated the history of the people inhabiting the country, I have preferred to retain on the map the aboriginal name. By a meridional observation, the latitude is 41 deg. 45' 59".

In the afternoon we took our way directly across the spurs from the point of the mountain, where we had several ridges to cross; and, although the road was not rendered bad by the nature of the ground, it was made extremely rough by the stiff tough bushes of ***artemisia tridentata***, [Footnote: The greater portion of our subsequent journey was through a region where this shrub constituted the tree of the country; and, as it will often be mentioned in occasional descriptions, the word ***artemisia*** only will be used, without the specific name.] in this country commonly called sage.

This shrub now began to make its appearance in compact fields; and we were about to quit for a long time this country of excellent pasturage and brilliant flowers. Ten or twelve buffalo bulls were seen during the afternoon; and we were surprised by the appearance of a large red ox. We gathered around him as if he had been an old acquaintance, with all our domestic feelings as much awakened as if we had come in sight of an old farm-house. He had probably made his escape from some party of emigrants on Green river; and, with a vivid remembrance of some old green field, be was pursuing the straightest course for the frontier that the country admitted. We carried him along with us as a prize; and, when it was found in the morning that he had wandered off, I would not let him be pursued, for I would rather have gone through a starving time of three entire days, than let him be killed after he had successfully run the gauntlet so far among the Indians. I have been told by Mr. Bent's people of an ox born and raised at St. Vrain's fort, which made his escape from them at Elm grove, near the frontier, having come in that year with the wagons. They were on their way out, and saw occasionally places where he had eaten and laid down to rest; but did not see him for about 700 miles, when they overtook him on the road, traveling along to the fort, having unaccountably escaped Indians and every other mischance.

We encamped at evening on the principal fork of Medicine Bow river, near to an isolated mountain called the Medicine *Butte*, which appeared to be about 1,800 feet above the plain, from which it rises abruptly, and was still white, nearly to its base, with a great quantity of snow. The streams were timbered with the long-leaved, cottonwood and red willow; and during the afternoon a species of onion was very abundant. I obtained here an immersion of the first satellite of Jupiter, which, corresponding very nearly with the chronometer, placed us in longitude 106 deg. 47' 25". The latitude, by observation, was 41 deg. 37' 16"; elevation above the sea, 7,800 feet, and distance from St. Vrain's fort, 147 miles.

3d.--There was a white frost last night; the morning is clear and cool. We were early on the road, having breakfasted before sunrise, and in a few miles' travel entered the pass of the Medicine *Butte*, through which led a broad trail, which had been recently traveled by a very large party. Immediately in the pass, the road was broken by ravines, and we were obliged to clear a way through groves of aspens, which generally made their appearance when we reached elevated regions. According to the barometer, this was 8,300 feet; and while we were detained in opening a road, I obtained a meridional observation of the sun, which gave 41 deg. 35' 48" for the latitude of the pass. The Medicine *Butte* is isolated by a small tributary of the North fork of the Platte, but the mountains approach each other very nearly; the stream running at their feet. On the south they are smooth, with occasional streaks of pine; but the butte itself is ragged, with escarpments of red feldspathic granite, and dark with pines; the snow reaching from the summit to within a few hundred feet of the trail. The granite here was more compact and durable than that in the formation which we had passed through a few days before to the eastward of

Laramie. Continuing our way over a plain on the west side of the pass, where the road was terribly rough with artemisia, we made our evening encampment on the creek, where it took a northern direction, unfavorably to the course we were pursuing. Bands of buffalo were discovered as we came down upon the plain; and Carson brought into the camp a cow which had the fat on the fleece two inches thick. Even in this country of rich pasturage and abundant game, it is rare that a hunter chances upon a finer animal. Our voyage had already been long, but this was the first good buffalo meat we had obtained. We traveled to-day 26 miles.

4th.--The morning was clear and calm; and, leaving the creek, we traveled towards the North fork of the Platte, over a plain which was rendered rough and broken by ravines. With the exception of some thin grasses, the sandy soil here was occupied almost exclusively by artemisia, with its usual turpentine odor. We had expected to meet with some difficulty in crossing the river, but happened to strike it where there was a very excellent ford, and halted to noon on the left bank, two hundred miles from St. Vrain's fort. The hunters brought in pack-animals loaded with fine meat. According to our imperfect knowledge of the country, there should have been a small affluent to this stream a few miles higher up; and in the afternoon we continued our way among the river hills, in the expectation of encamping upon it in the evening. The ground proved to be so exceedingly difficult, broken up into hills, terminating in escarpments and broad ravines, five hundred or six hundred feet deep, with sides so precipitous that we could scarcely find a place to descend, that, towards sunset, I turned directly in towards the river, and, after nightfall, entered a sort of ravine. We were obliged to feel our way, and clear a road in the darkness; the surface being much broken, and the progress of the carriages being greatly obstructed by the artemisia, which had a luxuriant growth of four to six feet in height. We had scrambled along this gulley for several hours, during which we had knocked off the carriage-lamps, broken a thermometer and several small articles, when, fearing to lose something of more importance, I halted for the night at ten o'clock. Our animals were turned down towards the river, that they might pick up what little grass they could find; and after a little search, some water was found in a small ravine, and improved by digging. We lighted up the ravine with fires of artemisia, and about midnight sat down to a supper which we were hungry enough to find delightful--although the buffalo-meat was crusted with sand, and the coffee was bitter with the wormwood taste of the artemisia leaves.

A successful day's hunt had kept our hunters occupied until late, and they slept out, but rejoined us at daybreak, when, finding ourselves only about a mile from the river, we followed the ravine down, and camped in a cottonwood grove on a beautiful grassy bottom, where our animals indemnified themselves for the scanty fare of the past night. It was quite a pretty and pleasant place; a narrow strip of prairie, about five hundred yards long, terminated at the ravine where we entered by high precipitous hills closing in upon the river, and at the upper end by a ridge of low rolling hills.

In the precipitous bluffs were displayed a succession of strata containing fossil vegetable remains, and several beds of coal. In some of the beds the coal did not appear to be perfectly mineralized, and in some of the seams it was compact, and remarkably lustrous. In these latter places, there were also thin layers of a very fine white salts, in powder. As we had a large supply of meat in the camp, which it was necessary to dry, and the surrounding country appeared to be well stocked with buffalo, which it was probable, after a day or two, we would not see again until our return to the Mississippi waters, I determined to make here a provision of dried meat, which would be necessary for our subsistence in the region we were about entering, which was said to be nearly destitute of game. Scaffolds were accordingly soon erected, fires made, and the meat cut into thin slices to be dried; and all were busily occupied, when the camp was thrown into a sudden tumult, by a charge from about seventy mounted Indians, over the low hills at the upper end of the little bottom. Fortunately, the guard, who was between them and our animals, had caught a glimpse of an Indian's head, as he raised himself in his stirrups to look over the hill, a moment before he made the charge, and succeeded in turning the band into the camp, as the Indians charged into the bottom with the usual yell. Before they reached us, the grove on the verge of the little bottom was occupied by our people, and the Indians brought to a sudden halt, which they made in time to save themselves from a howitzer shot, which would undoubtedly have been very effective in such a compact body; and further proceedings were interrupted by their signs for peace. They proved to be a war party of Arapaho and Cheyenne Indians, and informed us that they had charged upon the camp under the belief that we were hostile Indians, and had discovered their mistake only at the moment of the attack--an excuse which policy required us to receive as true, though under the full conviction that the display of our little howitzer, and our favorable position in the grove, certainly saved our horses, and probably ourselves, from their marauding intentions. They had been on a war party, and had been defeated, and were consequently in the state of mind which aggravates their innate thirst for plunder and blood. Their excuse, however, was taken in good part, and the usual evidences of friendship interchanged. The pipe went round, provisions were spread, and the tobacco and goods furnished the customary presents, which they look for even from traders, and much more from government authorities.

They were returning from an expedition against the Shoshonee Indians, one of whose villages they had surprised, at Bridger's fort, on Ham's fork of Green river, (in the absence of the men, who were engaged in an antelope surround,) and succeeded in carrying off their horses, and taking several scalps. News of the attack reached the Snakes immediately, who pursued and overtook them, and recovered their horses; and, in the running fight which ensued, the Arapahoes had lost several men killed, and a number wounded, who were coming on more slowly with a party in the rear. Nearly all the horses they had brought off were the property of the whites at the fort. After remaining until nearly sunset, they took their departure; and the excitement which their arrival had afforded subsided into our usual quiet, a little enlivened by the vigilance rendered necessary by the neighborhood of our uncertain visitors. At noon the thermometer was at 75 deg., at sunset 70 deg., and the evening clear. Elevation above the sea 6,820 feet; latitude 41 deg. 36' 00"; longitude 107 deg. 22' 27".

6th.--At sunrise the thermometer was 46 deg., the morning being clear and calm. We traveled to-day over an extremely rugged country, barren and uninteresting--nothing to be seen but artemisia bushes; and, in the evening, found a grassy spot among the hills, kept green by several springs, where we encamped late. Within a few hundred yards was a very pretty little stream of clear cool water, whose green banks looked refreshing among the dry, rocky hills. The hunters brought in a fat mountain sheep, (***ovis montana***.)

Our road the next day was through a continued and dense field of ***artemisia***, which now entirely covered the country in such a luxuriant growth that it was difficult and laborious for a man on foot to force his way through, and nearly impracticable for our light carriages. The region through which we were traveling was a high plateau, constituting the dividing ridge between the waters of the Atlantic and Pacific oceans, and extending to a considerable distance southward, from the neighborhood of the Table rock, at the southern side of the South Pass. Though broken up into rugged and rocky hills of a dry and barren nature, it has nothing of a mountainous character; the small streams which occasionally occur belonging neither to the Platte nor the Colorado, but losing themselves either in the sand or in small lakes. From an eminence, in the afternoon, a mountainous range became visible in the north, in which were recognised some rocky peaks belonging to the range of the Sweet Water valley; and, determining to abandon any further attempt to struggle through this almost impracticable country, we turned our course directly north, towards a pass in the valley of the Sweet Water river. A shaft of the gun-carriage was broken during the afternoon, causing a considerable delay; and it was late in an unpleasant evening before we succeeded in finding a very poor encampment, where there was a little water in a deep trench of a creek, and some scanty grass among the shrubs. All the game here consisted of a few straggling buffalo bulls, and during the day there had been but very little grass, except in some green spots where it had collected around springs or shallow lakes. Within fifty miles of the Sweet Water, the country changed into a vast saline plain, in many places extremely level, occasionally resembling the flat sandy beds of shallow lakes. Here the vegetation consisted of a shrubby growth, among which were several varieties of **chenopodiaceous** plants; but the characteristic shrub was **Fremontia vermicularis**, with smaller saline shrubs growing with singular luxuriance, and in many places holding exclusive possession of the ground.

On the evening of the 8th we encamped on one of these fresh-water lakes, which the traveler considers himself fortunate to find; and the next day, in latitude, by observation, 42 deg. 20' 06", halted to noon immediately at the foot of the southern side of the range which walls in the Sweet Water valley, on the head of a small tributary to that river.

Continuing in the afternoon our course down the stream, which here cuts directly through the ridge, forming a very practicable pass, we entered the valley; and, after a march of about nine miles, encamped on our familiar river, endeared to us by the acquaintance of the previous expedition--the night having already closed in with a cold rain-storm. Our camp was about twenty miles above the Devil's gate, which we had been able to see in coming down the plain; and, in the course of the night, the clouds broke away around Jupiter for a short time; during which we obtained an emersion of the first satellite, the result of which agreed very nearly with the chronometer, giving for the mean longitude 107 deg. 50' 07"; elevation above the sea 6,040 feet; and distance from St. Vrain's fort, by the road we had Just traveled, 315 miles.

Here passes the road to Oregon; and the broad smooth highway, where the numerous heavy wagons of the emigrants had entirely beaten and crushed the artemisia, was a happy exchange to our poor animals, for the sharp rocks and tough shrubs among which they had been toiling so long; and we moved up the valley rapidly and pleasantly. With very little deviation from our route of the preceding year, we continued up the valley; and on the evening of the 12th encamped on the Sweet Water, at a point where the road turns off to cross to the plains of Green river. The increased coolness of the weather indicated that we had attained a greater elevation, which the barometer here placed at 7,220 feet; and during the night water froze in the lodge.

The morning of the 13th was clear and cold, there being a white-frost, and the thermometer, a little before sunrise, standing at 26.5 deg.. Leaving this encampment, (our last on the waters which flow towards the rising sun,) we took our way along the upland, towards the dividing ridge which separates the Atlantic from the Pacific waters, and crossed it by a road some miles further south than the one we had followed on our return in 1842. We crossed very near the Table mountain, at the southern extremity of the South Pass, which is near twenty miles in width, and already traversed by several different roads. Selecting, as well as I could, in the scarcely distinguishable ascent, what might be considered the dividing ridge in this remarkable depression in the mountain, I took a barometrical observation, which gave 7,490 feet for the elevation above the Gulf of Mexico. You will remember that, in my report of 1842, I estimated the elevation of this pass at about 7,000 feet; a correct observation with a good barometer enables me to give it with more precision. Its importance, as the great gate through which commerce and traveling may hereafter pass between the valley of the Mississippi and the North Pacific, justifies a precise notice of its locality and distance from leading points, in addition to this statement of its elevation. As stated in the report of 1842, its latitude, at the point where we crossed, is 42 deg. 24' 32"; its longitude 109 deg. 26' 00"; its distance from the mouth of the Kansas, by the common traveling route, 962 miles; from the mouth of the Great Platte, along the valley of that river, according to our survey of 1842, 882 miles; and its distance from St. Louis about 400 miles more by the Kansas, and about 700 by the Great Platte route; these additions being steamboat conveyance in both instances. From this pass to the mouth of the Oregon is about 1,400 miles by the common traveling route; so that under a general point of view, it may be assumed to be about half-way between the Mississippi and the Pacific ocean, on the common traveling route. Following a hollow of slight and easy descent, in which was very soon formed a little tributary to the Gulf of California, (for the waters which flow west from the South Pass go to this gulf,) we made our usual halt four miles from the pass, in latitude, by observation, 42 deg. 19' 53". Entering here the valley of Green river--the great Colorado of the West-- and inclining very much to the southward along the streams which form the Sandy river, the road led for several days over dry and level uninteresting plains; to which a low scrubby growth of artemisia gave a uniform dull grayish color; and on the evening of the 15th we encamped in the Mexican territory, on the left bank of Green river, 69 miles from the South Pass, in longitude 110 deg. 05' 05", and latitude 41 deg. 53' 54", distant 1,031 miles from the mouth of the Kansas. This is the emigrant road to Oregon, which bears much to the southward, to avoid the mountains about the western heads of Green river--the **Rio Verde** of the Spaniards.

16th.--Crossing the river, here about 400 feet wide, by a very good ford, we continued to descend for seven or eight miles on a pleasant road along the right bank of the stream, of which the islands and shores are handsomely timbered with cottonwood. The refreshing appearance of the broad river, with its timbered shores and green wooded islands, in contrast to its dry and sandy plains, probably obtained for it the name of Green river, which was bestowed on it by the Spaniards who first came into this country to trade some 25 years ago. It was then familiarly known as the Seeds-ke-dee-agie, or Prairie Hen (*tetrao urophasianus*) river; a name which it received from the Crows, to whom its upper waters belong, and on which this bird is still very abundant. By the Shoshonee and Utah Indians, to whom belongs, for a considerable distance below, the country where we were now traveling, it was called the Bitter Root river, from a great abundance in its valley of a plant which affords them one of their favorite roots. Lower down, from Brown's hole to the southward, the river runs through lofty chasms, walled in by precipices of **red** rock; and even among the wilder tribes which inhabit that portion of its course, I have heard it called by Indian refugees from the California settlements the Rio **Colorado**. We halted to noon at the upper end of a large bottom, near some old houses, which had been a trading post, in lat. 41 deg. 46' 54". At this place the elevation of the river above the sea is 6,230 feet. That of Lewis's fork of the Columbia at Fort Hall is, according to our subsequent observations, 4,500 feet. The descent of each stream is rapid, but that of the Colorado is but little known, and that little derived from vague report. Three hundred miles of its lower part, as it approaches the Gulf of California, is reported to be smooth and tranquil; but its upper part is manifestly broken into many falls and rapids. From many descriptions of trappers, it is probable that in its foaming course among its lofty precipices it presents many scenes of wild grandeur; and though offering many temptations, and often discussed, no trappers have been found bold enough to undertake a voyage which has so certain a prospect of a fatal termination. The Indians have strange stories of beautiful valleys abounding with beaver, shut up among inaccessible walls of rock in the lower course of the river; and to which the neighboring Indians, in their occasional wars with the Spaniards and among themselves, drive their herds of cattle and flocks of sheep, leaving them to pasture in perfect security.

The road here leaves the river, which bends considerably to the east; and in the afternoon we resumed our westerly course, passing over a somewhat high and broken country; and about sunset, after a day's travel of 26 miles, reached Black's fork of the Green river--a shallow stream, with a somewhat sluggish current, about 120 feet wide, timbered principally with willow, and here and there an occasional large tree. At three in the morning I obtained an observation of an emersion of the first satellite of Jupiter, with other observations. The heavy wagons have so completely pulverized the soil, that clouds of fine light dust are raised by the slightest wind, making the road sometimes very disagreeable.

17th.--Leaving our encampment at six in the morning, we traveled along the bottom, which is about two miles wide, bordered by low hills, in which the strata contained handsome and very distinct vegetable fossils. In a gully a short distance farther up the river, and underlying these, was exposed a stratum of an impure or argillaceous limestone. Crossing on the way Black's fork, where it is one foot deep and forty wide, with clear water and a pebbly bed, in nine miles we reached Ham's fork, a tributary to the former stream, having now about sixty feet breadth, and a few inches depth of water. It is wooded with thickets of red willow, and in the bottom is a tolerably strong growth of grass. The road here makes a traverse of twelve miles across a bend of the river. Passing in the way some remarkable hills, two or three hundred feet high, with frequent and nearly vertical escarpments of a green stone, consisting of an argillaceous carbonate of lime, alternating with strata of an iron-brown limestone, and worked into picturesque forms by wind and rain, at two in the afternoon we reached the river again, having made to-day 21 miles. Since crossing the great dividing ridge of the Rocky mountains, plants have been very few in variety, the country being covered principally with artemisia.

18th.--We passed on the road, this morning, the grave of one of the emigrants, being the second we had seen since falling into their trail; and halted to noon on the river, a short distance above.

The Shoshonee woman took leave of us here, expecting to find some of her relations at Bridger's fort, which is only a mile or two distant, on a fork of this stream. In the evening we encamped on a salt creek, about fifteen feet wide, having to-day traveled 32 miles.

I obtained an emersion of the first satellite under favorable circumstances, the night being still and clear.

One of our mules died here, and in this portion of our journey we lost six or seven of our animals. The grass which the country had lately afforded was very poor and insufficient; and animals which have been accustomed to grain become soon weak and unable to labor, when reduced to no other nourishment than grass. The American horses (as those are usually called which are brought to this country from the States) are not of any serviceable value until after they have remained a winter in the country, and become accustomed to live entirely on grass.

19th.--Desirous to avoid every delay not absolutely necessary, I sent on Carson in advance to Fort Hall this morning, to make arrangements for a small supply of provisions. A few miles from our encampment, the road entered a high ridge, which the trappers called the "little mountain," connecting the Utah with the Wind

River chain; and in one of the hills near which we passed I remarked strata of a conglomerate formation, fragments of which were scattered over the surface. We crossed a ridge of this conglomerate, the road passing near a grove of low cedar, and descending upon one of the heads of Ham's fork, called Muddy, where we made our mid-day halt. In the river hills at this place, I discovered strata of fossiliferous rock, having an ***oolitic structure***, which, in connection with the neighboring strata, authorize us to believe that here, on the west side of the Rocky mountains, we find repeated the modern formations of Great Britain and Europe, which have hitherto been wanting to complete the system of North American geology.

In the afternoon we continued our road, and searching among the hills a few miles up the stream, and on the same bank, I discovered, among the alternate beds of coal and clay, a stratum of white indurated clay, containing very clear and beautiful impressions of vegetable remains. This was the most interesting fossil locality I had met in the country, and I deeply regretted that time did not permit me to remain a day or two in the vicinity; but I could not anticipate the delays to which I might be exposed in the course of our journey--or, rather, I knew that they were many and inevitable; and after remaining here only about an hour, I hurried off, loaded with as many specimens as I could conveniently carry.

Coal made its appearance occasionally in the hills during the afternoon, and was displayed in rabbit burrows in a kind of gap, through which we passed over some high hills, and we descended to make our encampment on the same stream, where we found but very poor grass. In the evening a fine cow, with her calf, which had strayed off from some emigrant party, was found several miles from the road, and brought into camp; and as she gave an abundance of milk, we enjoyed to-night an excellent cup of coffee. We traveled to-day 28 miles, and, as has been usual since crossing the Green river, the road has been very dusty, and the weather smoky and oppressively hot. Artemisia was characteristic among the few plants.

20th.--We continued to travel up the creek by a very gradual ascent and a very excellent grassy road, passing on the way several small forks of the stream. The hills here are higher, presenting escarpments of party-colored and apparently clay rocks, purple, dark-red, and yellow, containing strata of sandstone and limestone with shells, with a bed of cemented pebbles, the whole overlaid by beds of limestone. The alternation of red and yellow gives a bright appearance to the hills, one of which was called by our people the Rainbow hill, and the character of the country became more agreeable, and traveling far more pleasant, as now we found timber and very good grass. Gradually ascending, we reached the lower level of a bed of white limestone, lying upon a white clay, on the upper line of which the whole road is abundantly supplied with beautiful cool springs, gushing out a foot in breadth and several inches deep, directly from the hill- side.

At noon we halted at the last main fork of the creek, at an elevation of 7,200 feet, and in latitude, by observation, 41 deg. 39' 45"; and in the afternoon continued on the same excellent road, up the left or northern fork of the stream, towards its head, in a pass which the barometer placed at 8,230 feet above the sea. This is a connecting ridge between the Utah or Bear River mountains and the Wind River chain of the Rocky mountains, separating the waters of the Gulf of California on the east, and those on the west belonging more directly to the Pacific, from a vast interior basin whose rivers are collected into numerous lakes having no outlet to the ocean. From the summit of this pass, the highest which the road crosses between the Mississippi and the Western ocean, our view was over a very mountainous region, whose rugged appearance was greatly increased by the smoky weather, through which the broken ridges were dark and dimly seen. The ascent to the summit of the gap was occasionally steeper than the national road in the Alleghanies; and the descent, by way of a spur on the western side, is rather precipitous, but the pass may still be called a good one. Some thickets of the willow in the hollows below deceived us into the expectation of finding a camp at our usual hour at the foot of the mountain; but we found them without water, and continued down a ravine, and encamped about dark at a place where the springs began again to make their appearance, but where our animals fared badly; the stock of the emigrants having razed the grass as completely as if we were again in the midst of the buffalo.

21st.--An hour's travel this morning brought us into the fertile and picturesque valley of Bear river, the principal tributary to the Great Salt lake. The stream is here two hundred feet wide, fringed with willows and occasional groups of hawthorns. We were now entering a region which, for us, possessed a strange and extraordinary interest. We were upon the waters of the famous lake which forms a salient point among the remarkable geographical features of the country, and around which the vague and superstitious accounts of the trappers had thrown a delightful obscurity, which we anticipated pleasure in dispelling, but which, in the mean time, left a crowded field for the exercise of our imagination.

In our occasional conversations with the few old hunters who had visited the region, it had been a subject of frequent speculation; and the wonders which they related were not the less agreeable because they were highly exaggerated and impossible.

Hitherto this lake had been seen only by trappers who were wandering through the country in search of new beaver-streams, caring very little for geography; its islands had never been visited; and none were to be found who had entirely made the circuit of its shores; and no instrumental observations or geographical survey, of any description, had ever been made anywhere in the neighboring region. It was generally supposed that it had no visible outlet; but among the trappers, including those in my own camp, were many who believed that somewhere on its surface was a terrible whirlpool, through which its waters found their way to the ocean by some subterranean communication. All these things had made a frequent subject of discussion in our desultory conversations around the fires at night; and my own mind had become tolerably well filled with their indefinite pictures, and insensibly colored with their romantic descriptions, which, in the pleasure of excitement, I was well disposed to believe, and half expected to realize.

Where we descended into this beautiful valley, it is three to four miles in breadth, perfectly level, and bounded by mountainous ridges, one above another, rising suddenly from the plain.

We continued our road down the river, and at night encamped with a family of emigrants--two men, women, and several children--who appeared to be bringing up the rear of the great caravan. I was struck with the fine appearance of their cattle, some six or eight yoke of oxen, which really looked as well as if they had been all the summer at work on some good farm. It was strange to see one small family traveling along through such a country, so remote from civilization. Some nine years since, such a security might have been a fatal one, but since their disastrous defeats in the country a little north, the Blackfeet have ceased to visit these waters. Indians however, are very uncertain in their localities; and the friendly feelings, also, of those now inhabiting it may be changed.

According to barometrical observation at noon, the elevation Of the valley was 6,400 feet above the sea; and our encampment at night in latitude 42 deg. 03' 47", and longitude 111 deg. 10' 53", by observation--the day's journey having been 26 miles. This encampment was therefore within the territorial limit of the United States; our traveling, from the time we entered the valley of the Green river, on the 15th of August, having been south of the 42d degree of north latitude, and consequently on Mexican territory; and this is the route all the emigrants now travel to Oregon.

The temperature at sunset was 65 deg.; and at evening there was a distant thunder-storm, with a light breeze from the north.

Antelope and elk were seen during the day on the opposite prairie; and there were ducks and geese in the river.

The next morning, in about three miles from our encampment, we reached Smith's fork, a stream of clear water, about 50 feet in breadth. It is timbered with cottonwood, willow, and aspen, and makes a beautiful debouchement through a pass about 600 yards wide, between remarkable mountain hills, rising abruptly on either side, and forming gigantic columns to the gate by which it enters Bear River valley. The bottoms, which below Smith's fork had been two miles wide, narrowed as we advanced to a gap 500 yards wide, and during the greater part of the day we had a winding route, the river making very sharp and sudden bends, the mountains steep and rocky, and the valley occasionally so narrow as only to leave space for a passage through.

We made our halt at noon in a fertile bottom, where the common blue flax was growing abundantly, a few miles below the mouth of Thomas's fork, one of the larger tributaries of the river.

Crossing, in the afternoon, the point of a narrow spur, we descended into a beautiful bottom, formed by a lateral valley, which presented a picture of home beauty that went directly to our hearts. The edge of the wood, for several miles along the river, was dotted with the white covers of emigrant wagons, collected in groups at different camps, where the smoke was rising lazily from the fires, around which the women were occupied in preparing the evening meal, and the children playing in the grass; and herds of cattle, grazing about in the bottom, had an air of quiet security, and civilized comfort, that made a rare sight for the traveler in such a remote wilderness.

In common with all the emigration, they had been reposing for several days in this delightful valley, in order to recruit their animals on its luxuriant pasturage after their long journey, and prepare them for the hard travel along the comparatively sterile banks of the Upper Columbia. At the lower end of this extensive bottom, the river passes through an open canon, where there were high vertical rocks to the water's edge, and the road here turns up a broad valley to the right. It was already near sunset; but, hoping to reach the river again before night, we continued our march along the valley, finding the road tolerably good, until we arrived at a point where it crosses the ridge by an ascent of a mile in length, which was so very steep and difficult for the gun and carriage, that we did not reach the summit until dark.

It was absolutely necessary to descend into the valley for water and grass; and we were obliged to grope our way in the darkness down a very steep, bad mountain, reaching the river at about ten o'clock. It was late before our animals were gathered into the camp, several of those which were very weak being necessarily left to pass the night on the ridge; and we sat down again to a midnight supper. The road, in the morning, presented an animated appearance. We found that we had encamped near a large party of emigrants; and a few miles below, another party was already in motion. Here the valley had resumed its usual breadth, and the river swept off along the mountains on the western side, the road continuing directly on.

In about an hour's travel we met several Shoshonee Indians, who informed us that they belonged to a large village which had just come into the valley from the mountain to the westward, where they had been hunting antelope and gathering service-berries. Glad at the opportunity of seeing one of their villages, and in the hope of purchasing from them a few horses, I turned immediately off into the plain towards their encampment, which was situated on a small stream near the river.

We had approached within something more than a mile of the village, when suddenly a single horseman emerged from it at full speed, followed by another and another in rapid succession; and then party after party poured into the plain, until, when the foremost rider reached us, all the whole intervening plain was occupied by a mass of horsemen, which came charging down upon us with guns and naked swords, lances, and bows and arrows-- Indians entirely naked, and warriors fully dressed for war, with the long red streamers of their war-bonnets reaching nearly to the ground, all mingled together in the bravery of savage warfare. They had been thrown into a sudden tumult by the appearance of our flag, which, among these people, is regarded as an emblem of hostility--it being usually borne by the Sioux and the neighboring mountain Indians, when they come here to war; and we had, accordingly been mistaken for a body of their enemies. A few words from the chief quieted the excitement; and the whole band, increasing every moment in number, escorted us to their encampment, where the chief pointed out a place for us to encamp, near his own lodge, and we made known our purpose in visiting the village. In a very short time we purchased eight horses, for which we gave in exchange blankets, red and blue cloth, beads, knives, and tobacco, and the usual other articles of Indian traffic. We obtained from them also a considerable quantity of berries, of different kinds, among which service-berries were the most abundant; and several kinds of roots and seeds, which we could eat with pleasure, as any kind of vegetable food was gratifying to us. I ate here, for the first time, the **_kooyah_**, or **_tobacco-root_**, (**_valeriana edulis_**,)--the principal edible root among the Indians who inhabit the upper waters of the streams on the western side of the mountains. It has a very strong and remarkably peculiar taste and odor, which I can compare to no other vegetable that I am acquainted with, and which to some persons is extremely offensive. It was characterized by Mr. Preuss as the most horrid food he had ever put in his mouth; and when, in the evening, one of the chiefs sent his wife to me with a portion which she had prepared as a delicacy to regale us, the odor immediately drove him out of the lodge; and frequently afterwards he used to beg that when those who liked it had taken what they desired, it might be sent away. To others, however, the taste is rather an agreeable one; and I was afterwards glad when it formed an addition to our scanty meals. It is full of nutriment; and in its unprepared state is said by the Indians to have very strong poisonous qualities, of which it is deprived by a peculiar process, being baked in the ground for about two days.

The morning of the 24th was disagreeably cool, with an easterly wind, and very smoky weather. We made a late start from the village, and, regaining the road, (on which, during all the day, were scattered the emigrant wagons,) we continued on down the valley of the river, bordered by high and mountainous hills, on which fires are seen at the summit. The soil appears generally good, although, with the grasses, many of the plants are dried up, probably on account of the great heat and want of rain. The common blue flax of cultivation, now almost entirely in seed--

only a scattered flower here and there remaining--is the most characteristic plant of the Bear River valley. When we encamped at night, on the right bank of the river, it was growing as in a sown field. We had traveled during the day twenty-two miles, encamping in latitude (by observation) 42 deg. 36' 56", chronometric longitude 111 deg. 42' 05".

In our neighborhood the mountains appeared extremely rugged, giving still greater value to this beautiful natural pass.

25th.--This was a cloudless but smoky autumn morning, with a cold wind from the southeast, and a temperature of 45 deg. at sunrise. In a few miles I noticed, where a little stream crossed the road, fragments of **scoriated basalt** scattered about--the first volcanic rock we had seen, and which now became a characteristic rock along our future road. In about six miles' travel from our encampment, we reached one of the points in our journey to which we had always looked forward with great interest--the famous **Beer springs**. The place in which they are situated is a basin of mineral waters enclosed by the mountains, which sweep around a circular bend of Bear river, here at its most northern point, and which, from a northern, in the course of a few miles acquires a southern direction towards the GREAT SALT LAKE. A pretty little stream of clear water enters the upper part of the basin, from an open valley in the mountains, and, passing through the bottom, discharges into Bear river. Crossing this stream, we descended a mile below, and made our encampment in a grove of cedar immediately at the Beer springs, which, on account of the effervescing gas and acid taste, have received their name from the voyageurs and trappers of the country, who, in the midst of their rude and hard lives, are fond of finding some fancied resemblance to the luxuries they rarely have the fortune to enjoy.

Although somewhat disappointed in the expectations which various descriptions had led me to form of unusual beauty of situation and scenery, I found it altogether a place of very great interest; and a traveler for the first time in a volcanic region remains in a constant excitement, and at every step is arrested by something remarkable and new. There is a confusion of interesting objects gathered together in a small space. Around the place of encampment the Beer springs were numerous; but, as far as we could ascertain, were confined entirely to that locality in the bottom. In the bed of the river, in front, for a space of several hundred yards, they were very abundant; the effervescing gas rising up and agitating the water in countless bubbling columns. In the vicinity round about were numerous springs of an entirely different and equally marked mineral character. In a rather picturesque spot about 1,300 yards below our encampment, and immediately on the river bank, is the most remarkable spring of the place. In an opening on the rock, a white column of scattered water is thrown up, in form like a *jet-d'eau*, to a variable height of about three feet, and, though it is maintained in a constant supply, its greatest height is only attained at regular intervals, according to the action of the force below. It is accompanied by a subterranean noise, which, together with the motion of the water, makes very much the impression of a steamboat in motion; and, without knowing that it had been already previously so called, we gave to it the name of the **Steamboat spring**. The rock through which it is forced is slightly raised in a convex manner, and gathered at the opening into an urn-mouthed form, and is evidently formed by continued deposition from the water, and colored bright red by oxide of iron. An analysis of this deposited rock, which I subjoin, will give you some idea of the properties of the water, which, with the exception of the Beer springs, is the mineral water of the place[1]. It is a hot spring, and the water has a pungent and disagreeable metallic taste, leaving a burning effect on the tongue. Within perhaps two yards of the *jet-d'eau* is a small hole of about an inch in diameter, through which, at regular intervals, escapes a blast of hot air, with a light wreath of smoke, accompanied by a regular noise. This hole had been noticed by Dr. Wislizenus, a gentleman who had several years since passed by this place, and who remarked, with very nice observation, that smelling the gas which issued from the orifice produced a sensation of giddiness and nausea. Mr. Preuss and myself repeated the observation, and were so well satisfied with its correctness, that we did not find it pleasant to continue the experiment, as the sensation of giddiness which it produced

1   ANALYSIS.
Carbonate of lime -   - - 92.55
Carbonate of magnesia - 0.42
Oxide of iron - - - -   - 1.05

Silica- - - - - -}
Alumina - - - - -}-   - - 5.98
Water and loss- -}   _____
                      100.00

was certainly strong and decided. A huge emigrant wagon, with a large and diversified family had overtaken us and halted to noon at our encampment; and, while we were sitting at the spring, a band of boys and girls, with two or three young men, came up, one of whom I asked to stoop down and smell the gas, desirous to satisfy myself further of its effects. But his natural caution had been awakened by the singular and suspicious features of the place, and he declined my proposal decidedly, and with a few indistinct remarks about the devil, whom he seemed to consider the ***genius loci***. The ceaseless motion and the play of the fountain, the red rock and the green trees near, make this a picturesque spot.

A short distance above the spring, and near the foot of the same spur, is a very remarkable, yellow-colored rock, soft and friable, consisting principally of carbonate of lime and oxide of iron, of regular structure, which is probably a fossil coral. The rocky bank along the shore between the Steamboat spring and our encampment, along which is dispersed the water from the hills, is composed entirely of strata of a calcareous ***tufa***, with the remains of moss and reed-like grasses, which is probably the formation of springs. The ***Beer*** or ***Soda springs***, which have given name to this locality, are agreeable, but less highly flavored than the Boiling springs at the foot of Pike's peak, which are of the same character. They are very numerous, and half hidden by tufts of grass, which we amused ourselves in removing and searching about for more highly impregnated springs. They are some of them deep, and of various sizes--sometimes several yards in diameter, and kept in constant motion by columns of escaping gas. By analysis, one quart of the water contains as follows:

Grains.

Sulphate of magnesia------------ 12.10
Sulphate of lime---------------- 2.12
Carbonate of lime--------------- 3.86
Carbonate of magnesia----------- 3.22
Chloride of calcium------------- 1.33
Chloride of magnesium----------- 1.12
Chloride of sodium-------------- 2.24
Vegetable extractive matter, &c-- 0.85
———
26.84

The carbonic acid, originally contained in the water, had mainly escaped before it was subjected to analysis; and it was not, therefore, taken into consideration.

In the afternoon I wandered about among the cedars, which occupy the greater part of the bottom towards the mountains. The soil here has a dry and calcined appearance; in some places, the open grounds are covered with saline efflorescences, and there are a number of regularly-shaped and very remarkable hills, which are formed of a succession of convex strata that have been deposited by the waters of extinct springs, the orifices of which are found on their summits, some of them having the form of funnel- shaped cones. Others of these remarkably-shaped hills are of a red-colored earth, entirely bare, and composed principally of carbonate of lime, with oxide of iron, formed in the same manner. Walking near one of them, on the summit of which the springs were dry, my attention was attracted by an underground noise, around which I circled repeatedly, until I found the spot from beneath which it came; and, removing the red earth, discovered a hidden spring, which was boiling up from below, with the same disagreeable metallic taste as the Steamboat spring. Continuing up the bottom, and crossing the little stream which has been already mentioned, I visited several remarkable red and white hills, which had attracted my attention from the road in the morning. These are immediately upon the stream, and, like those already mentioned, are formed by the deposition of successive strata from the springs. On their summits, the orifices through which the waters had been discharged were so large, that they resembled miniature craters, being some of them several feet in diameter, circular, and regularly formed as if by art. At a former time, when these dried-up fountains were all in motion, they must have made a beautiful display on a grand scale; and nearly all this basin appears to me to have been formed under their action, and should be called the ***place of fountains***. At the foot of one of these hills, or rather on its side near the base, are several of these small limestone columns, about one foot in diameter at the base, and tapering upwards to a height of three or four feet; and on the summit the water is boiling up and bubbling over, constantly adding to the height of the little obelisks. In some, the water only boils up, no longer overflowing, and has here the same taste as at the Steamboat spring. The observer will remark a gradual subsidence in the water, which formerly supplied the fountains; as on all the summits of the hills the springs are now dry, and are found only low down upon their sides, or on the surrounding plain.

A little higher up the creek its banks are formed by strata of very heavy and hard scoriaceous basalt, having a bright metallic lustre when broken. The mountains overlooking the plain are of an entirely different geological character. Continuing on, I walked to the summit of one of them, where the principal rock was a granular quartz. Descending the mountains, and returning towards the camp along the base of the ridge which skirts the plain, I found, at the foot of a mountain spur, and issuing from a compact rock of a dark blue color, a great number of springs having the same pungent and disagreeably metallic taste already mentioned, the water of which was collected into a very remarkable basin, whose singularity, perhaps, made it appear to me very beautiful. It is large--perhaps fifty yards in circumference; and in it the water is contained, at an elevation of several feet above the surrounding ground, by a wall of calcareous ***tufa***, composed principally of the remains of mosses, three or four, and sometimes ten feet high. The water within is very clear and pure, and three or four feet deep, where it could be measured, near the wall; and at a considerably low level, is another pond or basin of very clear water, and apparently of considerable depth, from the bottom of which the gas was escaping in bubbling columns at many places. This water was collected into a small stream, which, in a few hundred yards, sank under ground, reappearing among the rocks between the two great springs near the river, which it entered by a little fall.

Late in the afternoon I set out on my return to the camp, and, crossing in the way a large field of salt that was several inches deep, found on my arrival that our emigrant friends, who had been encamped in company with us, had resumed their journey, and the road had again assumed its solitary character. The temperature of the largest of the *Beer* springs at our encampment was 65 deg. at sunset, that of the air being 62.5 deg.. Our barometric observation gave 5,840 feet for the elevation above the gulf, being about 500 feet lower than the Boiling springs, which are of a similar nature, at the foot of Pike's peak. The astronomical observations gave for our latitude 42 deg. 39' 57", and 111 deg. 46' 00" for the longitude. The night was very still and cloudless, and I sat up for an observation of the first satellite of Jupiter, the emersion of which took place about midnight; but fell asleep at the telescope, awaking just a few minutes after the appearance of the star.

The morning of the 26th was calm, and the sky without clouds, but smoky, and the temperature at sunrise 28.5 deg.. At the same time, the temperature of the large Beer spring, where we were encamped, was 56 deg.; that of the Steamboat spring 87 deg., and that of the steam-hole, near it, 81.5 deg.. In the course of the morning, the last wagons of the emigration passed by, and we were again left in our place, in the rear.

Remaining in camp until nearly 11 o'clock, we traveled a short distance down the river, and halted to noon on the bank, at a point where the road quits the valley of Bear river, and, crossing a ridge which divides the Great basin from the Pacific waters, reaches Fort Hall, by way of the Portneuf river, in a distance of probably fifty miles, or two and a half days' journey for wagons. An examination of the great lake which is the outlet of this river, and the principal feature of geographical interest in the basin, was one of the main objects contemplated in the general plan of our survey, and I accordingly determined at this place to leave the road, and, after having completed a reconnoissance of the lake, regain it subsequently at Fort Hall. But our little stock of provisions had again become extremely low; we had only dried meat sufficient for one meal, and our supply of flour and other comforts was entirely exhausted. I therefore immediately dispatched one of the party, Henry Lee, with a note to Carson, at Fort Hall, directing him to load a pack-horse with whatever could be obtained there in the way of provisions, and endeavor to overtake me on the river. In the mean time, we had picked up along the road two tolerably well-grown calves, which would have become food for wolves, and which had probably been left by some of the earlier emigrants, none of those we had met having made any claim to them; and on these I mainly relied for support during our circuit to the lake.

In sweeping around the point of the mountain which runs down into the bend, the river here passes between perpendicular walls of basalt, which always fix the attention, from the regular form in which it occurs, and its perfect distinctness from the surrounding rocks among which it had been placed. The mountain, which is rugged and steep, and, by our measurement, 1,400 feet above the river directly opposite the place of our halt, is called the **Sheep-rock**--probably because a flock of the mountain sheep (***ovis montana***) had been seen on the craggy point.

As we were about resuming our march in the afternoon, I was attracted by the singular appearance of an isolated hill with a concave summit, in the plain, about two miles from the river, and turned off towards it, while the camp proceeded on its way southward in search of the lake. I found the thin and stony soil of the plain entirely underlaid by the basalt which forms the river walls; and when I reached the neighborhood of the hill, the surface of the plain was rent into frequent fissures and chasms of the same scoriated volcanic rock, from 40 to 60 feet deep, but which there was not sufficient light to penetrate entirely, and which I had not time to descend. Arrived at the summit of the hill, I found that it terminated in a very perfect crater, of an oval, or nearly circular form, 360 paces in circumference, and 60 feet at the greatest depth. The walls, which were perfectly vertical, and disposed like masonry in a very regular manner, were composed of a brown-colored scoriaceous lava, similar to the light scoriaceous lava of Mt. Etna, Vesuvius, and other volcanoes. The faces of the walls were reddened and glazed by the fire, in which they had been melted, and which had left them contorted and twisted by its violent action.

Our route luring the afternoon was a little rough, being (in the direction we had taken) over a volcanic plain, where our progress was sometimes obstructed by fissures, and black beds, composed of fragments of the rock. On both sides, the mountains appeared very broken, but tolerably well timbered.

Crossing a point of ridge which makes in to the river, we fell upon it again before sunset, and encamped on the right bank, opposite to the encampment of three lodges of Snake Indians. They visited us during the evening, and we obtained from them a small quantity of roots of different kinds, in exchange for goods. Among them was a sweet root of very pleasant flavor, having somewhat the taste of preserved quince. My endeavors to become acquainted with the plants which furnish to the Indians a portion of their support, were only gradually successful, and after long and persevering attention; and even after obtaining, I did not succeed in preserving them until they could be satisfactorily determined. In this portion of the journey, I found this particular root cut up into small pieces, that it was only to be identified by its taste, when the bulb was met with in perfect form among the Indians lower down on the Columbia, among whom it is the highly celebrated kamas. It was long afterwards, on our return through Upper California, that I found the plant itself in bloom, which I supposed to furnish the kamas root, (*camassia esculenta*.) The root diet had a rather mournful effect at the commencement, and one of the calves was killed this evening for food. The animals fared well on rushes.

27th.--The morning was cloudy, with appearance of rain, and the thermometer at sunrise at 29 deg.. Making an unusually early start, we crossed the river at a good ford; and, following for about three hours a trail which led along the bottom, we entered a labyrinth of hills below the main ridge, and halted to noon in the ravine of a pretty little stream, timbered with cottonwood of a large size, ash-leaved maple, with cherry and other shrubby trees. The hazy weather, which had prevented any very extended views since entering the Green River valley, began now to disappear. There was a slight rain in the earlier part of the day, and at noon, when the thermometer had risen to 79.5 deg., we had a bright sun, with blue sky and scattered *cumuli*. According to the barometer, our halt there among the hills was at an elevation of 5,320 feet. Crossing a dividing ridge in the afternoon, we followed down another little Bear River tributary, to the point where it emerged on an open green flat among the hills, timbered with groves, and bordered with cane thickets, but without water. A pretty little rivulet coming out of the hillside, and overhung by tall flowering plants of a species I had not hitherto seen, furnished us with a good camping-place. The evening was cloudy, the temperature at sunset 69 deg., and the elevation 5,140 feet. Among the plants occurring along the road during the day, *epinettes des prairies* (grindelia squarraso) was in considerable abundance, and is among the very few plants remaining in bloom--the whole country having now an autumnal appearance, in the crisp and yellow plants, and dried-up grasses. Many cranes were seen during the day, with a few antelope, very shy and wild.

28th.--During the night we had a thunder-storm, with moderate rain, which has made the air this morning very clear, the thermometer being at 55 deg.. Leaving our encampment at the **Cane spring**, and quitting the trail on which we had been traveling, and which would probably have afforded us a good road to the lake, we crossed some very deep ravines, and, in about an hour's traveling, again reached the river. We were now in a valley five or six miles wide, between mountain ranges, which, about thirty miles below, appeared to close up and terminate the valley, leaving for the river only a very narrow pass, or canon, behind which we imagined we would find the broad waters of the lake. We made the usual halt at the mouth of a small clear stream, having a slightly mineral taste, (perhaps of salt,) 4,760 feet above the gulf. In the afternoon we climbed a very steep sandy hill; and after a slow and winding day's march of 27 miles, encamped at a slough on the river. There were great quantities of geese and, ducks, of which only a few were shot; the Indians having probably made them very wild. The men employed themselves in fishing but caught nothing. A skunk, (*mephitis Americana*,) which was killed in the afternoon, made a supper for one of the messes. The river is bordered occasionally with fields of cane, which we regarded as an indication of our approach to a lake-country. We had frequent showers of rain during the night, with thunder.

29th.--The thermometer at sunrise was 54 deg., with air from the NW., and dark rainy clouds moving on the horizon; rain squalls and bright sunshine by intervals. I rode ahead with Basil to explore the country, and, continuing about three miles along the river, turned directly off on a trail running towards three marked gaps in the bordering range, where the mountains appeared cut through their bases, towards which the river plain rose gradually. Putting our horses into a gallop on some fresh tracks which showed very plainly in the wet path, we came suddenly upon a small party of Shoshonee Indians, who had fallen into the trail from the north. We could only communicate by signs; but they made us understand that the road through the chain was a very excellent one, leading into a broad valley which ran to the southward. We halted to noon at what may be called the gate of the pass; on either side of which were huge mountains of rock, between which stole a little pure water stream, with a margin just sufficiently large for our passage. From the river, the plain had gradually risen to an altitude of 5,500 feet, and, by meridian observation, the latitude of the entrance was 42 deg..

In the interval of our usual halt, several of us wandered along up the stream to examine the pass more at leisure. Within the gate, the rocks receded a little back, leaving a very narrow, but most beautiful valley, through which the little stream wound its way, hidden by the different kinds of trees and shrubs--aspen, maple, willow, cherry, and elder; a fine verdure of smooth short grass spread over the remaining space to the bare sides of the rocky walls. These were of a blue limestone, which constitutes the mountain here; and opening directly on the grassy bottom were several curious caves, which appeared to be inhabited by root- diggers. On one side was gathered a heap of leaves for a bed, and they were dry, open, and pleasant. On the roofs of the caves I remarked bituminous exudations from the rock.

The trail was an excellent one for pack-horses; but as it sometimes crossed a shelving point, to avoid the shrubbery we were obliged in several places to open a road for the carriage through the wood. A squaw on horseback, accompanied by five or six dogs, entered the pass in the afternoon; but was too much terrified at finding herself in such unexpected company to make any pause for conversation, and hurried off at a good pace--being, of course, no further disturbed than by an accelerating shout. She was well and showily dressed, and was probably going to a village encamped somewhere near, and evidently did not belong to the tribe of *root-diggers*. We now had entered a country inhabited by these people; and as in the course of the voyage we shall frequently meet with them in various stages of existence, it will be well to inform you that, scattered over the great region west of the Rocky mountains, and south of the Great Snake river, are numerous Indians whose subsistence is almost solely derived from roots and seeds, and such small animals as chance and great good fortune sometimes bring within their reach. They are miserably poor, armed only with bows and arrows, or clubs; and, as the country they inhabit is almost destitute of game, they have no means of obtaining better arms. In the northern part of the region just mentioned, they live generally in solitary families; and farther to the south they are gathered together in villages. Those who live together in villages, strengthened by association, are in exclusive possession of the more genial and richer parts of the country; while the others are driven to the ruder mountains, and to the more inhospitable parts of the country. But by simply observing, in accompanying us along our road, you will become better acquainted with these people than we could make you in any other than a very long description, and you will find them worthy of your interest.

Roots, seeds, and grass, every vegetable that affords any nourishment, and every living animal thing, insect or worm, they eat. Nearly approaching to the lower animal creation, their sole employment is to obtain food; and they are constantly occupied in struggling to support existence.

The most remarkable feature of the pass is the **Standing rock**, which has fallen from the cliffs above, and standing perpendicularly near the middle of the valley, presents itself like a watch-tower in the pass. It will give you a tolerably correct idea of the character of the scenery in this country, where generally the mountains rise abruptly up from comparatively unbroken plains and level valleys; but it will entirely fail in representing the picturesque beauty of this delightful place, where a green valley, full of foliage and a hundred yards wide, contrasts with naked crags that spire up into a blue line of pinnacles 3,000 feet above, sometimes crested with cedar and pine, and sometimes ragged and bare.

The detention that we met with in opening the road, and perhaps a willingness to linger on the way, made the afternoon's travel short; and about two miles from the entrance, we passed through another gate, and encamped on the stream at the junction of a little fork from the southward, around which the mountains stooped more gently down, forming a small open cove.

As it was still early in the afternoon, Basil and myself in one direction, and Mr. Preuss in another, set out to explore the country, and ascended different neighboring peaks, in the hope of seeing some indications of the lake; but though our elevation afforded magnificent views, the eye ranging over a large extent of Bear river, with the broad and fertile **Cache valley** in the direction of our search, was only to be seen a bed of apparently impracticable mountains. Among these, the trail we had been following turned sharply to the northward, and it began to be doubtful if it would not lead us away from the object of our destination; but I nevertheless determined to keep it, in the belief that it would eventually bring us right. A squall of rain drove us out of the mountain, and it was late when we reached the camp. The evening closed in with frequent showers of rain, with some lightning and thunder.

30th.--We had constant thunder-storms during the night, but in the morning the clouds were sinking to the horizon, and the air was clear and cold, with the thermometer at sunrise at 39 deg.. Elevation by barometer 5,580 feet. We were in motion early, continuing up the little stream without encountering any ascent where a horse would not easily gallop; and, crossing a slight dividing ground at the summit, descended upon a small stream, along which continued the same excellent road. In riding through the pass, numerous cranes were seen; and prairie hens, or grouse, (***bonasia umbellus***,) which lately had been rare, were very abundant.

This little affluent brought us to a larger stream, down which we traveled through a more open bottom, on a level road, where heavily-laden wagons could pass without obstacle. The hills on the right grew lower, and, on entering a more open country, we discovered a Shoshonee village; and being desirous to obtain information, and purchase from them some roots and berries, we halted on the river, which was lightly wooded with cherry, willow, maple, service-berry, and aspen. A meridian observation of the sun, which I obtained here, gave 42 deg. 14' 22" for our latitude, and the barometer indicated a height of 5,170 feet. A number of Indians came immediately over to visit us, and several men were sent to the village with goods, tobacco, knives, cloth, vermilion, and the usual trinkets, to exchange for provisions. But they had no game of any kind; and it was difficult to obtain any roots from them, as they were miserably poor, and had but little to spare from their winter stock of provisions. Several of the Indians drew aside their blankets, showing me their lean and bony figures; and I would not any longer tempt them with a display of our merchandise to part with their wretched subsistence, when they gave as a reason that it would expose them to temporary starvation. A great portion of the region inhabited by this nation, formerly abounded in game--the buffalo ranging about in herds, as we had found them on the eastern waters, and the plains dotted with scattered bands of antelope; but so rapidly have they disappeared within a few years, that now, as we journeyed along, an occasional buffalo skull and a few wild antelope were all that remained of the abundance which had covered the country with animal life.

The extraordinary rapidity with which the buffalo is disappearing from our territories will not appear surprising when we remember the great scale on which their destruction is yearly carried on. With inconsiderable exceptions, the business of the American trading-posts is carried on in their skins; every year the Indian villages make new lodges, for which the skin of the buffalo furnishes the material; and in that portion of the country where they are still found, the Indians derive their entire support from them, and slaughter them with a thoughtless and abominable extravagance. Like the Indians themselves, they have been a characteristic of the Great West; and as, like them, they are visibly diminishing, it will be interesting to throw a glance backward through the last twenty years, and give some account of their former distribution through the country, and the limit of their western range.

The information is derived principally from Mr. Fitzpatrick, supported by my own personal knowledge and acquaintance with the country. Our knowledge does not go farther back than the spring of 1824, at which time the buffalo were spread in immense numbers over the Green River and Bear River valleys, and through all the country lying between the Colorado, or Green river of the Gulf of California, and Lewis's fork of the Columbia river; the meridian of Fort Hall then forming the western limit of their range. The buffalo then remained for many years in that country, and frequently moved down the valley of the Columbia, on both sides of the river as far as the ***Fishing falls***. Below this point they never descended in any numbers. About the year 1834 or 1835 they began to diminish very rapidly, and continued to decrease until 1838 or 1840, when, with the country we have just described, they entirely abandoned all the waters of the Pacific north of Lewis's fork of the Columbia. At that time, the Flathead Indians were in the habit of finding their buffalo on the heads of Salmon river, and other streams of the Columbia; but now they never meet with them farther west than the three forks of the Missouri, or the plains of the Yellow-stone river.

In the course of our journey it will be remarked that the buffalo have not so entirely abandoned the waters of the Pacific, in the Rocky-Mountain region south of the Sweet Water, as in the country north of the Great Pass. This partial distribution can only be accounted for in the great pastoral beauty of that country, which bears marks of having been one of their favorite haunts, and by the fact that the white hunters have more frequented the northern than the southern region--it being north of the South Pass that the hunters, trappers, and traders, have had their rendezvous for many years past; and from that section also the greater portion of the beaver and rich furs were taken, although always the most dangerous as well as the most profitable hunting-ground.

In that region lying between the Green or Colorado river and the head- waters of the Rio del Norte, over the ***Yampah, Kooyah, White***, and ***Grand*** rivers--all of which are the waters of the Colorado--the buffalo never extended so far to the westward as they did on the waters of the Columbia; and only in one or two instances have they been known to descend as far west as the mouth of White river. In traveling through the country west of the Rocky mountains, observation readily led me to the impression that the buffalo had, for the first time, crossed that range to the waters of the Pacific only a few years prior to the period we are considering; and in this opinion I am sustained by Mr. Fitzpatrick, and the older trappers in that country. In the region west of the Rocky mountains, we never meet with any of the ancient vestiges which, throughout all the country lying upon their eastern waters, are found in the ***great highways***, continuous for hundreds of miles, always several inches, and sometimes several feet in depth, which the buffalo have made in crossing from one river to another, or in traversing the mountain ranges. The Snake Indians, more particularly those low down upon Lewis's fork, have always been very grateful to the American trappers, for the great kindness (as they frequently expressed it) which they did to them, in driving the buffalo so low down the Columbia river.

The extraordinary abundance of the buffalo on the east side of the Rocky mountains, and their extraordinary diminution, will be made clearly evident from the following statement: At any time between the years 1824 and 1836, a traveler might start from any given point south or north in the Rocky Mountain range, journeying by the most direct route to the Missouri river; and, during the whole distance, his road would always be among large bands of buffalo, which would never be out of his view until he arrived almost within sight of the abodes of civilization.

At this time, the buffalo occupy but a very limited space, principally along the eastern base of the Rocky mountains, sometimes extending at their southern extremity to a considerable distance into the plains between the Platte and Arkansas rivers, and along the eastern frontier of New Mexico as far south as Texas.

The following statement, which I owe to the kindness of Mr. Sanford, a partner in the American Fur Company, will further illustrate this subject, by extensive knowledge acquired during several years of travel through the region inhabited by the buffalo:

"The total amount of robes annually traded by ourselves and others will not be found to differ much from the following statement:

Robes.

American Fur Company	70,000
Hudson's Bay Company	10,000
All other companies, probably	10,000
Making a total of	90,000

as an average annual return for the last eight or ten years.

"In the northwest, the Hudson's Bay Company purchase from the Indians but a very small number--their only market being Canada, to which the cost of transportation nearly equals the produce of the furs; and it is only within a very recent period that they have received buffalo robes in trade; and out of the great number of buffalo annually killed throughout the extensive region inhabited by the Camanches and other kindred tribes, no robes whatever are furnished for trade. During only four months of the year, (from November until March,) the skins are good for dressing; those obtained in the remaining eight months are valueless to traders; and the hides of bulls are never taken off or dressed as robes at any season. Probably not more than one-third of the skins are taken from the animals killed, even when they are in good season, the labor of preparing and dressing the robes being very great; and it is seldom that a lodge trades more than twenty skins in a year. It is during the summer months, and in the early part of autumn, that the greatest number of buffalo are killed, and yet at this time a skin is never taken for the purpose of trade."

From these data, which are certainly limited, and decidedly within bounds, the reader is left to draw his own inference of the immense number annually killed.

In 1842, I found the Sioux Indians of the Upper Platte ***demontes***, as their

French traders expressed it, with the failure of the buffalo; and in the following year, large villages from the Upper Missouri came over to the mountains at the heads of the Platte, in search of them. The rapidly progressive failure of their principal, and almost their only means of subsistence, has created great alarm among them; and at this time there are only two modes presented to them, by which they see a good prospect for escaping starvation: one of these is to rob the settlements along the frontier of the States; and the other is to form a league between the various tribes of the Sioux nation, the Cheyennes, and Arapahoes, and make war against the Crow nation, in order to take from them their country, which is now the best buffalo country in the west. This plan they now have in consideration; and it would probably be a war of extermination, as the Crows have long been advised of this state of affairs, and say that they are perfectly prepared. These are the best warriors in the Rocky mountains, and are now allied with the Snake Indians; and it is probable that their combination would extend itself to the Utahs, who have long been engaged in war against the Sioux. It is in this section of country that my observation formerly led me to recommend the establishment of a military post.

The farther course of our narrative will give fuller and more detailed information of the present disposition of the buffalo in the country we visited.

Among the roots we obtained here, I could distinguish only five or six different kinds; and the supply of the Indians whom we met consisted principally of yampah, (***anethum graveolens***,) tobacoo-root, (***valeriana***,) and a large root of a species of thistle, (***circium Virginianum***,) which now is occasionally abundant and is a very agreeably flavored vegetable.

We had been detained so long at the village, that in the afternoon we made only five miles, and encamped on the same river after a day's journey of 19 miles. The Indians informed us that we should reach the big salt water after having slept twice and traveling in a south direction. The stream had here entered nearly a level plain or valley, of good soil, eight or ten miles broad, to which no termination was to be seen, and lying between ranges of mountains which, on the right, were grassy and smooth, unbroken by rock, and lower than on the left, where they were rocky and bald, increasing in height to the southward. On the creek were fringes of young willows, older trees being rarely found on the plains, where the Indians burn the surface to produce better grass. Several magpies (***pica Hudsopica***) were seen on the creek this afternoon; and a rattlesnake was killed here, the first which had been seen since leaving the eastern plains. Our camp to-night had such a hungry appearance that I suffered the little cow to be killed, and divided the roots and berries among the people. A number of Indians from the village encamped near.

The weather the next morning was clear, the thermometer at sunrise at 44.5 deg.; and, continuing down the valley, in about five miles we followed the little creek of our encampment to its junction with a larger stream, called **Roseaux**, or Reed river. Immediately opposite, on the right, the range was gathered into its highest peak, sloping gradually low, and running off to a point apparently some forty or fifty miles below. Between this (now become the valley stream) and the foot of the mountains, we journeyed along a handsome sloping level, which frequent springs from the hills made occasionally miry, and halted to noon at a swampy spring, where there were good grass and abundant rushes. Here the river was forty feet wide, with a considerable current, and the valley a mile and a half in breadth; the soil being generally good, of a dark color, and apparently well adapted to cultivation. The day had become bright and pleasant, with the thermometer at 71 deg.. By observation, our latitude was 41 deg. 59' 31", and the elevation above the sea 4,670 feet. On our left, this afternoon, the range at long intervals formed itself into peaks, appearing to terminate, about forty miles below, in a rocky cape, beyond which several others were faintly visible; and we were disappointed when, at every little rise, we did not see the lake. Towards evening, our way was somewhat obstructed by fields of *artemisia*, which began to make their appearance here, and we encamped on the Roseaux, the water of which had acquired a decidedly salt taste, nearly opposite to a canon gap in the mountains, through which the Bear river enters this valley. As we encamped, the night set in dark and cold, with heavy rain, and the artemisia, which was our only wood, was so wet that it would not burn. A poor, nearly starved dog, with a wound in his side from a ball, came to the camp, and remained with us until the winter, when he met a very unexpected fate.

SEPTEMBER.

1st.--The morning was squally and cold; the sky scattered over with clouds; and the night had been so uncomfortable, that we were not on the road until eight o'clock. Traveling between Roseaux and Bear rivers, we continued to descend the valley, which gradually expanded, as we advanced, into a level plain, of good soil, about 25 miles in breadth, between mountains 3,000 and 4,000 feet high, rising suddenly to the clouds, which all day rested upon the peaks. These gleamed out in the occasional sunlight, mantled with the snow, which had fallen upon them, while it rained on us in the valley below, of which the elevation here was 4,500 feet above the sea. The country before us plainly indicated that we were approaching the lake, though, as the ground we were traveling afforded no elevated point, nothing of it as yet could be seen; and at a great distance ahead were several isolated mountains resembling islands, which they were afterwards found to be. On this upper plain, the grass was everywhere dead; and among the shrubs with which it was almost exclusively occupied, (artemisia being the most abundant,) frequently occurred handsome clusters of several species of **dieteria** in bloom. **Purshia tridentata** was among the frequent shrubs. Descending to the bottoms of Bear river, we found good grass for the animals, and encamped about 300 yards above the mouth of Roseaux, which here makes its junction, without communicating any of its salty taste to the main stream, of which the water remains perfectly pure. On the river are only willow thickets, (**salix longifolia**,) and in the bottoms the abundant plants are canes, soldiago, and helianthi, and along the banks of Roseaux are fields of **malva rotundifolia**. At sunset the thermometer was at 54.5 deg., and the evening clear and calm; but I deferred making any use of it until one o'clock in the morning, when I endeavored to obtain an emersion of the first satellite; but it was lost in a bank of clouds, which also rendered our usual observations indifferent.

Among the useful things which formed a portion of our equipage, was an India-rubber boat, 18 feet long, made somewhat in the form of a bark canoe of the northern lakes. The sides were formed by two air-tight cylinders, eighteen inches in diameter, connected with others forming the bow and stern. To lessen the danger from accidents to the boat, these were divided into four different compartments, and the interior space was sufficiently large to contain five or six persons, and a considerable weight of baggage. The Roseaux being too deep to be forded, our boat was filled with air, and in about one hour all the equipage of the camp, carriage and gun included, ferried across. Thinking that perhaps in the course of the day we might reach the outlet of the lake, I got into the boat with Basil Lajeunesse, and paddled down Bear river, intending at night to rejoin the party, which in the mean time proceeded on its way. The river was from sixty to one hundred yards broad, and the water so deep, that even on the comparatively shallow points we could not reach the bottom with 15 feet. On either side were alternately low bottoms and willow points, with an occasional high prairie; and for five or six hours we followed slowly the winding course of the river, which crept along with a sluggish current among frequent ***detours*** several miles around, sometimes running for a considerable distance directly up the valley. As we were stealing quietly down the stream, trying in vain to get a shot at a strange large bird that was numerous among the willows, but very shy, we came unexpectedly upon several families of **Root-Diggers**, who were encamped among the rushes on the shore, and appeared very busy about several weirs or nets which had been rudely made of canes and rushes for the purpose of catching fish. They were very much startled at our appearance, but we soon established an acquaintance; and finding that they had some roots, I promised to send some men with goods to trade with them. They had the usual very large heads, remarkable among the Digger tribe, with matted hair, and were almost entirely naked: looking very poor and miserable, as if their lives had been spent in the rushes where they were, beyond which they seemed to have very little knowledge of any thing. From the words we could comprehend, their language was that of the Snake Indians.

Our boat moved so heavily, that we had made very little progress; and, finding that it would be impossible to overtake the camp, as soon as we were sufficiently far below the Indians, we put to the shore near a high prairie bank, hauled up the boat, and ***cached*** our effects in the willows. Ascending the bank, we found that our desultory labor had brought us only a few miles in a direct line; and, going out into the prairie, after a search we found the trail of the camp, which was nowhere in sight, but had followed the general course of the river in a large circular sweep which it makes at this place. The sun was about three hours high when we found the trail; and as our people had passed early in the day, we had the prospect of a vigorous walk before us. Immediately where we landed, the high arable plain on which we had been traveling, for several days past, terminated in extensive low flats, very generally occupied by salt marshes, or beds of shallow lakes, whence the water had in most places evaporated, leaving their hard surface incrusted with a shining white residuum; and absolutely covered with very small ***univalve*** shells. As we advanced, the whole country around us assumed this appearance; and there was no other vegetation than the shrubby chenopodiaceous and other apparently saline plants, which were confined to the rising grounds. Here and there, on the river bank, which was raised like a levee above the flats through which it ran, was a narrow border of grass and short black- burnt willows; the stream being very deep and sluggish, and sometimes six hundred to eight hundred feet wide. After a rapid walk of about fifteen miles, we caught sight of the camp-fires among clumps of willows, just as the sun had sunk behind the mountains on the west side of the valley, filling the clear sky with a golden yellow. These last rays, to us so precious, could not have revealed a more welcome sight. To the traveler and the hunter, a camp-fire in the lonely wilderness is always cheering; and to ourselves, in our present situation, after a hard march in a region of novelty, approaching the **debouches** of a river, in a lake of almost fabulous reputation, it was doubly so. A plentiful supper of aquatic birds, and the interest of the scene, soon dissipated fatigue; and I obtained during the night emersions of the second, third, and fourth satellites of Jupiter, with observations for time and latitude.

3d.--The morning was clear, with a light air from the north, and the thermometer at sunrise at 45.5 deg.. At three in the morning, Basil was sent back with several men and horses for the boat, which, in a direct course across the flats, was not ten miles distant; and in the mean time there was a pretty spot of grass here for the animals. The ground was so low that we could not get high enough to see across the river, on account of the willows; but we were evidently in the vicinity of the lake, and the water-fowl made this morning a noise like thunder. A pelican (**pelecanus onocrotalus**) was killed as he passed by, and many geese and ducks flew over the camp. On the dry salt marsh here is scarce any other plant than **salicornia herbacea**.

In the afternoon the men returned with the boat, bringing with them a small quantity of roots and some meat, which the Indians had told them was bear-meat.

Descending the river for about three miles, in the afternoon, we found a bar to any further traveling in that direction--the stream being spread out in several branches, and covering the low grounds with water, where the miry nature of the bottom did not permit any further advance. We were evidently on the border of the lake, although the rushes and canes which covered the marshes prevented any view; and we accordingly encamped at the little **delta** which forms the mouth of

Bear river--a long arm of the lake stretching up to the north, between us and the opposite mountains. The river was bordered with a fringe of willows and canes, among which were interspersed a few plants; and scattered about on the marsh was a species of ***uniola***, closely allied to ***U. spicata*** of our sea-coast. The whole morass was animated with multitudes of water-fowl, which appeared to be very wild--rising for the space of a mile round about at the sound of a gun, with a noise like distant thunder. Several of the people waded out into the marshes, and we had to-night a delicious supper of ducks, geese, and plover.

Although the moon was bright, the night was otherwise favorable; and I obtained this evening an emersion of the first satellite, with the usual observations. A mean result, depending on various observations made during our stay in the neighborhood, places the mouth of the river in longitude 112 deg. 19' 30" west from Greenwich; latitude 41 deg. 30' 22"; and, according to the barometer, in elevation 4,200 feet above the Gulf of Mexico. The night was clear, with considerable dew, which I had remarked every night since the first of September. The next morning, while we were preparing to start, Carson rode into the camp with flour and a few other articles of light provision sufficient for two or three days--a scanty but very acceptable supply. Mr. Fitzpatrick had not yet arrived, and provisions were very scarce, and difficult to be had at Fort Hall, which had been entirely exhausted by the necessities of the emigrants. He brought me also a letter from Mr. Dwight, who, in company with several emigrants, had reached that place in advance of Mr. Fitzpatrick, and was about continuing his journey to Vancouver.

Returning about five miles up the river, we were occupied until nearly sunset in crossing to the left bank--the stream, which in the last five or six miles of its course is very much narrower than above, being very deep immediately at the banks; and we had great difficulty in getting our animals over. The people with the baggage were easily crossed in the boat, and we encamped on the left bank where we crossed the river. At sunset the thermometer was at 75 deg., and there was some rain during the night, with a thunder-storm at a distance.

5th.--Before us was evidently the bed of the lake, being a great salt marsh, perfectly level and bare, whitened in places by saline efflorescences, with here and there a pool of water, and having the appearance of a very level seashore at low tide. Immediately along the river was a very narrow strip of vegetation, consisting of willows, helianthi, roses, flowering vines, and grass; bordered on the verge of the great marsh by a fringe of singular plants, which appear to be a shrubby salicornia, or a genus allied to it.

About 12 miles to the southward was one of those isolated mountains, now appearing to be a kind of peninsula; and towards this we accordingly directed our course, as it probably afforded a good view of the lake; but the deepening mud as we advanced forced us to return towards the river, and gain the higher ground at the foot of the eastern mountains. Here we halted for a few minutes at noon, on a beautiful little stream of pure and remarkably clear water, with a bed of rock *in situ*, on which was an abundant water-plant with a white blossom. There was good grass in the bottoms; and, amidst a rather luxuriant growth, its banks were bordered with a large showy plant, (*eupatorium purpureum*,) which I here saw for the first time. We named the stream **Clear creek**.

We continued our way along the mountain, having found here a broad plainly-beaten trail, over what was apparently the shore of the lake in the spring; the ground being high and firm, and the soil excellent, and covered with vegetation, among which a leguminous plant (*glycyrrhiza lepidota*) was a characteristic plant. The ridge here rises abruptly to the height of about 4,000 feet, its face being very prominently marked with a massive stratum of rose-colored granular quartz, which is evidently an altered sedimentary rock, the lines of deposition being very distinct. It is rocky and steep--divided into several mountains--and the rain in the valley appears to be always snow on their summits at this season. Near a remarkably rocky point of the mountain, at a large spring of pure water, were several hackberry-trees, (*celtis*,) probably a new species, the berries still green; and a short distance farther, thickets of sumach, (*rhus*.)

On the plain here I noticed blackbirds and grouse. In about seven miles from Clear creek, the trail brought us to a place at the foot of the mountain where there issued, with considerable force, 10 or 12 hot springs, highly impregnated with salt. In one of these the thermometer stood at 136 deg., and in another at 132.5 deg., and the water, which was spread in pools over the low ground, was colored red.

An analysis of the red earthy matter deposited in the bed of the stream from the springs, gives the following result:

Peroxide of iron-- ----- 33.50
Carbonate of magnesia-- 2.40
Carbonate of lime------ 50.43
Sulphate of lime------- 2.00
Chloride of sodium----- 3.45
Silica and alumina------ 3.00
Water and loss---------- 5.22

100.00 deg.

At this place the trail we had been following turned to the left, apparently with a view of entering a gorge in the mountain, from which issued the principal fork of a large and comparatively well-timbered stream, called Weber's fork. We accordingly turned off towards the lake, and encamped on this river, which was 100 to 150 feet wide, with high banks, and very clear pure water, without the slightest indication of salt.

6th.--Leaving the encampment early, we again directed our course for the peninsular **butte** across a low shrubby plain, crossing in the way a slough-like creek with miry banks, and wooded with thickets of thorn, (*crataegus*,) which were loaded with berries. This time we reached the butte without any difficulty, and, ascending to the summit, immediately at our feet beheld the object of our anxious search--the waters of the Inland Sea, stretching in still and solitary grandeur far beyond the limit of our vision. It was one of the great points of the exploration; and as we looked eagerly over the lake in the first emotions of excited pleasure, I am doubtful if the followers of Balboa felt more enthusiasm when, from the heights of the Andes, they saw for the first time the great Western ocean. It was certainly a magnificent object, and a noble ***terminus*** to this part of our expedition; and to travelers so long shut up among mountain ranges, a sudden view over the expanse of silent waters had in it something sublime. Several large islands raised their high rocky heads out of the waves; but whether or not they were timbered, was still left to our imagination, as the distance was too great to determine if the dark hues upon them were woodland or naked rock. During the day the clouds had been gathering black over the mountains to the westward, and, while we were looking, a storm burst down with sudden fury upon the lake, and entirely hid the inlands from our view. So far as we could see, along the shores there was not a solitary tree, and but little appearance of grass; and on Weber's fork, a few miles below our last encampment, the timber was gathered into groves, and then disappeared entirely. As this appeared to be the nearest point to the lake, where a suitable camp could be found, we directed our course to one of the groves, where we found a handsome encampment, with good grass and an abundance of rushes, (*equisetum hyemale*.) At sunset the thermometer was at 55 deg.; the evening clear and calm, with some cumuli.

7th.--The morning was calm and clear, with a temperature at sunrise of 39.5 deg.. The day was spent in active preparation for our intended voyage on the lake. On the edge of the stream a favorable spot was selected in a grove, and, felling the timber, we made a strong *coral*, or horse- pen, for the animals, and a little fort for the people who were to remain. We were now probably in the country of the Utah Indians, though none reside on the lake. The India-rubber boat was repaired with prepared cloth and gum, and filled with air, in readiness for the next day.

The provisions which Carson brought with him being now exhausted, and our stock reduced to a small quantity of roots, I determined to retain with me only a sufficient number of men for the execution of our design; and accordingly seven were sent back to Fort Hall, under the guidance of Francois Lajeunesse, who, having been for many years a trapper in the country, was considered an experienced mountaineer. Though they were provided with good horses, and the road was a remarkably plain one of only four days' journey for a horse-man, they became bewildered, (as we afterwards learned,) and, losing their way, wandered about the country in parties of one or two, reaching the fort about a week afterwards. Some straggled in of themselves, and the others were brought in by Indians who had picked them up on Snake river, about sixty miles below the fort, traveling along the emigrant road in full march for the Lower Columbia. The leader of this adventurous party was Francois.

Hourly barometrical observations were made during the day, and, after the departure of the party for Fort Hall, we occupied ourselves in continuing our little preparations, and in becoming acquainted with the country in the vicinity. The bottoms along the river were timbered with several kinds of willow, hawthorn, and fine cottonwood-trees (***populus canadensis***) with remarkably large leaves, and sixty feet in height by measurement.

We formed now but a small family. With Mr. Preuss and myself, Carson, Bernier, and Basil Lajeunesse, had been selected for the boat expedition-- the first attempted on this interior sea; and Badeau, with Derosier, and Jacob, (the colored man,) were to be left in charge of the camp. We were favored with most delightful weather. To-night there was a brilliant sunset of golden orange and green, which left the western sky clear and beautifully pure; but clouds in the east made me lose an occultation. The summer frogs were singing around us; and the evening was very pleasant, with a temperature of 60 deg.--a night of a more southern autumn. For our supper we had ***yampah***, the most agreeably flavored of the roots, seasoned by a small fat duck, which had come in the way of Jacob's rifle. Around our fire to-night were many speculations on what to-morrow would bring forth, and in our busy conjectures we fancied that we should find every one of the large islands a tangled wilderness of trees and shrubbery, teeming with game of every description that the neighboring region afforded, and which the foot of a white man or Indian had never violated. Frequently, during the day, clouds had rested on the summits of their lofty mountains, and we believed that we should find clear streams and springs of fresh water; and we indulged in anticipations of the luxurious repasts with which we were to indemnify ourselves for past privations. Neither, in our discussions, were the whirlpool and other mysterious dangers forgotten, which Indian and hunters' stories attributed to this unexplored lake. The men had found that, instead of being strongly sewed, (like that of the preceding year, which had so triumphantly rode the canons of the upper Great Platte,) our present boat was only pasted together in a very insecure manner, the maker having been allowed so little time in the construction, that he was obliged to crowd the labor of two months into several days. The insecurity of the boat was sensibly felt by us; and, mingled with the enthusiasm and excitement that we all felt at the prospect of an undertaking which had never before been accomplished, was a certain impression of danger, sufficient to give a serious character to our conversation. The momentary view which had been had of the lake the day before, its great extent and rugged islands, dimly seen amidst the dark waters in the obscurity of the sudden storm, were calculated to heighten the idea of undefined danger with which the lake was generally associated.

8th.--A calm, clear day, with a sunrise temperature of 41 deg.. In view of our present enterprise, a part of the equipment of the boat had been made to consist in three air-tight bags, about three feet long, and capable each of containing five gallons. These had been filled with water the night before, and were now placed in the boat, with our blankets and instruments, consisting of a sextant, telescope, spy-glass, thermometer, and barometer.

We left the camp at sunrise, and had a very pleasant voyage down the river, in which there was generally eight or ten feet of water, deepening as we neared the mouth in the latter part of the day. In the course of the morning we discovered that two of the cylinders leaked so much as to require one man constantly at the bellows, to keep them sufficiently full of air to support the boat. Although we had made a very early start, we loitered so much on the way--stopping every now and then, and floating silently along, to get a shot at a goose or duck--that it was late in the day when we reached the outlet. The river here divided into several branches, filled with fluvials, and so very shallow that it was with difficulty we could get the boat along, being obliged to get out and wade. We encamped on a low point among rushes and young willows, where was a quantity of drift-wood, which served for our fires. The evening was mild and clear; we made a pleasant bed of young willows; and geese and ducks enough had been killed for an abundant supper at night, and for breakfast the next morning. The stillness of the night was enlivened by millions of water-fowl. Lat. (by observation) 41 deg. 11' 26"; and long. 112 deg. 11' 30".

9th.--The day was clear and calm; the thermometer at sunrise at 49 deg.. As is usual with the trappers on the eve of any enterprise, our people had made dreams, and theirs happened to be a bad one--one which always preceded evil--and consequently they looked very gloomy this morning; but we hurried through our breakfast, in order to made an early start, and have all the day before us for our adventure. The channel in a short distance became so shallow that our navigation was at an end, being merely a sheet of soft mud, with a few inches of water, and sometimes none at all, forming the low-water shore of the lake. All this place was absolutely covered with flocks of screaming plover. We took off our clothes, and, getting overboard, commenced dragging the boat--making, by this operation, a very curious trail, and a very disagreeable smell in stirring up the mud, as we sank above the knee at every step. The water here was still fresh, with only an insipid and disagreeable taste, probably derived from the bed of fetid mud. After proceeding in this way about a mile, we came to a small black ridge on the bottom, beyond which the water became suddenly salt, beginning gradually to deepen, and the bottom was sandy and firm. It was a remarkable division, separating the fresh waters of the rivers from the briny water of the lake, which was entirely ***saturated*** with common salt. Pushing our little vessel across the narrow boundary, we sprang on board, and at length were afloat on the waters of the unknown sea.

We did not steer for the mountainous islands, but directed our course towards a lower one, which it had been decided we should first visit, the summit of which was formed like the crater at the upper end of Bear River valley. So long as we could touch the bottom with our paddles, we were very gay; but gradually, as the water deepened, we became more still in our frail batteau of gum-cloth distended with air, and with pasted seams. Although the day was very calm, there was a considerable swell on the lake; and there were white patches of foam on the surface, which were slowly moving to the southward, indicating the set of a current in that direction, and recalling the recollection of the whirlpool stories. The water continued to deepen as we advanced--the lake becoming almost transparently clear, of an extremely beautiful bright-green color; and the spray, which was thrown into the boat and over our clothes, was directly converted into a crust of common salt, which covered also our hands and arms. "Captain," said Carson, who for some time had been looking suspiciously at some whitening appearances outside the nearest islands, "what are those yonder?--won't you just take a look with the glass?" We ceased paddling for a moment, and found them to be the caps of the waves that were beginning to break under the force of a strong breeze that was coming up the lake.

The form of the boat seemed to be an admirable one, and it rode on the waves like a water-bird; but, at the same time, it was extremely slow in its progress. When we were a little more than half way across the reach, two of the divisions between the cylinders gave way, and it required the constant use of the bellows to keep in a sufficient quantity of air. For a long time we scarcely seemed to approach our island, but gradually we worked across the rougher sea of the open channel, into the smoother water under the lee of the island, and began to discover that what we took for a long row of pelicans, ranged on the beach, were only low cliffs whitened with salt by the spray of the waves; and about noon we reached the shore, the transparency of the water enabling us to see the bottom at a considerable depth.

It was a handsome broad beach where we landed, behind which the hill, into which the island was gathered, rose somewhat abruptly; and a point of rock at one end enclosed it in a sheltering way; and as there was an abundance of drift-wood along the shore, it offered us a pleasant encampment. We did not suffer our frail boat to touch the sharp rocks, but, getting overboard, discharged the baggage, and, lifting it gently out of the water, carried it to the upper part of the beach, which was composed of very small fragments of rock.

Among the successive banks of the beach, formed by the action of the waves, our attention, as we approached the island, had been attracted by one 10 to 20 feet in breadth, of a dark-brown color. Being more closely examined, this was found to be composed, to the depth of seven or eight and twelve inches, entirely of the ***larvae*** of insects, or, in common language; of the skins of worms, about the size of a grain of oats, which had been washed up by the waters of the lake.

Alluding to this subject some months afterwards, when traveling through a more southern portion of this region, in company with Mr. Joseph Walker, an old hunter, I was informed by him, that, wandering with a party of men in a mountain country east of the great California range, he surprised a party of several Indian families encamped near a small salt lake, who abandoned their lodges at his approach, leaving every thing behind them. Being in a starving condition, they were delighted to find in the abandoned lodges a number of skin bags, containing a quantity of what appeared to be fish, dried and pounded. On this they made a hearty supper, and were gathering around an abundant breakfast the next morning, when Mr. Walker discovered that it was with these, or a similar worm, that the bags had been filled. The stomachs of the stout trappers were not proof against their prejudices, and the repulsive food was suddenly rejected. Mr. Walker had further opportunities of seeing these worms used as an article of food; and I am inclined to think they are the same as those we saw, and appear to be a product of the salt lakes. It may be well to recall to your mind that Mr. Walker was associated with Capt. Bonneville in his expedition to the Rocky mountains, and has since that time remained in the country, generally residing in some one of the Snake villages, when not engaged in one of his numerous trapping expeditions, in which he is celebrated as one of the best and bravest leaders who have ever been in the country.

The cliffs and masses of rock along the shore were whitened by an incrustation of salt where the waves dashed up against them; and the evaporating water, which had been left in holes and hollows on the surface of the rocks, was covered with a crust of salt about one-eighth of an inch in thickness. It appeared strange that, in the midst of this grand reservoir, one of our greatest wants lately had been salt. Exposed to be more perfectly dried in the sun, this became very white and fine, having the usual flavor of very excellent common salt, without any foreign taste; but only a little was collected for present use, as there was in it a number of small black insects.

Carrying with us the barometer and other instruments, in the afternoon we ascended to the highest point of the island--a bare, rocky peak, eight hundred feet above the lake. Standing on the summit, we enjoyed an extended view of the lake, enclosed in a basin of rugged mountains, which sometimes left marshy flats and extensive bottoms between them and the shore, and in other places came directly down into the water with bold and precipitous bluffs. Following with our glasses the irregular shores, we searched for some indications of a communication with other bodies of water, or the entrance of other rivers; but the distance was so great that we could make out nothing with certainty. To the southward, several peninsular mountains, 3,000 or 4,000 feet high, entered the lake, appearing, so far as the distance and our position enabled us to determine, to be connected by flats and low ridges with the mountains in the rear. These are probably the islands usually indicated on maps of this region as entirely detached from the shore. The season of our operations was when the waters were at their lowest stage. At the season of high waters in the spring, it is probable that the marshes and low grounds are overflowed, and the surface of the lake considerably greater. In several places the view was of unlimited extent--here and there a rocky islet appearing above the waters, at a great distance; and beyond, every thing was vague and undefined. As we looked over the vast expanse of water spread out beneath us, and strained our eyes along the silent shores over which hung so much doubt and uncertainty, and which were so full of interest to us, I could hardly repress the almost irresistible desire to continue our explorations; but the lengthening snow on the mountains was a plain indication of the advancing season, and our frail linen boat appeared so insecure that I was unwilling to trust our lives to the uncertainties of the lake. I therefore unwillingly resolved to terminate our survey here, and remain satisfied for the present with what we had been able to add to the unknown geography of the region. We felt pleasure, also, in remembering that we were the first who, in the traditionary annals of the country, had visited the islands, and broken, with the cheerful sound of human voices, the long solitude of the place. From the point where we were standing, the ground fell off on every side to the water, giving us a perfect view of the island, which is twelve or thirteen miles in circumference, being simply a rocky hill, on which there is neither water nor trees of any kind; although the ***Fremontia vermicularis***, which was in great abundance, might easily be taken for timber at a distance. The plant seemed here to delight in a congenial air, growing in extraordinary luxuriance seven to eight feet high, and was very abundant on the upper parts of the island, where it was almost the only plant. This is eminently a saline shrub; its leaves have a salt taste; and it luxuriates in saline soils, where it is usually a characteristic. It is widely diffused over all this country. A chenopodiaceous shrub, which is a new species of OBIONE, (O. rigida, *Torr. and Frem*.,) was equally characteristic of the lower parts of the island. These two are the striking plants on the island, and belong to a class of plants which form a prominent feature in the vegetation of this country. On the lower parts of the island, also, a prickly pear of very large size was frequent. On the shore, near the water, was a woolly species of ***phaca***; and a new species of umbelliferous plant (*leptotaemia*) was scattered about in very considerable abundance. These constituted all the vegetation that now appeared upon the island.

    I accidentally left on the summit the brass cover to the object end of my spyglass: and as it will probably remain there undisturbed by Indians, it will furnish matter of speculation to some future traveler. In our excursions about the island, we did not meet with any kind of animal; a magpie, and another larger bird, probably attracted by the smoke of our fire, paid us a visit from the shore, and were the only living things seen during our stay. The rock constituting the cliffs along the shore, where we were encamped, is a talcous rock, or steatite, with brown spar.

    At sunset, the temperature was 70 deg.. We had arrived just in time to obtain a meridian altitude of the sun, and other observations were obtained this evening, which placed our camp in latitude 41 deg. 10' 42", and longitude 112 deg. 21' 05" from Greenwich. From a discussion of the barometrical observations made during our stay on the shores of the lake, we have adopted 4,200 feet for its elevation above the Gulf of Mexico. In the first disappointment we felt from the dissipation of our dream of the fertile islands, I called this ***Disappointment island***.

Out of the drift-wood, we made ourselves pleasant little lodges, open to the water; and, after having kindled large fires to excite the wonder of any straggling savage on the lake shores, lay down, for the first time in a long journey, in perfect security; no one thinking about his arms. The evening was extremely bright and pleasant; but the wind rose during the night, and the waves began to break heavily on the shore, making our island tremble. I had not expected in our inland journey to hear the roar of an ocean surf; and the strangeness of our situation, and the excitement we felt in the associated interest of the place, made this one of the most interesting nights I made during our long expedition.

In the morning, the surf was breaking heavily on the shore, and we were up early. The lake was dark and agitated, and we hurried through our scanty breakfast, and embarked--having first filled one of the buckets with water from the lake, of which it was intended to make salt. The sun had risen by the time we were ready to start; and it was blowing a strong gale of wind, almost directly off the shore, and raising a considerable sea, in which our boat strained very much. It roughened as we got away from the island, and it required all the efforts of the men to make any head against the wind and sea, the gale rising with the sun; and there was danger of being blown into one of the open reaches beyond the island. At the distance of half a mile from the beach, the depth of the water was 16 feet, with a clay bottom; but, as the working of the boat was very severe labor, and during the operation of sounding it was necessary to cease paddling, during which the boat lost considerable way, I was unwilling to discourage the men, and reluctantly gave up my intention of ascertaining the depth and the character of the bed. There was a general shout in the boat when we found ourselves in one fathom, and we soon after landed on a low point of mud, immediately under the butte of the peninsula, where we unloaded the boat, and carried the baggage about a quarter of a mile to firmer ground. We arrived just in time for meridian observation, and carried the barometer to the summit of the butte, which is 500 feet above the lake. Mr. Preuss set off on foot for the camp, which was about nine miles distant; Basil accompanying him, to bring back horses for the boat and baggage.

The rude-looking shelter we raised on the shore, our scattered baggage and boat lying on the beach, made quite a picture; and we called this the **Fisherman's camp**. **Lynosiris graveolens**, and another new species of OBIONE, (O. confertifolia--Torr. & Frem.,) were growing on the low grounds, with interspersed spots of an unwholesome salt grass, on a saline clay soil, with a few other plants.

The horses arrived late in the afternoon, by which time the gale had increased to such a height that a man could scarcely stand before it; and we were obliged to pack our baggage hastily, as the rising water of the lake had already reached the point where we were halted. Looking back as we rode off, we found the place of recent encampment entirely covered. The low plain through which we rode to the camp was covered with a compact growth of shrubs of extraordinary size and luxuriance. The soil was sandy and saline; flat places, resembling the beds of ponds, that were bare of vegetation, and covered with a powdery white salt, being interspersed among the shrubs. Artemisia tridentata was very abundant, but the plants were principally saline; a large and vigorous chenopodiaceous shrub, five to eight feet high, being characteristic, with Fremontia vermicularis, and a shrubby plant which seems to be a new *salicornia*. We reached the camp in time to escape a thunder-storm which blackened the sky, and were received with a discharge of the howitzer by the people, who, having been unable to see any thing of us on the lake, had begun to feel some uneasiness.

11th.--To-day we remained at this camp, in order to obtain some further observations, and to boil down the water which had been brought from the lake, for a supply of salt. Roughly evaporated over the fire, the five gallons of water yielded fourteen pints of very fine-grained and very white salt, of which the whole lake may be regarded as a saturated solution. A portion of the salt thus obtained has been subjected to analysis, giving, in 100 parts, the following proportions.

Analysis of the salt.

Chloride of sodium, (common salt,) --- 97.80
Chloride of calcium, -------------------- 0.61
Chloride of magnesium, --------------- 0.24
Sulphate of soda, ---------------------- 0.23
Sulphate of lime, ---------------------- 1.12

100.00

Glancing your eye along the map, you will see a small stream entering **Utah lake**, south of the Spanish fork, and the first waters of that lake which our road of 1844 crosses in coming up from the southward. When I was on this stream with Mr. Walker in that year, he informed me that on the upper part of the river are immense beds of rock-salt of very great thickness, which he had frequently visited. Farther to the southward, the rivers which are affluent to the Colorado, such as the Rio Virgen, and Gila river, near their mouths, are impregnated with salt by the cliffs of rock-salt between which they pass. These mines occur in the same ridge in which, about 120 miles to the northward, and subsequently in their more immediate neighborhood, we discovered the fossils belonging to the oolitic period, and they are probably connected with that formation, and are the deposite from which the Great Lake obtains its salt. Had we remained longer, we should have found them in its bed, and in the mountains around its shores. By observation the latitude of this camp is 41 deg. 15' 50", and longitude 112 deg. 06" 43".

The observations made during our stay give for the rate of the chronometer 31.72", corresponding almost exactly with the rate obtained at St. Vrain's fort. Barometrical observations were made almost hourly during the day. This morning we breakfasted on yampah, and had only kamas for supper; but a cup of good coffee still distinguished us from our **Digger** acquaintances.

12th.--The morning was clear and calm, with a temperature at sunrise of 32 deg.. We resumed our journey late in the day, returning by nearly the same route which we had traveled in coming to the lake; and, avoiding the passage of Hawthorn creek, struck the hills a little below the hot salt- springs. The flat plain we had here passed over consisted alternately of tolerably good sandy soil and of saline plats. We encamped early on Clear creek, at the foot of the high ridge; one of the peaks of which we ascertained by measurement to be 4,210 feet above the lake, or about 8,400 feet above the sea. Behind these front peaks the ridge rises towards the Bear River mountains, which are probably as high as the Wind River chain. This creek is here unusually well timbered with a variety of trees. Among them were birch, (*betula*,) the narrow-leaved poplar, (*populus angustifolia*,) several kinds of willow, (*solix*,) hawthorn, (*crataegus*,) alder, (*alnus viridis*,) and *cerasus*, with an oak allied to *quercus alba*, but very distinct from that or any other species in the United States.

We had to-night a supper of sea-gulls, which Carson killed near the lake. Although cool, the thermometer standing at 47 deg., musquitoes were sufficiently numerous to be troublesome this evening.

13th.--Continuing up the river valley, we crossed several small streams; the mountains on the right appearing to consist of the blue limestone which we had observed in the same ridge to the northward, alternating here with a granular quartz already mentioned. One of these streams, which forms a smaller lake near the river, was broken up into several channels; and the irrigated bottom of fertile soil was covered with innumerable flowers, among which were purple fields of *eupatorium purpureum*, with helianthi, a handsome solidago, (*S. canadensis*,) and a variety of other plants in bloom. Continuing along the foot of the hills, in the afternoon we found five or six hot-springs gushing out together, beneath a conglomerate, consisting principally of fragments of a grayish-blue limestone, efflorescing a salt upon the surface. The temperature of these springs was 134 deg., and the rocks in the bed were colored with a red deposite, and there was common salt crystallized on the margin. There was also a white incrustation upon leaves and roots, consisting principally of carbonate of lime. There were rushes seen along the road this afternoon, and the soil under the hills was very black, and apparently very good; but at this time the grass is entirely dried up. We encamped on Bear river, immediately below a cut-off, the canon by which the river enters this valley bearing north by compass. The night was mild, with a very clear sky; and I obtained a very excellent observation of an occultation of Tau. Arietis, with other observations. Both immersion and emersion of the star were observed; but, as our observations have shown, the phase at the bright limb generally gives incorrect longitudes, and we have adopted the result obtained from the emersion at the dark limb, without allowing any weight to the immersion. According to these observations, the longitude is 112 deg. 05' 12", and the latitude 41 deg. 42' 43". All the longitudes on the line of our outward journey, between St. Vrain's fort and the Dalles of the Columbia, which were not directly determined by satellites, have been chronometrically referred to this place.

The people to-day were rather low-spirited, hunger making them very quiet and peaceable; and there was rarely an oath to be heard in the camp--not even a solitary **enfant de garce**. It was time for the men with an expected supply of provisions from Mr. Fitzpatrick to be in the neighborhood; and the gun was fired at evening, to give notice of our locality, but met with no response.

14th.--About four miles from this encampment, the trail led us down to the river, where we unexpectedly found an excellent ford--the stream being widened by an island, and not yet disengaged from the hills at the foot of the range. We encamped on a little creek where we had made a noon halt in descending the river. The night was very clear and pleasant, the sunset temperature being 67 deg..

The people this evening looked so forlorn, that I gave them permission to kill a fat young horse which I had purchased with goods from the Snake Indians, and they were very soon restored to gayety and good humor. Mr. Preuss and myself could not yet overcome some remains of civilized prejudices, and preferred to starve a little longer; feeling as much saddened as if a crime had been committed.

The next day we continued up the valley, the soil being sometimes very black and good, occasionally gravelly, and occasionally a kind of naked salt plains. We found on the way this morning a small encampment of two families of Snake Indians, from whom we purchased a small quantity of **kooyah**. They had piles of seeds, of three different kinds, spread out upon pieces of buffalo robe; and the squaws had just gathered about a bushel of the root of a thistle, (*circium Virginianum*.) They were about the ordinary size of carrots, and, as I have previously mentioned, are sweet and well flavored, requiring only a long preparation. They had a band of twelve or fifteen horses, and appeared to be growing in the sunshine with about as little labor as the plants they were eating.

Shortly afterwards we met an Indian on horseback who had killed an antelope, which we purchased of him for a little powder and some balls. We crossed the Roseaux, and encamped on the left bank; halting early for the pleasure of enjoying a wholesome and abundant supper, and were pleasantly engaged in protracting our unusual comfort, when Tabeau galloped into the camp with news that Mr. Fitzpatrick was encamped close by us, with a good supply of provisions--flour, rice, and dried meat, and even a little butter. Excitement to-night made us all wakeful; and after a breakfast before sunrise the next morning, we were again on the road, and, continuing up the valley, crossed some high points of hills, and halted to noon on the same stream, near several lodges of Snake Indians, from whom we purchased about a bushel of service-berries, partially dried. By the gift of a knife, I prevailed upon a little boy to show me the ***kooyah*** plant, which proved to be ***valeriana edulis***. The root which constitutes the ***kooyah***, is large, of a very bright yellow color, with the characteristic odor, but not so fully developed as in the prepared substance. It loves the rich moist soil of river bottoms, which was the locality in which I always afterwards found it. It was now entirely out of bloom; according to my observation, flowering in the months of May and June. In the afternoon we entered a long ravine leading to a pass in the dividing ridge between the waters of Bear river and the Snake river, or Lewis's fork of the Columbia; our way being very much impeded, and almost entirely blocked up, by compact fields of luxuriant artemisia. Taking leave at this point of the waters of Bear river, and of the geographical basin which encloses the system of rivers and creeks which belong to the Great Salt Lake, and which so richly deserves a future detailed and ample exploration, I can say of it, in general terms, that the bottoms of this river, (Bear,) and of some of the creeks which I saw, form a natural resting and recruiting station for travelers, now, and in all time to come. The bottoms are extensive; water excellent; timber sufficient; the soil good, and well adapted to grains and grasses suited to such an elevated region. A military post, and a civilized settlement, would be of great value here; grass and salt so much abound. The lake will furnish exhaustless supplies of salt. All the mountains here are covered with a valuable nutritious grass, called bunch-grass, from the form in which it grows, which has a second growth in the fall. The beasts of the Indians were fat upon it; our own found it a good subsistence; and its quantity will sustain any amount of cattle, and make this truly a bucolic region.

We met here an Indian family on horseback, which had been out to gather service-berries, and were returning loaded. This tree was scattered about on the hills; and the upper part of the pass was timbered with aspen, (*populus trem.*;) the common blue flowering-flax occurring among the plants. The approach to the pass was very steep, and the summit about 6,300 feet above the sea--probably only an uncertain approximation, as at the time of observation it was blowing a violent gale of wind from the northwest, with *cumuli* scattered in masses over the sky, the day otherwise bright and clear. We descended, by a steep slope, into a broad open valley--good soil--from four to five miles wide, coming down immediately upon one of the head-waters of the Pannack river, which here loses itself in swampy ground. The appearance of the country here is not very interesting. On either side is a regular range of mountains of the usual character, with a little timber, tolerably rocky on the right, and higher and more smooth on the left, with still higher peaks looking out above the range. The valley afforded a good level road, but it was late when it brought us to water, and we encamped at dark. The north-west wind had blown up very cold weather, and the artemisia, which was our firewood to-night, did not happen to be very abundant. This plant loves a dry, sandy soil, and cannot grow in the good bottoms where it is rich and moist, but on every little eminence, where water does not rest long, it maintains absolute possession. Elevation above the sea about 5,100 feet.

At night scattered fires glimmered along the mountains, pointing out camps of the Indians; and we contrasted the comparative security in which we traveled through this country with the guarded vigilance we were compelled to exert among the Sioux and other Indians on the eastern side of the Rocky mountains.

At sunset the thermometer was at 50 deg., and at midnight at 30 deg..

17th.--The morning sky was calm and clear, the temperature at daylight being 25 deg., and at sunrise 20 deg.. There is throughout this country a remarkable difference between the morning and mid-day temperatures, which at this season was very generally 40 deg. or 50 deg., and occasionally greater; and frequently, after a very frosty morning, the heat in a few hours would render the thinnest clothing agreeable. About noon we reached the main fork. The Pannack river was before us, the valley being here 11/2 miles wide, fertile, and bordered by smooth hills, not over 500 feet high, partly covered with cedar; a high ridge, in which there is a prominent peak, rising behind those on the left. We continued to descend this stream, and found on it at night a warm and comfortable camp. Flax occurred so frequently during the day as to be almost a characteristic, and the soil appeared excellent. The evening was gusty, with a temperature at sunset of 59 deg.. I obtained, about midnight, an observation of an emersion of the first satellite, the night being calm and very clear, the stars remarkably bright, and the thermometer at 30 deg.. Longitude, from mean of satellite and chronometer, 112 deg. 29' 52", and latitude, by observation, 42 deg. 44' 40".

18th.--The day clear and calm, with a temperature of 25 deg. at sunrise. After traveling seven or eight miles, we emerged on the plains of the Columbia, in sight of the famous "*Three Buttes*," a well-known landmark in the country, distant about 45 miles. The French word *butte*, which so often occurs in this narrative, is retained from the familiar language of the country, and identifies the objects to which it refers. It is naturalized in the region of the Rocky mountains, and, even if desirable to render it in English, I know of no word which would be its precise equivalent. It is applied to the detached hills and ridges which rise rapidly, and reach too high to be called hills or ridges, and not high enough to be called mountains. **Knob**, as applied in the western states, is their descriptive term in English. **Cerro** is the Spanish term; but no translation, or periphrasis, would preserve the identity of these picturesque landmarks, familiar to the traveler, and often seen at a great distance. Covered as far as could be seen with artemisia, the dark and ugly appearance of this plain obtained for it the name of **Sage Desert**; and we were agreeably surprised, on reaching the Portneuf river, to see a beautiful green valley with scattered timber spread out beneath us, on which, about four miles distant, were glistening the white walls of the fort. The Portneuf runs along the upland plain nearly to its mouth, and an abrupt descent of perhaps two hundred feet brought us down immediately upon the stream, which at the ford is one hundred yards wide, and three feet deep, with clear water, a swift current, and gravelly bed; but a little higher up the breadth was only about thirty-five yards, with apparently deep water.

In the bottom I remarked a very great number of springs and sloughs, with remarkably clear water and gravel beds. At sunset we encamped with Mr. Talbot and our friends, who came on to Fort Hall when we went to the lake, and whom we had the satisfaction to find all well, neither party having met with any mischance in the interval of our separation. They, too, had had their share of fatigue and scanty provisions, as there had been very little game left on the trail of the populous emigration; and Mr. Fitzpatrick had rigidly husbanded our stock of flour and light provisions, in view of the approaching winter and the long journey before us.

19th.--This morning the sky was very dark and gloomy, and at daylight it began snowing thickly, and continued all day, with cold, disagreeable weather. At sunrise the temperature was 43 deg.. I rode up to the fort, and purchased from Mr. Grant (the officer in charge of the post) several very indifferent horses, and five oxen, in very fine order, which were received at the camp with great satisfaction: and, one being killed at evening, the usual gayety and good humor were at once restored. Night came in stormy.

20th.--We had a night of snow and rain, and the thermometer at sunrise was at 34 deg.; the morning was dark, with a steady rain, and there was still an inch of snow on the ground, with an abundance on the neighboring hills and mountains. The sudden change in the weather was hard for our animals, who trembled and shivered in the cold--sometimes taking refuge in the timber, and now and then coming out and raking the snow off the ground for a little grass, or eating the young willows.

21st.--Ice made tolerably thick during this night, and in the morning the weather cleared up very bright, with a temperature at sunrise of 29 deg.; and I obtained a meridian observation for latitude at the fort, with observations for time. The sky was again covered in the afternoon, and the thermometer at sunset 48 deg..

22d.--The morning was cloudy and unpleasant, and at sunrise a cold rain commenced, with a temperature of 41 deg..

The early approach of winter, and the difficulty of supporting a large party, determined me to send back a number of the men who had become satisfied that they were not fitted for the laborious service and frequent privation to which they were necessarily exposed, and which there was reason to believe would become more severe in the further extension of the voyage. I accordingly called them together, and, informing them of my intention to continue our journey during the ensuing winter, in the course of which they would probably be exposed to considerable hardship, succeeded in prevailing on a number of them to return voluntarily. These were: Charles de Forrest, Henry Lee, J. Campbell, Wm. Creuss, A. Vasquez; A. Pera,

Patrick White, B. Tesson, M. Creely, Francois Lajeunesse, Basil Lajeunesse. Among these I regretted very much to lose Basil Lajeunesse, one of the best men in my party, who was obliged, by the condition of his family, to be at home in the coming winter. Our preparations having been completed in the interval of our stay here, both parties were ready this morning to resume their respective routes.

Except that there is a greater quantity of wood used in its construction, Fort Hall very much resembles the other trading posts which have already been described to you, and would be another excellent post of relief for the emigration. It is in the low rich bottom of a valley, apparently 20 miles long, formed by the confluence of Portneuf river with Lewis's fork of the Columbia, which it enters about nine miles below the fort, and narrowing gradually to the mouth of the Pannack river, where it has a breadth of only two or three miles. Allowing 50 miles for the road from the *Beer springs* of Bear river to Fort Hall, its distance along the *traveled* road from the town of Westport, on the frontier of Missouri, by way of Fort Laramie and the great South Pass, is 1,323 miles. Beyond this place, on the line of road along the *barren* valley of the Upper Columbia, there does not occur, for a distance of nearly 300 miles to the westward, a fertile spot of ground sufficiently large to produce the necessary quantity of grain, or pasturage enough to allow even a temporary repose to the emigrants. On their recent passage, they had been able to obtain, at very high prices and in insufficient quantity, only such assistance as could be afforded by a small and remote trading- post--and that a foreign one--which, in the supply of its own wants, had necessarily drawn around it some of the resources of civilization, but which obtained nearly all its supplies from the distant depot of Vancouver, by a difficult water-carriage of 250 miles up the Columbia river, and a land-carriage by pack-horses of 600 miles. An American military post, sufficiently strong to give to their road a perfect security against the Indian tribes, who are unsettled in locality and very *uncertain* in their disposition, and which, with the necessary facilities for the repair of their equipage, would be able to afford them relief in stock and grain from the produce of the post, would be of extraordinary value to the emigration. Such a post (and all others which may be established on the line to Oregon) would naturally form the *nucleus* of a settlement, at which supplies and repose would be obtained by the emigrant, or trading caravans, which may hereafter traverse these elevated, and, in many places, desolate and inhospitable regions.

I subjoin an analysis of the soil in the river bottom near Fort Hall, which will be of assistance in enabling you to form some correct idea of its general character in the neighboring country. I characterize it as good land, but the analysis will show its precise properties.

Analysis of the Soil.

```
Silicina -------------------- 68.55
Alumina -------------------- 7.45
Carbonate of lime ---------- 8.51
Carbonate of magnesia ----- 5.09
Oxide of iron --------------- 1.40
Organic vegetable matter -- 4.74
Water and loss ------------- 4.26
                             _____
                             100.00
```

Our observations place this post in longitude 112 deg. 29' 54", latitude 43 deg. 01' 30", and the elevation above the sea, 4,500 feet.

Taking leave of the homeward party, we resumed our journey down the valley, the weather being very cold, and the rain coming in hard gusts, which the wind blew directly in our faces. We forded the Portneuf in a storm of rain, the water in the river being frequently up to the axles, and about 110 yards wide. After the gust, the weather improved a little, and we encamped about three miles below, at the mouth of the Pannack river, on Lewis's fork, which here has a breadth of about 120 yards. The temperature at sunset was 42 deg.; the sky partially covered with dark, rainy clouds.

23d.--The temperature at sunrise was 32 deg.; the morning dark, and snow falling steadily and thickly, with a light air from the southward. Profited of being obliged to remain in camp, to take hourly barometrical observations from sunrise to midnight. The wind at eleven o'clock set in from the north-ward in heavy gusts, and the snow changed into rain. In the afternoon, when the sky brightened, the rain had washed all the snow from the bottoms; but the neighboring mountains, from summit to foot, were luminously white--an inauspicious commencement of the autumn, of which this was the first day.

24th.--The thermometer at sunrise was 35 deg., and a blue sky in the west promised a fine day. The river bottoms here are narrow and swampy, with frequent sloughs; and after crossing the Pannack, the road continued along the uplands, rendered very slippery by the soil of wet clay, and entirely covered with artemisia bushes, among which occur frequent fragments of obsidian. At noon we encamped in a grove of willows, at the upper end of a group of islands about half a mile above the ***American falls*** of Snake river. Among the willows here, were some bushes of Lewis and Clarke's currant, (***ribes aureum***.) The river here enters between low mural banks, which consist of a fine vesicular trap-rock, the intermediate portions being compact and crystalline. Gradually becoming higher in its downward course, these banks of scoriated volcanic rock form, with occasional interruptions, its characteristic feature along the whole line to the Dalles of the Lower Columbia, resembling a chasm which had been rent through the country, and which the river had afterwards taken for its bed. The immediate valley of the river is a high plain covered with black rocks and artemisias. In the south is a bordering range of mountains, which, although not very high, are broken and covered with snow; and at a great distance to the north is seen the high, snowy line of the Salmon river mountains, in front of which stand out prominently in the plain the three isolated rugged-looking mountains commonly known as the ***Three Buttes***. Between the river and the distant Salmon river range, the plain is represented by Mr. Fitzpatrick as so entirely broken up and rent into chasms as to be impracticable for a man even on foot. In the sketch annexed, the point of view is low, but it conveys very well some idea of the open character of the country, with the buttes rising out above the general line. By measurement, the river above is 870 feet wide, immediately contracted at the fall in the form of a lock, by jutting piles of scoriaceous basalt, over which the foaming river must present a grand appearance at the time of high water. The evening was clear and pleasant, with dew; and at sunset the temperature was 54 deg.. By observation, the latitude is 42 deg. 47' 05", and the longitude 112 deg. 40' 13". A few hundred yards below the falls, and on the left bank of the river is an escarpment from which we obtained some specimens.

25th.--Thermometer at sunrise 47 deg.. The day came in clear, with a strong gale from the south, which commenced at eleven of the last night. The road to-day led along the river which is full of rapids and small falls. Grass is very scanty and along the rugged banks are scattered cedars, with an abundance of rocks and sage. We traveled fourteen miles, and encamped in the afternoon near the river, on a rocky creek, the bed of which was entirely occupied with boulders of a very large size. For the last three or four miles the right bank of the river has a palisaded appearance. One of the oxen was killed here for food. The thermometer at evening was at 55 deg., the sky almost overcast, and the barometer indicated an elevation of 4,400 feet.

26th.--Rain during the night, and the temperature at sunrise 42 deg.. Traveling along the river, in about four miles we reached a picturesque stream, to which we gave the name of Fall creek. It is remarkable for the many falls which occur in a short distance; and its bed is composed of a calcareous tufa, or vegetable rock, composed principally of the remains of reeds and mosses, resembling that at the *Basin spring*, on Bear river.

The road along the river bluffs had been occasionally very bad; and imagining that some rough obstacles rendered such a detour necessary, we followed for several miles a plain wagon-road leading up this stream, until we reached a point whence it could be seen making directly towards a low place in the range on the south side of the valley, and we became immediately aware that we were on a trail formed by a party of wagons, in company with whom we had encamped at Elm grove, near the frontier of Missouri, and which you will remember were proceeding to Upper California under the direction of Mr. Jos. Chiles. At the time of their departure, no practicable passes were known in the southern Rocky mountains within the territory of the United States; and the probable apprehension of difficulty in attempting to pass near the settled frontier of New Mexico, together with the desert character of the unexplored region beyond, had induced them to take a more northern and circuitous route by way of the Sweet Water pass and Fort Hall. They had still between them and the valley of the Sacramento a great mass of mountains, forming the *Sierra Nevada*, here commonly known as the *Great California mountain*, and which were at this time considered as presenting an impracticable barrier to wheeled-carriages. Various considerations had suggested to them a division of the party; and a greater portion of the camp, including the wagons, with the mail and other stores, were now proceeding under the guidance of Mr. Joseph Walker, who had engaged to conduct them, by a long sweep to the southward, around what is called the ***point of the mountain***; and, crossing through a pass known only to himself, gain the banks of the Sacramento by the valley of the San Joaquin. It was a long and a hazardous journey for a party in which there were women and children. Sixty days was the shortest period of time in which they could reach the point of the mountain, and their route lay through a country inhabited by wild and badly-disposed Indians, and very poor in game; but the leader was a man possessing great and intimate knowledge of the Indians, with an extraordinary firmness and decision of character. In the mean time, Mr. Chiles had passed down the Columbia with a party of ten or twelve men, with the intention of reaching the settlements on the Sacramento by a more direct course, which indefinite information from hunters had indicated in the direction of the head-waters of the ***Riviere aux Malheurs***; and having obtained there a reinforcement of animals, and a supply of provisions, meet the wagons before they should have reached the point of the mountain, at a place which had been previously agreed upon. In the course of our narrative, we shall be able to give you some information of the fortunes which attended the movements of these adventurous travelers.

Having discovered our error, we immediately regained the line along the river, which the road quitted about noon, and encamped at five o'clock on the stream called Raft river, (***Riviere aux Cajeux***,) having traveled only 13 miles. In the north, the Salmon River mountains are visible at a very far distance; and on the left, the ridge in which Raft river heads is about 20 miles distant, rocky, and tolerably high. Thermometer at sunset 44 deg., with a partially clouded sky, and a sharp wind from the S.W.

27th.--It was now no longer possible, as in our previous journey, to travel regularly every day, and find at any moment a convenient place for repose at noon or a camp at night; but the halting-places were now generally fixed along the road, by the nature of the country, at places where, with water, there was a little scanty grass. Since leaving the American falls, the road had frequently been very bad; the many short, steep ascents, exhausting the strength of our worn-out animals, requiring always at such places the assistance of the men to get up each cart, one by one; and our progress with twelve or fourteen wheeled-carriages, though light and made for the purpose, in such a rocky country, was extremely slow; and I again determined to gain time by a division of the camp. Accordingly, to-day, the parties again separated, constituted very much as before--Mr. Fitzpatrick remaining in charge of the heavier baggage.

The morning was calm and clear, with a white frost, and the temperature at sunrise 24 deg..

To-day the country had a very forbidding appearance; and, after traveling 20 miles over a slightly undulating plain, we encamped at a considerable spring, called Swamp creek, rising in low grounds near the point of a spur from the mountain. Returning with a small party in a starving condition from the westward 12 or 14 years since, Carson had met here three or four buffalo bulls, two of which were killed. They were among the pioneers which had made the experiment of colonizing in the valley of the Columbia, and which had failed, as heretofore stated. At sunset the thermometer was at 46 deg., and the evening was overcast, with a cool wind from the S.E., and to-night we had only sage for firewood. Mingled with the artemisia was a shrubby and thorny chenopodiaceous plant.

28th.-Thermometer at sunrise 40 deg.. The wind rose early to a gale from the west, with a very cold driving rain; and, after an uncomfortable day's ride of 25 miles, we, were glad when at evening we found a sheltered camp, where there was an abundance of wood, at some elevated rocky islands covered with cedar, near the commencement of another long canon of the river. With the exception of a short detention at a deep little stream called Goose creek, and some occasional rocky places, we had to-day a very good road; but the country has a barren appearance, sandy, and densely covered with the artemisias from the banks of the river to the foot of the mountains. Here I remarked, among the sage bushes, green bunches of what is called the second growth of grass. The river to-day has had a smooth appearance, free from rapids, with a low sandy hill-slope bordering the bottoms, in which there is a little good soil. Thermometer at sunset 45 deg., blowing a gale, and disagreeably cold.

29th.--The thermometer at sunrise 36 deg., with a bright sun, and appearance of finer weather. The road for several miles was *extremely* rocky, and consequently bad; but, entering after this a sandy country, it became very good, with no other interruption than the sage bushes, which covered the river plain as far as the eye could reach, and, with their uniform tint of dark gray, gave to the country a gloomy and sombre appearance. All the day the course of the river has been between walls of the black volcanic rock, a dark line of the escarpment on the opposite side pointing out its course, and sweeping along in foam at places where the mountains which border the valley present always on the left two ranges, the lower one a spur of the higher; and, on the opposite side, the Salmon River mountains are visible at a great distance. Having made 24 miles, we encamped about five o'clock on Rock creek--a stream having considerable water, a swift current, and wooded with willow.

30th.--Thermometer at sunrise 28 deg.. In its progress towards the river, this creek soon enters a chasm of the volcanic rock, which in places along the wall presents a columnar appearance; and the road becomes extremely rocky whenever it passes near its banks. It is only about twenty feet wide where the road crosses it, with a deep bed, and steep banks, covered with rocky fragments, with willows and a little grass on its narrow bottom. The soil appears to be full of calcareous matter, with which the rocks are incrusted. The fragments of rock which had been removed by the emigrants in making a road, where we ascended from the bed of this creek, were whitened with lime; and during the afternoon's march I remarked in the soil a considerably quantity of calcareous concretions. Towards evening the sages became more sparse, and the clear spaces were occupied by tufts of green grass. The river still continued its course through a trough, or open canon; and towards sunset we followed the trail of several wagons which had turned in towards Snake river, and encamped, as they had done, on the top of the escarpment. There was no grass here, the soil among the sage being entirely naked; but there is occasionally a little bottom along the river, which a short ravine of rocks, at rare intervals, leaves accessible; and by one of these we drove our animals down, and found some tolerably good grass bordering the water.

Immediately opposite to us, a subterranean river bursts out directly from the face of the escarpment, and falls in white foam to the river below. The main river is enclosed with mural precipices, which form its characteristic feature along a great portion of its course. A melancholy and strange-looking country--one of fracture, and violence, and fire.

We had brought with us, when we separated from the camp, a large gaunt ox, in appearance very poor; but, being killed to-night, to the great joy of the people, he was found to be remarkably fat. As usual at such occurrences, the evening was devoted to gayety and feasting; abundant fare now made an epoch among us; and in this laborious life, in such a country as this, our men had but little else to enjoy. The temperature at sunset was 65 deg., with a clear sky and a very high wind. By the observation of the evening, the encampment was in longitude 114 deg. 25' 04", and in latitude 42 deg. 38' 44".

OCTOBER.

1st.--The morning clear, with wind from the west, and the thermometer at 55 deg.. We descended to the bottoms, taking with us the boat, for the purpose of visiting the fall in the opposite cliffs; and while it was being filled with air, we occupied ourselves in measuring the river, which is 1,786 feet in breadth, with banks 200 feet high. We were surprised, on our arrival at the opposite side, to find a beautiful basin of clear water, formed by the falling river, around which the rocks were whitened by some saline incrustation. Here the Indians had constructed wicker dams, although I was informed that the salmon do not ascend the river so far; and its character below would apparently render it impracticable.

The ascent of the steep hill-side was rendered a little difficult by a dense growth of shrubs and fields of cane; and there were frequent hidden crevices among the rocks, where the water was heard rushing below; but we succeeded in reaching the main stream, which, issuing from between strata of the trap-rock in two principal branches, produced almost immediately a torrent, 22 feet wide, and white with foam. It is a picturesque spot of singular beauty, overshadowed by bushes, from under which the torrent glances, tumbling into the white basin below, where the clear water contrasted beautifully with the muddy stream of the river. Its outlet was covered with a rank growth of canes, and a variety of unusual plants, and nettles, (*urtica canabina*,) which, before they were noticed, had set our hands and arms on fire. The temperature of the spring was 58 deg., while that of the river was 51 deg.. The perpendicular height of the place at which this stream issues is 45 feet above the river, and 162 feet below the summit of the precipice--making nearly 200 feet for the height of the wall. On the hill-side here was obtained a specimen consisting principally of fragments of the shells of small crustacea, and which was probably formed by deposition from these springs, proceeding from some lake or river in the highlands above.

We resumed our journey at noon, the day being hot and bright; and, after a march of 17 miles, encamped at sunset on the river, near several lodges of Snake Indians.

Our encampment was about one mile below the ***Fishing falls***--a series of cataracts with very inclined planes, which are probably so named because they form a barrier to the ascent of the salmon; and the great fisheries, from which the inhabitants of this barren region almost entirely derive a subsistence, commence at this place. These appeared to be unusually gay savages, fond of loud laughter; and, in their apparent good nature and merry character, struck me as being entirely different from the Indians we had been accustomed to see. From several who visited our camp in the evening, we purchased, in exchange for goods, dried salmon. At this season they are not very fat, but we were easily pleased. The Indians made us comprehend, that when the salmon came up the river in the spring, they are so abundant that they merely throw in their spears at random, certain of bringing out a fish.

These poor people are but slightly provided with winter clothing; there is but little game to furnish skins for the purpose; and of a little animal which seemed to be the most numerous, it required 20 skins to make a covering to the knees. But they are still a joyous, talkative race, who grow fat and become poor with the salmon, which at least never fail them-- the dried being used in the absence of the fresh. We are encamped immediately on the river bank, and with the salmon jumping up out of the water, and Indians paddling about in boats made of rushes, or laughing around the fires, the camp to-night has quite a lively appearance.

The river at this place is more open than for some distance above, and, for the time, the black precipices have disappeared, and no calcareous matter is visible in the soil. The thermometer at sunset 74 deg., clear and calm.

2d.--The sunrise temperature was 48 deg.; the weather clear and calm. Shortly after leaving the encampment, we crossed a stream of clear water, with a variable breadth of 10 to 25 yards, broken by rapids, and lightly wooded with willow, and having a little grass on its small bottom-land. The barrenness of the country is in fine contrast to-day with the mingled beauty and grandeur of the river, which is more open than hitherto, with a constant succession of falls and rapids. Over the edge of the black cliffs, and out from their faces, are falling numberless streams and springs; and all the line of the river is in motion with the play of the water. In about seven miles we reached the most beautiful and picturesque fall I had seen on the river.

On the opposite side, the vertical fall is perhaps 18 feet high; and nearer, the sheet of foaming water is divided and broken into cataracts, where several little islands on the brink and in the river above, give it much picturesque beauty, and make it one of those places the traveler turns again and again to fix in his memory. There were several lodges of Indians here, from whom we traded salmon. Below this place the river makes a remarkable bend; and the road, ascending the ridge, gave us a fine view of the river below, intersected at many places by numerous fish dams. In the north, about 50 miles distant, were some high snowy peaks of the Salmon River mountains; and in the northeast, the last peak of the range was visible at the distance of perhaps 100 miles or more. The river hills consist of very broken masses of sand, covered everywhere with the same interminable fields of sage, and occasionally the road is very heavy. We now frequently saw Indians, who were strung along the river at every little rapid where fish are to be caught, and the cry **haggai, haggai**, (fish,) was constantly heard whenever we passed near their huts, or met them in the road. Very many of them were oddly and partially dressed in overcoat, shirt, waistcoat, or pantaloons, or whatever article of clothing they had been able to procure in trade from the emigrants; for we had now entirely quitted the country where hawks' bells, beads, and vermilion were the current coin, and found that here only useful articles, and chiefly clothing, were in great request. These, however, are eagerly sought after; and for a few trifling pieces of clothing, travelers may procure food sufficient to carry them to the Columbia.

We made a long stretch across the upper plain, and encamped on the bluff, where the grass was very green and good, the soil of the upper plains containing a considerable proportion of calcareous matter. This green freshness of the grass was very remarkable for the season of the year. Again we heard the roar of the fall in the river below, where the water in an unbroken volume goes over a descent of several feet. The night is clear, and the weather continues very warm and pleasant, with a sunset temperature of 70 deg..

3d.--The morning was pleasant, with a temperature at sunrise of 42 deg.. The road was broken by ravines among the hills, and in one of these, which made the bed of a dry creek, I found a fragmentary stratum, or brecciated conglomerate, consisting of flinty slate pebbles, with fragments of limestone containing fossil shells.

On the left, the mountains are visible at the distance of 20 or 30 miles, appearing smooth and rather low; but at intervals higher peaks look out from beyond, and indicate that the main ridge, which we are leaving with the course of the river, and which forms the northern boundary of the Great Basin, still maintains its elevation. About two o'clock we arrived at the ford where the road crosses to the right bank of Snake river. An Indian was hired to conduct us through the ford, which proved impracticable for us, the water sweeping away the howitzer and nearly drowning the mules, which we were obliged to extricate by cutting them out of the harness. The river here is expanded into a little bay, in which there are two islands, across which is the road of the ford; and the emigrants had passed by placing two of their heavy wagons abreast of each other, so as to oppose a considerable mass against the body of water. The Indians informed us that one of the men, in attempting to turn some cattle which had taken a wrong direction, was carried off by the current and drowned. Since their passage, the water had risen considerably; but, fortunately, we had a resource in a boat, which was filled with air and launched; and at seven o'clock we were safely encamped on the opposite bank, the animals swimming across, and the carriage, howitzer, and baggage of the camp, being carried over in the boat. At the place where we crossed, above the islands, the river had narrowed to a breadth of 1,049 feet by measurement, the greater portion of which was from six to eight feet deep. We were obliged to make our camp where we landed, among the Indian lodges, which are semicircular huts made of willow, thatched over with straw, and open to the sunny south. By observation, the latitude of our encampment on the right bank of the river was 42 deg. 55' 58"; chronometric longitude 115 deg. 04' 46", and the traveled distance from Fort Hall 208 miles.

4th.--Calm, pleasant day, with the thermometer at sunrise at 47 deg.. Leaving the river at a considerable distance to the left, and following up the bed of a rocky creek, with occasional holes of water, in about six miles we ascended, by a long and rather steep hill, to a plain 600 feet above the river, over which we continued to travel during the day, having a broken ridge 2,000 or 3,000 feet high on the right. The plain terminates, where we ascended, in an escarpment of vesicular trap-rock, which supplies the fragments of the creek below. The sky clouded over with a strong wind from the northwest, with a few drops of rain and occasional sunlight, threatening a change.

Artemisia still covers the plain, but ***Purshia tridentata*** makes its appearance here on the hill-sides and on bottoms of the creeks--quite a tree in size, larger than the artemisia. We crossed several hollows with a little water in them, and improved grass; and, turning off from the road in the afternoon in search of water, traveled about three miles up the bed of a willow creek, towards the mountain, and found a good encampment, with wood and grass, and little ponds of water in the bed of the creek; which must be of more importance at other seasons, as we found there several old fixtures for fishing. There were many holes on the creek prairie, which had been made by the Diggers in search of roots.

Wind increased to a violent gale from the N.W., with a temperature at sunset of 57 deg..

5th..--The morning was calm and clear, and at sunrise the thermometer was at 32 deg.. The road to-day was occasionally extremely rocky, with hard volcanic fragments, and our traveling very slow. In about nine miles the road brought us to a group of smoking hot springs, with a temperature of 164 deg.. There were a few helianthi in bloom, with some other low plants, and the place was green round about; the ground warm and the air pleasant, with a summer atmosphere that was very grateful in a day of high and cold, searching wind. The rocks were covered with a white and red incrustation; and the water has on the tongue the same unpleasant effect as that of the Basin spring on Bear river. They form several branches, and bubble up with force enough to raise the small pebbles several inches. The following is an analysis of the deposite with which the rocks are incrusted:

```
Silica------------------------- 72.55
Carbonate of lime------------ 14.60
Carbonate of magnesia ------  1.20
Oxide of iron------------------ 4.65
Alumina----------------------- 0.70

Chloride of sodium, &c.-- }
Sulphate of soda---------- }---- 1.10
Sulphate of lime, &c.----- }

Organic vegetable matter- }---- 5.20
Water and loss------------- }
                              _____
                              100.00
```

These springs are near the foot of the ridge, (a dark and rugged-looking mountain,) in which some of the nearer rocks have a reddish appearance, and probably consist of a reddish-brown trap, fragments of which were scattered along the road after leaving the spring. The road was now about to cross the point of this mountain, which we judged to be a spur from the Salmon River range. We crossed a small creek, and encamped about sunset on a stream, which is probably Lake river. This is a small stream, some five or six feet broad, with a swift current, timbered principally with willows and some few cottonwoods. Along the banks were canes, rosebushes, and clematis, with Purshia tridentata and artemisias on the upper bottom. The sombre appearance of the country is somewhat relieved in coming unexpectedly from the dark rocks upon these green and wooded water- courses, sunk in chasms; and, in the spring, the contrasted effect must make them beautiful.

The thermometer at sunset 47 deg., and the night threatening snow.

6th.--The morning warm, the thermometer 46 deg. at sunrise, and sky entirely clouded. After traveling about three miles over an extremely rocky road, the volcanic fragments began to disappear; and, entering among the hills at the point of the mountain, we found ourselves suddenly in a granite country. Here, the character of the vegetation was very much changed; the artemisia disappeared almost entirely, showing only at intervals towards the close of the day, and was replaced by Purshia tridentata, with flowering shrubs, and small fields of **dieteria divaricata,** which gave bloom and gayety to the hills. These were everywhere covered with a fresh and green short grass, like that of the early spring. This is the fall or second growth, the dried grass having been burnt off by the Indians; and wherever the fire has passed, the bright, green color is universal. The soil among the hills is altogether different from that of the river plain, being in many places black, in others sandy and gravelly, but of a firm and good character, appearing to result from the decomposition of the granite rocks, which is proceeding rapidly.

In quitting for a time the artemisia (sage) through which we had been so long voyaging, and the sombre appearance of which is so discouraging, I have to remark, that I have been informed that in Mexico wheat is grown upon the ground which produces this shrub; which, if true, relieves the soil from the character of sterility imputed to it. Be this as it may, there is no dispute about the grass, which is almost universal on the hills and mountains, and always nutritious, even in its dry state. We passed on the way masses of granite on the slope of the spur, which was very much weathered and abraded. This is a white feldspathic granite, with small scales of black mica; smoky quartz and garnets appear to constitute this portion of the mountain.

The road at noon reached a broken ridge, on which were scattered many boulders or blocks of granite; and, passing very small streams, where, with a little more than the usual timber, was sometimes gathered a little wilderness of plants, we encamped on a small stream, after a march of 22 miles, in company with a few Indians. Temperature at sunset 51 deg.; and the night was partially clear, with a few stars visible through drifting white clouds. The Indians made an unsuccessful attempt to steal a few horses from us--a thing of course with them, and to prevent which the traveler is on perpetual watch.

7th.--The day was bright, clear, pleasant, with a temperature of 45 deg.; and we breakfasted at sunrise, the birds singing in the trees as merrily as if we were in the midst of summer. On the upper edge of the hills on the opposite side of the creek, the black volcanic rock appears; and ascending these, the road passed through a basin, around which the hills swept in such a manner as to give it the appearance of an old crater. Here were strata and broken beds of black scoriated rock, and hills composed of the same, on the summit of one of which there was an opening resembling a rent. We traveled to-day through a country resembling that of yesterday, where, although the surface was hilly, the road was good, being firm, and entirely free from rocks and artemisia. To our left, below, was the great sage plain; and on the right were the near mountains, which presented a smoothly-broken character, or rather a surface waved into numberless hills. The road was occasionally enlivened by meeting Indians, and the day was extremely beautiful and pleasant; and we were pleased to be free from the sage, even for a day. When we had traveled about eight miles, we were nearly opposite to the highest portion of the mountains on the left side of the Smoke River valley; and, continuing on a few miles beyond, we came suddenly in sight of the broad green line of the valley of the **Riviere Boisee**, (wooded river,) black near the gorge where it debouches into the plains, with high precipices of basalt, between walls of which it passes, on emerging from the mountains. Following with the eye its upward course, it appears to be shut in among lofty mountains, confining its valley in a very rugged country.

Descending the hills, after traveling a few miles along the high plain, the road brought us down upon the bottoms of the river, which is a beautiful, rapid stream, with clear mountain water; and, as the name indicates, well wooded with some varieties of timber--among which are handsome cottonwoods. Such a stream had become quite a novelty in this country, and we were delighted this afternoon to make a pleasant camp under fine old trees again. There were several Indian encampments scattered along the river; and a number of their inhabitants, in the course of the evening, came to the camp on horseback with dried and fresh fish, to trade. The evening was clear, and the temperature at sunset 57 deg..

At the time of the first occupation of this region by parties engaged in the fur-trade, a small party of men, under the command of ----- Reid, constituting all the garrison of a small fort on this river, were surprised and massacred by the Indians; and to this event the stream owes its occasional name of **Reid's river**. On the 8th we traveled about 26 miles, the ridge on the right having scattered pines on the upper parts; and, continuing the next day our road along the river bottom, after a day's travel of 24 miles, we encamped in the evening on the right bank of the river, a mile above the mouth, and early the next morning arrived at Fort **_Boise_**. This is a simple dwelling-house on the right bank of Snake river, about a mile below the mouth of Riviere Boisee; and on our arrival we were received with an agreeable hospitality by Mr. Payette, an officer of the Hudson's Bay Company, in charge of the fort, all of whose garrison consisted in a Canadian **_engage_**.

Here the road recrosses the river, which is broad and deep; but, with our good boat, aided by two canoes, which were found at the place, the camp was very soon transferred to the left bank. Here we found ourselves again surrounded by the sage; artemisia tridentata, and the different shrubs which during our voyage had always made their appearance abundantly on saline soils, being here the prevailing and almost the only plants. Among them the surface was covered with the usual saline efflorescences, which here consist almost entirely of carbonate of soda, with a small portion of chloride of sodium. Mr. Payette had made but slight attempts at cultivation, his efforts being limited to raising a few vegetables, in which he succeeded tolerably well; the post being principally supported by salmon. He was very hospitable and kind to us, and we made a sensible impression upon all his comestibles; but our principal inroad was into the dairy, which was abundantly supplied, stock appearing to thrive extremely well; and we had an unusual luxury in a present of fresh butter, which was, however, by no means equal to that of Fort Hall--probably from some accidental cause. During the day we remained here, there were considerable numbers of miserable, half-naked Indians around the fort, who had arrived from the neighboring mountains. During the summer, the only subsistence of these people is derived from the salmon, of which they are not provident enough to lay up a sufficient store for the winter, during which many of them die from absolute starvation.

Many little accounts and scattered histories, together with an acquaintance which I gradually acquired of their modes of life, had left the aboriginal inhabitants of this vast region pictured in my mind as a race of people whose great and constant occupation was the means of procuring a subsistence; and though want of space and other reasons will prevent me from detailing the many incidents which made this familiar to me, this great feature among the characteristics of the country will gradually be forced upon your mind.

Pointing to the group of Indians who had just arrived from the mountains on the left side of the valley, and who were regarding our usual appliances of civilization with an air of bewildered curiosity, Mr. Payette informed me that, every year since his arrival at this post, he had unsuccessfully endeavored to induce these people to lay up a store of salmon for their winter provision. While the summer weather and the salmon lasted, they lived contentedly and happily, scattered along the different streams where fish are to be found; and as soon as the winter snows began to, fall, little smokes would be seen rising among the mountains, where they would be found in miserable groups, starving out the winter; and sometimes, according to the general belief, reduced to the horror of cannibalism--the strong, of course, preying on the weak. Certain it is they are driven to any extremity for food, and eat every insect, and every creeping thing, however loathsome and repulsive. Snails, lizards, ants-- all are devoured with the readiness and greediness of mere animals.

In common with all the other Indians we had encountered since reaching the Pacific waters, these people use the Shoshonee or Snake language, which you will have occasion to remark, in the course of the narrative, is the universal language over a very extensive region.

On the evening of the 10th, I obtained, with the usual observations, a very excellent emersion of the first satellite, agreeing very nearly with the chronometer. From these observations, the longitude of the fort is 116 deg. 47' 00", latitude 43 deg. 49' 22", and elevation above the sea 2,100 feet.

Sitting by the fire on the river bank, and waiting for the immersion of the satellite, which did not take place until after midnight, we heard the monotonous song of the Indians, with which they accompany a certain game of which they are very fond. Of the poetry we could not judge, but the music was miserable.

11th.--The morning was clear, with a light breeze from the east, and a temperature at sunrise of 33 deg.. A part of a bullock purchased at the fort, together with the boat, to assist him in crossing, was left here for Mr. Fitzpatrick, and at 11 o'clock we resumed our journey; and directly leaving the river, and crossing the artemisia plain, in several ascents we reached the foot of a ridge, where the road entered a dry sandy hollow, up which it continued to the head; and, crossing a dividing ridge, entered a similar one. We met here two poor emigrants, (Irishmen,) who had lost their horses two days since--probably stolen by the Indians; and were returning to the fort, in hopes to hear something of them there. They had recently had nothing to eat; and I halted to unpack an animal, and gave them meat for their dinner. In this hollow, the artemisia is partially displaced on the hill-sides by grass; and descending it -- miles, about sunset we reached the **Riviere aux Malheurs**, (the unfortunate or unlucky river,)--a considerable stream, with an average breadth of 50 feet, and, at this time, 18 inches' depth of water.

The bottom lands were generally one and a half mile broad, covered principally with long dry grass; and we had difficulty to find sufficient good grass for the camp. With the exception of a bad place of a few hundred yards long, which occurred in rounding a point of hill to reach the ford of the river, the road during the day had been very good.

12th.--The morning was clear and calm, and the thermometer at sunrise 23 deg.. My attention was attracted by a smoke on the right side of the river, a little below the ford, where I found, on the low banks near the water, a considerable number of hot springs, in which the temperature of the water was 193 deg.. The ground, which was too hot for the naked foot, was covered above and below the springs with an incrustation of common salt, very white and good, and fine-grained.

Leading for five miles up a broad dry branch of the Malheurs river, the road entered a sandy hollow, where the surface was rendered firm by the admixture of other rock; being good and level until arriving near the head of the ravine, where it became a little rocky, and we met with a number of sharp ascents over an undulating surface. Crossing here a dividing ridge, it becomes an excellent road of gradual descent down a very marked hollow; in which, after ten miles, willows began to appear in the dry bed of a head of the **Riviere aux Bouleaux**, (Birch river;) and descending seven miles, we found, at its junction with another branch, a little water, not very good or abundant, but sufficient, in case of necessity, for a camp. Crossing Birch river, we continued for about four miles across a point of hill; the country on the left being entirely mountainous, with no level spot to be seen; whence we descended to Snake river--here a fine- looking stream, with a large body of water and a smooth current; although we hear the roar, and see below us the commencement of rapids, where it enters among the hills. It forms here a deep bay, with a low sand island in the midst; and its course among the mountains is agreeably exchanged for the black volcanic rock. The weather during the day had been very bright and extremely hot; but, as usual, so soon as the sun went down, it was necessary to put on overcoats.

I obtained this evening an observation of an emersion of the first satellite, and our observations of the evening place this encampment in latitude 44 deg. 17' 36", and longitude 116 deg. 56' 45", which is the mean of the results from the satellite and chronometer. The elevation above the sea is 1,880 feet. At this encampment, the grass is scanty and poor.

13th.--The morning was bright, with the temperature at sunrise 28 deg.. The horses had strayed off during the night, probably in search of grass; and, after a considerable delay, we had succeeded in finding all but two, when, about nine o'clock, we heard the sound of an Indian song and drum approaching; and shortly after, three Cayuse Indians appeared in sight, bringing with them the two animals. They belonged to a party which had been on a buffalo-hunt in the neighborhood of the Rocky mountains, and were hurrying home in advance. We presented them with some tobacco and other things, with which they appeared well satisfied, and, moderating their pace, traveled in company with us.

We were now about to leave the valley of the great southern branch of the Columbia river, to which the absence of timber, and the scarcity of water, give the appearance of a desert, to enter a mountainous region, where the soil is good, and in which the face of the country is covered with nutritious grasses and dense forest--land embracing many varieties of trees peculiar to the country, and on which the timber exhibits a luxuriance of growth unknown to the eastern part of the continent and to Europe. This mountainous region connects itself in the southward and westward with the elevated country belonging to the Cascade or California range; and, as will be remarked in the course of the narrative, forms the eastern limit of the fertile and timbered lands along the desert and mountainous region included within the Great Basin--a term which I apply to the intermediate region between the Rocky mountains and the next range, containing many lakes, with their own system of rivers and creeks, (of which the Great Salt is the principal,) and which have no connection with the ocean, or the great rivers which flow into it. This Great Basin is yet to be adequately explored. And here, on quitting the banks of a sterile river, to enter on arable mountains, the remark may be made, that, on this western slope of our continent, the usual order or distribution of good and bad soil is often reversed; the river and creek bottoms being often sterile, and darkened with the gloomy and barren artemisia; while the mountain is often fertile, and covered with rich grass, pleasant to the eye, and good for flocks and herds.

Leaving entirely the Snake river, which is said henceforth to pursue its way through canons, amidst rocky and impracticable mountains, where there is no possibility of traveling with animals, we ascended a long and steep hill; and crossing the dividing ridge, came down into the valley of **Burnt** river, which here looks like a hole among the hills. The average breadth of the stream here is thirty feet; it is well fringed with the usual small timber; and the soil in the bottoms is good, with better grass than we had lately been accustomed to see.

We now traveled through a very mountainous country; the stream running rather in a ravine than a valley, and the road is decidedly bad and dangerous for single wagons, frequently crossing the stream where the water is sometimes deep; and all the day the animals were fatigued in climbing up and descending a succession of steep ascents, to avoid the precipitous hill-sides; and the common trail, which leads along the mountain-side at places where the river strikes the base, is sometimes bad even for a horseman. The mountains along this day's journey were composed, near the river, of a slaty calcareous rock in a metamorphic condition. It appears originally to have been a slaty sedimentary limestone, but its present condition indicates that it has been altered, and has become partially crystalline-- probably from the proximity of volcanic rocks. But though traveling was slow and fatiguing to the animals, we were delighted with the appearance of the country, which was green and refreshing after our tedious journey down the parched valley of Snake river. The mountains were covered with good bunch-grass, (*festuca*;) the water of the streams was cold and pure; their bottoms were handsomely wooded with various kinds of trees; and huge and lofty picturesque precipices where the river cut through the mountain.

We found in the evening some good grass and rushes; and encamped among large timber, principally birch, which had been recently burnt, and blackened, and almost destroyed by fire. The night was calm and tolerably clear, with the thermometer at sunset at 59 deg.. Our journey to-day was about twenty miles.

14th.--The day was clear and calm, with a temperature at sunrise of 46 deg.. After traveling about three miles up the valley, we found the river shut up by precipices in a kind of canon, and the road makes a circuit over the mountains. In the afternoon we reached the river again, by another little ravine; and, after traveling along it for a few miles, left it enclosed among rude mountains; and, ascending a smaller branch; encamped on it about five o'clock, very much elevated above the valley. The view was everywhere limited by mountains, on which were no longer seen the black and barren rocks, but a fertile soil, with excellent grass, and partly well covered with pine. I have never seen a wagon-road equally bad in the same space, as this of yesterday and to-day. I noticed where one wagon had been overturned twice, in a very short distance; and it was surprising to me that those wagons which were in the rear, and could not have had much assistance, got through at all. Still, there is no mud; and the road has one advantage, in being perfectly firm. The day had been warm and very pleasant, and the night was perfectly clear.

15th.--The thermometer at daylight was 42 deg., and at sunrise 40 deg.; clouds, which were scattered over all the sky, disappeared with the rising sun. The trail did not much improve until we had crossed the dividing-ground between the ***Brulee*** (Burnt) and Powder rivers. The rock displayed on the mountains, as we approached the summit, was a compact trap, decomposed on the exposed surfaces, and apparently an altered argillaceous sandstone, containing small crystalline nodules of anolcime, apparently filling cavities originally existing. From the summit here, the whole horizon shows high mountains; no high plain or level is to be seen; and on the left, from south around by the west to north, the mountains are black with pines; while, through the remaining space to the eastward, they are bald, with the exception of some scattered pines. You will remark that we are now entering a region where all the elevated parts are covered with dense and heavy forests. From the dividing grounds we descended by a mountain road to Powder river, on an old bed of which we encamped. Descending from the summit, we enjoyed a picturesque view of high rocky mountains on the right, illuminated by the setting sun.

From the heights we had looked in vain for a well known landmark on Powder river, which had been described to me by Mr. Payette as *l'arbre seul*, (the lone tree;) and, on arriving at the river, we found a fine tall pine stretched on the ground, which had been felled by some inconsiderate emigrant axe. It had been a beacon on the road for many years past. Our Cayuses had become impatient to reach their homes, and traveled on ahead to day; and this afternoon we were visited by several

Indians who belonged to the tribes on the Columbia. They were on horseback, and were out on a hunting excursion, but had obtained no better game than a large gray hare, of which each had some six or seven hanging to his saddle. We were also visited by an Indian who had his lodge and family in the mountain to the left. He was in want of ammunition, and brought with him a beaver-skin to exchange, and which he valued at six charges of powder and ball. I learned from him that there are very few of these animals remaining in this part of the country.

The temperature at sunset was 61 deg., and the evening clear. I obtained, with other observations, an immersion and emersion of the third satellite. Elevation 3,100 feet.

16th.--For several weeks the weather in the daytime has been very beautiful, clear, and warm; but the nights, in comparison, are very cold. During the night there was ice a quarter of an inch thick in the lodge; and at daylight the thermometer was at 16 deg., and the same at sunrise, the weather being calm and clear. The annual vegetation now is nearly gone, almost all the plants being out of bloom.

Last night two of our horses had run off again, which delayed us until noon, and we made to-day but a short journey of 13 miles, the road being very good, and encamped in a fine bottom of Powder river.

The thermometer at sunset was at 61 deg., with an easterly wind, and partially clear sky; and the day has been quite pleasant and warm, though more cloudy than yesterday; and the sun was frequently faint, but it grew finer and clearer towards evening.

17th.--Thermometer at sunrise 25 deg.. The weather at daylight was fine, and the sky without a cloud; but these came up, or were formed by the sun, and at seven were thick over all the sky. Just now, this appears to be the regular course--clear and brilliant during the night, and cloudy during the day. There is snow yet visible in the neighboring mountains, which yesterday extended along our route to the left, in a lofty and dark-blue range, having much the appearance of the Wind River mountains. It is probable that they have received their name of the **Blue mountains** from the dark-blue appearance given to them by the pines. We traveled this morning across the affluents to Powder river, the road being good, firm, and level, and the country became constantly more pleasant and interesting. The soil appeared to be very deep, and is black and extremely good, as well among the hollows of the hills on the elevated plats, as on the river bottoms, the vegetation being such as is usually found in good ground. The following analytical result shows the precise qualities of this soil, and will justify to science the character of fertility which the eye attributes to it:

Analysis of Powder river soil.

Silica	72.30
Alumina	6.25
Carbonate of lime	6.86
Carbonate of magnesia	4.62
Oxide of iron	1.20
Organic matter	4.50
Water and loss	4.27
	100.00

From the waters of this stream, the road ascended by a good and moderate ascent to a dividing ridge, but immediately entered upon ground covered with fragments of an altered silicious slate, which are in many places large, and render the road racking to a carriage. In this rock the planes of deposition are distinctly preserved, and the metamorphism is evidently due to the proximity of volcanic rocks. On either side, the mountains here are densely covered with tall and handsome trees; and, mingled with the green of a variety of pines, is the yellow of the European larch, (*pinus larix*,) which loses its leaves in the fall. From its present color, we were enabled to see that it forms a large proportion of the forests on the mountains, and is here a magnificent tree, attaining sometimes the height of 200 feet, which I believe is elsewhere unknown. About two in the afternoon we reached a high point of the dividing ridge, from which we obtained a good view of the **Grand Rond**--a beautiful level basin, or mountain valley, covered with good grass, on a rich soil, abundantly watered, and surrounded by high and well-timbered mountains-- and its name descriptive of its form--the great circle. It is a place--one of the few we have seen on our journey so far--where a farmer would delight to establish himself, if he were content to live in the seclusion which it imposes. It is about 20 miles in diameter, and may, in time, form a superb county. Probably with the view of avoiding a circuit, the wagons had directly descended into the **Rond** by the face of a hill so very rocky and continuously steep as to be apparently impracticable, and, following down on their trail, we encamped on one of the branches of the Grand Rond river, immediately at the foot of the hill. I had remarked, in descending, some very white spots glistening on the plain, and, going out in that direction after we had encamped, I found them to be the bed of a dry salt lake, or marsh, very firm and bare, which was covered thickly with a fine white powder, containing a large quantity of carbonate of soda, (thirty-three in one hundred parts.)

The old grass had been lately burnt off from the surrounding hills, and, wherever the fire had passed, there was a recent growth of strong, green, and vigorous grass; and the soil of the level prairie, which sweeps directly up to the foot of the surrounding mountains, appears to be very rich, producing flax spontaneously and luxuriantly in various places.

Analysis of Grand Rond soil.

Silica,	70.81
Alumina,	10.97
Lime and magnesia,	1.38
Oxide of iron,	2.21
Vegetable matter, partly decomposed,	8.16
Water and loss,	5.46
Phosphate of lime,	1.01
	100.00

The elevation of this encampment is 2,940 feet above the sea.

18th.--It began to rain an hour before sunrise, and continued until ten o'clock; the sky entirely overcast, and the temperature at sunrise 48 deg..

We resumed our journey somewhat later than usual, travelling in a nearly north direction across the beautiful valley; and about noon reached a place on one of the principal streams, where I had determined to leave the emigrant trail, in the expectation of finding a more direct and better road across the Blue mountains. At this place the emigrants appeared to have held some consultation as to their further route, and finally turned directly off to the left; reaching the foot of the mountain in about three miles, which they ascended by a hill as steep and difficult as that by which we had yesterday descended to the Rond. Quitting, therefore, this road, which, after a very rough crossing, issues from the mountains by the heads of the *Umatilah* river, we continued our northern course across the valley, following an Indian trail which had been indicated to me by Mr. Payette, and encamped at the northern extremity of the Grand Rond, on a slough-like stream of very deep water, without any apparent current. There are some pines here on the low hills at the creek; and in the northwest corner of the Rond is a very heavy body of timber, which descends into the plain. The clouds, which had rested very low along the mountain sides during the day, rose gradually up in the afternoon; and in the evening the sky was almost entirely clear, with a temperature at sunset of 47 deg.. Some indifferent observations placed the camp in longitude 117 deg. 28' 26", latitude 45 deg. 26' 47"; and the elevation was 2,600 feet above the sea.

19th.--This morning the mountains were hidden by fog; there was a heavy dew during the night, in which the exposed thermometer at daylight stood at 32 deg., and at sunrise the temperature was 35 deg..

We passed out of the Grand Rond by a fine road along the creek, which, for a short distance, runs in a kind of rocky chasm. Crossing a low point, which was a little rocky, the trail conducted into the open valley of the stream--a handsome place for farms; the soil, even of the hills, being rich and black. Passing through a point of pines, which bore evidences of being very much frequented by the Indians, and in which the trees were sometimes apparently 200 feet high, and three to seven feet in diameter, we halted for a few minutes in the afternoon at the foot of the Blue mountains, on a branch of the Grand Rond river, at an elevation of 2,700 feet. Resuming our journey, we commenced the ascent of the mountains through an open pine forest of large and stately trees, among which the balsam pine made its appearance; the road being good, with the exception of one steep ascent, with a corresponding descent, which might both have been easily avoided by opening the way for a short distance through the timber. It would have been well had we encamped on the stream where we had halted below, as the night overtook us on the mountain, and we were obliged to encamp without water, and tie up the animals to the trees for the night. We halted on a smooth open place of a narrow ridge, which descended very rapidly to a ravine or piny hollow, at a considerable distance below; and it was quite a pretty spot, had there been water near. But the fires at night look very cheerless after a day's march, when there is no preparation for supper going on; and, after sitting some time around the blazing logs, Mr. Preuss and Carson, with several others, volunteered to take the India-rubber buckets and go down into the ravine in search of water. It was a very difficult way in the darkness down the slippery side of the steep mountain, and harder still to climb about half a mile up again; but they found the water, and the cup of coffee (which it enabled us to make) and bread were only enjoyed with greater pleasure.

At sunset the temperature was 46 deg.; the evening remarkably clear; and I obtained an emersion of the first satellite, which does not give a good result, although the observation was a very good one. The chronometric longitude was 117 deg. 28' 34", latitude 45 deg. 38' 07", and we had ascended to an elevation of 3,830 feet. It appeared to have snowed yesterday on the mountains, their summits showing very white to-day.

20th.--There was a heavy white frost during the night, and at sunrise the temperature was 37 deg..

The animals had eaten nothing during the night; and we made an early start, continuing our route among the pines, which were more dense than yesterday, and still retained their magnificent size. The larches cluster together in masses on the side of the mountains, and their yellow foliage contrasts handsomely with the green of the balsam and other pines. After a few miles we ceased to see any pines, and the timber consisted of several varieties of spruce, larch, and balsam pine, which have a regularly conical figure. These trees appeared from 60 to nearly 200 feet in height; the usual circumference being 10 to 12 feet, and in the pines sometimes 21 feet. In open places near the summit, these trees became less high and more branching, the conical form having a greater base. The instrument carriage occasioned much delay, it being frequently necessary to fell trees and remove the fallen timber. The trail we were following led up a long spur, with a very gradual and gentle rise. At the end of three miles, we halted at an open place near the summit, from which we enjoyed a fine view over the mountainous country where we had lately traveled, to take a barometrical observation at the height of 4,460 feet.

After traveling occasionally through open places in the forest, we were obliged to cut a way through a dense body of timber, from which we emerged on an open mountain-side, where we found a number of small springs, and encamped after a day's journey of ten miles. Our elevation here was 5,000 feet.

21st.--There was a very heavy white frost during the night, and the thermometer at sunrise was 30 deg..

We continued to travel through the forest, in which the road was rendered difficult by fallen trunks, and obstructed by many small trees, which it was necessary to cut down. But these are only accidental difficulties, which could easily be removed, and a very excellent road may be had through this pass, with no other than very moderate ascents or declivities. A laborious day, which had advanced us only six miles on the road, brought us in the afternoon to an opening in the forest, in which there was a fine mountain meadow, with good grass, and a large clear-water stream--one of the head branches of the ***Umatilah*** river. During this day's journey, the barometer was broken; and the elevations above the sea, hereafter given, depend upon the temperature of boiling water. Some of the white spruces which I measured to-day were twelve feet in circumference, and one of the larches ten; but eight feet was the average circumference of those measured along the road. I held in my hand a tape line as I walked along, in order to form some correct idea of the size of the timber. Their height appeared to be from 100 to 180, and perhaps 200 feet, and the trunks of the larches were sometimes 100 feet without a limb; but the white spruces were generally covered with branches nearly to the root. All these trees have their branches, particularly the lower ones, declining.

22d.--The white frost this morning was like snow on the ground; the ice was a quarter of an inch thick on the creek, and the thermometer at sunrise was at 20 deg.. But, in a few hours, the day became warm and pleasant, and our road over the mountains was delightful and full of enjoyment.

The trail passed sometimes through very thick young timber, in which there was much cutting to be done; but, after traveling a few miles, the mountains became more bald, and we reached a point from which there was a very extensive view in the northwest. We were on the western verge of the Blue mountains, long spurs of which, very precipitous on either side extended down into the valley, the waters of the mountain roaring between them. On our right was a mountain plateau, covered with a dense forest; and to the westward, immediately below us, was the great *Nez Perce* (pierced nose) prairie, in which dark lines of timber indicated the course of many affluents to a considerable stream that was pursuing its way across the plain towards what appeared to be the Columbia river. This I knew to be the Walahwalah river, and occasional spots along its banks, which resembled clearings, were supposed to be the mission or Indian settlements; but the weather was smoky and unfavorable to far views with the glass. The rock displayed here in the escarpments is a compact amorphous trap, which appears to constitute the mass of the Blue mountains in this latitude; and all the region of country through which we have traveled since leaving the Snake river has been the seat of violent and extensive igneous action. Along the Burnt River valley, the strata are evidently sedimentary rocks, altered by the intrusion of volcanic products, which in some instances have penetrated and essentially changed their original condition. Along our line of route from this point to the California mountains, there seems but little essential change. All our specimens of sedimentary rocks show them much altered, and volcanic productions appear to prevail throughout the whole intervening distance.

The road now led along the mountain side, around heads of the precipitous ravines; and keeping men ahead to clear the road, we passed alternately through bodies of timber and small open prairies, and encamped in a large meadow, in view of the great prairie below.

At sunset the thermometer was at 40 deg., and the night was very clear and bright. Water was only to be had here by descending a bad ravine, into which we drove our animals, and had much trouble with them in a very close growth of small pines. Mr. Preuss had walked ahead and did not get into the camp this evening. The trees here maintained their size, and one of the black spruces measured 15 feet in circumference. In the neighborhood of the camp, pines have reappeared here among the timber.

23d.--The morning was very clear; there had been a heavy white frost during the night, and at sunrise the thermometer was at 31 deg..

After cutting through two thick bodies of timber, in which I noticed some small trees of **hemlock** spruce, (*perusse*) the forest became more open, and we had no longer any trouble to clear a way. The pines here were 11 or 12 feet in circumference, and about 110 feet high, and appeared to love the open grounds. The trail now led along one of the long spurs of the mountain, descending gradually towards the plain; and after a few miles traveling, we emerged finally from the forest, in full view of the plain below, and saw the snowy mass of Mount Hood, standing high out above the surrounding country at the distance of 180 miles. The road along the ridge was excellent, and the grass very green and good; the old grass having been burnt off early in the autumn. About 4 o'clock in the afternoon we reached a little bottom of the Walahwalah river, where we found Mr. Preuss, who yesterday had reached this place, and found himself too far in advance of the camp to return. The stream here has just issued from the narrow ravines, which are walled with precipices, in which the rock has a brown and more burnt appearance than above.

At sunset the thermometer was at 48 deg., and our position was in longitude 118 deg. 00' 39", and in latitude 45 deg. 53' 35".

The morning was clear, with a temperature at sunrise of 24 deg.. Crossing the river, we traveled over a hilly country with a good bunch-grass; the river bottom, which generally contains the best soil in other countries, being here a sterile level of rocks and pebbles. We had found the soil in the Blue mountains to be of excellent quality, and it appeared also to be good here among the lower hills. Reaching a little eminence over which the trail passed, we had an extensive view along the course of the river, which was divided and spread over its bottom in a network of water, receiving several other tributaries from the mountains. There was a band of several hundred horses grazing on the hills about two miles ahead; and as we advanced on the road we met other bands, which Indians were driving out to pasture also on the hills. True to its general character, the reverse of other countries, the hills and mountains here were rich in grass, the bottoms barren and sterile.

In six miles we crossed a principal fork, below which the scattered waters of the river were gathered into one channel; and, passing on the way several unfinished houses; and some cleared patches, where corn and potatoes were cultivated, we reached, in about eight miles further, the missionary establishment of Dr. Whitman, which consisted at this time of one *adobe* house-- *i.e.*, built of unburnt bricks as in Mexico.

I found Dr. Whitman absent on a visit to the *Dalles* of the Columbia; but had the pleasure to see a fine-looking family of emigrants, men, women, and children, in robust health, all indemnifying themselves for previous scanty fare, in a hearty consumption of potatoes, which are produced here of a remarkably good quality. We were disappointed in our expectation of obtaining corn-meal or flour at this station, the mill belonging to the mission having been lately burned down; but an abundant supply of excellent potatoes banished regrets, and furnished a grateful substitute for bread. A small town of Nez Perce Indians gave an inhabited and even a populous appearance to the station; and, after remaining about an hour, we continued our route and encamped on the river about four miles below, passing on the way an emigrant encampment.

Temperature at sunset, 49 deg..

25th..--The weather was pleasant, with a sunrise temperature of 36 deg.. Our road to-day had nothing in it of interest; and the country offered to the eye only a sandy, undulating plain, through which a scantily-timbered river takes its course. We halted about three miles above the mouth, on account of grass; and the next morning arrived at the Nez Perce fort, one of the trading establishments of the Hudson Bay Company, a few hundred yards above the junction of the Walahwalah with the Columbia river. Here we had the first view of this river, and found it about 1,200 yards wide, and presenting the appearance of a fine, navigable stream. We made our camp in a little grove of willows on the Walahwalah, which are the only trees to be seen in the neighborhood; but were obliged to send the animals back to the encampment we had left, as there was scarcely a blade of grass to be found. The post is on the bank of the Columbia, on a plain of bare sands, from which the air was literally filled with clouds of dust and sand, during one of the few days we remained here; this place being one of the several points on the river which are distinguished for prevailing high winds, that come from the sea. The appearance of the post and country was without interest, except that we here saw, for the first time, the great river on which the course of events for the last half century has been directing attention and conferring historical fame. The river is, indeed, a noble object, and has here attained its full magnitude. About nine miles above, and in sight from the heights about this post, is the junction of the two great forks which constitute the main stream--that on which we had been traveling from Fort Hall, and known by the names of Lewis's fork, Shoshonee, and Snake river; and the North fork, which has retained the name of Columbia, as being the main stream.

We did not go up to the junction, being pressed for time; but the union of two large streams, coming one from the southeast, and the other from the northeast, and meeting in what may be treated as the geographical centre of the Oregon valley, thence doubling the volume of water to the ocean, while opening two great lines of communication with the interior continent, constitutes a feature in the map of the country which cannot be overlooked; and it was probably in reference to this junction of waters, and these lines of communication, that this post was established. They are important lines, and, from the structure of the country, must forever remain so,--one of them leading to the South Pass and to the valley of the Mississippi, the other to the pass at the head of the Athabasca river, and to the countries drained by the waters of the Hudson Bay. The British fur companies now use both lines; the Americans, in their emigration to Oregon, have begun to follow the one which leads towards the United States. Bateaux from tide-water ascend to the junction, and thence high up the North fork, or Columbia. Land conveyance only is used upon the line of Lewis's fork. To the emigrants to Oregon, the Nez Perce is a point of great interest, as being, to those who choose it, the termination of their overland journey. The broad expanse of the river here invites them to embark on its bosom; and the lofty trees of the forest furnish the means of doing so.

From the South Pass to this place is about 1,000 miles; and as it is about the same distance from that pass to the Missouri river at the mouth of the Kansas, it may be assumed that 2,000 miles is the ***necessary*** land travel in crossing from the United States to the Pacific ocean on this line. From the mouth of the Great Platte it would be about 100 miles less.

Mr. McKinley, the commander of the post, received us with great civility; and both to myself, and the heads of the emigrants who were there at the time, extended the rights of hospitality in a comfortable dinner to which he invited us.

By a meridional altitude of the sun, the only observation that the weather permitted us to obtain, the mouth of the Walahwalah river is in latitude 46 deg. 03' 46"; and, by the road we had traveled, 612 miles from Fort Hall. At the time of our arrival, a considerable body of emigrants, under the direction of Mr. Applegate, a man of considerable resolution and energy, had nearly completed the building of a number of Mackinaw boats, in which they proposed to continue their further voyage down the Columbia. I had seen, in descending the Walahwalah river, a fine drove of several hundred cattle, which they had exchanged for California cattle, to be received at Vancouver, and which are considered a very inferior breed. The other portion of the emigration had preferred to complete their journey by land along the banks of the Columbia, taking their stock and wagons with them.

Having reinforced our animals with eight fresh horses, hired from the post, and increased our stock of provisions with dried salmon, potatoes, and a little beef, we resumed our journey down the left bank of the Columbia, being guided on our road by an intelligent Indian boy, whom I had engaged to accompany us as far as the Dalles.

From an elevated point over which the road led, we obtained another far view of Mount Hood, 150 miles distant. We obtained on the river bank an observation of the sun at noon, which gave for the latitude 45 deg. 58' 08". The country to-day was very unprepossessing, and our road bad; and as we toiled slowly along through deep loose sands, and over fragments of black volcanic rock, our laborious traveling was strongly contrasted with the rapid progress of Mr. Applegate's fleet of boats, which suddenly came gliding swiftly down the broad river, which here chanced to be tranquil and smooth. At evening we encamped on the river bank, where there was very little grass, and less timber. We frequently met Indians on the road, and they were collected at every favorable spot along the river.

29th.--The road continued along the river, and in the course of the day Mount St. Helens, another snowy peak of the Cascade range, was visible. We crossed the Umatilah river at a fall near its mouth. This stream is of the same class as the Walah-walah river, with a bed of volcanic rock, in places split into fissures. Our encampment was similar to that of yesterday; there was very little grass, and no wood. The Indians brought us some pieces for sale, which were purchased to make our fires.

31st.--By observation, our camp is in latitude 45 deg. 50' 05", and longitude 119 deg. 22' 18". The night has been cold, and we have white frost this morning, with a temperature at daylight of 25 deg., and at sunrise of 24 deg.. The early morning was very clear, and the stars bright; but, as usual, since we are on the Columbia, clouds formed immediately with the rising sun. The day continued fine, the east being covered with scattered clouds, but the west remaining clear, showing the remarkable cone-like peak of Mount Hood brightly drawn against the sky. This was in view all day in the southwest, but no other peaks of the range were visible. Our road was a bad one, of very loose, deep sand. We met on the way a party of Indians unusually well-dressed. They appeared intelligent, and, in our slight intercourse, impressed me with the belief that they possessed some aptitude for acquiring languages.

We continued to travel along the river, the stream being interspersed with many sand-bars (it being the season of low water) and with many islands, and an apparently good navigation. Small willows were the only wood; rock and sand the prominent geological feature. The rock of this section is a very compact and tough basalt, occurring in strata which have the appearance of being broken into fragments, assuming the form of columnar hills, and appearing always in escarpments, with the broken fragments strewed at the base and over the adjoining country.

We made a late encampment on the river, and used to-night the *purshia tridentata* for firewood. Among the rocks which formed the bank, was very good green grass. Latitude 45 deg. 44' 23", longitude 119 deg. 45' 09".

NOVEMBER.

1st.--Mount Hood is glowing in the sunlight this morning, and the air is pleasant, with a temperature of 38 deg.. We continued down the river, and, passing through a pretty green valley, bounded by high precipitous rocks, encamped at the lower end.

On the right shore, the banks of the Columbia are very high and steep; the river is 1,690 feet broad, and dark bluffs of rock give it a picturesque appearance.

2d.--The river here entered among bluffs, leaving no longer room for a road; and we accordingly left it, and took a more inland way among the river hills--on which we had no sooner entered, than we found a great improvement in the country. The sand had disappeared, and the soil was good, and covered with excellent grass, although the surface was broken into high hills, with uncommonly deep valleys. At noon we crossed John Day's river, a clear and beautiful stream, with a swift current and a bed of rolled stones. It is sunk in a deep valley, which is characteristic of all the streams in this region; and the hill we descended to reach it well deserves the name of mountain. Some of the emigrants had encamped on the river, and others at the summit of the farther hill, the ascent of which had probably cost their wagons a day's labor; and others again had halted for the night a few miles beyond, where they had slept without water. We also encamped in a grassy hollow without water; but, as we had been forewarned of this privation by the guide, the animals had all been watered at the river, and we had brought with us a sufficient quantity for the night.

3d.--After two hours' ride through a fertile, hilly country, covered, as all the upland here appears to be, with good green grass, we descended again into the river bottom, along which we resumed our sterile road, and in about four miles reached the ford of the Fall river, (***Riviere aux Chutes***,) a considerable tributary to the Columbia. We had heard, on reaching the Nez Perce fort, a repetition of the account in regard to the unsettled character of the Columbia Indians at the present time; and to our little party they had at various points manifested a not very friendly disposition, in several attempts to steal our horses. At this place I expected to find a badly-disposed band, who had plundered a party of 14 emigrant men a few days before, and taken away their horses; and accordingly we made the necessary preparation for our security, but happily met with no difficulty.

The river was high, divided into several arms, with a rocky island at its outlet into the Columbia, which at this place it rivalled in size, and apparently derived its highly characteristic name, which is received from one of its many falls some forty miles up the river. It entered the Columbia with a roar of falls and rapids, and is probably a favorite fishing station among the Indians, with whom both banks of the river were populous; but they scarcely paid any attention to us. The ford was very difficult at this time, and, had they entertained any bad intentions, they were offered a good opportunity to carry them out, as I drove directly into the river, and during the crossing the howitzer was occasionally several feet under water, and a number of the men appeared to be more often below than above. Our guide was well acquainted with the ford, and we succeeded in getting every thing safe over to the left bank. We delayed here only a short time to put the gun in order, and, ascending a long mountain hill, resumed our route again among the interior hills.

The roar of the ***Falls of the Columbia*** is heard from the heights, where we halted a few moments to enjoy a fine view of the river below. In the season of high water, it would be a very interesting object to visit, in order to witness what is related of the annual submerging of the fall under the waters which back up from the basin below, constituting a great natural lock at this place. But time had become an object of serious consideration; and the Falls, in their present state, had been seen and described by many.

After a day's journey of 17 miles, we encamped among the hills on a little clear stream, where, as usual, the Indians immediately gathered round us. Among them was a very old man, almost blind from age, with long and very white hair. I happened of my own accord to give this old man a present of tobacco, and was struck with the impression which my unpropitiated notice made on the Indians, who appeared in a remarkable manner acquainted with the real value of goods, and to understand the equivalents of trade. At evening, one of them spoke a few words to his people, and, telling me that we need entertain no uneasiness in regard to our animals, as none of them would be disturbed, they went all quietly away. In the morning, when they again came to the camp, I expressed to them the gratification we felt at their reasonable conduct, making them a present of some large knives and a few smaller articles.

4th.--The road continued among the hills, and, reaching an eminence, we saw before us, watered by a clear stream, a tolerably large valley, through which the trail passed.

In comparison with the Indians of the Rocky mountains and the great eastern plain, these are disagreeably dirty in their habits. Their huts were crowded with half-naked women and children, and the atmosphere within was any thing but pleasant to persons who had just been riding in the fresh morning air. We were somewhat amused with the scanty dress of a woman, who, in common with the others, rushed out of the huts on our arrival, and who, in default of other covering, used a child for a fig- leaf.

The road in about half an hour passed near an elevated point, from which we overlooked the valley of the Columbia for many miles, and saw in the distance several houses surrounded by fields, which a chief, who had accompanied us from the village, pointed out to us as the Methodist missionary station.

In a few miles we descended to the river, which we reached at one of its remarkably interesting features, known as the ***Dalles of the Columbia***. The whole volume of the river at this place passed between the walls of a chasm, which has the appearance of having been rent through the basaltic strata which form the valley-rock of the region. At the narrowest place we found the breadth, by measurement, 58 yards, and the average height of the walls above the water 25 feet; forming a trough between the rocks--whence the name, probably applied by a Canadian voyageur. The mass of water, in the present low state of the river, passed swiftly between, deep and black, and curled into many small whirlpools and counter currents, but unbroken by foam, and so still that scarcely the sound of a ripple was heard. The rock, for a considerable distance from the river, was worn over a large portion of its surface into circular holes and well-like cavities, by the abrasion of the river, which, at the season of high waters, is spread out over the adjoining bottoms.

In the recent passage through this chasm, an unfortunate event had occurred to Mr. Applegate's party, in the loss of one of their boats, which had been carried under water in the midst of the ***Dalles***, and two of Mr. Applegate's children and one man drowned. This misfortune was attributed only to want of skill in the steersman, as at this season there was no impediment to navigation; although the place is entirely impassable at high water, when boats pass safely over the great falls above, in the submerged state in which they then find themselves.

The basalt here is precisely the same as that which constitutes the rock of the valley higher up the Columbia, being very compact, with a few round cavities.

We passed rapidly three or four miles down the level valley and encamped near the mission. The character of the forest growth here changes, and we found ourselves, with pleasure, again among oaks and other forest-trees of the east, to which we had long been strangers; and the hospitable and kind reception with which we were welcomed among our country people at the mission, aided the momentary illusion of home.

Two good-looking wooden dwelling-houses, and a large schoolhouse, with stables, barn, and garden, and large cleared fields between the houses and the river bank, on which were scattered the wooden huts of an Indian village, gave to the valley the cheerful and busy air of civilization, and had in our eyes an appearance of abundant and enviable comfort.

Our land journey found here its western termination. The delay involved in getting our camp to the right bank of the Columbia, and in opening a road through the continuous forest to Vancouver, rendered a journey along the river impracticable; and on this side the usual road across the mountain required strong and fresh animals, there being an interval of three days in which they could obtain no food. I therefore wrote immediately to Mr. Fitzpatrick, directing him to abandon the carts at the Walahwalah missionary station, and, as soon as the necessary pack-saddles could be made, which his party required, meet me at the Dalles, from which point I proposed to commence our homeward journey. The day after our arrival being Sunday, no business could be done at the mission; but on Monday, Mr. Perkins assisted me in procuring from the Indians a large canoe, in which I designed to complete our journey to Vancouver, where I expected to obtain the necessary supply of provisions and stores for our winter journey. Three Indians, from the family to whom the canoe belonged, were engaged to assist in working her during the voyage, and, with them, our water party consisted of Mr. Preuss and myself, with Bernier and Jacob Dodson. In charge of the party which was to remain at the Dalles I left Carson, with instructions to occupy the people in making pack-saddles and refitting their equipage. The village from which we were to take the canoe was on the right bank of the river, about ten miles below, at the mouth of the Tinanens creek: and while Mr. Preuss proceeded down the river with the instruments, in a little canoe paddled by two Indians, Mr. Perkins accompanied me with the remainder of the party by land. The last of the emigrants had just left the Dalles at the time of our arrival, traveling some by water and others by land, making ark-like rafts, on which they had embarked their families and households, with their large wagons and other furniture, while their stock were driven along the shore.

For about five miles below the Dalles, the river is narrow, and probably very deep; but during this distance it is somewhat open, with grassy bottoms on the left. Entering, then, among the lower mountains of the Cascade range, it assumes a general character, and high and steep rocky hills shut it in on either side, rising abruptly in places, to the height of fifteen hundred feet above the water, and gradually acquiring a more mountainous character as the river approaches the Cascades.

After an hour's travel, when the sun was nearly down, we searched along the shore for a pleasant place, and halted to prepare supper. We had been well supplied by our friends at the mission with delicious salted salmon, which had been taken at the fattest season; also, with potatoes, bread, coffee, and sugar. We were delighted at a change in our mode of traveling and living. The canoe sailed smoothly down the river; at night we encamped upon the shore, and a plentiful supply of comfortable provisions supplied the first of wants. We enjoyed the contrast which it presented to our late toilsome marchings, our night watchings, and our frequent privation of food. We were a motley group, but all happy: three unknown Indians; Jacob, a colored man; Mr. Preuss, a German; Bernier, creole French; and myself.

Being now upon the ground explored by the South Sea expedition under Captain Wilkes, and having accomplished the object of uniting my survey with his, and thus presenting a connected exploration from the Mississippi to the Pacific, and the winter being at hand, I deemed it necessary to economize time by voyaging in the night, as is customary here, to avoid the high winds, which rise with the morning, and decline with the day.

Accordingly, after an hour's halt, we again embarked, and resumed our pleasant voyage down the river. The wind rose to a gale after several hours; but the moon was very bright, and the wind was fair, and the canoe glanced rapidly down the stream, the waves breaking into foam alongside; and our night voyage, as the wind bore us rapidly along between the dark mountains, was wild and interesting. About midnight we put to the shore on a rocky beach, behind which was a dark looking pine forest. We built up large fires among the rocks, which were in large masses round about; and, arranging our blankets on the most sheltered places we could find, passed a delightful night.

After an early breakfast, at daylight we resumed our journey, the weather being clear and beautiful, and the river smooth and still. On either side the mountains are all pine-timbered, rocky, and high. We were now approaching one of the marked features of the lower Columbia where the river forms a great *cascade*, with a series of rapids, in breaking through the range of mountains to which the lofty peaks of Mount Hood and St. Helens belong, and which rise as great pillars of snow on either side of the passage. The main branch of the *Sacramento* river, and the *Tlamath*, issue in cascades from this range; and the Columbia, breaking through it in a succession of cascades, gives the idea of cascades to the whole range; and hence the name of CASCADE RANGE, which it bears, and distinguishes it from the Coast Range lower down. In making a short turn to the south, the river forms the cascades in breaking over a point of agglomerated masses of rock, leaving a handsome bay to the right, with several rocky, pine-covered islands, and the mountains sweep at a distance around a cove where several small streams enter the bay. In less than an hour we halted on the left bank, about five minutes' walk above the cascades, where there were several Indian huts, and where our guides signified it was customary to hire Indians to assist in making the ***portage***. When traveling with a boat as light as a canoe, which may easily be carried on the shoulders of the Indians, this is much the better side of the river for the portage, as the ground here is very good and level, being a handsome bottom, which I remarked was covered (***as was now always the case along the river***) with a growth of green and fresh- looking grass. It was long before we could come to an understanding with the Indians; but to length, when they had first received the price of their assistance in goods, they went vigorously to work; and, in a shorter time than had been occupied in making our arrangements, the canoe, instruments, and baggage, were carried through (a distance of about half a mile) to the bank below the main cascade, where we again embarked, the water being white with foam among ugly rocks, and boiling into a thousand whirlpools. The boat passed with great rapidity, crossing and recrossing in the eddies of the current. After passing through about two miles of broken water, we ran some wild-looking rapids, which are called the Lower Rapids, being the last on the river, which below is tranquil and smooth--a broad, magnificent stream. On a low broad point on the right bank of the river, at the lower end of these rapids, were pitched many tents of the emigrants, who were waiting here for their friends from above, or for boats and provisions which were expected from Vancouver. In our passage down the rapids, I had noticed their camps along the shore, or transporting their goods across the portage. This portage makes a head of navigation, ascending the river. It is about two miles in length; and above, to the Dalles, is 45 miles of smooth and good navigation.

We glided on without further interruption between very rocky and high steep mountains, which sweep along the river valley at a little distance, covered with forests of pine, and showing occasionally lofty escarpments of red rock. Nearer, the shore is bordered by steep escarped hills end huge vertical rocks, from which the waters of the mountain reach the river in a variety of beautiful falls, sometimes several hundred feet in height. Occasionally along the river occurred pretty bottoms, covered with the greenest verdure of the spring. To a professional farmer, however, it does not offer many places of sufficient extent to be valuable for agriculture; and after passing a few miles below the Dalles, I had scarcely seen a place on the south shore where wagons could get to the river. The beauty of the scenery was heightened by the continuance of very delightful weather, resembling the Indian summer of the Atlantic. A few miles below the cascades we passed a singular isolated hill; and in the course of the next six miles occurred five very pretty falls from the heights on the left bank, one of them being of a very picturesque character; and towards sunset we reached a remarkable point of rocks, distinguished, on account of prevailing high winds, and the delay it frequently occasions to the canoe navigation, by the name of *Cape Horn*. It borders the river in a high wall of rock, which comes boldly down into deep water; and in violent gales down the river, and from the opposite shore, which is the prevailing direction of strong winds, the water is dashed against it with considerable violence. It appears to form a serious obstacle to canoe traveling; and I was informed by Mr. Perkins, that in a voyage up the river he had been detained two weeks at this place, and was finally obliged to return to Vancouver.

The winds of this region deserve a particular study. They blow in currents, which show them to be governed by fixed laws; and it is a problem how far they may come from the mountains, or from the ocean through the breaks in the mountains which let out the river.

The hills here had lost something of their rocky appearance, and had already begun to decline. As the sun went down, we searched along the river for an inviting spot; and, finding a clean rocky beach, where some large dry trees were lying on the ground, we ran our boat to the shore; and, after another comfortable supper, ploughed our way along the river in darkness. Heavy clouds covered the sky this evening, and the wind began to sweep in gusts among the trees, as if bad weather were coming. As we advanced, the hills on both sides grew constantly lower; on the right, retreating from the shore, and forming a somewhat extensive bottom of intermingled prairie and wooded land. In the course of a few hours, and opposite to a small stream corning in from the north, called the *Tea Prairie* river, the highlands on the left declined to the plains, and three or four miles more disappeared entirely on both sides, and the river entered the low country. The river had gradually expanded; and when we emerged from the highlands, the opposite shores were so distant as to appear indistinct in the uncertainty of the light. About ten o'clock our pilots halted, apparently to confer about the course; and, after a little hesitation, pulled directly across an open expansion of the river, where the waves were somewhat rough for a canoe, the wind blowing very fresh. Much to our surprise, a few minutes afterwards we ran aground. Backing off our boat, we made repeated trials at various places to cross what appeared to be a point of shifting sand-bars, where we had attempted to shorten the way by a cut-off. Finally, one of our Indians got into the water, and waded about until he found a channel sufficiently deep, through which we wound along after him, and in a few minutes again entered the deep water below. As we paddled rapidly down the river, we heard the noise of a saw-mill at work on the right bank; and, letting our boat float quietly down, we listened with pleasure to the unusual sounds, and before midnight, encamped on the bank of the river, about a mile above Fort Vancouver. Our fine dry weather had given place to a dark cloudy night. At midnight it began to rain; and we found ourselves suddenly in the gloomy and humid season, which, in the narrow region lying between the Pacific and the Cascade mountains, and for a considerable distance along the coast, supplies the place of winter.

In the morning, the first object that attracted my attention was the barque Columbia, lying at anchor near the landing. She was about to start on a voyage to England, and was now ready for sea; being detained only in waiting the arrival of the express bateaux, which descend the Columbia and its north fork with the overland mail from Canada and Hudson's Bay, which had been delayed beyond the usual time. I immediately waited upon Dr. McLaughlin, the executive officer of the Hudson Bay Company, in the territory west of the Rocky mountains, who received me with the courtesy and hospitality for which he has been eminently distinguished, and which makes a forcible and delightful impression on a traveler from the long wilderness from which we had issued. I was immediately supplied by him with the necessary stores and provisions to refit and support my party in our contemplated winter journey to the States; and also with a Mackinaw boat and canoes, manned with Canadian and Iroquois voyageurs and Indians, for their transportation to the Dalles of the Columbia. In addition to this efficient kindness in furnishing me with these necessary supplies, I received from him a warm and gratifying sympathy in the suffering which his great experience led him to anticipate for us in our homeward journey, and a letter of recommendation and credit for any officers of the Hudson Bay Company into whose posts we might be driven by unexpected misfortune.

Of course, the future supplies for my party were paid for, bills on the Government of the United States being readily taken; but every hospitable attention was extended to me, and I accepted an invitation to take a room in the fort, "*and to make myself at home while I stayed.*"

I found many American emigrants at the fort; others had already crossed the river into their land of promise--the Walahmette valley. Others were daily arriving; and all of them have been furnished with shelter, so far as it could be afforded by the buildings connected with the establishment. Necessary clothing and provisions (the latter to be returned in kind from the produce of their labor) were also furnished. This friendly assistance was of very great value to the emigrants, whose families were otherwise exposed to much suffering in the winter rains, which had now commenced; at the same time they were in want of all the common necessaries of life. Those who had taken a water conveyance at the Nez Perce fort continued to arrive safely, with no other accident than has been already mentioned. The party which had crossed over the Cascade mountains were reported to have lost a number of their animals; and those who had driven their stock down the Columbia had brought them safely in, and found for them a ready and very profitable market, and were already proposing to return to the States in the spring for another supply. In the space of two days our preparations had been completed, and we were ready to set out on our return. It would have been very gratifying to have gone down to the Pacific, and, solely in the interest and love of geography, to have seen the ocean on the western as well as on the eastern side of the continent, so as to give a satisfactory completeness to the geographical picture which had been formed in our minds; but the rainy season had now regularly set in, and the air was filled with fogs and rain, which left no beauty in any scenery, and obstructed observations. The object of my instructions had been entirely fulfilled in having connected our reconnoissance with the surveys of Captain Wilkes; and although it would have been agreeable and satisfactory to terminate here also our ruder astronomical observations, I was not, for such a reason, justified to make a delay in waiting for favorable weather.

Near sunset of the 10th, the boats left the fort, and encamped after making only a few miles. Our flotilla consisted of a Mackinaw barge and three canoes--one of them that in which we had descended the river; and a party in all of twenty men. One of the emigrants, Mr. Burnet, of Missouri, who had left his family and property at the Dalles, availed himself of the opportunity afforded by the return of our boats to bring them down to Vancouver. This gentleman, as well as the Messrs. Applegate, and others of the emigrants whom I saw, possessed intelligence and character, with the moral and intellectual stamina, as well as the enterprise, which give solidity and respectability to the foundation of colonies.

11th.--The morning was rainy and misty. We did not move with the practised celerity of my own camp; and it was nearly nine o'clock when our motley crew had finished their breakfast and were ready to start. Once afloat, however, they worked steadily and well, and we advanced at a good rate up the river; and in the afternoon a breeze sprung up, which enabled us to add a sail to the oars. At evening we encamped on a warm-looking beach, on the right bank, at the foot of the high river-hill, immediately at the lower end of Cape Horn. On the opposite shore is said to be a singular hole in the mountain, from which the Indians believe comes the wind producing these gales. It is called the Devil's hole; and the Indians, I was told, had been resolving to send down one of their slaves to explore the region below. At dark, the wind shifted into its stormy quarter, gradually increasing to a gale from the southwest; and the sky becoming clear, I obtained a good observation of an emersion of the first satellite; the result of which being an absolute observation, I have adopted for the longitude of the place.

12th.--The wind during the night had increased to so much violence that the broad river this morning was angry and white; the waves breaking with considerable force against this rocky wall of the cape. Our old Iroquois pilot was unwilling to risk the boats around the point, and I was not disposed to hazard the stores of our voyage for the delay of a day. Further observations were obtained during the day, giving for the latitude of the place 45 deg. 33' 09"; and the longitude obtained from the satellite is 122 deg. 6' 15".

13th.--We had a day of disagreeable and cold rain and, late in the afternoon, began to approach the rapids of the cascades. There is here a high timbered island on the left shore, below which, in descending, I had remarked, in a bluff of the river, the extremities of trunks of trees, appearing to be imbedded in the rock. Landing here this afternoon, I found, in the lower part of the escarpment, a stratum of coal and forest- trees, imbedded between strata of altered clay, containing the remains of vegetables, the leaves of which indicate that the plants wore dicotyledonous. Among these, the stems of some of the ferns are not mineralized, but merely charred, retaining still their vegetable structure and substance; and in this condition a portion of the trees remain. The indurated appearance and compactness of the strata, as well, perhaps, as the mineralized condition of the coal, are probably due to igneous action. Some portions of the coal precisely resemble in aspect the canal coal of England, and, with the accompanying fossils, have been referred to the tertiary formation.

These strata appear to rest upon a mass of agglomerated rock, being but a few feet above the water of the river; and over them is the escarpment of perhaps 80 feet, rising gradually in the rear towards the mountains. The wet and cold evening, and near approach of night, prevented me from making any other than a slight examination.

The current was now very swift, and we were obliged to **cordelle** the boat along the left shore, where the bank was covered with large masses of rocks. Night overtook us at the upper end of the island, a short distance below the cascades, and we halted on the open point. In the mean time, the lighter canoes, paddled altogether by Indians, had passed ahead, and were out of sight. With them was the lodge, which was the only shelter we had, with most of the bedding and provisions. We shouted, and fired guns; but all to no purpose, as it was impossible for them to hear above the roar of the river; and we remained all night without shelter, the rain pouring down all the time. The old voyageurs did not appear to mind it much, but covered themselves up as well as they could, and lay down on the sand- beach, where they remained quiet until morning. The rest of us spent a rather miserable night; and, to add to our discomfort, the incessant rain extinguished our fires; and we were glad when at last daylight appeared, and we again embarked.

Crossing to the right bank, we **cordelled** the boat along the shore, there being no longer any use of the paddles, and put into a little bay below the upper rapids. Here we found a lodge pitched, and about 20 Indians sitting around a blazing fire within, making a luxurious breakfast with salmon, bread, butter, sugar, coffee, and other provisions. In the forest, on the edge of the high bluff overlooking the river, is an Indian graveyard, consisting of a collection of tombs, in each of which were the scattered bones of many skeletons. The tombs were made of boards, which were ornamented with many figures of men and animals of the natural size-- from their appearance, constituting the armorial device by which, among Indians, the chiefs are usually known.

The masses of rock displayed along the shores of the ravine in the neighborhood of the cascades, are clearly volcanic products. Between this cove, which I called Graveyard bay, and another spot of smooth water above, on the right, called Luders bay, sheltered by a jutting point of huge rocky masses at the foot of the cascades, the shore along the intervening rapids is lined with precipices of distinct strata of red and variously-colored lavas, in inclined positions.

The masses of rock forming the point at Luders bay consist of a porous trap, or basalt--a volcanic product of a modern period. The rocks belong to agglomerated masses, which form the immediate ground of the cascades, and have been already mentioned as constituting a bed of cemented conglomerate rocks, appearing at various places along the river. Here they are scattered along the shores, and through the bed of the river, wearing the character of convulsion, which forms the impressive and prominent feature of the river at this place.

Wherever we came in contact with the rocks of these mountains, we found them volcanic, which is probably the character of the range; and at this time, two of the great snowy cones, Mount Regnier and St. Helens, were in action. On the 23d of the preceding November, St. Helens had scattered its ashes, like a white fall of snow, over the Dalles of the Columbia, 50 miles distant. A specimen of these ashes was given to me by Mr. Brewer, one of the clergymen at the Dalles.

The lofty range of the Cascade mountains forms a distinct boundary between the opposite climates of the regions along its western and eastern bases. On the west, they present a barrier to the clouds of fog and rain which roll up from the Pacific ocean and beat against their rugged sides, forming the rainy season of the winter in the country along the coast. Into the brighter skies of the region along their eastern base, this rainy winter never penetrates; and at the Dalles of the Columbia the rainy season is unknown, the brief winter being limited to a period of about two months, during which the earth is covered with the slight snows of a climate remarkably mild for so high a latitude. The Cascade range has an average distance of about 130 miles from the sea-coast. It extends far both north and south of the Columbia, and is indicated to the distant observer, both in course and position, by the lofty volcanic peaks which rise out of it, and which are visible to an immense distance.

During several days of constant rain, it kept our whole force laboriously employed in getting our barge and canoes to the upper end of the Cascades. The portage ground was occupied by emigrant families; their thin and insufficient clothing, bareheaded and barefooted children, attesting the length of their journey, and showing that they had, in many instances, set out without a due preparation of what was indispensable.

A gentleman named Luders, a botanist from the city of Hamburg, arrived at the bay I have called by his name while we were occupied in bringing up the boats. I was delighted to meet at such a place a man of kindred pursuits; but we had only the pleasure of a brief conversation, as his canoe, under the guidance of two Indians, was about to run the rapids; and I could not enjoy the satisfaction of regaling him with a breakfast, which, after his recent journey, would have been an extraordinary luxury. All of his few instruments and baggage were in the canoe, and he hurried around by land to meet it at the Graveyard bay; but he was scarcely out of sight, when, by the carelessness of the Indians, the boat was drawn into the midst of the rapids, and glanced down the river, bottom up, with a loss of every thing it contained. In the natural concern I felt for his misfortune, I gave to the little cove the name of Luders bay.

15th.--We continued to-day our work at the portage.

About noon, the two barges of the express from Montreal arrived at the upper portage landing, which, for large boats, is on the right bank of the river. They were a fine-looking crew, and among them I remarked a fresh- looking woman and her daughter, emigrants from Canada. It was satisfactory to see the order and speed with which these experienced water-men effected the portage, and passed their boats over the cascades. They had arrived at noon, and in the evening they expected to reach Vancouver. These bateaux carry the express of the Hudson Bay Company to the highest navigable point of the North Fork of the Columbia, whence it is carried by an overland party to Lake Winipec, where it is divided; part going to Montreal, and part to Hudson Bay. Thus a regular communication is kept up between three very remote points.

The Canadian emigrants were much chagrined at the change of climate, and informed me that, only a few miles above, they had left a country of bright blue sky and a shining sun. The next morning the upper parts of the mountains which directly overlook the cascades, were white with the freshly fallen snow, while it continued to rain steadily below.

Late in the afternoon we finished the portage, and, embarking again, moved a little distance up the right bank, in order to clear the smaller rapids of the cascades, and have a smooth river for the next morning. Though we made but a few miles, the weather improved immediately; and though the rainy country and the cloudy mountains were close behind, before us was the bright sky; so distinctly is climate here marked by a mountain boundary.

17th.--We had to-day an opportunity to complete the sketch of that portion of the river down which we had come by night.

Many places occur along the river, where the stumps, or rather portions of the trunks of pine-trees, are standing along the shore, and in the water, where they may be seen at a considerable depth below the surface, in the beautifully clear water. These collections of dead trees are called on the Columbia the ***submerged forest***, and are supposed to have been created by the effects of some convulsion which formed the cascades, and which, by damming up the river, placed these trees under water and destroyed them. But I venture to presume that the cascades are older than the trees; and as these submerged forests occur at five or six places along the river, I had an opportunity to satisfy myself that they have been formed by immense landslides from the mountains, which here closely shut in the river, and which brought down with them into the river the pines of the mountain. At one place, on the right bank, I remarked a place where a portion of one of these slides seemed to have planted itself, with all the evergreen foliage, and the vegetation of the neighboring hill, directly amidst the falling and yellow leaves of the river trees. It occurred to me that this would have been a beautiful illustration to the eye of a botanist.

Following the course of a slide, which was very plainly marked along the mountain, I found that in the interior parts the trees were in their usual erect position; but at the extremity of the slide they were rocked about, and thrown into a confusion of inclinations.

About 4 o'clock in the afternoon we passed a sandy bar in the river, whence we had an unexpected view of Mount Hood, bearing directly south by compass.

During the day we used oar and sail, and at night had again a delightful camping ground, and a dry place to sleep upon.

18th.--The day again was pleasant and bright. At 10 o'clock we passed a rock island, on the right shore of the river, which the Indians use as a burial ground; and halting for a short time, about an hour afterwards, at the village of our Indian friends, early in the afternoon we arrived again at the Dalles.

Carson had removed the camp up the river a little nearer to the hills, where the animals had better grass. We found every thing in good order, and arrived just in time to partake of an excellent roast of California beef. My friend, Mr. Gilpin, had arrived in advance of the party. His object in visiting this country had been to obtain correct information of the Walahmette settlements; and he had reached this point in his journey, highly pleased with the country over which he had traveled, and with invigorated health. On the following day he continued his journey, in our returning boats, to Vancouver.

The camp was now occupied in making the necessary preparations for our homeward journey, which, though homeward, contemplated a new route, and a great circuit to the south and southeast, and the exploration of the Great Basin between the Rocky mountains and the *Sierra Nevada*. Three principal objects were indicated, by report or by maps, as being on this route; the character or existence of which I wished to ascertain and which I assumed as landmarks, or leading points, on their projected line of return. The first of those points was the *Tlamath* lake, on the table-land between the head of Fall river, which comes to the Columbia, and the Sacramento, which goes to the Bay of San Francisco; and from which lake a river of the same name makes its way westwardly direct to the ocean. This lake and river are often called *Klamet*, but I have chosen to write its name according to the Indian pronunciation. The position of this lake, on the line of inland communication between Oregon and California; its proximity to the demarcation boundary of latitude 42 deg.; its imputed double character of lake, or meadow, according to the season of the year; and the hostile and warlike character attributed to the Indians about it--all made it a desirable object to visit and examine. From this lake our course was intended to be about southeast, to a reported lake called Mary's, at some days' journey in the Great Basin; and thence, still on southeast, to the reputed *Buenaventura* river, which has had a place in so many maps, and countenanced the belief of the existence of a great river flowing from the Rocky mountains to the Bay of San Francisco. From the Buenaventura the next point was intended to be in that section of the Rocky mountains which includes the heads of Arkansas river, and of the opposite waters of the Californian gulf; and thence down the Arkansas to Bent's fort, and home. This was our projected line of return--a great part of it absolutely new to geographical, botanical, and geological science--and the subject of reports in relation to lakes, rivers, deserts, and savages hardly above the condition of mere wild animals, which inflamed desire to know what this *terra incognita* really contained.

It was a serious enterprise, at the commencement of winter, to undertake the traverse of such a region, and with a party consisting only of twenty- five persons, and they of many nations--American, French, German, Canadian, Indian, and colored--and most of those young, several being under twenty-one years of age. All knew that a strange country was to be explored, and dangers and hardships to be encountered; but no one blenched at the prospect. On the contrary, courage and confidence animated the whole party. Cheerfulness, readiness, subordination, prompt obedience, characterized all; nor did any extremity of peril and privation, to which we were afterwards exposed, ever belie, or derogate from, the fine spirit of this brave and generous commencement. The course of the narrative will show at what point, and for what reasons, we were prevented from the complete execution of this plan, after having made considerable progress upon it, and how we were forced by desert plains and mountain ranges, and deep snows, far to the south, and near to the Pacific ocean, and along the western base of the Sierra Nevada, where, indeed, a new and ample field of exploration opened itself before us. For the present, we must follow the narrative, which will first lead us south along the valley of Fall river, and the eastern base of the Cascade range, to the Tlamath lake, from which, or its margin, three rivers go in three directions--one west, to the ocean; another north, to the Columbia; the third south, to California.

For the support of the party, I had provided at Vancouver a supply of provisions for not less than three months, consisting principally of flour, peas, and tallow--the latter being used in cooking; and, in addition to this, I had purchased at the mission some California cattle, which were to be driven on the hoof. We had 104 mules and horses--part of the latter procured from the Indians about the mission; and for the sustenance of which, our reliance was upon the grass which we should find, and the soft porous wood which was to be substituted when there was none.

Mr. Fitzpatrick, with Mr. Talbot and the remainder of the party, arrived on the 21st; and the camp was now closely engaged in the labor of preparation. Mr. Perkins succeeded in obtaining as a guide to the Tlamath lake two Indians--one of whom had been there, and bore the marks of several wounds he had received from some of the Indians in the neighborhood; and the other went along for company. In order to enable us to obtain horses, he dispatched messengers to the various Indian villages in the neighborhood, informing them that we were desirous to purchase, and appointing a day for them to bring them in.

We made, in the mean time, several excursions in the vicinity. Mr. Perkins walked with Mr. Preuss and myself to the heights, about nine miles distant, on the opposite side of the river, whence, in fine weather, an extensive view may be had over the mountains, including seven great peaks of the Cascade range; but clouds, on this occasion, destroyed the anticipated pleasure, and we obtained bearings only to three that were visible--Mount Regnier, St. Helens, and Mount Hood. On the heights, about one mile south of the mission, a very fine view may be had of Mount Hood and St. Helens. In order to determine their position with as much accuracy as possible, the angular distances of the peaks were measured with the sextant, at different fixed points from which they could be seen.

The Indians brought in their horses at the appointed time, and we succeeded in obtaining a number in exchange for goods; but they were relatively much higher here, where goods are plenty and at moderate prices, than we had found them in the more eastern part of our voyage. Several of the Indians inquired very anxiously to know if we had any ***dollars***; and the horses we procured were much fewer in number than I had desired, and of thin, inferior quality; the oldest and poorest being those that were sold to us. These horses, as ever in our journey you will have occasion to remark, are valuable for hardihood and great endurance.

24th.--At this place one of the men was discharged; and at the request of Mr. Perkins, a Chinook Indian, a lad of nineteen, who was extremely desirous to "see the whites," and make some acquaintance with our institutions, was received into the party under my special charge, with the understanding that I would again return him to his friends. He had lived for some time in the household of Mr. Perkins, and spoke a few words of the English language.

25th.--We were all up early, in the excitement of turning towards home. The stars were brilliant, and the morning cold, the thermometer at daylight 26 deg..

Our preparations had been fully completed, and to-day we commenced our journey. The little wagon which had hitherto carried the instruments, I judged it necessary to abandon; and it was accordingly presented to the mission. In all our long traveling, it had never been overturned or injured by any accident of the road; and the only things broken were the glass lamps, and one of the front panels, which had been kicked out by an unruly Indian horse. The howitzer was the only wheeled carriage now remaining. We started about noon, when the weather had become disagreeably cold, with flurries of snow. Our friend Mr. Perkins, whose kindness had been active and efficient during our stay, accompanied us several miles on our road, when he bade us farewell, and consigned us to the care of our guides. Ascending to the uplands beyond the southern fork of the ***Tinanens*** creek, we found the snow lying on the ground in frequent patches, although the pasture appeared good, and the new short grass was fresh and green. We traveled over high, hilly land, and encamped on a little branch of Tinanens creek, where there were good grass and timber. The southern bank was covered with snow, which was scattered over the bottom; and the little creek, its borders lined with ice, had a chilly and wintry look. A number of Indians had accompanied us so far on our road, and remained with us during the night. Two bad-looking fellows, who were detected in stealing, were tied and laid before the fire, and guard mounted over them during the night. The night was cold, and partially clear.

26th.--The morning was cloudy and misty, and but a few stars visible. During the night water froze in the tents, and at sunrise the thermometer was at 20 deg.. Left camp at 10 o'clock, the road leading along tributaries of the Tinanens, and being, so far, very good. We turned to the right at the fork of the trail, ascending by a steep ascent along a spur to the dividing grounds between this stream and the waters of Fall river. The creeks we had passed were timbered principally with oak and other deciduous trees. Snow lies everywhere here on the ground, and we had a slight fall during the morning; but towards noon the bright sky yielded to a bright sun.

This morning we had a grand view of St. Helens and Regnier: the latter appeared of a conical form, and very lofty, leading the eye far up into the sky. The line of the timbered country is very distinctly marked here, the bare hills making with it a remarkable contrast. The summit of the ridge commanded a fine view of the Taih prairie, and the stream running through it, which is a tributary to the Fall river, the chasm of which is visible to the right. A steep descent of a mountain hill brought us down into the valley, and we encamped on the stream after dark, guided by the light of fires, which some naked Indians, belonging to a village on the opposite side, were kindling for us on the bank. This is a large branch of the Fall river. There was a broad band of thick ice some fifteen feet wide on either bank, and the river current is swift and bold. The night was cold and clear, and we made our astronomical observation this evening with the thermometer at 20 deg..

In anticipation of coming hardship, and to spare our horses, there was much walking done to-day; and Mr. Fitzpatrick and myself made the day's journey on foot. Somewhere near the mouth of this stream are the falls from which the river takes its name.

27th.--A fine view of Mount Hood this morning; a rose-colored mass of snow, bearing S. 85 deg. W. by compass. The sky is clear, and the air cold; the thermometer 2.5 deg. below zero, the trees and bushes glittering white, and the rapid stream filled with floating ice.

Stiletsi and *the White Crane*, two Indian chiefs who had accompanied us thus far, took their leave, and we resumed our journey at 10 o'clock. We ascended by a steep hill from the river bottom, which is sandy, to a volcanic plain, around which lofty hills sweep in a regular form. It is cut up by gullies of basaltic rock, escarpments of which appear everywhere in the hills. This plain is called the Taih prairie, and is sprinkled with some scattered pines. The country is now far more interesting to a traveler than the route along the Snake and Columbia rivers. To our right we had always the mountains, from the midst of whose dark pine forests the isolated snowy peaks were looking out like giants. They served us for grand beacons to show the rate at which we advanced in our journey. Mount Hood was already becoming an old acquaintance, and, when we ascended the prairie, we obtained a bearing to Mount Jefferson, S. 23 deg. W. The Indian superstition has peopled these lofty peaks with evil spirits, and they have never yet known the tread of a human foot. Sternly drawn against the sky, they look so high and steep, so snowy and rocky, that it appears almost impossible to climb them; but still a trial would have its attractions for the adventurous traveler. A small trail takes off through the prairie, towards a low point in the range, and perhaps there is here a pass into the Wahlamette valley.

Crossing the plain, we descended by a rocky hill into the bed of a tributary of Fall river, and made an early encampment. The water was in holes, and frozen over; and we were obliged to cut through the ice for the animals to drink. An ox, which was rather troublesome to drive, was killed here for food.

The evening was fine, the sky being very clear, and I obtained an immersion of the third satellite, with a good observation of an emersion of the first; the latter of which gives for the longitude, 121 deg. 02' 43"; the latitude, by observation, being 45 deg. 06' 45". The night was cold--the thermometer during the observations standing at 9 deg..

28th.--The sky was clear in the morning, but suddenly clouded over, and at sunrise it began to snow, with the thermometer at 18 deg..

We traversed a broken high country, partly timbered with pine, and about noon crossed a mountainous ridge, in which, from the rock occasionally displayed, the formation consists of compact lava. Frequent tracks of elk were visible in the snow. On our right, in the afternoon, a high plain, partially covered with pine, extended about ten miles, to the foot of the Cascade mountains.

At evening we encamped in a basin narrowly surrounded by rocky hills, after a day's journey of twenty-one miles. The surrounding rocks are either volcanic products, or highly altered by volcanic action, consisting of quartz and reddish-colored silicious masses.

29th.--We emerged from the basin, by a narrow pass, upon a considerable branch of Fall river, running to the eastward through a narrow valley. The trail, descending this stream, brought us to a locality of hot springs, which were on either bank. Those on the left, which were formed into deep handsome basins, would have been delightful baths, if the outer air had not been so keen, the thermometer in these being at 89 deg.. There were others on the opposite side, at the foot of an escarpment, in which the temperature of the water was 134 deg.. These waters deposited around the spring a brecciated mass of quartz and feldspar, much of it of a reddish color.

We crossed the stream here, and ascended again to a high plain, from an elevated point of which we obtained a view of six of the great peaks-- Mount Jefferson, followed to the southward by two others of the same class; and succeeding, at a still greater distance to the southward, were three other lower peaks, clustering together in a branch ridge. These, like the great peaks, were snowy masses, secondary only to them; and, from the best examination our time permitted, we are inclined to believe that the range to which they belong is a branch from the great chain which here bears to the westward. The trail, during the remainder of the day, followed near to the large stream on the left, which was continuously walled in between high rocky banks. We halted for the night on a little by-stream.

30th.--Our journey to-day was short. Passing over a high plain, on which were scattered cedars, with frequent beds of volcanic rock in fragments interspersed among the grassy grounds, we arrived suddenly on the verge of the steep and rocky descent to the valley of the stream we had been following, and which here ran directly across our path, emerging from the mountains on the right. You will remark that the country is abundantly watered with large streams, which pour down from the neighboring range.

These streams are characterized by the narrow and chasm-like valleys in which they run, generally sunk a thousand feet below the plain. At the verge of this plain, they frequently commence in vertical precipices of basaltic rock, and which leave only casual places at which they can be entered by horses. The road across the country, which would otherwise be very good, is rendered impracticable for wagons by these streams. There is another trail among the mountains, usually followed in the summer, which the snows now compelled us to avoid; and I have reason to believe that this, passing nearer the heads of these streams, would afford a much better road.

At such places, the gun-carriage was unlimbered, and separately descended by hand. Continuing a few miles up the left bank of the river, we encamped early in an open bottom among the pines, a short distance below a lodge of Indians. Here, along the river the bluffs present escarpments seven or eight hundred feet in height, containing strata of a very fine porcelain clay, overlaid, at the height of about five hundred feet, by a massive stratum of compact basalt one hundred feet in thickness, which again is succeeded above by other strata of volcanic rocks. The clay strata are variously colored, some of them very nearly as white as chalk, and very fine-grained. Specimens brought from these have been subjected to microscopical examination by Professor Bailey, of West Point, and are considered by him to constitute one of the most remarkable deposites of fluviatile infusoria on record. While they abound in genera and species which are common in fresh water, but which rarely thrive where the water is even brackish, not one decidedly marine form is to be found among them; and their fresh-water origin is therefore beyond a doubt. It is equally certain that they lived and died at the situation where they were found, as they could scarcely have been transported by running waters without an admixture of sandy particles; from which, however, they are remarkably free. Fossil infusoria of a fresh-water origin had been previously detected by Mr. Bailey, in specimens brought by Mr. James D. Dana from the tertiary formation of Oregon. Most of the species in those specimens differed so much from those now living and known, that he was led to infer that they might belong to extinct species, and considered them also as affording proof of an alteration, in the formation from which they were obtained, of fresh and salt-water deposits, which, common enough in Europe, had not hitherto been noticed in the United States. Coming evidently from a locality entirely different, our specimens show very few species in common with those brought by Mr. Dana, but bear a much closer resemblance to those inhabiting the northeastern states. It is possible that they are from a more recent deposite; but the presence of a few remarkable forms which are common to the two localities renders it more probable that there is no great difference in their age.

I obtained here a good observation of an emersion of the second satellite; but clouds, which rapidly overspread the sky, prevented the usual number of observations. Those which we succeeded in obtaining, are, however, good; and give for the latitude of the place 44 deg. 35' 23", and for the longitude from the satellite 121 deg. 10' 25".

DECEMBER.

1st.--A short distance above our encampment, we crossed the river, which was thickly lined along its banks with ice. In common with all these mountain-streams the water was very clear and the current swift. It was not everywhere fordable, and the water was three or four feet deep at our crossing, and perhaps a hundred feet wide. As was frequently the case at such places, one of the mules got his pack, consisting of sugar, thoroughly wet, and turned into molasses. One of the guides informed me that this was a "salmon-water," and pointed out several ingeniously-contrived places to catch the fish; among the pines in the bottom I saw an immense one, about twelve feet in diameter. A steep ascent from the opposite bank delayed us again; and as, by the information of our guides, grass would soon become very scarce, we encamped on the height of land, in a marshy place among the pines, where there was an abundance of grass. We found here a single Nez Perce family, who had a very handsome horse in their drove, which we endeavored to obtain in exchange for a good cow; but the man "had two hearts," or, rather, he had one and his wife had another: she wanted the cow, but he loved the horse too much to part with it. These people attach great value to cattle, with which they are endeavoring to supply themselves.

2d.--In the first rays of the sun, the mountain peaks this morning presented a beautiful appearance, the snow being entirely covered with a hue of rosy gold. We traveled to-day over a very stony, elevated plain, about which were scattered cedar and pine, and encamped on another branch of Fall river. We were gradually ascending to a more elevated region, which would have been indicated by the rapidly increasing quantities of snow and ice, had we not known it by other means. A mule, which was packed with our cooking-utensils, wandered off among the pines unperceived, and several men were sent back to search for it.

3d.--Leaving Mr. Fitzpatrick with the party, I went ahead with the howitzer and a few men, in order to gain time, as our progress with the gun was necessarily slower. The country continued the same--very stony, with cedar and pine; and we rode on until dark, when we encamped on a hill-side covered with snow, which we used to-night for water, as we were unable to reach any stream.

4th.--Our animals had taken the back track, although a great number were hobbled; and we were consequently delayed until noon. Shortly after we had left this encampment, the mountain trail from the Dalles joined that on which we were traveling. After passing for several miles over an artemisia plain, the trail entered a beautiful pine forest, through which we traveled for several hours; and about 4 o'clock descended into the valley of another large branch, on the bottom of which were spaces of open pines, with occasional meadows of good grass, in one of which we encamped. The stream is very swift and deep, and about 40 feet wide, and nearly half frozen over. Among the timber here, are larches 140 feet high, and over three feet in diameter. We had to-night the rare sight of a lunar rainbow.

5th.--To-day the country was all pine forest, and beautiful weather made our journey delightful. It was too warm at noon for winter clothes; and the snow, which lay everywhere in patches through the forest, was melting rapidly. After a few hours' ride, we came upon a fine stream in the midst of the forest, which proved to be the principal branch of the Fall river. It was occasionally 200 feet wide--sometimes narrowed to 50 feet--the waters very clear, and frequently deep. We ascended along the river, which sometimes presented sheets of foaming cascades--its banks occasionally blackened with masses of scoriated rock--and found a good encampment on the verge of open bottom, which had been an old camping-ground of the Cayuse Indians. A great number of deer-horns were lying about, indicating game in the neighborhood. The timber was uniformly large, some of the pines measuring 22 feet in circumference at the ground, and 12 to 13 feet at six feet above.

In all our journeying, we had never traveled through a country where the rivers were so abounding in falls; and the name of this stream is singularly characteristic. At every place where we come in the neighborhood of the river, is heard the roaring of falls. The rock along the banks of the stream, and the ledge over which it falls, is a scoriated basalt, with a bright metallic fracture. The stream goes over in one clear pitch, succeeded by a foaming cataract of several hundred yards. In a little bottom above the falls, a small stream discharges into an ***entonnoir***, and disappears below.

We made an early encampment, and in the course of the evening Mr. Fitzpatrick joined us here with the lost mule. Our lodge-poles were nearly worn out, and we found here a handsome set, leaning against one of the trees, very white, and cleanly scraped. Had the owners been here, we would have purchased them; but as they were not, we merely left the old ones in their place, with a small quantity of tobacco.

6th.--The morning was frosty and clear. We continued up the stream on undulating forest ground, over which there was scattered much falling timber. We met here a village of Nez Perce Indians, who appeared to be coming down from the mountains, and had with them fine bands of horses. With them were a few Snake Indians of the root-digging species. From the forest we emerged into an open valley ten or twelve miles wide, through which the stream was flowing tranquilly, upwards of two hundred feet broad, with occasional islands, and bordered with fine broad bottoms. Crossing the river, which here issues from a great mountain ridge on the right, we continued up the southern and smaller branch over a level country, consisting of fine meadow-land, alternating with pine forests, and encamped on it early in the evening. A warm sunshine made the day pleasant.

7th.--To-day we had good traveling ground, the trail leading sometimes over rather sandy soils in the pine forest, and sometimes over meadow-land along the stream. The great beauty of the country in summer constantly suggested itself to our imaginations; and even now we found it beautiful, as we rode along these meadows, from half a mile to two miles wide. The rich soil and excellent water, surrounded by noble forests, make a picture that would delight the eye of a farmer.

I observed to-night an occultation of *a Geminorum*; which, although at the bright limb of the moon, appears to give a very good result, that has been adopted for the longitude. The occultation, observations of satellites, and our position deduced from daily surveys with the compass, agree remarkably well together, and mutually support and strengthen each other. The latitude of the camp is 43 deg. 30' 36"; and longitude, deduced from the occultation, 121 deg. 33' 50".

8th.--To-day we crossed the last branch of the Fall river, issuing, like all the others we had crossed, in a southwesterly direction from the mountains. Our direction was a little east of south, the trail leading constantly through pine forests. The soil was generally bare, consisting, in greater part, of a yellowish-white pumice-stone, producing varieties of magnificent pines, but not a blade of grass; and to-night our horses were obliged to do without food, and use snow for water. These pines are remarkable for the red color of the bolls; and among them occurs a species of which the Indians had informed me when leaving the Dalles. The unusual size of the cone (16 or 18 inches long) had attracted their attention; and they pointed it out to me among the curiosities of the country. They are more remarkable for their large diameter than their height, which usually averages only about 120 feet. The leaflets are short--only two or three inches long, and five in a sheath; the bark of a red color.

9th.--The trail leads always through splendid pine forests. Crossing dividing grounds by a very fine road, we descended very gently towards the south. The weather was pleasant, and we halted late. The soil was very much like that of yesterday; and on the surface of a hill near our encampment, were displayed beds of pumice-stone; but the soil produced no grass, and again the animals fared badly.

10th.--The country began to improve; and about eleven o'clock we reached a spring of cold water on the edge of a savannah, or grassy meadow, which our guides informed us was an arm of the Tlamath lake; and a few miles further we entered upon an extensive meadow, or lake of grass, surrounded by timbered mountains. This was the Tlamath lake. It was a picturesque and beautiful spot, and rendered more attractive to us by the abundant and excellent grass, which our animals, after traveling through pine forests, so much needed; but the broad sheet of water which constitutes a lake was not to be seen. Overlooking it, immediately west, were several snowy knobs, belonging to what we have considered a branch of the Cascade range. A low point, covered with pines, made out into the lake, which afforded us a good place for an encampment, and for the security of our horses, which were guarded in view on the open meadow. The character of courage and hostility attributed to the Indians in this quarter induced more than usual precaution; and, seeing smokes rising from the middle of the lake (or savannah) and along the opposite shores, I directed the howitzer to be fired. It was the first time our guides had seen it discharged; and the bursting of the shell at a distance, which was something like the second fire of the gun, amazed and bewildered them with delight. It inspired them with triumphant feelings; but on the camps at a distance the effect was different, for the smokes in the lake and on the shores immediately disappeared.

The point on which we were encamped forms, with the opposite eastern shore, a narrow neck, connecting the body of the lake with a deep cove or bay which receives the principal affluent stream, and over the greater part of which the water (or rather ice) was at this time dispersed in shallow pools. Among the grass, and scattered over the prairie lake, appeared to be similar marshes. It is simply a shallow basin, which, for a short period at the time of melting snows, is covered with water from the neighboring mountains; but this probably soon runs off, and leaves for the remainder of the year a green savannah, through the midst of which the river Tlamath, which flows to the ocean, winds its way to the outlet on the southwestern side.

11th.--No Indians made their appearance, and I determined to pay them a visit. Accordingly the people were gathered together, and we rode out towards the village in the middle of the lake which one of our guides had previously visited. It could not be directly approached, as a large part of the lake appeared a marsh; and there were sheets of ice among the grass on which our horses could not keep their footing. We therefore followed the guide for a considerable distance along the forest; and then turned off towards the village, which we soon began to see was a few large huts, on the tops of which were collected the Indians. When we had arrived within half a mile of the village, two persons were seen advancing to meet us; and, to please the fancy of our guides, we ranged ourselves into a long line, riding abreast, while they galloped ahead to meet the strangers.

We were surprised, on riding up, to find one of them a woman, having never before known a squaw to take any part in the business of war. They were the village chief and his wife, who, in excitement and alarm at the unusual event and appearance, had come out to meet their fate together. The chief was a very prepossessing Indian, with handsome features, and a singularly soft and agreeable voice--so remarkable as to attract general notice.

The huts were grouped together on the bank of the river which, from being spread out in a shallow marsh at the upper end of the lake, was collected here into a single stream. They were large round huts, perhaps 20 feet in diameter, with rounded tops, on which was the door by which they descended into the interior. Within, they were supported by posts and beams.

Almost like plants, these people seem to have adapted themselves to the soil, and to be growing on what the immediate locality afforded. Their only subsistence at the time appeared to be a small fish, great quantities of which, that had been smoked and dried, were suspended on strings about the lodge. Heaps of straw were lying around; and their residence in the midst of grass and rushes had taught them a peculiar skill in converting this material to useful purposes. Their shoes were made of straw or grass, which seemed well adapted for a snowy country; and the women wore on their heads a closely-woven basket, which made a very good cap. Among other things, were party-colored mats about four feet square, which we purchased to lay on the snow under our blankets, and to use for table-cloths.

Numbers of singular-looking dogs, resembling wolves, were sitting on the tops of the huts; and of these we purchased a young one, which, after its birthplace, was named Tlamath. The language spoken by these Indians is different from that of the Shoshonee and Columbia River tribes; and otherwise than by signs they cannot understand each other. They made us comprehend that they were at war with the people who lived to the southward and to the eastward; but I could obtain from them no certain information. The river on which they live enters the Cascade mountains on the western side of the lake, and breaks through them by a passage impracticable for travelers; but over the mountains, to the northward, are passes which present no other obstacle than in the almost impenetrable forests. Unlike any Indians we had previously seen, these wore shells in their noses. We returned to our camp, after remaining here an hour or two, accompanied by a number of Indians.

In order to recruit a little the strength of our animals, and obtain some acquaintance with the locality, we remained here for the remainder of the day. By observation, the latitude of the camp was 42 deg. 56' 51", and the diameter of the lake, or meadow, as has been intimated, about 20 miles. It is a picturesque and beautiful spot, and, under the hand of cultivation, might become a little paradise. Game is found in the forest, timbered and snowy mountains skirt it, and fertility characterizes it. Situated near the heads of three rivers, and on the line of inland communication with California, and near to Indians noted for treachery, it will naturally, in the progress of the settlement of Oregon, become a point for military occupation and settlement.

From Tlamath lake, the further continuation of our voyage assumed a character of discovery and exploration, which, from the Indians here, we could obtain no information to direct, and where the imaginary maps of the country, instead of assisting, exposed us to suffering and defeat. In our journey across the desert, Mary's lake, and the famous Buenaventura river, were two points on which I relied to recruit the animals and repose the party. Forming, agreeably to the best maps in my possession, a connected water-line from the Rocky mountains to the Pacific ocean, I felt no other anxiety than to pass safely across the intervening desert to the banks of the Buenaventura, where, in the softer climate of a more southern latitude, our horses might find grass to sustain them, and ourselves be sheltered from the rigors of winter, and from the inhospitable desert. The guides who had conducted us thus far on our journey were about to return; and I endeavored in vain to obtain others to lead us, even for a few days, in the direction (east) which we wished to go. The chief to whom I applied alleged the want of horses, and the snow on the mountains across which our course would carry us, and the sickness of his family, as reasons for refusing to go with us.

12th.--This morning the camp was thronged with Tlamath Indians from the southeastern shore of the lake; but, knowing the treacherous disposition which is a remarkable characteristic of the Indians south of the Columbia, the camp was kept constantly on its guard. I was not unmindful of the disasters which Smith and other travelers had met with in this country, and therefore was equally vigilant in guarding against treachery and violence.

According to the best information I had been able to obtain from the Indians, in a few days' traveling we should reach another large water, probably a lake, which they indicated exactly in the course we were about to pursue. We struck our tents at 10 o'clock, and crossed the lake in a nearly east direction, where it has the least extension--the breadth of the arm being here only about a mile and a half. There were ponds of ice, with but little grass, for the greater part of the way, and it was difficult to get the pack-animals across, which fell frequently, and could not get up with their loads, unassisted. The morning was very unpleasant, snow falling at intervals in large flakes, and the sky dark. In about two hours we succeeded in getting the animals over; and, after traveling another hour along the eastern shore of the lake, we turned up into a cove where there was a sheltered place among the timber, with good grass, and encamped. The Indians, who had accompanied us so far, returned to their village on the south-eastern shore. Among the pines here, I noticed some five or six feet in diameter.

13th.--The night has been cold; the peaks around the lake gleam out brightly in the morning sun, and the thermometer is at zero. We continued up the hollow formed by a small affluent to the lake, and immediately entered an open pine forest on the mountain. The way here was sometimes obstructed by fallen trees, and the snow was four to twelve inches deep. The mules at the gun pulled heavily, and walking was a little laborious. In the midst of the wood, we heard the sound of galloping horses, and were agreeably surprised by the unexpected arrival of our Tlamath chief with several Indians. He seemed to have found his conduct inhospitable in letting the strangers depart without a guide through the snow, and had come, with a few others, to pilot us a day or two on the way. After traveling in an easterly direction through the forest for about four hours, we reached a considerable stream, with a border of good grass; and here, by the advice of our guides, we encamped. It is about thirty feet wide, and two to four feet deep, the water clear, with some current; and, according to the information of our Indians, is the principal affluent to the lake, and the head-water of the Tlamath river.

A very clear sky enabled me to obtain here to-night good observations, including an emersion of the first satellite of Jupiter, which gave for the long. 121 deg. 20' 42", and for the lat. 42 deg. 51' 26". This emersion coincides remarkably well with the result obtained from an occultation at the encampment of December 7th to 8th, 1843; from which place, the line of our survey gives an easting of 13 miles. The day's journey was 12 miles.

14th.--Our road was over a broad mountain, and we rode seven hours in a thick snow-storm, always through pine forests, when we came down upon the head-waters of another stream, on which there was grass. The snow lay deep on the ground, and only the high swamp-grass appeared above. The Indians were thinly clad, and I had remarked during the day that they suffered from cold. This evening they told me that the snow was getting too deep on the mountain, and I could not induce them to go any farther. The stream we had struck issued from the mountain in an easterly direction, turning to the southward a short distance below; and, drawing its course upon the ground, they made us comprehend that it pursued its way for a long distance in that direction, uniting with many other streams, and gradually becoming a great river. Without the subsequent information, which confirmed the opinion, we became immediately satisfied that this water formed the principal stream of the Sacramento river; and, consequently, that this main affluent of the bay of San Francisco had its source within the limits of the United States, and opposite a tributary to the Columbia, and near the head of the Tlamath river, which goes to the ocean north of 42 deg., and within the United States.

15th.--A present, consisting of useful goods, afforded much satisfaction to our guides; and, showing them the national flag, I explained that it was a symbol of our nation; and they engaged always to receive it in a friendly manner. The chief pointed out a course, by following which we would arrive at the big water, where no more snow was to be found. Traveling in a direction N. 60 deg. E. by compass, which the Indians informed me would avoid a bad mountain to the right, we crossed the Sacramento where it turned to the southward, and entered a grassy level plain--a smaller Grand Rond; from the lower end of which the river issued into an inviting country of low rolling hills. Crossing a hard-frozen swamp on the farther side of the Rond, we entered again the pine forest, in which very deep snow made our traveling slow and laborious. We were slowly but gradually ascending a mountain; and, after a hard journey of seven hours, we came to some naked places among the timber, where a few tufts of grass showed above the snow, on the side of a hollow; and here we encamped. Our cow, which every day got poorer, was killed here, but the meat was rather tough.

16th.--We traveled this morning through snow about three feet deep, which, being crusted, very much cut the feet of our animals. The mountain still gradually rose; we crossed several spring heads covered with quaking asp; otherwise it was all pine forest. The air was dark with falling snow, which everywhere weighed down the trees. The depths of the forest were profoundly still; and below, we scarcely felt a breath of the wind which whirled the snow through their branches. I found that it required some exertion of constancy to adhere steadily to one course through the woods, when we were uncertain how far the forest extended, or what lay beyond; and, on account of our animals, it would be bad to spend another night on the mountain. Towards noon the forest looked clear ahead, appearing suddenly to terminate; and beyond a certain point we could see no trees. Riding rapidly ahead to this spot, we found ourselves on the verge of a vertical and rocky wall of the mountain. At our feet--more than a thousand feet below--we looked into a green prairie country, in which a beautiful lake, some twenty miles in length, was spread along the foot of the mountains, its shores bordered with green grass. Just then the sun broke out among the clouds, and illuminated the country below; while around us the storm raged fiercely. Not a particle of ice was to be seen on the lake, or snow on its borders, and all was like summer or spring. The glow of the sun in the valley below brightened up our hearts with sudden pleasure; and we made the woods ring with joyful shouts to those behind; and gradually, as each came up, he stopped to enjoy the unexpected scene. Shivering on snow three feet deep, and stiffening in a cold north wind, we exclaimed at once that the names of Summer Lake and Winter Ridge should be applied to these two proximate places of such sudden and violent contrast.

We were now immediately on the verge of the forest land, in which we had been traveling so many days; and, looking forward to the east, scarce a tree was to be seen. Viewed from our elevation, the face of the country exhibited only rocks and grass, and presented a region in which the artemisia became the principal wood, furnishing to its scattered inhabitants fuel for their fires, building material for their huts, and shelter for the small game which ministers to their hunger and nakedness. Broadly marked by the boundary at the mountain wall, and immediately below us, were the first waters of that Great Interior Basin which has the Wahsatch and Bear River mountains for its eastern, and the Sierra Nevada for its western rim; and the edge of which we had entered upwards of three months before, at the Great Salt Lake.

When we had sufficiently admired the scene below, we began to think about descending, which here was impossible, and we turned towards the north, traveling always along the rocky wall. We continued on for four or five miles, making ineffectual attempts at several places; and at length succeeded in getting down at one which was extremely difficult of descent. Night had closed in before the foremost reached the bottom, and it was dark before we all found ourselves together in the valley. There were three or four half-dead dry cedar-trees on the shore, and those who first arrived kindled bright fires to light on the others. One of the mules rolled over and over two or three hundred feet into a ravine, but recovered himself without any other injury than to his pack; and the howitzer was left midway the mountain until morning. By observation, the latitude of this encampment is 42 deg. 57' 22". It delayed us until near noon the next day to recover ourselves and put every thing in order; and we made only a short camp along the western shore of the lake, which, in the summer temperature we enjoyed to-day, justified the name we had given it. Our course would have taken us to the other shore, and over the highlands beyond; but I distrusted the appearance of the country, and decided to follow a plainly-beaten Indian trail leading along this side of the lake. We were now in a country where the scarcity of water and of grass makes traveling dangerous, and great caution was necessary.

18th.--We continued on the trail along the narrow strip of land between the lake and the high rocky wall, from which we had looked down two days before. Almost every half mile we crossed a little spring, or stream of pure cold water, and the grass was certainly as fresh and green as in the early spring. From the white efflorescence along the shore of the lake, we were enabled to judge that the water was impure, like that of lakes we subsequently found, but the mud prevented us from approaching it. We encamped near the eastern point of the lake, where there appeared between the hills a broad and low connecting hollow with the country beyond. From a rocky hill in the rear, I could see, marked out by a line of yellow dried grass, the bed of a stream, which probably connected the lake with other waters in the spring.

The observed latitude of this encampment is 42 deg. 42' 37".

19th.--After two hours' ride in an easterly direction, through a low country, the high ridge with pine forest still to our right, and a rocky and bald but lower one on the left, we reached a considerable fresh-water stream, which issues from the piny mountains. So far as we had been able to judge, between this stream and the lake we had crossed dividing grounds, and there did not appear to be any connection, as might be inferred from the impure condition of the lake water.

The rapid stream of pure water, roaring along between banks overhung with aspens and willows, was a refreshing and unexpected sight; and we followed down the course of the stream, which brought us soon into a marsh, or dry lake, formed by the expanding waters of the stream. It was covered with high reeds and rushes, and large patches of ground had been turned up by the squaws in digging for roots, as if a farmer had been preparing the land for grain. I could not succeed in finding the plant for which they had been digging. There were frequent trails, and fresh tracks of Indians; and, from the abundant signs visible, the black-tailed hare appears to be numerous here. It was evident that, in other seasons, this place was a sheet of water. Crossing this marsh towards the eastern hills, and passing over a bordering plain of heavy sands, covered with artemisia, we encamped before sundown on the creek, which here was very small, having lost its water in the marshy grounds. We found here tolerably good grass. The wind to-night was high, and we had no longer our huge pine fires, but were driven to our old resource of small dried willows and artemisia. About 12 miles ahead, the valley appears to be closed in by a high, dark-looking ridge.

20th.--Traveling for a few hours down the stream this morning, we turned the point of a hill on our left, and came suddenly in sight of another and much larger lake, which, along its eastern shore, was closely bordered by the high black ridge which walled it in by a precipitous face on this side. Throughout this region the face of the country is characterized by these precipices of black volcanic rock, generally enclosing the valleys of streams, and frequently terminating the hills. Often, in the course of our journey, we would be tempted to continue our road up the gentle ascent of a sloping hill, which, at the summit, would terminate abruptly in a black precipice. Spread out over a length of 20 miles, the lake, when we first came in view, presented a handsome sheet of water, and I gave to it the name of Lake Abert, in honor of the chief of the corps to which I belonged. The fresh-water stream we had followed emptied into the lake by a little fall; and I was doubtful for a moment whether to go on, or encamp at this place. The miry ground in the neighborhood of the lake did not allow us to examine the water conveniently, and, being now on the borders of a desert country, we were moving cautiously. It was, however, still early in the day, and I continued on trusting either that the water would be drinkable or that we should find some little spring from the hill-side. We were following an Indian trail which led along the steep rocky precipice--a black ridge along the western shore holding out no prospect whatever. The white efflorescences which lined the shore like a bank of snow, and the disagreeable odor which filled the air as soon as we came near, informed us too plainly that the water belonged to one of those fetid salt lakes which are common in this region. We continued until late in the evening to work along the rocky shore, but, as often afterwards, the dry, inhospitable rock deceived us; and, halting on the lake, we kindled up fires to guide those who were straggling along behind. We tried the water, but it was impossible to drink it, and most of the people to- night lay down without eating; but some of us, who had always a great reluctance to close the day without supper, dug holes along the shore, and obtained water, which, being filtered, was sufficiently palatable to be used, but still retained much of its nauseating taste. There was very little grass for the animals, the shore being lined with a luxuriant growth of chenopodiaceous shrubs, which burned with a quick bright flame, and made our firewood.

The next morning we had scarcely traveled two hours along the shore, when we reached a place where the mountains made a bay, leaving at their feet a low bottom around the lake. Here we found numerous hillocks covered with rushes, in the midst of which were deep holes, or springs, of pure water; and the bottom was covered with grass, which, although of a salt and unwholesome quality, and mixed with saline efflorescences, was still abundant, and made a good halting-place to recruit our animals, and we accordingly encamped here for the remainder of the day. I rode ahead several miles to ascertain if there was any appearance of a water-course entering the lake, but found none, the hills preserving their dry character, and the shore of the lake sprinkled with the same white powdery substance, and covered with the same shrubs. There were flocks of ducks on the lake, and frequent tracks of Indians along the shore, where the grass had been recently burnt by their fires.

We ascended the bordering mountain, in order to obtain a more perfect view of the lake, in sketching its figure: hills sweep entirely around its basin, from which the waters have no outlet.

22d.--To-day we left this forbidding lake. Impassable rocky ridges barred our progress to the eastward, and I accordingly bore off towards the south, over an extensive sage-plain. At a considerable distance ahead, and a little on our left, was a range of snowy mountains, and the country declined gradually towards the foot of a high and nearer ridge, immediately before us, which presented the feature of black precipices now becoming common to the country. On the summit of the ridge, snow was visible; and there being every indication of a stream at its base, we rode on until after dark, but were unable to reach it, and halted among the sage-bushes on the open plain, without either grass or water. The two India-rubber bags had been filled with water in the morning, which afforded sufficient for the camp; and rain in the night formed pools, which relieved the thirst of the animals. Where we encamped on the bleak sandy plain, the Indians had made huts or circular enclosures, about four feet high and twelve feet broad, of artemisia bushes. Whether these had been forts or houses, or what they had been doing in such a desert place, we could not ascertain.

23d.--The weather is mild; the thermometer at daylight 38 deg.; the wind having been from the southward for several days. The country has a very forbidding appearance, presenting to the eye nothing but sage, and barren ridges. We rode up towards the mountain, along the foot of which we found a lake, that we could not approach on account of the mud; and, passing around its southern end, ascended the slope at the foot of the ridge, where in some hollows we had discovered bushes and small trees--in such situations, a sure sign of water. We found here several springs, and the hill-side was well sprinkled with a species of *festuca*--a better grass than we had found for many days. Our elevated position gave us a good view over the country, but we discovered nothing very encouraging. Southward, about ten miles distant, was another small lake, towards which a broad trail led along the ridge; and this appearing to afford the most practicable route, I determined to continue our journey in that direction.

24th.--We found the water at the lake tolerably pure, and encamped at the farther end. There were some good grass and canes along the shore, and the vegetables at this place consisted principally of chenopodiaceous shrubs.

25th.--We were roused on Christmas morning by a discharge from the small-arms and howitzer, with which our people saluted the day; and the name of which we bestowed on the lake. It was the first time, perhaps, in this remote and desolate region, in which it had been so commemorated. Always, on days of religious or national commemoration, our voyageurs expect some unusual allowance; and having nothing else, I gave them each a little brandy, (which was carefully guarded, as one of the most useful articles a traveler can carry,) with some coffee and sugar, which here, where every eatable was a luxury, was sufficient to make them a feast. The day was sunny and warm; and resuming our journey, we crossed some slight dividing grounds into a similar basin, walled in on the right by a lofty mountain ridge. The plainly-beaten trail still continued, and occasionally we passed camping-grounds of the Indians, which indicated to me that we were on one of the great thoroughfares of the country. In the afternoon I attempted to travel in a more eastern direction; but after a few laborious miles, was beaten back into the basin by an impassable country. There were fresh Indian tracks about the valley, and last night a horse was stolen. We encamped on the valley bottom, where there was some cream-like water in ponds, colored by a clay soil, and frozen over. Chenopodiaceous shrubs constituted the growth, and made again our firewood. The animals were driven to the hill, where there was tolerably good grass.

26th.--Our general course was again south. The country consists of larger or smaller basins, into which the mountain waters run down, forming small lakes: they present a perfect level, from which the mountains rise immediately and abruptly. Between the successive basins, the dividing grounds are usually very slight; and it is probable that in the seasons of high water, many of these basins are in communication. At such times there is evidently an abundance of water, though now we find scarcely more than the dry beds. On either side, the mountains, though not very high, appear to be rocky and sterile. The basin in which we were traveling declined towards the southwest corner, where the mountains indicated a narrow outlet; and, turning round a rocky point or cape, we continued up a lateral branch valley, in which we encamped at night, on a rapid, pretty little stream of fresh water, which we found unexpectedly among the sage, near the ridge, on the right side of the valley. It was bordered with grassy bottoms and clumps of willows; the water partially frozen. This stream belongs to the basin we had left. By a partial observation to-night, our camp was found to be directly on the 42d parallel. To-night a horse belonging to Carson, one of the best we had in the camp, was stolen by the Indians.

27th.--We continued up the valley of the stream, the principal branch of which here issues from a bed of high mountains. We turned up a branch to the left, and fell into an Indian trail, which conducted us by a good road over open bottoms along the creek, where the snow was five or six inches deep. Gradually ascending, the trail led through a good broad pass in the mountain, where we found the snow about one foot deep. There were some remarkably large cedars in the pass, which were covered with an unusual quantity of frost, which we supposed might possibly indicate the neighborhood of water; and as, in the arbitrary position of Mary's lake, we were already beginning to look for it, this circumstance contributed to our hope of finding it near. Descending from the mountain, we reached another basin, on the flat lake bed of which we found no water, and encamped among the sage on the bordering plain, where the snow was still about one foot deep. Among this the grass was remarkably green, and to- night the animals fared tolerably well.

28th.--The snow being deep, I had determined, if any more horses were stolen, to follow the tracks of the Indians into the mountains, and put a temporary check to their sly operations; but it did not occur again.

Our road this morning lay down a level valley, bordered by steep mountainous ridges, rising very abruptly from the plain. Artemisia was the principal plant, mingled with Fremontia and the chenopodiaceous shrubs. The artemisia was here extremely large, being sometimes a foot in diameter, and eight feet high. Riding quietly along over the snow, we came suddenly upon smokes rising among these bushes; and, galloping up, we found two huts, open at the top, and loosely built of sage, which appeared to have been deserted at the instant; and, looking hastily around, we saw several Indians on the crest of the ridge near by, and several others scrambling up the side. We had come upon them so suddenly, that they had been well-nigh surprised in their lodges. A sage fire was burning in the middle; a few baskets made of straw were lying about, with one or two rabbit-skins; and there was a little grass scattered about, on which they had been lying. "Tabibo--bo!" they shouted from the hills--a word which, in the Snake language, signifies *white*--and remained looking at us from behind the rocks. Carson and Godey rode towards the hill, but the men ran off like deer. They had been so much pressed, that a woman with two children had dropped behind a sage-bush near the lodge, and when Carson accidentally stumbled upon her, she immediately began screaming in the extremity of fear, and shut her eyes fast to avoid seeing him. She was brought back to the lodge, and we endeavored in vain to open a communication with the men. By dint of presents, and friendly demonstrations, she was brought to calmness; and we found that they belonged to the Snake nation, speaking the language of that people. Eight or ten appeared to live together, under the same little shelter; and they seemed to have no other subsistence than the roots or seeds they might have stored up, and the hares which live in the sage, and which they are enabled to track through the snow, and are very skilful in killing. Their skins afford them a little scanty covering. Herding together among bushes, and crouching almost naked over a little sage fire, using their instinct only to procure food, these may be considered, among human beings, the nearest approach to the animal creation. We have reason to believe that these had never before seen the face of a white man.

The day had been pleasant, but about two o'clock it began to blow; and crossing a slight dividing ground we encamped on the sheltered side of a hill, where there was good bunch-grass, having made a day's journey of 24 miles. The night closed in, threatening snow; but the large sage-bushes made bright fires.

29th.--The morning mild, and at 4 o'clock it commenced snowing. We took our way across a plain, thickly covered with snow, towards a range of hills in the southeast. The sky soon became so dark with snow, that little could be seen of the surrounding country; and we reached the summit of the hills in a heavy snow-storm. On the side we had approached, this had appeared to be only a ridge of low hills and we were surprised to find ourselves on the summit of a bed of broken mountains, which, as far as the weather would permit us to see, declined rapidly to some low country ahead, presenting a dreary and savage character; and for a moment I looked around in doubt on the wild and inhospitable prospect, scarcely knowing what road to take which might conduct us to some place of shelter for the night.

Noticing among the hills the head of a grassy hollow, I determined to follow it, in the hope that it would conduct us to a stream. We followed a winding descent for several miles, the hollow gradually broadening into little meadows, and becoming the bed of a stream as we advanced; and towards night we were agreeably surprised by the appearance of a willow grove, where we found a sheltered camp, with water and excellent and abundant grass. The grass, which was covered by the snow on the bottom, was long and green, and the face of the mountain had a more favorable character in its vegetation, being smoother, and covered with good bunch-grass. The snow was deep, and the night very cold. A broad trail had entered the valley from the right, and a short distance below the camp were the tracks where a considerable party of Indians had passed on horseback, who had turned out to the left, apparently with the view of crossing the mountains to the eastward.

30th.--After following the stream for a few hours in a southeasterly direction, it entered a canon where we could not follow; but, determined not to leave the stream, we searched a passage below, where we could regain it, and entered a regular narrow valley. The water had now more the appearance of a flowing creek; several times we passed groves of willows, and we began to feel ourselves out of all difficulty. From our position, it was reasonable to conclude that this stream would find its outlet in Mary's lake, and conduct us into a better country. We had descended rapidly, and here we found very little snow. On both sides, the mountains showed often stupendous and curious-looking rocks, which at several places so narrowed the valley, that scarcely a pass was left for the camp. It was a singular place to travel through--shut up in the earth, a sort of chasm, the little strip of grass under our feet, the rough walls of bare rock on either hand, and the narrow strip of sky above. The grass to-night was abundant, and we encamped in high spirits.

31st.--After an hour's ride this morning, our hopes were once more destroyed. The valley opened out, and before us again lay one of the dry basins. After some search, we discovered a high-water outlet, which brought us in a few miles, and by a descent of several hundred feet, into a long, broad basin, in which we found the bed of the stream, and obtained sufficient water by cutting the ice. The grass on the bottoms was salt and unpalatable.

Here we concluded the year 1843, and our new year's eve was rather a gloomy one. The result of our journey began to be very uncertain; the country was singularly unfavorable to travel; the grasses being frequently of a very unwholesome character, and the hoofs of our animals were so worn and cut by the rocks, that many of them were lame, and could scarcely be got along.

JANUARY.

New Year's day, 1844.--We continued down the valley, between a dry-looking black ridge on the left, and a more snowy and high one on the right. Our road was bad along the bottom, being broken by gullies and impeded by sage, and sandy on the hills, where there is not a blade of grass, nor does any appear on the mountains. The soil in many places consists of a fine powdery sand, covered with a saline efflorescence; and the general character of the country is desert. During the day we directed our course towards a black cape, at the foot of which a column of smoke indicated hot springs.

2d.--We were on the road early. The face of the country was hidden by falling snow. We traveled along the bed of the stream, in some places dry, in others covered with ice; the traveling being very bad, through deep fine sand, rendered tenacious by a mixture of clay. The weather cleared up a little at noon, and we reached the hot springs of which we had seen the vapor the day before. There was a large field of the usual salt grass here, peculiar to such places. The country otherwise is a perfect barren, without a blade of grass, the only plant being some dwarf Fremontias. We passed the rocky cape, a jagged broken point, bare and torn. The rocks are volcanic, and the hills here have a burnt appearance--cinders and coal occasionally appearing as at a blacksmith's forge. We crossed the large dry bed of a muddy lake in a southeasterly direction, and encamped at night, without water and without grass, among sage-bushes covered with snow. The heavy road made several mules give out to-day; and a horse, which had made the journey from the States successfully, thus far, was left on the trail.

3d.--A fog, so dense that we could not see a hundred yards, covered the country, and the men that were sent out after the horses were bewildered and lost; and we were consequently detained at camp until late in the day. Our situation had now become a serious one. We had reached and run over the position where, according to the best maps in my possession, we should have found Mary's lake or river. We were evidently on the verge of the desert which had been reported to us; and the appearance of the country was so forbidding, that I was afraid to enter it, and determined to bear away to the southward, keeping close along the mountains, in the full expectation of reaching the Buenaventura river. This morning I put every man in the camp on foot--myself, of course, among the rest--and in this manner lightened by distribution the loads of the animals. We traveled seven or eight miles along the ridge bordering the valley, and encamped where there were a few bunches of grass on the bed of a hill-torrent, without water. There were some large artemisias; but the principal plants are chenopodiaceous shrubs. The rock composing the mountains is here changed suddenly into white granite. The fog showed the tops of the hills at sunset, and stars enough for observations in the early evening, and then closed over us as before. Latitude by observation, 40 deg. 48' 15".

4th.--The fog to-day was still more dense, and the people again were bewildered. We traveled a few miles around the western point of the ridge, and encamped where there were a few tufts of grass, but no water. Our animals now were in a very alarming state, and there was increased anxiety in the camp.

5th.--Same dense fog continued, and one of the mules died in camp this morning. I have had occasion to remark, on such occasions as these, that animals which are about to die leave the band, and, coming into the camp; lie down about the fires. We moved to a place where there was a little better grass, about two miles distant. Taplin, one of our best men, who had gone out on a scouting excursion, ascended a mountain near by, and to his surprise emerged into a region of bright sunshine, in which the upper parts of the mountain were glowing, while below all was obscured in the darkest fog.

6th.--The fog continued the same, and, with Mr. Preuss and Carson, I ascended the mountain, to sketch the leading features of the country as some indication of our future route, while Mr. Fitzpatrick explored the country below. In a very short distance we had ascended above the mist, but the view obtained was not very gratifying. The fog had partially cleared off from below when we reached the summit; and in the southwest corner of a basin communicating with that in which we had encamped, we saw a lofty column of smoke, 16 miles distant, indicating the presence of hot springs. There, also, appeared to be the outlet of those draining channels of the country; and, as such places afforded always more or less grass, I determined to steer in that direction. The ridge we had ascended appeared to be composed of fragments of white granite. We saw here traces of sheep and antelope.

Entering the neighboring valley, and crossing the bed of another lake, after a hard day's travel over ground of yielding mud and sand, we reached the springs, where we found an abundance of grass, which, though only tolerably good, made this place, with reference to the past, a refreshing and agreeable spot.

This is the most extraordinary locality of hot springs we had met during the journey. The basin of the largest one has a circumference of several hundred feet; but there is at one extremity a circular space of about fifteen feet in diameter, entirely occupied by the boiling water. It boils up at irregular intervals, and with much noise. The water is clear, and the spring deep: a pole about sixteen feet long was easily immersed in the centre; but we had no means of forming a good idea of the depth. It was surrounded on the margin with a border of **green** grass, and near the shore the temperature of the water was 206 deg.. We had no means of ascertaining that of the centre, where the heat was greatest; but, by dispersing the water with a pole, the temperature at the margin was increased to 208 deg., and in the centre it was doubtless higher. By driving the pole towards the bottom, the water was made to boil up with increased force and noise. There are several other interesting places, where water and smoke or gas escape; but they would require a long description. The water is impregnated with common salt, but not so much as to render it unfit for general cooking; and a mixture of snow made it pleasant to drink.

In the immediate neighborhood, the valley bottom is covered almost exclusively with chenopodiaceous shrubs, of greater luxuriance, and larger growth, than we have seen them in any preceding part of the journey.

I obtained this evening some astronomical observations.

Our situation now required caution. Including those which gave out from the injured condition of their feet, and those stolen by Indians, we had lost, since leaving the Dalles of the Columbia, fifteen animals; and of these, nine had been left in the last few days. I therefore determined, until we should reach a country of water and vegetation, to feel our way ahead, by having the line of route explored some fifteen or twenty miles in advance, and only to leave a present encampment when the succeeding one was known.

Taking with me Godey and Carson, I made to-day a thorough exploration of the neighboring valleys, and found in a ravine, in the bordering mountains, a good encamping place, where was water in springs, and a sufficient quantity of grass for a night. Overshadowing the springs were some trees of the sweet cottonwood, which, after a long interval of absence, we saw again with pleasure; regarding them as harbingers of a better country. To us, they were eloquent of green prairies and buffalo. We found here a broad and plainly-marked trail, on which there were tracks of horses, and we appeared to have regained one of the thoroughfares which pass by the watering-places of the country. On the western mountains of the valley, with which this of the boiling spring communicates, we remarked scattered cedars--probably indicating that we were on the borders of the timbered region extending to the Pacific. We reached the camp at sunset, after a day's ride of about 40 miles. The horses we rode were in good order, being of some that were kept for emergencies, and rarely used.

Mr. Preuss had ascended one of the mountains, and occupied the day in sketching the country; and Mr. Fitzpatrick had found, a few miles distant, a hollow of excellent grass and pure water, to which the animals were driven, as I remained another day to give them an opportunity to recruit their strength. Indians appear to be everywhere prowling about like wild animals, and there is a fresh trail across the snow in the valley near.

Latitude of the boiling springs, 40 deg. 39' 46".

On the 9th we crossed over to the cottonwood camp. Among the shrubs on the hills were a few bushes of ***ephedra occidentalis***, which afterwards occurred frequently along the road, and, as usual, the lowlands were occupied with artemisia. While the party proceeded to this place, Carson and myself reconnoitred the road in advance, and found another good encampment for the following day.

10th.--We continued our reconnoissance ahead, pursuing a south direction in the basin along the ridge; the camp following slowly after. On a large trail there is never any doubt of finding suitable places for encampments. We reached the end of the basin, where we found, in a hollow of the mountain which enclosed it, an abundance of good bunch-grass. Leaving a signal for the party to encamp, we continued our way up the hollow, intending to see what lay beyond the mountain. The hollow was several miles long, forming a good pass; the snow deepening to about a foot as we neared the summit. Beyond, a defile between the mountains descended rapidly about two thousand feet; and, filling up all the lower space, was a sheet of green water, some twenty miles broad. It broke upon our eyes like the ocean. The neighboring peaks rose high above us, and we ascended one of them to obtain a better view. The waves were curling in the breeze, and their dark-green color showed it to be a body of deep water. For a long time we sat enjoying the view, for we had become fatigued with mountains, and the free expanse of moving waves was very grateful. It was set like a gem in the mountains, which, from our position, seemed to enclose it almost entirely. At the western end it communicated with the line of basins we had left a few days since; and on the opposite side it swept a ridge of snowy mountains, the foot of the great Sierra. Its position at first inclined us to believe it Mary's lake, but the rugged mountains were so entirely discordant with descriptions of its low rushy shores and open country, that we concluded it some unknown body of water, which it afterwards proved to be.

On our road down, the next day, we saw herds of mountain sheep, and encamped on a little stream at the mouth of the defile, about a mile from the margin of the water, to which we hurried down immediately. The water is so slightly salt, that, at first, we thought it fresh, and would be pleasant to drink when no other could be had. The shore was rocky--a handsome beach, which reminded us of the sea. On some large ***granite*** boulders that were scattered about the shore, I remarked a coating of calcareous substance, in some places a few inches, and in others a foot in thickness. Near our camp, the hills, which were of primitive rock, were also covered with this substance, which was in too great quantity on the mountains along the shore of the lake to have been deposited by water, and has the appearance of having been spread over the rocks in mass[2].

Where we had halted appeared to be a favorite camping-place for Indians.

13th.--We followed again a broad Indian trail along the shore of the lake to

---

2   The label attached to a specimen of this rock was lost; but I append an analysis of that which, from memory, I judge to be the specimen:

Carbonate of lime	77.31
Carbonate of magnesia	5.25
Oxide of iron	1.60
Alumina	1.05
Silica	8.55
Organic matter, water, and loss	6.24

	100.00

the southward. For a short space we had room enough in the bottom; but, after traveling a short distance, the water swept the foot of the precipitous mountains, the peaks of which are about 3,000 feet above the lake. The trail wound along the base of these precipices, against which the water dashed below, by a way nearly impracticable for the howitzer. During a greater part of the morning the lake was nearly hid by a snow- storm, and the waves broke on the narrow beach in a long line of foaming serf, five or six feet high. The day was unpleasantly cold, the wind driving the snow sharp against our faces; and, having advanced only about 12 miles, we encamped in a bottom formed by a ravine, covered with good grass, which was fresh and green.

We did not get the howitzer into camp, but were obliged to leave it on the rocks until morning. We saw several flocks of sheep, but did not succeed in killing any. Ducks were riding on the waves, and several large fish were seen. The mountain sides were crusted with the calcareous cement previously mentioned. There were chenopodiaceous and other shrubs along the beach; and, at the foot of the rocks, an abundance of ***ephedra occidentalis***, whose dark-green color makes them evergreens among the shrubby growth of the lake. Towards evening the snow began to fall heavily, and the country had a wintry appearance.

The next morning the snow was rapidly melting under a warm sun. Part of the morning was occupied in bringing up the gun; and, making only nine miles, we encamped on the shore, opposite a very remarkable rock in the lake, which had attracted our attention for many miles. It rose, according to our estimate, 600 feet above the water, and, from the point we viewed it, presented a pretty exact outline of the great pyramid of Cheops. Like other rocks along the shore, it seemed to be incrusted with calcareous cement. This striking feature suggested a name for the lake, and I called it Pyramid Lake; and though it may be deemed by some a fanciful resemblance, I can undertake to say that the future traveler will find much more striking resemblance between this rock and the pyramids of Egypt, than there is between them and the object from which they take their name.

The elevation of this lake above the sea is 4,890 feet, being nearly 700 feet higher than the Great Salt lake, from which it lies nearly west, and distant about eight degrees of longitude. The position and elevation of this lake make it an object of geographical interest. It is the nearest lake to the western rim, as the Great Salt lake is to the eastern rim, of the Great Basin which lies between the base of the Rocky mountains and the Sierra Nevada--and the extent and character of which, its whole circumference and contents, it is so desirable to know.

The last of the cattle which had been driven from the Dalles was killed here for food, and was still in good condition.

15th.--A few poor-looking Indians made their appearance this morning, and we succeeded in getting one into the camp. He was naked, with the exception of a tunic of hare-skins. He told us that there was a river at the end of the lake, but that he lived in the rocks near by. From the few words our people could understand, he spoke a dialect of the Snake language; but we were not able to understand enough to know Whether the river ran in or out, or what was its course; consequently, there still remained a chance that this might be Mary's lake.

Groves of large cottonwood, which we could see at the mouth of the river, indicated that it was a stream of considerable size, and, at all events, we had the pleasure to know that now we were in a country where human beings could live. Accompanied by the Indian, we resumed our road, passing on the way several caves in the rock where there were baskets and reeds, but the people had disappeared. We saw also horse-tracks along the shore.

Early in the afternoon, when we were approaching the groves at the mouth of the river, three or four Indians met us on the trail. We had an explanatory conversation in signs, and then we moved on together towards the village, which the chief said was encamped on the bottom.

Reaching the groves, we found the ***inlet*** of a large freshwater stream, and all at once were satisfied that it was neither Mary's river nor the waters of the Sacramento, but that we had discovered a large interior lake, which the Indians informed us had no outlet. It is about 35 miles long, and, by the mark of the water-line along the shore, the spring level is about 12 feet above its present waters. The chief commenced speaking in a loud voice as we approached; and parties of Indians, armed with bows and arrows, issued from the thickets. We selected a strong place for our encampment--a grassy bottom, nearly enclosed by the river, and furnished with abundant firewood. The village, a collection of straw huts, was a few hundred yards higher up. An Indian brought in a large fish to trade, which we had the inexpressible satisfaction to find was a salmon- trout; we gathered round him eagerly. The

Indians were amused with our delight, and immediately brought in numbers, so that the camp was soon stocked. Their flavor was excellent--superior, in fact, to that of any fish I have ever known. They were of extraordinary size--about as large as the Columbia River salmon--generally from two to four feet in length. From the information of Mr. Walker, who passed among some lakes lying more to the eastward, this fish is common to the streams of the inland lakes. He subsequently informed me that he had obtained them weighing six pounds when cleaned and the head taken off, which corresponds very well with the size of those obtained at this place. They doubtless formed the subsistence of these people, who hold the fishery in exclusive possession.

 I remarked that one of them gave a fish to the Indian we had first seen, which he carried off to his family. To them it was probably a feast; being of the Digger tribe, and having no share in the fishery, living generally on seeds and roots. Although this was a time of the year when the fish have not yet become fat, they were excellent, and we could only imagine what they are at the proper season. These Indians were very fat, and appeared to live an easy and happy life. They crowded into the camp more than was consistent with our safety, retaining always their arms; and, as they made some unsatisfactory demonstrations, they were given to understand that they would not be permitted to come armed into the camp; and strong guards were kept with the horses. Strict vigilance was maintained among the people, and one-third at a time were kept on guard during the night. There is no reason to doubt that these dispositions, uniformly preserved, conducted our party securely through Indians famed for treachery.

 In the mean time, such a salmon-trout feast as is seldom seen was going on in our camp; and every variety of manner in which fish could be prepared-- boiled, fried, and roasted in the ashes--was put into requisition; and every few minutes an Indian would be seen running off to spear a fresh one. Whether these Indians had seen whites before, we could not be certain; but they were evidently in communication with others who had, as one of them had some brass buttons, and we noticed several other articles of civilized manufacture. We could obtain from them but little information respecting the country. They made on the ground a drawing of the river, which they represented as issuing from another lake in the mountains three or four days distant, in a direction a little west of south; beyond which, they drew a mountain; and further still, two rivers; on one of which they told us that people like ourselves traveled. Whether they alluded to the settlements on the Sacramento, or to a party from the United States which had crossed the Sierra about three degrees to the southward, a few years since, I am unable to determine.

I tried unsuccessfully to prevail on some of them to guide us for a few days on the road, but they only looked at each other and laughed.

The latitude of our encampment, which may be considered the mouth of the inlet, is 39 deg. 51' 13" by our observations.

16th.--This morning we continued our journey along this beautiful stream, which we naturally called the Salmon Trout river. Large trails led up on either side; the stream was handsomely timbered with large cottonwoods; and the waters were very clear and pure. We were traveling along the mountains of the great Sierra, which rose on our right, covered with snow; but below the temperature was mild and pleasant. We saw a number of dams which the Indians had constructed to catch fish. After having made about 18 miles, we encamped under some large cottonwoods on the river bottom, where there was tolerably good grass.

17th.--This morning we left the river, which here issues from mountains on the west. With every stream I now expected to see the great Buenaventura; and Carson hurried eagerly to search, on every one we reached, for beaver cuttings, which he always maintained we should find only on waters that ran to the Pacific; and the absence of such signs was to him a sure indication that the water had no outlet from the Great Basin. We followed the Indian trail through a tolerably level country, with small sage-bushes, which brought us, after 20 miles' journey, to another large stream, timbered with cottonwood, and flowing also out of the mountains, but running more directly to the eastward.

On the way we surprised a family of Indians in the hills; but the man ran up the mountain with rapidity; and the woman was so terrified, and kept up such a continued screaming, that we could do nothing with her, and were obliged to let her go.

18th.--There were Indian lodges and fish-dams on the stream. There were no beaver cuttings on the river; but below, it turned round to the right; and, hoping that it would prove a branch of the Buenaventura, we followed it down for about three hours, and encamped.

I rode out with Mr. Fitzpatrick and Carson to reconnoitre the country, which had evidently been alarmed by the news of our appearance. This stream joined with the open valley of another to the eastward; but which way the main water ran, it was impossible to tell. Columns of smoke rose over the country at scattered intervals--signals by which the Indians here, as elsewhere, communicate to each other that enemies are in the country. It is a signal of ancient and very universal application among barbarians.

Examining into the condition of the animals when I returned into the camp, I found their feet so much cut up by the rocks, and so many of them lame, that it was evidently impossible that they could cross the country to the Rocky mountains. Every piece of iron that could be used for the purpose had been converted into nails, and we could make no further use of the shoes we had remaining. I therefore determined to abandon my eastern course, and to cross the Sierra Nevada into the valley of the Sacramento, wherever a practicable pass could be found. My decision was heard with joy by the people, and diffused new life throughout the camp.

Latitude, by observation, 39 deg. 24' 16".

19th.--A great number of smokes are still visible this morning, attesting at once the alarm our appearance had spread among these people, and their ignorance of us. If they knew the whites, they would understand that their only object in coming among them was to trade, which required peace and friendship; but they have nothing to trade--consequently, nothing to attract the white man; hence their fear and flight.

At daybreak we had a heavy snow; but set out, and, returning up the stream, went out of our way in a circuit over a little mountain; and encamped on the same stream, a few miles above, in latitude 39 deg. 19' 21" by observation.

20th.--To-day we continued up the stream, and encamped on it close to the mountains. The freshly fallen snow was covered with the tracks of Indians, who had descended from upper waters, probably called down by the smokes in the plain.

We ascended a peak of the range, which commanded a view of this stream behind the first ridge, where it was winding its course through a somewhat open valley, and I sometimes regret that I did not make the trial to cross here; but while we had fair weather below, the mountains were darkened with falling snow, and, feeling unwilling to encounter them, we turned away again to the southward. In that direction we traveled the next day over a tolerably level country, having always the high mountains on the west. There was but little snow or rock on the ground; and, after having traveled 24 miles, we encamped again on another large stream, running off to the northward and eastward, to meet that we had left. It ran through broad bottoms, having a fine meadow-land appearance.

Latitude 39 deg. 01' 53".

22d.--We traveled up the stream about fourteen miles, to the foot of the mountains, from which one branch issued in the southwest, the other flowing S.S.E. along their base. Leaving camp below, we ascended the range through which the first stream passed, in a canon; on the western side was a circular valley about 15 miles long, through which the stream wound its way, issuing from a gorge in the main mountain, which rose abruptly beyond. The valley looked yellow with faded grass; and the trail we had followed was visible, making towards the gorge, and this was evidently a pass; but again, while all was bright sunshine on the ridge and on the valley where we were, the snow was falling heavily in the mountains. I determined go still to the southward, and encamped on the stream near the forks, the animals being fatigued and the grass tolerably good.

The rock of the ridge we had ascended is a compact lava, assuming a granitic appearance and structure, and containing, in some places, small nodules of obsidian. So far as composition and aspect are concerned, the rock in other parts of the ridge appears to be granite; but it is probable that this is only a compact form of lava of recent origin.

By observation, the elevation of the encampment was 5,020 feet; and the latitude 38 deg. 49' 54".

23d.--We moved along the course of the other branch towards the southeast, the country affording a fine road; and, passing some slight dividing- grounds, descended towards the valley of another stream. There was a somewhat rough-looking mountain ahead, which it appeared to issue from, or to enter--we could not tell which; and as the course of the valley and the inclination of the ground had a favorable direction, we were sanguine to find here a branch of the Buenaventura; but were again disappointed, finding it an inland water, on which we encamped after a day's journey of 24 miles. It was evident that, from the time we descended into the plain at Summer lake, we had been flanking the great range of mountains which divided the Great Basin from the waters of the Pacific; and that the continued succession, and almost connection, of lakes and rivers which we encountered, were the drainings of that range. Its rains, springs, and snows, would sufficiently account for these lakes and streams, numerous as they were.

24th.--A man was discovered running towards the camp as we were about to start this morning, who proved to be an Indian of rather advanced age--a sort of forlorn hope, who seemed to have been worked up into the resolution of visiting the strangers who were passing through the country. He seized the hand of the first man he met as he came up, out of breath, and held on, as if to assure himself of protection. He brought with him, in a little skin bag, a few pounds of the seeds of a pine-tree, which to- day we saw for the first time, and which Dr. Torrey has described as a new species, under the name of ***pinus monophyllus***; in popular language it might be called the ***nut pine***. We purchased them all from him. The nut is oily, of very agreeable flavor, and must be very nutritious, as it constitutes the principal subsistence of the tribes among which we were now traveling. By a present of scarlet cloth, and other striking articles, we prevailed upon this man to be our guide of two days' journey. As clearly as possible by signs, we made him understand our object; and he engaged to conduct us in sight of a good pass which he knew. Here we ceased to hear the Shoshonee language--that of this man being perfectly unintelligible. Several Indians, who had been waiting to see what reception he would meet with, now came into camp; and, accompanied by the new-comers, we resumed our journey.

The road led us up the creek, which here becomes a rather rapid mountain stream, fifty feet wide, between dark-looking hills without snow; but immediately beyond them rose snowy mountains on either side, timbered principally with the nut pine. On the lower grounds, the general height of this tree is twelve to twenty feet, and eight inches the greatest diameter; it is rather branching, and has a peculiar and singular, but pleasant odor. We followed the river for only a short distance along a rocky trail, and crossed it at a dam which the Indians made us comprehend had been built to catch salmon trout. The snow and ice were heaped up against it three or four feet deep entirely across the stream.

Leaving here the stream, which runs through impassable canons, we continued our road over a very broken country, passing through a low gap between the snowy mountains. The rock which occurs immediately in the pass has the appearance of impure sandstone, containing scales of black mica. This may be only a stratified lava. On issuing from the gap, the compact lava, and other volcanic products usual in the country, again occurred. We descended from the gap into a wide valley, or rather basin, and encamped on a small tributary to the last stream, on which there was very good grass. It was covered with such thick ice, that it required some labor with pickaxes to make holes for the animals to drink. The banks are lightly wooded with willow, and on the upper bottoms are sage and Fremontia, with ***ephedra occidentalis***, which begins to occur more frequently. The day has been a summer one, warm and pleasant; no snow on the trail, which, as we are all on foot, makes traveling more agreeable. The hunters went into a neighboring mountain, but found no game. We have five Indians in camp to-night.

25th.--The morning was cold and bright, and as the sun rose the day became beautiful. A party of twelve Indians came down from the mountains to trade pine nuts, of which each one carried a little bag. These seemed now to be the staple of the country; and whenever we met an Indian, his friendly salutation consisted in offering a few nuts to eat and to trade; their only arms were bows and flint-pointed arrows. It appeared that in almost all the valleys the neighboring bands were at war with each other; and we had some difficulty in prevailing on our guides to accompany us on this day's journey, being at war with the people on the other side of a large snowy mountain which lay before us.

The general level of the country appeared to be getting higher, and we were gradually entering the heart of the mountains. Accompanied by all the Indians, we ascended a long ridge, and reached a pure spring at the edge of the timber, where the Indians had waylaid and killed an antelope, and where the greater part of them left us. Our pacific conduct had quieted their alarms; and though at war among each other, yet all confided in us-- thanks to the combined effects of power and kindness--for our arms inspired respect, and our little presents and good treatment conciliated their confidence. Here we suddenly entered snow six inches deep, and the ground was a little rocky, with volcanic fragments, the mountain appearing to be composed of such rock. The timber consists principally of nut pines, (***pinus monophyllus***,) which here are of larger size--12 to 15 inches in diameter; heaps of cones lying on the ground, where the Indians have gathered the seeds.

The snow deepened gradually as we advanced. Our guides wore out their moccasins; and putting one of them on a horse, we enjoyed the unusual sight of an Indian who could not ride. He could not even guide the animal, and appeared to have no knowledge of horses. The snow was three or four feet deep on the summit of the, pass; and from this point the guide pointed out our future road, declining to go any further. Below us was a little valley; and beyond this the mountains rose higher still, one ridge above another, presenting a rude and rocky outline. We descended rapidly to the valley: the snow impeded us but little; yet it was dark when we reached the foot of the mountain.

The day had been so warm that our moccasins were wet with melting snow; but here, as soon as the sun begins to decline, the air gets suddenly cold, and we had great difficulty to keep our feet from freezing--our moccasins being frozen perfectly stiff. After a hard day's march of 27 miles, we reached the river some time after dark, and found the snow about a foot deep on the bottom--the river being entirely frozen over. We found a comfortable camp, where there were dry willows abundant, and we soon had blazing fires. A little brandy, which I husbanded with great care, remained, and I do not know any medicine more salutary, or any drink (except coffee) more agreeable, than this in a cold night and after a hard day's march. Mr. Preuss questioned whether the famed nectar ever possessed so exquisite a flavor. All felt it to be a reviving cordial.

The next morning, when the sun had not yet risen over the mountains, the thermometer was at 2 deg. below zero; but the sky was bright and pure, and the weather changed rapidly into a pleasant day of summer. I remained encamped in order to examine the country, and allow the animals a day of rest, the grass being good and abundant under the snow.

The river is fifty or eighty feet wide, with a lively current, and very clear water. It forked a little above our camp, one of its branches coming directly from the south. At its head appeared to be a handsome pass; and from the neighboring heights we could see, beyond, a comparatively low and open country, which was supposed to form the valley of the Buenaventura. The other branch issued from a nearer pass, in a direction S. 75 deg. W., forking at the foot of the mountain, and receiving a part of its waters from a little lake. I was in advance of the camp when our last guides had left us; but, so far as could be understood, this was the pass which they had indicated, and, in company with Carson, to-day I set out to explore it. Entering the range, we continued in a northwesterly direction up the valley, which here bent to the right. It was a pretty open bottom, locked between lofty mountains, which supplied frequent streams as we advanced. On the lower part they were covered with nut-pine trees, and above with masses of pine, which we easily recognised, from the darker color of the foliage. From the fresh trails which occurred frequently during the morning, deer appeared to be remarkably numerous in the mountain.

We had now entirely left the desert country, and were on the verge of a region which, extending westward to the shores of the Pacific, abounds in large game, and is covered with a singular luxuriance of vegetable life.

The little stream grew rapidly smaller, and in about twelve miles we had reached its head, the last water coming immediately out of the mountain on the right; and this spot was selected for our next encampment. The grass showed well in sunny places; but in colder situations the snow was deep, and began to occur in banks, through which the horses found some difficulty in breaking a way.

To the left, the open valley continued in a southwesterly direction, with a scarcely perceptible ascent, forming a beautiful pass, the exploration of which we deferred until the next day, and returned to the camp.

To-day an Indian passed through the valley, on his way into the mountains, where he showed us was his lodge. We comprehended nothing of his language; and, though he appeared to have no fear, passing along in full view of the camp, he was indisposed to hold any communication with us, but showed the way he was going, and pointed for us to go on our road.

By observation, the latitude of this encampment was 38 deg. 18' 01", and the elevation above the sea 6,310 feet.

27th.--Leaving the camp to follow slowly, with directions to Carson to encamp at the place agreed on, Mr. Fitzpatrick and myself continued the reconnoissance. Arriving at the head of the stream, we began to enter the pass--passing occasionally through open groves of large pine-trees, on the warm side of the defile, where the snow had melted away, occasionally exposing a large Indian trail. Continuing along a narrow meadow, we reached, in a few miles, the gate of the pass, where there was a narrow strip of prairie, about 50 yards wide, between walls of granite rock. On either side rose the mountains, forming on the left a rugged mass, or nucleus, wholly covered with deep snow, presenting a glittering and icy surface. At the time, we supposed this to be the point into which they were gathered between the two great rivers, and from which the waters flowed off to the bay. This was the icy and cold side of the pass, and the rays of the sun hardly touched the snow. On the left, the mountains rose into peaks, but they were lower and secondary, and the country had a somewhat more open and lighter character. On the right were several hot springs, which appeared remarkable in such a place. In going through, we felt impressed by the majesty of the mountain, along the huge wall of which we were riding. Here there was no snow; but immediately beyond was a deep bank, through which we dragged our horses with considerable effort. We then immediately struck upon a stream, which gathered itself rapidly, and descended quick; and the valley did not preserve the open character of the other side, appearing below to form a canon. We therefore climbed one of the peaks on the right, leaving our horses below; but we were so much shut up that we did not obtain an extensive view, and what we saw was not very satisfactory, and awakened considerable doubt. The valley of the stream pursued a northwesterly direction, appearing below to turn sharply to the right, beyond which further view was cut off. It was, nevertheless, resolved to continue our road the next day down this valley, which we trusted still would prove that of the middle stream between the two great rivers. Towards the summit of this peak, the fields of snow were four or five feet deep on the northern side; and we saw several large hares, which had on their winter color, being white as the snow around them.

The winter day is short in the mountains, the sun having but a small space of sky to travel over in the visible part above our horizon; and the moment his rays are gone, the air is keenly cold. The interest of our work had detained us long, and it was after nightfall when we reached the camp.

28th.--To-day we went through the pass with all the camp, and, after a hard day's journey of twelve miles, encamped on a high point where the snow had been blown off, and the exposed grass afforded a scanty pasture for the animals. Snow and broken country together made our traveling difficult; we were often compelled to make large circuits, and ascend the highest and most exposed ridges, in order to avoid snow, which in other places was banked up to a great depth.

During the day a few Indians were seen circling around us on snow-shoes, and skimming along like birds; but we could not bring them within speaking distance.

Godey, who was a little distance from the camp, had sat down to tie his moccasins, when he heard a low whistle near, and, looking up, saw two Indians half hiding behind a rock about forty yards distant; they would not allow him to approach, but breaking into a laugh, skimmed off over the snow, seeming to have no idea of the power of firearms, and thinking themselves perfectly safe when beyond arm's length.

To-night we did not succeed in getting the howitzer into camp. This was the most laborious day we had yet passed through, the steep ascents and deep snow exhausting both men and animals. Our single chronometer had stopped during the day, and its error in time occasioned the loss of an eclipse of a satellite this evening. It had not preserved the rate with which we started from the Dalles, and this will account for the absence of longitudes along this interval of our journey.

29th.--From this height we could see, at a considerable distance below, yellow spots in the valley, which indicated that there was not much snow. One of these places we expected to reach to-night; and some time being required to bring up the gun, I went ahead with Mr. Fitzpatrick and a few men, leaving the camp to follow, in charge of Mr. Preuss. We followed a trail down a hollow where the Indians had descended, the snow being so deep that we never came near the ground; but this only made our descent the easier, and, when we reached a little affluent to the river, at the bottom, we suddenly found ourselves in presence of eight or ten Indians. They seemed to be watching our motions, and, like the others, at first were indisposed to let us approach, ranging themselves like birds on a fallen log, on the hill-side above our heads, where, being out of our reach, they thought themselves safe. Our friendly demeanor reconciled them, and, when we got near enough, they immediately stretched out to us handfuls of pine-nuts, which seemed an exercise of hospitality. We made them a few presents, and, telling us that their village was a few miles below, they went on to let their people know what we were. The principal stream still running through an impracticable canon, we ascended a very steep hill, which proved afterwards the last and fatal obstacle to our little howitzer, which was finally abandoned at this place. We passed through a small meadow a few miles below, crossing the river, which depth, swift current, and rock, made it difficult to ford; and, after a few more miles of very difficult trail, issued into a larger prairie bottom, at the farther end of which we encamped, in a position rendered strong by rocks and trees. The lower parts of the mountain were covered with the nut-pine. Several Indians appeared on the hill-side, reconnoitring the camp, and were induced to come in; others came in during the afternoon; and in the evening we held a council. The Indians immediately made it clear that the waters on which we were also belonged to the Great Basin, in the edge of which we had been since the 17th of December; and it became evident that we had still the great ridge on the left to cross before we could reach the Pacific waters.

We explained to the Indians that we were endeavoring to find a passage across the mountains into the country of the whites, whom we were going to see; and told them that we wished them to bring us a guide, to whom we would give presents of scarlet cloth, and other articles, which were shown to them. They looked at the reward we offered, and conferred with each other, but pointed to the snow on the mountain, and drew their hands across their necks, and raised them above their heads, to show the depth; and signified that it was impossible for us to get through. They made signs that we must go to the southward, over a pass through a lower range, which they pointed out: there, they said, at the end of one day's travel, we would find people who lived near a pass in the great mountain; and to that point they engaged to furnish us a guide. They appeared to have a confused idea, from report, of whites who lived on the other side of the mountain; and once, they told us, about two years ago, a party of twelve men like ourselves had ascended their river, and crossed to the other waters. They pointed out to us where they had crossed; but then, they said, it was summer time; but now it would be impossible. I believe that this was a party led by Mr. Chiles, one of the only two men whom I know to have passed through the California mountains from the interior of the Basin--Walker being the other; and both were engaged upwards of twenty days, in the summer time, in getting over. Chiles's destination was the bay of San Francisco, to which he descended by the Stanislaus river; and Walker subsequently informed me that, like myself, descending to the southward on a more eastern line, day after day he was searching for the Buenaventura, thinking that he had found it with every new stream, until, like me, he abandoned all idea of its existence, and, turning abruptly to the right, crossed the great chain. These were both western men, animated with the spirit of exploratory enterprise which characterizes that people.

The Indians brought in during the evening an abundant supply of pine-nuts, which we traded from them. When roasted, their pleasant flavor made them an agreeable addition to our now scanty store of provisions, which were reduced to a very low ebb. Our principal stock was in peas, which it is not necessary to say contain scarcely any nutriment. We had still a little flour left, some coffee, and a quantity of sugar, which I reserved as a defence against starvation.

The Indians informed us that at certain seasons they have fish in their waters, which we supposed to be salmon-trout: for the remainder of the year they live upon the pine-nuts, which form their great winter subsistence--a portion being always at hand, shut up in the natural storehouse of the cones. At present, they were presented to us as a whole people living upon this simple vegetable.

The other division of the party did not come in to-night, but encamped in the upper meadow, and arrived the next morning. They had not succeeded in getting the howitzer beyond the place mentioned, and where it had been left by Mr. Preuss, in obedience to my orders; and, in anticipation of the snow-banks and snow-fields still ahead, foreseeing the inevitable detention to which it would subject us, I reluctantly determined to leave it there for the time. It was of the kind invented by the French for the mountain part of their war in Algiers; and the distance it had come with us proved how well it was adapted to its purpose. We left it, to the great sorrow of the whole party, who were grieved to part with a companion which had made the whole distance from St. Louis, and commanded respect for us on some critical occasions, and which might be needed for the same purpose again.

30th.--Our guide, who was a young man, joined us this morning; and, leaving our encampment late in the day, we descended the river, which immediately opened out into a broad valley, furnishing good traveling ground. In a short distance we passed the village, a collection of straw huts; and a few miles below, the guide pointed out the place where the whites had been encamped, before they entered the mountain. With our late start we made but ten miles, and encamped on the low river-bottom, where there was no snow, but a great deal of ice; and we cut piles of long grass to lay under our blankets, and fires were made of large dry willows, groves of which wooded the stream. The river took here a northeasterly direction, and through a spur from the mountains on the left was the gap where we were to pass the next day.

31st.--We took our way over a gently rising ground, the dividing ridge being tolerably low; and traveling easily along a broad trail, in twelve or fourteen miles reached the upper part of the pass, when it began to snow thickly, with very cold weather. The Indians had only the usual scanty covering, and appeared to suffer greatly from the cold. All left us, except our guide. Half hidden by the storm, the mountains looked dreary; and, as night began to approach, the guide showed great reluctance to go forward. I placed him between two rifles, for the way began to be difficult. Traveling a little farther, we struck a ravine, which the Indian said would conduct us to the river; and as the poor fellow suffered greatly, shivering in the snow which fell upon his naked skin, I would not detain him any longer; and he ran off to the mountain, where he said was a hut near by. He had kept the blue and scarlet cloth I had given him tightly rolled up, preferring rather to endure the cold than to get them wet. In the course of the afternoon, one of the men had his foot frostbitten; and about dark we had the satisfaction to reach the bottoms of a stream timbered with large trees, among which we found a sheltered camp, with an abundance of such grass as the season afforded for the animals. We saw before us, in descending from the pass, a great continuous range, along which stretched the valley of the river; the lower parts steep, and dark with pines, while above it was hidden in clouds of snow. This we felt instantly satisfied was the central ridge of the Sierra Nevada, the great California mountain, which only now intervened between us and the waters of the bay. We had made a forced march of 26 miles, and three mules had given out on the road. Up to this point, with the exception of two stolen by Indians, we had lost none of the horses which had been brought from the Columbia river, and a number of these were still strong and in tolerably good order. We had now 67 animals in the band.

We had scarcely lighted our fires, when the camp was crowded with nearly naked Indians; some of them were furnished with long nets in addition to bows, and appeared to have been out on the sage hills to hunt rabbits. These nets were perhaps 30 to 40 feet long, kept upright in the ground by slight sticks at intervals, and were made from a kind of wild hemp, very much resembling in manufacture those common among the Indians of the Sacramento valley. They came among us without any fear, and scattered themselves about the fires, mainly occupied in gratifying their astonishment. I was struck by the singular appearance of a row of about a dozen, who were sitting on their haunches perched on a log near one of the fires, with their quick sharp eyes following every motion.

We gathered together a few of the most intelligent of the Indians, and held this evening an interesting council. I explained to them my intentions. I told them that we had come from a very far country, having been traveling now nearly a year, and that we were desirous simply to go across the mountain into the country of the other whites. There were two who appeared particularly intelligent--one, a somewhat old man. He told me that, before the snows fell, it was six sleeps to the place where the whites lived, but that now it was impossible to cross the mountain on account of the deep snow; and showing us, as the others had done, that it was over our heads, he urged us strongly to follow the course of the river, which he said would conduct us to a lake in which there were many large fish. There, he said, were many people; there was no snow on the ground; and we might remain there until the spring. From their descriptions, we were enabled to judge that we had encamped on the upper water of the Salmon Trout river. It is hardly necessary to say that our communication was only by signs, as we understood nothing of their language; but they spoke, notwithstanding, rapidly and vehemently, explaining what they considered the folly of our intentions, and urging us to go down to the lake. ***Tah-ve***, a word signifying snow, we very soon learned to know, from its frequent repetition. I told him that the men and the horses were strong, that we would break a road through the snow; and spreading before him our bales of scarlet cloth, and trinkets, showed him what we would give for a guide. It was necessary to obtain one, if possible; for I had determined here to attempt the passage of the mountain. Pulling a bunch of grass from the ground, after a short discussion among themselves, the old man made us comprehend, that if we could break through the snow, at the end of three days we would come down upon grass, which he showed us would be about six inches high, and where, the ground was entirely free. So far, he said, he had been in hunting for elk; but beyond that (and he closed his eyes) he had seen nothing; but there was one among them who had been to the whites, and, going out of the lodge, he returned with a young man of very intelligent appearance. Here, said he, is a young man who has seen the whites with his own eyes; and he swore, first by the sky, and then by the ground, that what he said was true. With a large present of goods, we prevailed upon this young man to be our guide, and he acquired among us the name of Melo--a word signifying friend, which they used very frequently. He was thinly clad, and nearly barefoot; his moccasins being about worn out. We gave him skins to make a new pair, and to enable him to perform his undertaking to us. The Indians remained in the camp during the night, and we kept the guide and two others to sleep in the lodge with us--Carson lying across the door, and having made them comprehend the use of our fire arms.

FEBRUARY.

1st.--The snow, which had intermitted in the evening, commenced falling again in the course of the night; and it snowed steadily all day. In the morning I acquainted the men with my decision, and explained to them that necessity required us to make a great effort to clear the mountains. I reminded them of the beautiful valley of the Sacramento, with which they were familiar from the descriptions of Carson, who had been there some fifteen years ago, and who, in our late privations, had delighted us in speaking of its rich pastures and abounding game, and drew a vivid contrast between its summer climate, less than a hundred miles distant, and the falling snow around us. I informed them (and long experience had given them confidence in my observations and good instruments) that almost directly west, and only about 70 miles distant, was the great farming establishment of Captain Sutter--a gentleman who had formerly lived in Missouri, and, emigrating to this country, had become the possessor of a principality. I assured them that, from the heights of the mountain before us, we should doubtless see the valley of the Sacramento river, and with one effort place ourselves again in the midst of plenty. The people received this decision with the cheerful obedience which had always characterized them, and the day was immediately devoted to the preparations necessary to enable us to carry it into effect. Leggins, moccasins, clothing--all were put into the best state to resist the cold. Our guide was not neglected. Extremity of suffering might make him desert; we therefore did the best we could for him. Leggins, moccasins, some articles of clothing, and a large green blanket, in addition to the blue and scarlet cloth, were lavished upon him, and to his great and evident contentment. He arrayed himself in all his colors, and, clad in green, blue, and scarlet, he made a gay-looking Indian; and, with his various presents, was probably richer and better clothed than any of his tribe had ever been before.

I have already said that our provisions were very low; we had neither tallow nor grease of any kind remaining, and the want of salt became one of our greatest privations. The poor dog which had been found in the Bear River valley, and which had been a *compagnon de voyage* ever since, had now become fat, and the mess to which it belonged, requested permission to kill it. Leave was granted. Spread out on the snow, the meat looked very good; and it made a strengthening meal for the greater part of the camp. Indians brought in two or three rabbits during the day, which were purchased from them.

The river was 40 to 70 feet wide, and now entirely frozen over. It was wooded with large cottonwood, willow, and *grain de boeuf*. By observation, the latitude of this encampment was 38 deg. 37' 18".

2d.--It had ceased snowing, and this morning the lower air was clear and frosty; and six or seven thousand feet above, the peaks of the Sierra now and then appeared among the rolling clouds, which were rapidly dispersing before the sun. Our Indian shook his head as he pointed to the icy pinnacles, shooting high up into the sky, and seeming almost immediately above us. Crossing the river on the ice, and leaving it immediately, we commenced the ascent of the mountain along the valley of a tributary stream. The people were unusually silent, for every man knew that our enterprise was hazardous; and the issue doubtful.

The snow deepened rapidly, and it soon became necessary to break a road. For this service, a party of ten was formed, mounted on the strongest horses, each man in succession opening the road on foot, or on horseback, until himself and his horse became fatigued, when he stepped aside, and, the remaining number passing ahead, he took his station in the rear. Leaving this stream, and pursuing a very direct course, we passed over an intervening ridge to the river we had left. On the way we passed two low huts entirely covered with snow, which might very easily have escaped observation. A family was living in each; and the only trail I saw in the neighborhood was from the door-hole to a nut-pine tree near, which supplied them with food and fuel. We found two similar huts on the creek where we next arrived; and, traveling a little higher up, encamped on its banks in about four feet depth of snow. Carson found near, an open hill-side, where the wind and the sun had melted the snow, leaving exposed sufficient bunch-grass for the animals to-night.

The nut-pines were now giving way to heavy timber, and there were some immense pines on the bottom, around the roots of which the sun had melted away the snow; and here we made our camp and built huge fires. To-day we had traveled 16 miles, and our elevation above the sea was 6,760 feet.

3d.--Turning our faces directly towards the main chain, we ascended an open hollow along a small tributary to the river, which, according to the Indians, issues from a mountain to the south. The snow was so deep in the hollow, that we were obliged to travel along the steep hill-sides, and over spurs, where the wind and sun had in places lessened the snow, and where the grass, which appeared to be in good quality along the sides of the mountains, was exposed. We opened our road in the same way as yesterday, but made only seven miles, and encamped by some springs at the foot of a high and steep hill, by which the hollow ascended to another basin in the mountain. The little stream below was entirely buried in snow. The springs were shaded by the boughs of a lofty cedar, which here made its first appearance; the usual height was 120 to 130 feet, and one that was measured near by was six feet in diameter.

There being no grass exposed here, the horses were sent back to that which we had seen a few miles below. We occupied the remainder of the day in beating down a road to the foot of the hill, a mile or two distant; the snow being beaten down when moist, in the warm part of the day, and then hard frozen at night, made a foundation that would bear the weight of the animals next morning. During the day several Indians joined us on snow-shoes. These were made of a circular hoop, about a foot in diameter, the interior space being filled with an open network of bark.

4th.--I went ahead early with two or three men, each with a led horse to break the road. We were obliged to abandon the hollow entirely, and work along the mountain-side, which was very steep, and the snow covered with an icy crust. We cut a footing as we advanced, and trampled a road through for the animals; but occasionally one plunged outside the trail, and slided along the field to the bottom, a hundred yards below. Late in the day we reached another bench in the hollow, where, in summer, the stream passed over a small precipice. Here was a short distance of dividing ground between the two ridges, and beyond an open basin, some ten miles across, whose bottom presented a field of snow. At the further or western side rose the middle crest of the mountain, a dark-looking ridge of volcanic rock.

The summit line presented a range of naked peaks, apparently destitute of snow and vegetation; but below, the face of the whole country was covered with timber of extraordinary size.

Towards a pass which the guide indicated here, we attempted in the afternoon to force a road; but after a laborious plunging through two or three hundred yards, our best horses gave out, entirely refusing to make any further effort, and, for the time, we were brought to a stand. The guide informed us that we were entering the deep snow, and here began the difficulties of the mountain; and to him, and almost to all, our enterprise seemed hopeless. I returned a short distance back, to the break in the hollow, where I met Mr. Fitzpatrick.

The camp had been occupied all the day in endeavoring to ascend the hill, but only the best horses had succeeded; the animals, generally, not having sufficient strength to bring themselves up without the packs; and all the line of road between this and the springs was strewed with camp-stores and equipage, and horses floundering in snow. I therefore immediately encamped on the ground with my own mess, which was in advance, and directed Mr. Fitzpatrick to encamp at the springs, and send all the animals, in charge of Tabeau, with a strong guard, back to the place where they had been pastured the night before. Here was a small spot of level ground, protected on one side by the mountain, and on the other sheltered by a little ridge of rock. It was an open grove of pines, which assimilated in size to the grandeur of the mountain, being frequently six feet in diameter.

To-night we had no shelter, but we made a large fire around the trunk of one of the huge pines; and covering the snow with small boughs, on which we spread our blankets, soon made ourselves comfortable. The night was very bright and clear, though the thermometer was only at 10 deg.. A strong wind, which sprang up at sundown, made it intensely cold; and this was one of the bitterest nights during the journey.

Two Indians joined our party here; and one of them, an old man, immediately began to harangue us, saying that ourselves and animals would perish in the snow; and that if we would go back, he would show us another and a better way across the mountain. He spoke in a very loud voice, and there was a singular repetition of phrases and arrangement of words, which rendered his speech striking and not unmusical.

We had now begun to understand some words, and, with the aid of signs, easily comprehended the old man's simple ideas. "Rock upon rock--rock upon rock--

snow upon snow," said he; "even if you get over the snow, you will not be able to get down from the mountains." He made us the sign of precipices, and showed us how the feet of the horses would slip, and throw them off from the narrow trails that led along their sides. Our Chinook, who comprehended even more readily than ourselves, and believed our situation hopeless, covered his head with his blanket, and began to weep and lament. "I wanted to see the whites," said he; "I came away from my own people to see the whites, and I wouldn't care to die among them, but here"--and he looked around into the cold night and gloomy forest, and, drawing his blanket over his head, began again to lament.

Seated around the tree, the fire illuminating the rocks and the tall bolls of the pines round about, and the old Indian haranguing, we presented a group of very serious faces.

5th.--The night had been too cold to sleep, and we were up very early. Our guide was standing by the fire with all his finery on; and seeing him shiver in the cold, I threw on his shoulders one of my blankets. We missed him a few minutes afterwards, and never saw him again. He had deserted. His bad faith and treachery were in perfect keeping with the estimate of Indian character, which a long intercourse with this people had gradually forced upon my mind.

While a portion of the camp were occupied in bringing up the baggage to this point, the remainder were busied in making sledges and snow-shoes. I had determined to explore the mountain ahead, and the sledges were to be used in transporting the baggage.

The mountains here consisted wholly of a white micaceous granite. The day was perfectly clear, and, while the sun was in the sky, warm and pleasant.

By observation our latitude was 38 deg. 42' 26"; and elevation by the boiling point, 7,400 feet.

6th.--Accompanied by Mr. Fitzpatrick, I set out to-day with a reconnoitring party on snow-shoes. We marched all in single file, trampling the snow as heavily as we could. Crossing the open basin, in a march of about ten miles we reached the top of one of the peaks, to the left of the pass indicated by our guide. Far below us, dimmed by the distance, was a large snowless valley, bounded on the western side, at the distance of about a hundred miles, by a low range of mountains, which Carson recognised with delight as the mountains bordering the coast. "There," said he, "is the little mountain--it is fifteen years since I saw it; but I am just as sure as if I had seen it yesterday." Between us, then, and this low coast range was the valley of the Sacramento; and no one who had not accompanied us through the incidents of our life for the last few months could realize the delight with which at last we looked down upon it. At the distance of apparently 30 miles beyond us were distinguished spots of prairie; and a dark line which could be traced with the glass, was imagined to be the course of the river; but we were evidently at a great height above the valley, and between us and the plains extended miles of snowy fields and broken ridges of pine-covered mountains.

It was late in the day when we turned towards the camp; and it grew rapidly cold as it drew towards night. One of the men became fatigued, and his feet began to freeze, and building a fire in the trunk of a dry old cedar, Mr. Fitzpatrick remained with him until his clothes could be dried, and he was in a condition to come on. After a day's march of 20 miles, we straggled into the camp one after another, at nightfall; the greater number excessively fatigued, only two of the party having ever traveled on snow-shoes before.

All our energies are now directed to getting our animals across the snow; and it was supposed that after all the baggage had been drawn with the sleighs over the trail we had made, it would be sufficiently hard to bear our animals. At several places between this point and the ridge, we had discovered some grassy spots, where the wind and sun had dispersed the snow from the sides of the hills, and these were to form resting-places to support the animals for a night in their passage across. On our way across we had set on fire several broken stumps, and dried trees, to melt holes in the snow for the camps. Its general depth was five feet; but we passed over places where it was 20 feet deep, as shown by the trees. With one party drawing sleighs loaded with baggage, I advanced to-day about four miles along the trail, and encamped at the first grassy spot, where we expected to bring our horses. Mr. Fitzpatrick, with another party, remained behind, to form an intermediate station between us and the animals.

8th.--The night has been extremely cold; but perfectly still, and beautifully clear. Before the sun appeared this morning, the thermometer was 3 deg. below zero; 1 deg. higher, when his rays struck the lofty peaks; and 0 deg. when they reached our camp.

Scenery and weather, combined, must render these mountains beautiful in summer; the purity and deep-blue color of the sky are singularly beautiful; the days are sunny and bright, and even warm in the noon hours; and if we could be free from the many anxieties that oppress us, even now we would be delighted here; but our provisions are getting fearfully scant. Sleighs arrived with baggage about ten o'clock; and leaving a portion of it here, we continued on for a mile and a half, and encamped at the foot of a long hill on this side of the open bottom.

Bernier and Godey, who yesterday morning had been sent to ascend a higher peak, got in, hungry and fatigued. They confirmed what we had already seen. Two other sleighs arrived in the afternoon; and the men being fatigued, I gave them all tea and sugar. Snow clouds began to rise in the S.S.W.; and, apprehensive of a storm, which would destroy our road, I sent the people back to Mr. Fitzpatrick, with directions to send for the animals in the morning. With me remained Mr. Preuss, Mr. Talbot, and Carson, with Jacob.

Elevation of the camp, by the boiling point, is 7,920 feet.

9th.--During the night the weather changed, the wind rising to a gale, and commencing to snow before daylight; before morning the trail was covered. We remained quiet in camp all day, in the course of which the weather improved. Four sleighs arrived towards evening, with the bedding of the men. We suffer much from the want of salt; and all the men are becoming weak from insufficient food.

10th.--Taplin was sent back with a few men to assist Mr. Fitzpatrick; and continuing on with three sleighs carrying a part of the baggage, we had the satisfaction to encamp within two and a half miles of the head of the hollow, and at the foot of the last mountain ridge. Here two large trees had been set on fire, and in the holes, where the snow had been melted away, we found a comfortable camp.

The wind kept the air filled with snow during the day; the sky was very dark in the southwest, though elsewhere very clear. The forest here has a noble appearance; and tall cedar is abundant; its greatest height being 130 feet, and circumference 20, three or four feet above the ground; and here I see for the first time the white pine, of which there are some magnificent trees. Hemlock spruce is among the timber, occasionally as large as eight feet in diameter, four feet above the ground; but, in ascending, it tapers rapidly to less than one foot at the height of eighty feet. I have not seen any higher than 130 feet, and the slight upper part is frequently broken off by the wind. The white spruce is frequent; and the red pine (***pinus colorado*** of the Mexicans) which constitutes the beautiful forest along the banks of the Sierra Nevada to the northward, is here the principal tree, not attaining a greater height than 140 feet, though with sometimes a diameter of 10. Most of these trees appeared to differ slightly from those of the same kind on the other side of the continent.

The elevation of the camp by the boiling point, is 8,050 feet. We are now 1,000 feet above the level of the South Pass in the Rocky mountains; and still we are not done ascending. The top of a flat ridge near was bare of snow, and very well sprinkled with bunch-grass, sufficient to pasture the animals two or three days; and this was to be their main point of support. This ridge is composed of a compact trap, or basalt of a columnar structure; over the surface are scattered large boulders of porous trap. The hills are in many places entirely covered with small fragments of volcanic rock.

Putting on our snow-shoes, we spent the afternoon in exploring a road ahead. The glare of the snow, combined with great fatigue, had rendered many of the people nearly blind; but we were fortunate in having some black silk handkerchiefs, which, worn as veils, very much relieved the eye.

11th.--High wind continued, and our trail this morning was nearly invisible--here and there indicated by a little ridge of snow. Our situation became tiresome and dreary, requiring a strong exercise of patience and resolution.

In the evening I received a message from Mr. Fitzpatrick, acquainting me with the utter failure of his attempt to get our mules and horses over the snow--the half-hidden trail had proved entirely too slight to support them, and they had broken through, and were plunging about or lying half buried in snow. He was occupied in endeavoring to get them back to his camp; and in the mean time sent to me for further instructions. I wrote to him to send the animals immediately back to their old pastures; and, after having made mauls and shovels, turn in all the strength of his party to open and beat a road through the snow, strengthening it with branches and boughs of the pines.

12th.--We made mauls, and worked hard at our end of the road all day. The wind was high, but the sun bright, and the snow thawing. We worked down the face of the hill, to meet the people at the other end. Towards sundown it began to grow cold, and we shouldered our mauls and trudged back to camp.

13th.--We continued to labor on the road; and in the course of the day had the satisfaction to see the people working down the face of the opposite hill, about three miles distant. During the morning we had the pleasure of a visit from Mr. Fitzpatrick, with the information that all was going on well. A party of Indians had passed on snow-shoes, who said they were going to the western side of the mountain after fish. This was an indication that the salmon were coming up the streams; and we could hardly restrain our impatience as we thought of them, and worked with increased vigor.

The meat train did not arrive this evening, and I gave Godey leave to kill our little dog, (Tlamath,) which he prepared in Indian fashion; scorching off the hair, and washing the skin with soap and snow, and then cutting it up into pieces, which were laid on the snow. Shortly afterwards, the sleigh arrived with a supply of horse-meat; and we had to-night an extraordinary dinner--pea-soup, mule, and dog.

14th.--The dividing ridge of the Sierra is in sight from this encampment. Accompanied by Mr. Preuss, I ascended to-day the highest peak to the right; from which we had a beautiful view of a mountain lake at our feet, about fifteen miles in length, and so entirely surrounded by mountains that we could not discover an outlet. We had taken with us a glass; but though we enjoyed an extended view, the valley was half hidden in mist, as when we had seen it before. Snow could be distinguished on the higher parts of the coast mountains; eastward, as far as the eye could extend, it ranged over a terrible mass of broken snowy mountains, fading off blue in the distance. The rock composing the summit consists of a very coarse, dark, volcanic conglomerate; the lower parts appeared to be of a slaty structure. The highest trees were a few scattering cedars and aspens. From the immediate foot of the peak, we were two hours reaching the summit, and one hour and a quarter in descending. The day had been very bright, still, and clear, and spring seems to be advancing rapidly. While the sun is in the sky, the snow melts rapidly, and gushing springs cover the face of the mountain in all the exposed places; but their surface freezes instantly with the disappearance of the sun.

I obtained to-night some observations; and the result from these, and others made during our stay, gives for the latitude 38 deg. 41' 57", longitude 120 deg. 25' 57", and rate of the chronometer 25.82".

16th.--We had succeeded in getting our animals safely to the first grassy hill;

and this morning I started with Jacob on a reconnoitring expedition beyond the mountain. We traveled along the crests of narrow ridges, extending down from the mountain in the direction of the valley, from which the snow was fast melting away. On the open spots was tolerably good grass; and I judged we should succeed in getting the camp down by way of these. Towards sundown we discovered some icy spots in a deep hollow; and, descending the mountain, we encamped on the head-water of a little creek, where at last the water found its way to the Pacific.

The night was clear and very long. We heard the cries of some wild animals, which had been attracted by our fire, and a flock of geese passed over during the night. Even these strange sounds had something pleasant to our senses in this region of silence and desolation.

We started again early in the morning. The creek acquired a regular breadth of about 20 feet, and we soon began to hear the rushing of the water below the icy surface, over which we traveled to avoid the snow; a few miles below we broke through, where the water was several feet deep, and halted to make a fire and dry our clothes. We continued a few miles farther, walking being very laborious without snow-shoes.

I was now perfectly satisfied that we had struck the stream on which Mr. Sutler lived; and, turning about, made a hard push, and reached the camp at dark. Here we had the pleasure to find all the remaining animals, 57 in number, safely arrived at the grassy hill near the camp; and here, also, we were agreeably surprised with the sight of an abundance of salt. Some of the horse-guard had gone to a neighboring hut for pine nuts, and discovered unexpectedly a large cake of very white fine-grained salt, which the Indians told them they had brought from the other side of the mountain; they used it to eat with their pine nuts, and readily sold it for goods.

On the 19th, the people were occupied in making a road and bringing up the baggage; and, on the afternoon of the next day, **February** 20, 1844, we encamped, with the animals and all the *materiel* of the camp, on the summit of the PASS in the dividing ridge, 1,000 miles by our traveled road from the Dalles to the Columbia.

The people, who had not yet been to this point, climbed the neighboring peak to enjoy a look at the valley.

The temperature of boiling water gave for the elevation of the encampment,

9,338 feet above the sea.

This was 2,000 feet higher than the South Pass in the Rocky mountains, and several peaks in view rose several thousand feet still higher. Thus, at the extremity of the continent, and near the coast, the phenomenon was seen of a range of mountains still higher than the great Rocky mountains themselves. This extraordinary fact accounts for the Great Basin, and shows that there must be a system of small lakes and rivers here scattered over a flat country, and which the extended and lofty range of the Sierra Nevada prevents from escaping to the Pacific ocean. Latitude 38 deg. 44'; longitude 120 deg. 28'.

Thus the Pass in the Sierra Nevada, which so well deserves its name of Snowy mountain, is eleven degrees west and about four degrees south of the South Pass.

21st.--We now considered ourselves victorious over the mountain; having only the descent before us, and the valley under our eyes, we felt strong hope that we should force our way down. But this was a case in which the descent was *not* facile. Still deep fields of snow lay between them, and there was a large intervening space of rough-looking mountains, through which we had yet to wind our way. Carson roused me this morning with an early fire, and we were all up long before day, in order to pass the snow-fields before the sun should render the crust soft. We enjoyed this morning a scene at sunrise, which even here was unusually glorious and beautiful. Immediately above the eastern mountains was repeated a cloud-formed mass of purple ranges, bordered with bright yellow gold; the peaks shot up into a narrow line of crimson cloud, above which the air was filled with a greenish orange; and over all was the singular beauty of the blue sky. Passing along a ridge which commanded the lake on our right, of which we began to discover an outlet through a chasm on the west, we passed over alternating open ground and hard-crusted snow-fields which supported the animals, and encamped on the ridge, after a journey of six miles. The grass was better than we had yet seen, and we were encamped in a clump of trees 20 or 30 feet high, resembling white pine. With the exception of these small clumps, the ridges were bare; and, where the snow found the support of the trees, the wind had blown it up into banks 10 or 15 feet high. It required much care to hunt out a practicable way, as the most open places frequently led to impassable banks.

We had hard and doubtful labor yet before us, as the snow appeared to be heavier where the timber began further down, with few open spots. Ascending a height, we traced out the best line we could discover for the next day's march, and had at least the consolation to see that the mountain descended rapidly. The day had been one of April--gusty, with a few occasional flakes of snow--which, in the afternoon, enveloped the upper mountain in clouds. We watched them anxiously, as now we dreaded a snow-storm. Shortly afterwards we heard the roll of thunder, and, looking towards the valley, found it enveloped in a thunder-storm. For us, as connected with the idea of summer, it had a singular charm, and we watched its progress with excited feelings until nearly sunset, when the sky cleared off brightly, and we saw a shining line of water directing its course towards another, a broader and larger sheet. We knew that these could be no other than the Sacramento and the Bay of San Francisco; but, after our long wandering in rugged mountains, where so frequently we had met with disappointments, and where the crossing of every ridge displayed some unknown lake or river, we were yet almost afraid to believe that we were at last to escape into the genial country of which we had heard so many glowing descriptions, and dreaded to find some vast interior lake, whose bitter waters would bring us disappointment. On the southern shore of what appeared to be the bay could be traced the gleaming line where entered another large stream; and again the Buenaventura rose up in our minds.

Carson had entered the valley along the southern side of the bay, and remembered perfectly to have crossed the mouth of a very large stream, which they had been obliged to raft; but the country then was so entirely covered with water from snow and rain, that he had been able to form no correct impressions of watercourses.

We had the satisfaction to know that at least there were people below. Fires were lit up in the valley just at night, appearing to be in answer to ours; and these signs of life renewed, in some measure, the gayety of the camp. They appeared so near, that we judged them to be among the timber of some of the neighboring ridges; but, having them constantly in view day after day, and night after night, we afterwards found them to be fires that had been kindled by the Indians among the *tulares*, on the shore of the bay, 80 miles distant.

Among the very few plants that appeared here, was the common blue flax. To-night a mule was killed for food.

22d.--Our breakfast was over long before day. We took advantage of the coolness of the early morning to get over the snow, which to-day occurred in very deep banks among the timber; but we searched out the coldest places, and the animals passed successfully with their loads over the hard crust. Now and then the delay of making a road occasioned much labor and loss of time. In the after part of the day, we saw before us a handsome grassy ridge point; and, making a desperate push over a snow-field 10 to 15 feet deep, we happily succeeded in getting the camp across, and encamped on the ridge, after a march of three miles. We had again the prospect of a thunder-storm below, and to-night we killed another mule-- now our only resource from starvation.

We satisfied ourselves during the day that the lake had an outlet between two ranges on the right; and with this, the creek on which I had encamped probably effected a junction below. Between these, we were descending.

We continued to enjoy the same delightful weather; the sky of the same beautiful blue, and such a sunset and sunrise as on our Atlantic coast we could scarcely imagine. And here among the mountains, 9,000 feet above the sea, we have the deep-blue sky and sunny climate of Smyrna and Palermo, which a little map before me shows are in the same latitude.

The elevation above the sea, by the boiling point, is 8,565 feet.

23d.--This was our most difficult day; we were forced off the ridges by the quantity of snow among the timber, and obliged to take to the mountain sides, where occasionally rocks and a southern exposure afforded us a chance to scramble along. But these were steep, and slippery with snow and ice; and the tough evergreens of the mountain impeded our way, tore our skins, and exhausted our patience. Some of us had the misfortune to wear moccasins with *parfleche* soles, so slippery that we could not keep our feet, and generally crawled across the snow-beds. Axes and mauls were necessary to-day, to make a road through the snow. Going ahead with Carson to reconnoitre the road, we reached in the afternoon the river which made the outlet of the lake. Carson sprang over, clear across a place where the stream was compressed among rocks, but the *parfleche* sole of my moccasin glanced from the icy rock, and precipitated me into the river. It was some few seconds before I could recover myself in the current, and Carson, thinking me hurt, jumped in after me, and we both had an icy bath. We tried to search awhile for my gun, which had been lost in the fall, but the cold drove us out; and making a large fire on the bank, after we had partially dried ourselves we went back to meet the camp. We afterwards found that the gun had been slung under the ice which lined the banks of the creek.

Using our old plan of breaking roads with alternate horses, we reached the creek in the evening, and encamped on a dry open place in the ravine.

Another branch, which we had followed, here comes in on the left; and from this point the mountain wall, on which we had traveled to-day, faces to the south along the right bank of the river, where the sun appears to have melted the snow; but the opposite ridge is entirely covered. Here, among the pines, the hill-side produces but little grass--barely sufficient to keep life in the animals. We had the pleasure to be rained upon this afternoon; and grass was now our greatest solicitude. Many of the men looked badly; and some this evening were giving out.

24th.--We rose at three in the morning for an astronomical observation, and obtained for the place a lat. of 38 deg. 46' 58"; long. 120 deg. 34' 20". The sky was clear and pure, with a sharp wind from the northeast, and the thermometer 2 deg. below the freezing point.

We continued down the south face of the mountain; our road leading over dry ground, we were able to avoid the snow almost entirely. In the course of the morning, we struck a footpath, which we were generally able to keep; and the ground was soft to our animals' feet, being sandy, or covered with mould. Green grass began to make its appearance, and occasionally we passed a hill scatteringly covered with it. The character of the forest continued the same; and, among the trees, the pine with sharp leaves and very large cones was abundant, some of them being noble trees. We measured one that had 10 feet diameter, though the height was not more than 130 feet. All along, the river was a roaring torrent, its fall very great; and, descending with a rapidity to which we had long been strangers, to our great pleasure oak-trees appeared on the ridge, and soon became very frequent; on these I remarked great quantities of mistletoe. Rushes began to make their appearance; and at a small creek where they were abundant, one of the messes was left with the weakest horses, while we continued on.

The opposite mountain-side was very steep and continuous--unbroken by ravines, and covered with pines and snow; while on the side we were traveling, innumerable rivulets poured down from the ridge. Continuing on, we halted a moment at one of these rivulets, to admire some beautiful evergreen-trees, resembling live-oak, which shaded the little stream. They were forty to fifty feet high, and two in diameter, with a uniform tufted top; and the summer green of their beautiful foliage, with the singing birds, and the sweet summer wind which was whirling about the dry oak leaves, nearly intoxicated us with delight; and we hurried on, filled with excitement, to escape entirely from the horrid region of inhospitable snow, to the perpetual spring of the Sacramento.

When we had traveled about ten miles, the valley opened a little to an oak and pine bottom, through which ran rivulets closely bordered with rushes, on which our half-starved horses fell with avidity; and here we made our encampment. Here the roaring torrent has already become a river, and we had descended to an elevation of 3,864 feet.

Along our road to-day the rock was a white granite, which appears to constitute the upper part of the mountains on both the eastern and western slopes; while between, the central is a volcanic rock.

Another horse was killed to-night, for food.

25th.--Believing that the difficulties of the road were passed, and leaving Mr. Fitzpatrick to follow slowly, as the condition of the animals required, I started ahead this morning with a party of eight, consisting of myself, Mr. Preuss and Mr. Talbot, Carson, Derosier, Towns, Proue, and Jacob. We took with us some of the best animals, and my intention was to proceed as rapidly as possible to the house of Mr. Sutter, and return to meet the party with a supply of provisions and fresh animals.

Continuing down the river, which pursued a very direct westerly course through a narrow valley, with only a very slight and narrow bottom-land, we made twelve miles, and encamped at some old Indian huts, apparently a fishing-place on the river. The bottom was covered with trees of deciduous foliage, and overgrown with vines and rushes. On a bench of the hill near by, was a hill of fresh green grass, six inches long in some of the tufts which I had the curiosity to measure. The animals were driven here; and I spent part of the afternoon sitting on a large rock among them, enjoying the pauseless rapidity with which they luxuriated on the unaccustomed food.

The forest was imposing to-day in the magnificence of the trees; some of the pines, bearing large cones, were 10 feet in diameter. Cedars also abounded, and we measured one 28 1/2 feet in circumference, four feet from the ground. This noble tree seemed here to be in its proper soil and climate. We found it on both sides of the Sierra, but most abundant on the west.

26th.--We continued to follow the stream, the mountains on either hand increasing in height as we descended, and shutting up the river narrowly in precipices, along which we had great difficulty to get our horses.

It rained heavily during the afternoon, and we were forced off the river to the heights above; whence we descended, at night-fall, the point of a spur between the river and a fork of nearly equal size, coming in from the right. Here we saw, on the lower hills, the first flowers in bloom, which occurred suddenly, and in considerable quantity--one of them a species of *gilia*.

The current in both streams (rather torrents than rivers) was broken by large boulders. It was late, and the animals fatigued; and not succeeding to find a ford immediately, we encamped, although the hill-side afforded but a few stray bunches of grass, and the horses, standing about in the rain, looked very miserable.

27th.--We succeeded in fording the stream, and made a trail by which we crossed the point of the opposite hill, which, on the southern exposure, was prettily covered with green grass, and we halted a mile from our last encampment. The river was only about 60 feet wide, but rapid, and occasionally deep, foaming among boulders, and the water beautifully clear. We encamped on the hill-slope, as there was no bottom level, and the opposite ridge is continuous, affording no streams.

We had with us a large kettle; and a mule being killed here, his head was boiled in it for several hours, and made a passable soup for famished people.

Below, precipices on the river forced us to the heights, which we ascended by a steep spur 2,000 feet high. My favorite horse, Proveau, had become very weak, and was scarcely able to bring himself to the top. Traveling here was good, except in crossing the ravines, which were narrow, steep, and frequent. We caught a glimpse of a deer, the first animal we had seen; but did not succeed in approaching him. Proveau could not keep up, and I left Jacob to bring him on, being obliged to press forward with the party, as there was no grass in the forest. We grew very anxious as the day advanced and no grass appeared, for the lives of our animals depended on finding it to-night. They were in just such a condition that grass and repose for the night enabled them to get on the next day. Every hour we had been expecting to see open out before us the valley, which, from the mountain above, seemed almost at our feet. A new and singular shrub, which had made its appearance since crossing the mountain, was very frequent to- day. It branched out near the ground, forming a clump eight to ten feet high, with pale-green leaves, of an oval form; and the body and branches had a naked appearance, as if stripped of the bark, which is very smooth and thin, of a chocolate color, contrasting well with the pale green of the leaves. The day was nearly gone; we had made a hard day's march, and found no grass. Towns became light-headed, wandering off into the woods without knowing where he was going, and Jacob brought him back.

Near night-fall we descended into the steep ravine of a handsome creek 30 feet wide, and I was engaged in getting the horses up the opposite hill, when I heard a shout from Carson, who had gone ahead a few hundred yards-- "Life yet," said he, as he came up, "life yet; I have found a hill-side sprinkled with grass enough for the night." We drove along our horses, and encamped at the place about dark, and there was just room enough to make a place for shelter on the edge of the stream. Three horses were lost to- day--Proveau; a fine young horse from the Columbia, belonging to Charles Towns; and another Indian horse, which carried our cooking utensils. The two former gave out, and the latter strayed off into the woods as we reached the camp.

29th.--We lay shut up in the narrow ravine, and gave the animals a necessary day; and men were sent back after the others. Derosier volunteered to bring up Proveau, to whom he knew I was greatly attached, as he had been my favorite horse on both expeditions. Carson and I climbed one of the nearest mountains; the forest land still extended ahead, and the valley appeared as far as ever. The pack-horse was found near the camp; but Derosier did not get in.

MARCH.

1st.--Derosier did not get in during the night, and leaving him to follow, as no grass remained here, we continued on over the uplands, crossing many small streams, and camped again on the river, having made six miles. Here we found the hillside covered (although lightly) with fresh green grass; and from this time forward we found it always improving and abundant.

We made a pleasant camp on the river hill, where were some beautiful specimens of the chocolate-colored shrub, which were a foot in diameter near the ground, and fifteen to twenty feet high. The opposite ridge runs continuously along, unbroken by streams. We are rapidly descending into the spring, and we are leaving our snowy region far behind; every thing is getting green; butterflies are swarming; numerous bugs are creeping out, wakened from their winter's sleep; and the forest flowers are coming into bloom. Among those which appeared most numerously today was ***dodecatheon dentatum***.

We began to be uneasy at Derosier's absence, fearing he might have been bewildered in the woods. Charles Towns, who had not yet recovered his mind, went to swim in the river, as if it were summer, and the stream placid, when it was a cold mountain torrent foaming among the rocks. We were happy to see Derosier appear in the evening. He came in, and, sitting down by the fire, began to tell us where he had been. He imagined he had been gone several days, and thought we were still at the camp where he had left us; and we were pained to see that his mind was deranged. It appeared that he had been lost in the mountain, and hunger and fatigue, joined to weakness of body and fear of perishing in the mountains, had crazed him. The times were severe when stout men lost their minds from extremity of suffering--when horses died--and when mules and horses, ready to die of starvation, were killed for food. Yet there was no murmuring or hesitation.

A short distance below our encampment the river mountains terminated in precipices, and, after a fatiguing march of only a few miles, we encamped on a bench where there were springs, and an abundance of the freshest grass. In the mean time, Mr. Preuss continued on down the river, and, unaware that we had encamped so early in the day, was lost. When night arrived, and he did not come in, we began to understand what had happened to him; but it was too late to make any search.

3d.--We followed Mr. Preuss' trail for a considerable distance along the river, until we reached a place where he had descended to the stream below and encamped. Here we shouted and fired guns, but received no answer; and we concluded that he had pushed on down the stream. I determined to keep out from the river, along which it was nearly impracticable to travel with animals, until it should form a valley. At every step the country improved in beauty; the pines were rapidly disappearing, and oaks became the principal trees of the forest. Among these, the prevailing tree was the evergreen oak, (which, by way of distinction, we call the *live- oak*;) and with these occurred frequently a new species of oak bearing a long slender acorn, from an inch to an inch and a half in length, which we now began to see formed the principal vegetable food of the inhabitants of this region. In a short distance we crossed a little rivulet, where were two old huts, and near by were heaps of acorn hulls. The ground round about was very rich, covered with an exuberant sward of grass; and we sat down for a while in the shade of the oaks, to let the animals feed. We repeated our shouts for Mr. Preuss; and this time were gratified with an answer. The voice grew rapidly nearer, ascending from the river; but when we expected to see him emerge, it ceased entirely. We had called up some straggling Indian--the first we had met, although for two days back we had seen tracks--who, mistaking us for his fellows, had been only undeceived on getting close up. It would have been pleasant to witness his astonishment; he would not have been more frightened had some of the old mountain spirits they are so much afraid of suddenly appeared in his path. Ignorant of the character of these people, we had now an additional cause of uneasiness in regard to Mr. Preuss; he had no arms with him, and we began to think his chance doubtful. We followed on a trail, still keeping out from the river, and descended to a very large creek, dashing with great velocity over a pre-eminently rocky bed, and among large boulders. The bed had sudden breaks, formed by deep holes and ledges of rock running across. Even here, it deserves the name of **Rock** creek, which we gave to it. We succeeded in fording it, and toiled about three thousand feet up the opposite hill. The mountains now were getting sensibly lower; but still there is no valley on the river, which presents steep and rocky banks; but here, several miles from the river, the country is smooth and grassy; the forest has no undergrowth; and in the open valleys of rivulets, or around spring-heads, the low groves of live-oak give the appearance of orchards in an old cultivated country. Occasionally we met deer, but had not the necessary time for hunting. At one of these orchard- grounds, we encamped about noon to make an effort for Mr. Preuss. One man took his way along a spur leading into the river, in hope to cross his trail; and another took our own back. Both were volunteers; and to the successful man was promised a pair of pistols--not as a reward, but as a token of gratitude for a service which would free us all from much anxiety.

    We had among our few animals a horse which was so much reduced, that, with traveling, even the good grass could nor save him; and, having nothing to eat, he was killed this afternoon. He was a good animal, and had made the journey round from Fort Hall.

Dodecatheon dentatum continued the characteristic plant in flower; and the naked-looking shrub already mentioned continued characteristic, beginning to put forth a small white blossom. At evening the men returned, having seen or heard nothing of Mr. Preuss; and I determined to make a hard push down the river the next morning and get ahead of him.

4th.--We continued rapidly along on a broad plainly-beaten trail, the mere traveling and breathing the delightful air being a positive enjoyment. Our road led along a ridge inclining to the river, and the air and the open grounds were fragrant with flowering shrubs; and in the course of the morning we issued on an open spur, by which we descended directly to the stream. Here the river issues suddenly from the mountains, which hitherto had hemmed it closely in; these now become softer, and change sensibly their character; and at this point commences the most beautiful valley in which we had ever traveled. We hurried to the river, on which we noticed a small sand beach, to which Mr. Preuss would naturally have gone. We found no trace of him, but, instead, were recent tracks of bare-footed Indians, and little piles of muscle-shells, and old fires where they had roasted the fish. We traveled on over the river grounds, which were undulating, and covered with grass to the river brink. We halted to noon a few miles beyond, always under the shade of the evergreen oaks, which formed open groves on the bottoms.

Continuing our road in the afternoon, we ascended to the uplands, where the river passes round a point of great beauty, and goes through very remarkable dalles, in character resembling those of the Columbia. Beyond, we again descended to the bottoms, where we found an Indian village, consisting of two or three huts; we had come upon them suddenly, and the people had evidently just run off. The huts were low and slight, made like beehives in a picture, five or six feet high, and near each was a crate, formed of interlaced branches and grass, in size and shape like a very large hogshead. Each of these contained from six to nine bushels. These were filled with the long acorns already mentioned, and in the huts were several neatly-made baskets, containing quantities of the acorns roasted. They were sweet and agreeably flavored, and we supplied ourselves with about half a bushel, leaving one of our shirts, a handkerchief, and some smaller articles, in exchange. The river again entered for a space among the hills, and we followed a trail leading across a bend through a handsome hollow behind. Here, while engaged in trying to circumvent a deer, we discovered some Indians on a hill several hundred yards ahead, and gave them a shout, to which they responded by loud and rapid talking and vehement gesticulation, but made no stop, hurrying up the mountain as fast as their legs could carry them. We passed on, and again encamped in a grassy grove.

The absence of Mr. Preuss gave me great concern; and, for a large reward, Derosier volunteered to go back on the trail. I directed him to search along the river, traveling upward for the space of a day and a half, at which time I expected he would meet Mr. Fitzpatrick, whom I requested to aid in the search; at all events, he was to go no farther, but return to this camp, where a *cache* of provisions was made for him.

Continuing the next day down the river, we discovered three squaws in a little bottom, and surrounded them before they could make their escape. They had large conical baskets, which they were engaged in filling with a small leafy plant (*erodium cicutarium*) just now beginning to bloom, and covering the ground like a sward of grass. These did not make any lamentations, but appeared very much impressed with our appearance, speaking to us only in a whisper, and offering us smaller baskets of the plant, which they signified to us was good to eat, making signs also that it was to be cooked by the fire. We drew out a little cold horse-meat, and the squaws made signs to us that the men had gone out after deer, and that we could have some by waiting till they came in. We observed that the horses ate with great avidity the herb which they had been gathering; and here also, for the first time, we saw Indians eat the common grass--one of the squaws pulling several tufts, and eating it with apparent relish. Seeing our surprise, she pointed to the horses; but we could not well understand what she meant, except, perhaps, that what was good for the one was good for the other.

We encamped in the evening on the shore of the river, at a place where the associated beauties of scenery made so strong an impression on us that we gave it the name of the Beautiful Camp. The undulating river shore was shaded with the live-oaks, which formed a continuous grove over the country, and the same grassy sward extended to the edge of the water, and we made our fires near some large granite masses which were lying among the trees. We had seen several of the acorn *caches* during the day, and here there were two which were very large, containing each, probably, ten bushels. Towards evening we heard a weak shout among the hills behind, and had the pleasure to see Mr. Preuss descending towards the camp. Like ourselves, he had traveled to-day 25 miles, but had seen nothing of Derosier. Knowing, on the day he was lost, that I was determined to keep the river as much as possible, he had not thought it necessary to follow the trail very closely, but walked on, right and left, certain to find it somewhere along the river, searching places to obtain good views of the country. Towards sunset he climbed down towards the river to look for the camp; but, finding no trail, concluded that we were behind, and walked back till night came on, when, being very much fatigued, he collected drift-wood and made a large fire among the rocks. The next day it became more serious and he encamped again alone, thinking that we must have taken some other course. To go back would have been madness in his weak and starved condition, and onward towards the valley was his only hope, always in expectation of reaching it soon. His principal means of subsistence were a few roots, which the hunters call sweet onions, having very little taste, but a good deal of nutriment, growing generally in rocky ground, and requiring a good deal of labor to get, as he had only a pocket-knife. Searching for these, he found a nest of big ants, which he let run on his hand, and stripped them off in his mouth; these had an agreeable acid taste. One of his greatest privations was the want of tobacco; and a pleasant smoke at evening would have been a relief which only a voyageur could appreciate. He tried the dried leaves of the live-oak, knowing that those of other oaks were sometimes used as a substitute; but these were too thick, and would not do. On the 4th he made seven or eight miles, walking slowly along the river, avoiding as much as possible to climb the hills. In little pools he caught some of the smallest kind of frogs, which he swallowed, not so much in the gratification of hunger, as in the hope of obtaining some strength. Scattered along the river were old fire- places, where the Indians had roasted muscles and acorns; but though he searched diligently, he did not there succeed in finding either. He had collected firewood for the night, when he heard, at some distance from the river, the barking of what he thought were two dogs, and walked in that direction as quickly as he was able, hoping to find there some Indian hut, but met only two wolves; and, in his disappointment, the gloom of the forest was doubled.

Traveling the next day feebly down the river, he found five or six Indians at the huts of which we have spoken: some were painting themselves black, and others roasting acorns. Being only one man, they did not run off, but received him kindly, and gave him a welcome supply of roasted acorns. He gave them his pocket-knife in return, and stretched out his hand to one of the Indians, who did not appear to comprehend the motion, but jumped back, as if he thought he was about to lay hold of him. They seemed afraid of him, not certain as to what he was.

Traveling on, he came to the place where we had found the squaws. Here he found our fire still burning, and the tracks of the horses. The sight gave him sudden hope and courage; and, following as fast as he could, joined us at evening.

6th.--We continued on our road through the same surpassingly beautiful country, entirely unequalled for the pasturage of stock by any thing we had ever seen. Our horses had now become so strong that they were able to carry us, and we traveled rapidly--over four miles an hour; four of us riding every alternate hour. Every few hundred yards we came upon a little band of deer; but we were too eager to reach the settlement, which we momentarily expected to discover, to halt for any other than a passing shot. In a few hours we reached a large fork, the northern branch of the river, and equal in size to that which we had descended. Together they formed a beautiful stream, 60 to 100 yards wide; which at first, ignorant of the nature of the country through which that river ran, we took to be the Sacramento.

We continued down the right bank of the river, traveling for a while over a wooded upland, where we had the delight to discover tracks of cattle. To the southwest was visible a black column of smoke, which we had frequently noticed in descending, arising from the fires we had seen from the top of the Sierra. From the upland we descended into broad groves on the river, consisting of the evergreen, and a new species of a white-oak, with a large tufted top, and three to six feet in diameter. Among these was no brushwood; and the grassy surface gave to it the appearance of parks in an old-settled country. Following the tracks of the horses and cattle, in search of people, we discovered a small village of Indians. Some of these had on shirts of civilized manufacture, but were otherwise naked, and we could understand nothing from them: they appeared entirely astonished at seeing us.

We made an acorn meal at noon, and hurried on; the valley being gay with flowers, and some of the banks being absolutely golden with the Californian poppy, (*escescholtzia crocea*.) Here the grass was smooth and green, and the groves very open; the large oaks throwing a broad shade among sunny spots. Shortly afterwards we gave a shout at the appearance, on a little bluff, of a neatly-built *adobe* house, with glass windows. We rode up, but, to our disappointment, found only Indians. There was no appearance of cultivation, and we could see no cattle; and we supposed the place had been abandoned. We now pressed on more eagerly than ever: the river swept round a large bend to the right; the hills lowered down entirely; and, gradually entering a broad valley, we came unexpectedly into a large Indian village, where the people looked clean, and wore cotton shirts and various other articles of dress. They immediately crowded around us, and we had the inexpressible delight to find one who spoke a little indifferent Spanish, but who at first confounded us by saying there were no whites in the country; but just then a well-dressed Indian came up, and made his salutations in very well-spoken Spanish. In answer to our inquiries, he informed us that we were upon the *Rio de los Americanos*, (the river of the Americans,) and that it joined the Sacramento river about ten miles below. Never did a name sound more sweetly! We felt ourselves among our countrymen; for the name of *American*, in these distant parts, is applied to the citizens of the United States. To our eager inquiries he answered, "I am a *vaquero* (cowherd) in the service of Capt. Sutter, and the people of this *rancheria* work for him." Our evident satisfaction made him communicative; and he went on to say that Capt. Sutter was a very rich man, and always glad to see his country people. We asked for his house.

He answered, that it was just over the hill before us; and offered, if we would wait a moment, to take his horse and conduct us to it. We readily accepted this civil offer. In a short distance we came in sight of the fort; and, passing on the way the house of a settler on the opposite side, (a Mr. Sinclair,) we forded the river; and in a few miles were met, a short distance from the fort, by Capt. Sutter himself. He gave us a most frank and cordial reception--conducted us immediately to his residence--and under his hospitable roof we had a night of rest, enjoyment, and refreshment, which none but ourselves could appreciate. But the party left in the mountains, with Mr. Fitzpatrick, were to be attended to; and the next morning, supplied with fresh horses and provisions, I hurried off to meet them. On the second day we met, a few miles below the forks of the Rio de los Americanos; and a more forlorn and pitiable sight than they presented, cannot well be imagined. They were all on foot--each man, weak and emaciated, leading a horse or mule as weak and emaciated as themselves. They had experienced great difficulty in descending the mountains, made slippery by rains and melting snows, and many horses fell over precipices, and were killed; and with some were lost the **packs** they carried. Among these, was a mule with the plants which we had collected since leaving Fort Hall, along a line of 2,000 miles' travel. Out of 67 horses and mules, with which we commenced crossing the Sierra, only 33 reached the valley of the Sacramento, and they only in a condition to be led along. Mr. Fitzpatrick and his party, traveling more slowly, had been able to make some little exertion at hunting, and had killed a few deer. The scanty supply was a great relief to them; for several had been made sick by the strange and unwholesome food which the preservation of life compelled them to use. We stopped and encamped as soon as we met; and a repast of good beef, excellent bread, and delicious salmon, which I had brought along, was their first relief from the sufferings of the Sierra, and their first introduction to the luxuries of the Sacramento. It required all our philosophy and forbearance to prevent **plenty** from becoming as hurtful to us now, as *scarcity* had been before.

The next day, March 8th, we encamped at the junction of the two rivers, the Sacramento and Americanos; and thus found the whole party in the beautiful valley of the Sacramento. It was a convenient place for the camp; and, among other things, was within reach of the wood necessary to make the pack-saddles, which we should need on our long journey home, from which we were farther distant now than we were four months before, when from the Dalles of the Columbia we so cheerfully took up the homeward line of march.

Captain Sutter emigrated to this country from the western part of Missouri in 1838-39, and formed the first settlement in the valley, on a large grant of land which he obtained from the Mexican Government. He had, at first, some trouble with the Indians; but, by the occasional exercise of well-timed authority, he has succeeded in converting them into a peaceable and industrious people. The ditches around his extensive wheat-fields; the making of the sun-dried bricks, of which his fort is constructed; the ploughing, harrowing, and other agricultural operations, are entirely the work of these Indians, for which they receive a very moderate compensation--principally in shirts, blankets, and other articles of clothing. In the same manner, on application to the chief of a village, he readily obtains as many boys and girls as he has any use for. There were at this time a number of girls at the fort, in training for a future woolen factory; but they were now all busily engaged in constantly watering the gardens, which the unfavorable dryness of the season rendered necessary. The occasional dryness of some seasons, I understood to be the only complaint of the settlers in this fertile valley, as it sometimes renders the crops uncertain. Mr. Sutter was about making arrangements to irrigate his lands by means of the Rio de los Americanos. He had this year sown, and altogether by Indian labor, three hundred fanegas of wheat.

A few years since, the neighboring Russian establishment of Ross, being about to withdraw from the country, sold to him a large number of stock, with agricultural and other stores, with a number of pieces of artillery and other munitions of war; for these, a regular yearly payment is made in grain.

The fort is a quadrangular ***adobe*** structure, mounting twelve pieces of artillery, (two of them brass,) and capable of admitting a garrison of a thousand men; this, at present, consists of forty Indians in uniform-- one of whom was always found on duty at the gate. As might naturally be expected, the pieces are not in very good order. The whites in the employment of Capt. Sutter, American, French, and German, amount, perhaps, to thirty men. The inner wall is formed into buildings, comprising the common quarters, with blacksmith and other workshops; the dwelling-house, with a large distillery-house, and other buildings, occupying more the centre of the area.

It is built upon a pond-like stream, at times a running creek communicating with the Rio de los Americanos, which enters the Sacramento about two miles below. The latter is here a noble river, about three hundred yards broad, deep and tranquil, with several fathoms of water in the channel, and its banks continuously timbered. There were two vessels belonging to Capt. Sutter at anchor near the landing--one a large two- masted lighter, and the other a schooner, which was shortly to proceed on a voyage to Fort Vancouver for a cargo of goods.

Since his arrival, several other persons, principally Americans, have established themselves in the valley. Mr. Sinclair, from whom I experienced much kindness during my stay, is settled a few miles distant, on the Rio de los Americanos. Mr.

Coudrois, a gentleman from Germany, has established himself on Feather river, and is associated with Capt. Sutter in agricultural pursuits. Among other improvements, they are about to introduce the cultivation of rape-seed, (***brassica rapus***,) which there is every reason to believe is admirably adapted to the climate and soil. The lowest average produce of wheat, as far as we can at present know, is thirty-five fanegas for one sown; but, as an instance of its fertility, it may be mentioned that Senor Valejo obtained, on a piece of ground where sheep had been pastured, 800 fanegas for eight sown. The produce being different in various places, a very correct idea cannot be formed.

An impetus was given to the active little population by our arrival, as we were in want of every thing. Mules, horses, and cattle, were to be collected; the horse-mill was at work day and night, to make sufficient flour; the blacksmith's shop was put in requisition for horse-shoes and bridle-bits; and pack-saddles, ropes, and bridles, and all the other little equipments of the camp, were again to be provided.

The delay thus occasioned was one of repose and enjoyment, which our situation required, and, anxious as we were to resume our homeward journey, was regretted by no one. In the mean time, I had the pleasure to meet with Mr. Chiles, who was residing at a farm on the other side of the river Sacramento, while engaged in the selection of a place for a settlement, for which he had received the necessary grant of land from the Mexican government.

It will be remembered that we had parted near the frontier of the states, and that he had subsequently descended the valley of Lewis's fork, with a party of ten or twelve men, with the intention of crossing the intermediate mountains to the waters of the Bay of San Francisco. In the execution of this design, and aided by subsequent information, he left the Columbia at the mouth of ***Malheur*** river, and, making his way to the head-waters of the Sacramento with a part of his company, traveled down that river to the settlements of Nueva Helvetia. The other party, to whom he had committed his wagons, and mill-irons, and saws, took a course further to the south, and the wagons and their contents were lost.

On the 22d we made a preparatory move, and encamped near the settlement of Mr. Sinclair, on the left bank of the Rio de los Americanos. I had discharged five of the party; Neal, the blacksmith, (an excellent workman, and an unmarried man, who had done his duty faithfully, and had been of very great service to me,) desired to remain, as strong inducements were offered here to mechanics.

Although at considerable inconvenience to myself, his good conduct induced me to comply with his request; and I obtained for him from Capt. Sutter, a present compensation of two dollars and a half per diem, with a promise that it should be increased to five, if he proved as good a workman as had been represented. He was more particularly an agricultural blacksmith. The other men were discharged with their own consent.

While we remained at this place, Derosier, one of our best men, whose steady good conduct had won my regard, wandered off from the camp, and never returned to it again, nor has he since been heard of.

24th.--We resumed our journey with an ample stock of provisions and a large cavalcade of animals, consisting of 130 horses and mules, and about 30 head of cattle, five of which were milch-cows. Mr. Sutter furnished us also with an Indian boy, who had been trained as a *vaquero*, and who would be serviceable in managing our cavalcade, great part of which were nearly as wild as buffalo, and who was, besides, very anxious to go along with us. Our direct course home was east, but the Sierra would force us south, above 500 miles of traveling, to a pass at the head of the San Joaquin river. This pass, reported to be good, was discovered by Mr. Joseph Walker, of whom I have already spoken, and whose name it might therefore appropriately bear. To reach it, our course lay along the valley of the San Joaquin--the river on our right, and the lofty wall of the impassable Sierra on the left. From that pass we were to move southeastwardly, having the Sierra then on the right, and reach the "*Spanish trail*," deviously traced from one watering-place to another, which constituted the route of the caravans from **Puebla de los Angelos**, near the coast of the Pacific, to **Santa Fe** of New Mexico. From the pass to this trail was 150 miles. Following that trail through a desert, relieved by some fertile plains indicated by the recurrence of the term *vegas*, until it turned to the right to cross the Colorado, our course would be northeast until we regained the latitude we had lost in arriving at Eutah lake, and thence to the Rocky mountains at the head of the Arkansas. This course of traveling, forced upon us by the structure of the country, would occupy a computed distance of 2,000 miles before we reached the head of the Arkansas--not a settlement to be seen upon it--and the names of places along it, all being Spanish or Indian, indicated that it had been but little trod by **American** feet. Though long, and not free from hardships, this route presented some points of attraction, in tracing the Sierra Nevada--turning the Great Basin, perhaps crossing its rim on the south--completely solving the problem of any river, except the Colorado, from the Rocky mountains on that part of our continent--and seeing the southern extremity of the Great Salt lake, of which the northern part had been examined the year before.

Taking leave of Mr. Sutter, who, with several gentlemen, accompanied us a few miles on our way, we traveled about 18 miles, and encamped on the **Rio de los Cosumnes**, a stream receiving its name from the Indians who live in its valley. Our road was through a level country, admirably suited to cultivation, and covered with groves of oak-trees, principally the evergreen-oak, and a large oak already mentioned, in form like those of the white-oak. The weather, which here, at this season, can easily be changed from the summer heat of the valley to the frosty mornings and bright days nearer the mountains, continued delightful for travelers, but unfavorable to the agriculturists, whose crops of wheat began to wear a yellow tinge from want of rain.

25th.--We traveled for 28 miles over the same delightful country as yesterday, and halted in a beautiful bottom at the ford of the **Rio de los Mukelemnes**, receiving its name from another Indian tribe living on the river. The bottoms on the stream are broad, rich, and extremely fertile, and the uplands are shaded with oak groves. A showy *lupinus*, of extraordinary beauty, growing four to five feet in height, and covered with spikes in bloom, adorned the banks of the river, and filled the air with a light and grateful perfume.

On the 26th we halted at the **Arroyo de las Calaveras**, (Skull creek,) a tributary to the San Joaquin--the previous two streams entering the bay between the San Joaquin and Sacramento rivers. This place is beautiful, with open groves of oak, and a grassy sward beneath, with many plants in bloom, some varieties of which seem to love the shade of the trees, and grow there in close small fields. Near the river, and replacing the grass, are great quantities of *ammole*, (soap plant,) the leaves of which are used in California for making, among other things, mats for saddle-cloths. A vine with a small white flower, (*melothria?*) called here **la yerba buena**, and which, from its abundance, gives name to an island and town in the bay, was to-day very frequent on our road--sometimes running on the ground or climbing the trees.

27th.--To-day we traveled steadily and rapidly up the valley; for, with our wild animals, any other gait was impossible, and making about five miles an hour. During the earlier part of the day, our ride had been over a very level prairie, or rather a succession of long stretches of prairie, separated by lines and groves of oak timber, growing along dry gullies, which are filled with water in seasons of rain; and, perhaps, also, by the melting snows. Over much of this extent, the vegetation was sparse; the surface showing plainly the action of water, which, in the season of flood, the Joaquin spreads over the valley. About one o'clock we came again among innumerable flowers; and a few miles further, fields of the beautiful blue-flowering *lupine*, which seems to love the neighborhood of water, indicated that we were approaching a stream. We here found this beautiful shrub in thickets, some of them being 12 feet in height. Occasionally three or four plants were clustered together, forming a grand bouquet, about 90 feet in circumference, and 10 feet high; the whole summit covered with spikes of flowers, the perfume of which is very sweet and grateful. A lover of natural beauty can imagine with what pleasure we rode among these flowering groves, which filled the air with a light and delicate fragrance. We continued our road for about a half a mile, interspersed through an open grove of live-oaks, which, in form, were the most symmetrical and beautiful we had yet seen in this country. The ends of their branches rested on the ground, forming somewhat more than a half sphere of very full and regular figure, with leaves apparently smaller than usual.

The Californian poppy, of a rich orange color, was numerous to-day. Elk and several bands of antelope made their appearance.

Our road was now one continued enjoyment; and it was pleasant riding among this assemblage of green pastures with varied flowers and scattered groves, and out of the warm green spring to look at the rocky and snowy peaks where lately we had suffered so much. Emerging from the timber, we came suddenly upon the Stanislaus river, where we hoped to find a ford, but the stream was flowing by, dark and deep, swollen by the mountain snows; its general breadth was about 50 yards.

We traveled about five miles up the river, and encamped without being able to find a ford. Here we made a large *coral*, in order to be able to catch a sufficient number of our wild animals to relieve those previously packed.

Under the shade of the oaks, along the river, I noticed ***erodium cicutarium*** in bloom, eight or ten inches high. This is the plant which we had seen the squaws gathering on the Rio de los Americanos. By the inhabitants of the valley it is highly esteemed for fattening cattle, which appear to be very fond of it. Here, where the soil begins to be sandy, it supplies to a considerable extent the want of grass.

Desirous, as far as possible, without delay, to include in our examination the San Joaquin river, I returned this morning down the Stanislaus for 17 miles, and again encamped without having found a fording-place. After following it for eight miles further the next morning, and finding ourselves in the vicinity of the San Joaquin, encamped in a handsome oak grove, and, several cattle being killed, we ferried over our baggage in their skins. Here our Indian boy, who probably had not much idea of where he was going, and began to be alarmed at the many streams which we were rapidly putting between him and the village, deserted.

Thirteen head of cattle took a sudden fright, while we were driving them across the river, and galloped off. I remained a day in the endeavor to recover them; but, finding they had taken the trail back to the fort, let them go without further effort. Here we had several days of warm and pleasant rain, which doubtless saved the crops below.

APRIL.

On the 1st of April, we made 10 miles across a prairie without timber, when we were stopped again by another large river, which is called the ***Rio de la Merced***, (river of our Lady of Mercy.) Here the country had lost its character of extreme fertility, the soil having become more sandy and light; but, for several days past, its beauty had been increased by the additional animation of animal life; and now, it is crowded with bands of elk and wild horses; and along the rivers are frequent fresh tracks of grizzly bear, which are unusually numerous in this country.

Our route had been along the timber of the San Joaquin, generally about eight miles distant, over a high prairie.

In one of the bands of elk seen to-day, there were about 200; but the larger bands, both of these and wild horses, are generally found on the other side of the river, which, for that reason, I avoided crossing. I had been informed below, that the droves of wild horses were almost invariably found on the western bank of the river; and the danger of losing our animals among them, together with the wish of adding to our reconnoissance the numerous streams which run down from the Sierra, decided me to travel up the eastern bank.

2d.--The day was occupied in building a boat, and ferrying our baggage across the river; and we encamped on the bank. A large fishing eagle was slowly sailing along, looking after salmon; and there were some pretty birds in the timber, with partridges, ducks and geese innumerable in the neighborhood. We were struck with the tameness of the latter bird at Helvetia, scattered about in flocks near the wheat-fields, and eating grass on the prairie; a horseman would ride by within 30 yards, without disturbing them.

3d.--To-day we touched several times the San Joaquin river--here a fine- looking tranquil stream, with a slight current, and apparently deep. It resembled the Missouri in color, with occasional points of white sand; and its banks, where steep, were a kind of sandy clay; its average width appeared to be about eighty yards. In the bottoms are frequent ponds, where our approach disturbed multitudes of wild fowl, principally geese. Skirting along the timber, we frequently started elk; and large bands were seen during the day, with antelope and wild horses. The low country and the timber rendered it difficult to keep the main line of the river; and this evening we encamped on a tributary stream, about five miles from its mouth. On the prairie bordering the San Joaquin bottoms, there occurred during the day but little grass, and in its place was a sparse and dwarf growth of plants; the soil being sandy, with small bare places and hillocks, reminded me much of the Platte bottoms; but, on approaching the timber, we found a more luxuriant vegetation, and at our camp was an abundance of grass and pea-vines.

The foliage of the oak is getting darker; and every thing, except that the weather is a little cool, shows that spring is rapidly advancing; and to- day we had quite a summer rain.

4th.--Commenced to rain at daylight, but cleared off brightly at sunrise. We ferried the river without any difficulty, and continued up the San Joaquin. Elk were running in bands over the prairie and in the skirt of the timber. We reached the river at the mouth of a large slough, which we were unable to ford, and made a circuit of several miles around. Here the country appears very flat; oak-trees have entirely disappeared, and are replaced by a large willow, nearly equal to it in size. The river is about a hundred yards in breadth, branching into sloughs, and interspersed with islands. At this time it appears sufficiently deep for a small steamer, but its navigation would be broken by shallows at low water. Bearing in towards the river, we were again forced off by another slough; and passing around, steered towards a clump of trees on the river, and finding there good grass, encamped. The prairies along the left bank are alive with immense droves of wild horses; and they had been seen during the day at every opening through the woods which afforded us a view across the river. Latitude, by observation, 37 deg. 08' 00"; longitude 120 deg. 45' 22".

5th--During the earlier part of the day's ride, the country presented a lacustrine appearance; the river was deep, and nearly on a level with the surrounding country; its banks raised like a levee, and fringed with willows. Over the bordering plain were interspersed spots of prairie among fields of *tule*, (bulrushes,) which in this country are called *tulares*, and little ponds. On the opposite side, a line of timber was visible which, according to information, points out the course of the slough, which at times of high water connects with the San Joaquin river-- a large body of water in the upper part of the valley, called the Tule lakes. The river and all its sloughs are very full, and it is probable that the lake is now discharging. Here elk were frequently started, and one was shot out of a band which ran around us. On our left, the Sierra maintains its snowy height, and masses of snow appear to descend very low towards the plains; probably the late rains in the valley were snow on the mountains. We traveled 37 miles, and encamped on the river. Longitude of the camp, 120 deg. 28' 34", and latitude, 36 deg. 49' 12".

6th.--After having traveled fifteen miles along the river, we made an early halt, under the shade of sycamore-trees. Here we found the San Joaquin coming down from the Sierra with a westerly course, and checking our way, as all its tributaries had previously done. We had expected to raft the river; but found a good ford, and encamped on the opposite bank, where droves of wild horses were raising clouds of dust on the prairie. Columns of smoke were visible in the direction of the Tule lakes to the southward--probably kindled in the tulares by the Indians, as signals that there were strangers in the valley.

We made, on the 7th, a hard march in a cold chilly rain from morning until night--the weather so thick that we traveled by compass. This was a *traverse* from the San Joaquin to the waters of the Tule lakes, and our road was over a very level prairie country. We saw wolves frequently during the day, prowling about after the young antelope, which cannot run very fast. These were numerous during the day, and two were caught by the people.

Late in the afternoon we discovered timber, which was found to be groves of oak-trees on a dry ***arroyo***. The rain, which had fallen in frequent showers, poured down in a storm at sunset, with a strong wind, which swept off the clouds, and left a clear sky. Riding on through the timber, about dark we found abundant water in small ponds, 20 to 30 yards in diameter, with clear deep water and sandy beds, bordered with bog rushes, (***juncus effusus***,) and a tall rush (***scirpus lacustris***) twelve feet high, and surrounded near the margin with willow-trees in bloom; among them one which resembled ***salix myricoides***. The oak of the groves was the same already mentioned, with small leaves, in form like those of the white-oak, and forming, with the evergreen-oak, the characteristic trees of the valley.

8th.--After a ride of two miles through brush and open groves, we reached a large stream, called the River of the Lake, resembling in size the San Joaquin, and being about 100 yards broad. This is the principal tributary to the Tule lakes, which collect all the waters in the upper part of the valley. While we were searching for a ford, some Indians appeared on the opposite bank, and having discovered that we were not Spanish soldiers, showed us the way to a good ford several miles above.

The Indians of the Sierra make frequent descents upon the settlements west of the Coast Range, which they keep constantly swept of horses; among them are many who are called Christian Indians, being refugees from Spanish missions. Several of these incursions occurred while we were at Helvetia. Occasionally parties of soldiers follow them across the Coast Range, but never enter the Sierra.

On the opposite side we found some forty or fifty Indians, who had come to meet us from the village below. We made them some small presents, and invited them to our encampment, which, after about three miles through fine oak groves, we made on the river. We made a fort, principally on account of our animals. The Indians brought otter-skins, and several kinds of fish, and bread made of acorns, to trade. Among them were several who had come to live among these Indians when the missions were broken up, and who spoke Spanish fluently. They informed us that they were called by the Spaniards ***mansitos***, (tame,) in distinction from the wilder tribes of the mountains. They, however, think themselves very insecure, not knowing at what unforeseen moment the sins of the latter may be visited upon them. They are dark-skinned, but handsome and intelligent Indians, and live principally on acorns and the roots of the tule, of which also their huts are made.

By observation, the latitude of the encampment is 36 deg. 24' 50", and longitude 119 deg. 41' 40".

9th.--For several miles we had very bad traveling over what is called rotten ground, in which the horses were frequently up to their knees. Making towards a line of timber, we found a small fordable stream, beyond which the country improved, and the grass became excellent; and crossing a number of dry and timbered *arroyos*, we traveled until late through open oak groves, and encamped among a collection of streams. These were running among rushes and willows; and, as usual, flocks of blackbirds announced our approach to water. We have here approached considerably nearer to the eastern Sierra, which shows very plainly, still covered with masses of snow, which yesterday and to-day has also appeared abundant on the Coast Range.

10th.--To-day we made another long journey of about forty miles, through a country uninteresting and flat, with very little grass and a sandy soil, in which several branches we crossed had lost their water. In the evening the face of the country became hilly; and, turning a few miles up towards the mountains, we found a good encampment on a pretty stream hidden among the hills, and handsomely timbered, principally with large cottonwoods, (*populus*, differing from any in Michaux's Sylva.) The seed-vessels of this tree were now just about bursting.

Several Indians came down the river to see us in the evening; we gave them supper, and cautioned them against stealing our horses; which they promised not to attempt.

11th.--A broad trail along the river here takes out among the hills. "Buen camino," (good road,) said one of the Indians, of whom we had inquired about the pass; and, following it accordingly, it conducted us beautifully through a very broken country, by an excellent way, which, otherwise, we should have found extremely bad. Taken separately, the hills present smooth and graceful outlines, but, together, make bad traveling ground. Instead of grass, the whole face of the country is closely covered with *erodium cicutarium*, here only two or three inches high. Its height and beauty varied in a remarkable manner with the locality, being, in many low places which we passed during the day, around streams and springs, two and three feet high. The country had now assumed a character of aridity; and the luxuriant green of these little streams, wooded with willow, oak, or sycamore, looked very refreshing among the sandy hills.

In the evening we encamped on a large creek, with abundant water. I noticed here in bloom, for the first time since leaving the Arkansas waters, the *Miribilis Jalapa*.

12th.--Along our road to-day the country was altogether sandy, and vegetation meager. *Ephedra occidentalis*, which we had first seen in the neighborhood of the Pyramid lake, made its appearance here, and in the course of the day became very abundant, and in large bushes. Towards the close of the afternoon, we reached a tolerably large river, which empties into a small lake at the head of the valley; it is about thirty-five yards wide, with a stony and gravelly bed, and the swiftest stream we have crossed since leaving the bay. The bottoms produced no grass, though well timbered with willow and cottonwood; and, after ascending several miles, we made a late encampment on a little bottom, with scanty grass. In greater part, the vegetation along our road consisted now of rare and unusual plants, among which many were entirely new.

Along the bottoms were thickets consisting of several varieties of shrubs, which made here their first appearance; and among these was *Garrya elliptica*, (Lindley,) a small tree belonging to a very peculiar natural order, and, in its general appearance, (growing in thickets,) resembling willow. It now became common along the streams, frequently supplying the place of *salix longifolia*.

13th.--The water was low, and a few miles above we forded the river at a rapid, and marched in a southeasterly direction over a less broken country. The mountains were now very near, occasionally looming out through fog. In a few hours we reached the bottom of a creek without water, over which the sandy beds were dispersed in many branches. Immediately where we struck it, the timber terminated; and below, to the right, it was a broad bed of dry and bare sands. There were many tracks of Indians and horses imprinted in the sand, which, with other indications, informed us was the creek issuing from the pass, and which we have called Pass creek. We ascended a trail for a few miles along the creek, and suddenly found a stream of water five feet wide, running with a lively current, but losing itself almost immediately. This little stream showed plainly the manner in which the mountain waters lose themselves in sand at the eastern foot of the Sierra, leaving only a parched desert and arid plains beyond. The stream enlarged rapidly, and the timber became abundant as we ascended.

A new species of pine made its appearance, with several kinds of oaks, and a variety of trees; and the country changing its appearance suddenly and entirely, we found ourselves again traveling among the old orchard-like places. Here we selected a delightful encampment in a handsome green oak hollow, where among the open bolls of the trees was an abundant sward of grass and pea-vines. In the evening a Christian Indian rode into the camp, well dressed, with long spurs, and a **sombreo**, and speaking Spanish fluently. It was an unexpected apparition, and a strange and pleasant sight in this desolate gorge of a mountain--an Indian face, Spanish costume, jingling spurs, and horse equipped after the Spanish manner. He informed me that he belonged to one of the Spanish missions to the south, distant two or three days' ride, and that he had obtained from the priests leave to spend a few days with his relations in the Sierra. Having seen us enter the pass, he had come down to visit us. He appeared familiarly acquainted with the country, and gave me definite and clear information in regard to the desert region east of the mountains. I had entered the pass with a strong disposition to vary my route, and to travel directly across towards the Great Salt lake, in the view of obtaining some acquaintance with the interior of the Great Basin, while pursuing a direct course for the frontier; but his representation, which described it as an arid and barren desert, that had repulsed by its sterility all the attempts of the Indians to penetrate it, determined me for the present to relinquish the plan, and agreeably to his advice, after crossing the Sierra, continue our intended route along its eastern base to the Spanish trail. By this route, a party of six Indians, who had come from a great river in the eastern part of the desert to trade with his people, had just started on their return. He would himself return the next day to **San Fernando**, and as our roads would be the same for two days, he offered his services to conduct us so far on our way. His offer was gladly accepted. The fog which had somewhat interfered with views in the valley, had entirely passed off, and left a clear sky. That which had enveloped us in the neighborhood of the pass proceeded evidently from fires kindled among the tulares by Indians living near the lakes, and which were intended to warn those in the mountains that there were strangers in the valley. Our position was in latitude 35 deg. 17' 12", and longitude 118 deg. 35' 03".

14th.--Our guide joined us this morning on the trail; and, arriving in a short distance at an open bottom where the creek forked, we continued up the right-hand branch, which was enriched by a profusion of flowers, and handsomely wooded with sycamore, oaks, cottonwood, and willow, with other trees, and some shrubby plants. In its long strings of balls, this sycamore differs from that of the United States, and is the ***platanus occidentalus*** of Hooker--a new species recently described among the plants collected in the voyage of the Sulphur. The cottonwood varied its foliage with white tufts, and the feathery seeds were flying plentifully through the air. Gooseberries, nearly ripe, were very abundant in the mountains; and as we passed the dividing grounds, which were not very easy to ascertain, the air was filled with perfume, as if we were entering a highly cultivated garden; and, instead of green, our pathway and the mountain sides were covered with fields of yellow flowers, which here was the prevailing color. Our journey to-day was in the midst of an advanced spring, whose green and floral beauty offered a delightful contrast to the sandy valley we had just left. All the day, snow was in sight on the butte of the mountain, which frowned down upon us on the right; but we beheld it now with feelings of pleasant security, as we rode along between green trees, and on flowers, with hummingbirds and other feathered friends of the traveler enlivening the serene spring air. As we reached the summit of this beautiful pass, and obtained a view into the eastern country, we saw at once that here was the place to take leave of all such pleasant scenes as those around us. The distant mountains were now bald rocks again, and below the land had any color but green. Taking into consideration the nature of the Sierra Nevada, we found this pass an excellent one for horses; and with a little labor, or perhaps with a more perfect examination of the localities, it might be made sufficiently practicable for wagons. Its latitude and longitude may be considered that of our last encampment, only a few miles distant. The elevation was not taken--our half-wild cavalcade making it troublesome to halt before night, when once started.

We here left the waters of the bay of San Francisco, and, though forced upon them contrary to my intentions, I cannot regret the necessity which occasioned the deviation. It made me well acquainted with the great range of the Sierra Nevada of the Alta California, and showed that this broad and elevated snowy ridge was a continuation of the Cascade Range of Oregon, between which and the ocean there is still another and a lower range, parallel to the former and to the coast, and which may be called the Coast Range. It also made me well acquainted with the basin of the San Francisco bay, and with the two pretty rivers and their valleys (the Sacramento and San Joaquin) which are tributary to that bay, and cleared up some points in geography on which error had long prevailed. It had been constantly represented, as I have already stated, that the bay of San Francisco opened far into the interior, by some river coming down from the base of the Rocky mountains, and upon which supposed stream the name of Rio Buenaventura had been bestowed. Our observations of the Sierra Nevada, in the long distance from the head of the Sacramento, to the head of the San Joaquin, and of the valley below it, which collects all the waters of the San Francisco bay, show that this neither is nor can be the case. No river from the interior does, or can, cross the Sierra Nevada--itself more lofty than the Rocky mountains; and as to the Buenaventura, the mouth of which seen on the coast gave the idea and the name of the reputed great river, it is, in fact, a small stream of no consequence, not only below the Sierra Nevada, but actually below the Coast Range--taking its rise within half a degree of the ocean, running parallel to it for about two degrees, and then falling into the Pacific near Monterey. There is no opening from the bay of San Francisco into the interior of the continent. The two rivers which flow into it are comparatively short, and not perpendicular to the coast, but lateral to it, and having their heads towards Oregon and southern California. They open lines of communication north and south, and not eastwardly; and thus this want of interior communication from the San Francisco bay, now fully ascertained, gives great additional value to the Columbia, which stands alone as the only great river on the Pacific slope of our continent which leads from the ocean to the Rocky mountains, and opens a line of communication from the sea to the valley of the Mississippi.

Four ***companeros*** joined our guide at the pass; and two going back at noon, the others continued on in company. Descending from the hills, we reached a country of fine grass, where the ***erodium cicutarium*** finally disappeared, giving place to an excellent quality of bunch-grass. Passing by some springs where there was a rich sward of grass among groves of large black-oak, we rode over a plain on which the guide pointed out a spot where a refugee Christian Indian had been killed by a party of soldiers which had unexpectedly penetrated into the mountains. Crossing a low sierra, and descending a hollow where a spring gushed out, we were struck by the sudden appearance of *yucca* trees, which gave a strange and southern character to the country, and suited well with the dry and desert region we were approaching. Associated with the idea of barren sands, their stiff and ungraceful form makes them to the traveler the most repulsive tree in the vegetable kingdom. Following the hollow, we shortly came upon a creek timbered with large black-oak, which yet had not put forth a leaf. There was a small rivulet of running water, with good grass.

15th.--The Indians who had accompanied the guide returned this morning, and I purchased from them a Spanish saddle and long spurs, as reminiscences of the time; and for a few yards of scarlet cloth they gave me a horse, which afterwards became food for other Indians.

We continued a short distance down the creek, in which our guide informed us that the water very soon disappeared, and turned directly to the southward along the foot of the mountain; the trail on which we rode appearing to describe the eastern limit of travel, where water and grass terminated. Crossing a low spur, which bordered the creek, we descended to a kind of plain among the lower spurs, the desert being in full view on our left, apparently illimitable. A hot mist lay over it to-day, through which it had a white and glistening appearance; here and there a few dry-looking *buttes* and isolated black ridges rose suddenly upon it. "There," said our guide, stretching out his hand towards it, "there are the great *llanos*, (plains,) *no hay agua; no hay zacate-- nada*: there is neither water nor grass--nothing; every animal that goes upon them, dies." It was indeed dismal to look upon, and to conceive so great a change in so short a distance. One might travel the world over, without finding a valley more fresh and verdant--more floral and sylvan-- more alive with birds and animals--more bounteously watered--than we had left in the San Joaquin: here within a few miles' ride, a vast desert plain spread before us, from which the boldest traveler turned away in despair.

Directly in front of us, at some distance to the southward, and running out in an easterly direction from the mountains, stretched a sierra, having at the eastern end (perhaps 50 miles distant) some snowy peaks, on which, by the information of our guide, snow rested all the year.

Our cavalcade made a strange and grotesque appearance; and it was impossible to avoid reflecting upon our position and composition in this remote solitude. Within two degrees of the Pacific ocean--already far south of the latitude of Monterey--and still forced on south by a desert on one hand, and a mountain range on the other--guided by a civilized Indian, attended by two wild ones from the Sierra--a Chinook from the Columbia, and our mixture of American, French, German--all armed--four or five languages heard at once--above a hundred horses and mules, half wild --American, Spanish, and Indian dresses and equipments intermingled--such was our composition. Our march was a sort of procession. Scouts ahead and on the flanks; a front and rear division; the pack-animals, baggage, and horned-cattle in the centre; and the whole stretching a quarter of a mile along our dreary path. In this form we journeyed, looking more as if we belonged to Asia than to the United States of America.

We continued in a southerly direction across the plain, to which, as well as to all the country, so far as we could see, the *yucca* trees gave a strange and singular character. Several new plants appeared, among which was a zygophyllaceous shrub, (***zygophyllum Californicum***, Torr. and Frem.,) sometimes ten feet in height; in form, and in the pliancy of its branches, it is rather a graceful plant. Its leaves are small, covered with a resinous substance; and, particularly when bruised and crushed, exhale a singular but very agreeable and refreshing odor. This shrub and the *yucca*, with many varieties of cactus, make the characteristic features in the vegetation for a long distance to the eastward. Along the foot of the mountain, 20 miles to the southward, red stripes of flowers were visible during the morning, which we supposed to be variegated sandstones. We rode rapidly during the day, and in the afternoon emerged from the *yucca* forest at the foot of an ***outlier*** of the Sierra before us, and came among the fields of flowers we had seen in the morning, which consisted principally of the rich orange-colored California poppy, mingled with other flowers of brighter tints. Reaching the top of the spur, which was covered with fine bunch-grass, and where the hills were very green, our guide pointed to a small hollow in the mountain before us, saying, "***a este piedra hay agua***." He appeared to know every nook in the country. We continued our beautiful road, and reached a spring in the slope at the foot of the ridge, running in a green ravine, among granite boulders; here nightshade, and borders of buckwheat, with their white blossoms around the granite rocks, attracted our notice as familiar plants. Several antelopes were seen among the hills, and some large hares. Men were sent back this evening in search of a wild mule with a valuable pack, which had managed (as they frequently do) to hide itself along the road.

By observation, the latitude of the camp is 34 deg. 41' 42", and longitude 118 deg. 20' 00". The next day the men returned with the mule.

17th.--Crossing the ridge by a beautiful pass of hollows, where several deer broke out of the thickets, we emerged at a small salt lake in a ***vallon*** lying nearly east and west, where a trail from the mission of ***San Buenaventura*** comes in. The lake is about 1,200 yards in diameter; surrounded on the margin by a white salty border, which, by the smell, reminded us slightly of Lake Abert. There are some cottonwoods, with willow and elder, around the lake; and the water is a little salt, although not entirely unfit for drinking. Here we turned directly to the eastward along the trail, which, from being seldom used, is almost imperceptible; and, after traveling a few miles, our guide halted, and, pointing to the hardly visible trail, "***aqui es camino***," said he, "***no se pierde--va siempre***." He pointed out a black ***butte*** on the plain at the foot of the mountain, where we would find water to encamp at night; and, giving him a present of knives and scarlet cloth, we shook hands and parted. He bore off south, and in a day's ride would arrive at San Fernando, one of several missions in this part of California, where the country is so beautiful that it is considered a paradise, and the name of its principal town (***Puebla de los Angeles***) would make it angelic. We continued on through a succession of valleys, and came into a most beautiful spot of flower fields; instead of green, the hills were purple and orange, with unbroken beds, into which each color was separately gathered. A pale straw-color, with a bright yellow, the rich red orange of the poppy mingled with fields of purple, covered the spot with a floral beauty; and, on the border of the sandy deserts, seemed to invite the traveler to go no farther. Riding along through the perfumed air, we soon after entered a defile overgrown with the ominous ***artemisia tridentata***, which conducted us into a sandy plain covered more or less densely with forests of ***yucca***.

Having now the snowy ridge on our right, we continued our way towards a dark ***butte***, belonging to a low sierra on the plain, and which our guide had pointed out for a landmark. Late in the day, the familiar growth of cottonwood, a line of which was visible ahead, indicated our approach to a creek, which we reached where the water spread out into sands, and a little below sank entirely. Here our guide had intended we should pass the night; but there was not a blade of grass, and, hoping to find nearer the mountain a little for the night, we turned up the stream. A hundred yards above, we found the creek a fine stream, sixteen feet wide, with a swift current. A dark night overtook us when we reached the hills at the foot of the ridge, and we were obliged to encamp without grass; tying up what animals we could secure in the darkness, the greater part of the wild ones having free range for the night. Here the stream was two feet deep, swift and clear, issuing from a neighboring snow peak. A few miles before reaching this creek, we had crossed a broad dry riverbed, which, nearer the hills, the hunters had found a bold and handsome stream.

18th.--Some parties were engaged in hunting up the scattered horses, and others in searching for grass above; both were successful, and late in the day we encamped among some spring-heads of the river, in a hollow which was covered with only tolerably good grasses, the lower ground being entirely overgrown with large bunches of the coarse stiff grass, (***carex sitchensis***.)

Our latitude, by observation, was 34 deg. 27' 03", and longitude 117 deg. 13' 00".

Traveling close along the mountain, we followed up, in the afternoon of the 19th, another stream, in hopes to find a grass-patch like that of the previous day, but were deceived; except some scattered bunch-grass, there was nothing but rock and sand; and even the fertility of the mountain seemed withered by the air of the desert. Among the few trees was the nut pine, (***pinus monophyllus***.)

Our road the next day was still in an easterly direction along the ridge, over very bad traveling ground, broken and confounded with crippled trees and shrubs; and, after a difficult march of eighteen miles, a general shout announced that we had struck the great object of our search--THE SPANISH TRAIL--which here was running directly north. The road itself, and its course, were equally happy discoveries to us. Since the middle of December we had continually been forced south by mountains and by deserts, and now would have to make six degrees of ***northing***, to regain the latitude on which we wished to cross the Rocky mountains. The course of the road, therefore, was what we wanted; and, once more, we felt like going homewards. A *road* to travel on, and the *right* course to go, were joyful consolations to us; and our animals enjoyed the beaten track like ourselves. Relieved from the rocks and brush, our wild mules started off at a rapid rate, and in fifteen miles we reached a considerable river, timbered with cottonwood and willow, where we found a bottom of tolerable grass. As the animals had suffered a great deal in the last few days, I remained here all next day, to allow them the necessary repose; and it was now necessary, at every favorable place, to make a little halt. Between us and the Colorado river we were aware that the country was extremely poor in grass, and scarce for water, there being many *jornadas*, (days' journey,) or long stretches of forty to sixty miles, without water, where the road was marked by bones of animals.

Although in California we had met with people who had passed over this trail, we had been able to obtain no correct information about it; and the greater part of what we had heard was found to be only a tissue of falsehoods. The rivers that we found on it were never mentioned, and others, particularly described in name and locality, were subsequently seen in another part of the country. It was described as a tolerably good sandy road, with so little rock as scarcely to require the animals to be shod; and we found it the roughest and rockiest road we had ever seen in the country, and which nearly destroyed our band of fine mules and horses. Many animals are destroyed on it every year by a disease called the foot- evil; and a traveler should never venture on it without having his animals well shod, and also carrying extra shoes.

Latitude 34 deg. 34' 11"; and longitude 117 deg. 13' 00".

The morning of the 22d was clear and bright, and a snowy peak to the southward shone out high and sharply defined. As has been usual since we crossed the mountains and descended into the hot plains, we had a gale of wind. We traveled down the right bank of the stream, over sands which are somewhat loose, and have no verdure, but are occupied by various shrubs. A clear bold stream, 60 feet wide, and several feet deep, had a strange appearance, running between perfectly naked banks of sand. The eye, however, is somewhat relieved by willows, and the beautiful green of the sweet cottonwoods with which it is well wooded. As we followed along its course, the river, instead of growing constantly larger, gradually dwindled away, as it was absorbed by the sand. We were now careful to take the old camping-places of the annual Santa Fe caravans, which, luckily for us, had not yet made their yearly passage. A drove of several thousand horses and mules would entirely have swept away the scanty grass at the watering places, and we should have been obliged to leave the road to obtain subsistence for our animals. After riding 20 miles in a north- easterly direction, we found an old encampment, where we halted.

By observation, the elevation of this encampment is 2,250 feet.

23d.--The trail followed still along the river, which, in the course of the morning, entirely disappeared. We continued along the dry bed, in which, after an interval of about 16 miles, the water reappeared in some low places, well timbered with cottonwood and willow, where was another of the customary camping-grounds. Here a party of six Indians came into camp, poor and hungry, and quite in keeping with the character of the country. Their arms were bows of unusual length, and each had a large gourd, strengthened with meshes of cord, in which he carried water. They proved to be the Mohahve Indians mentioned by our recent guide; and from one of them, who spoke Spanish fluently, I obtained some interesting information, which I would be glad to introduce here. An account of the people inhabiting this region would undoubtedly possess interest for the civilized world. Our journey homewards was fruitful in incident; and the country through which we traveled, although a desert, afforded much to excite the curiosity of the botanist; but limited time, and the rapidly advancing season for active operations, oblige me to omit all extended descriptions, and hurry briefly to the conclusion of this report.

The Indian who spoke Spanish had been educated for a number of years at one of the Spanish missions, and, at the breaking up of those establishments, had returned to the mountains, where he had been found by a party of **Mohahve** (sometimes called ***Amuchaba***) Indians, among whom he had ever since resided.

He spoke of the leader of the present party as "***mi amo***," (my master.) He said they lived upon a large river in the southeast, which the "soldiers called the Rio Colorado;" but that, formerly, a portion of them lived upon this river, and among the mountains which had bounded the river valley to the northward during the day, and that here along the river they had raised various kinds of melons. They sometimes came over to trade with the Indians of the Sierra, bringing with them blankets and goods manufactured by the Monquis and other Colorado Indians. They rarely carried home horses, on account of the difficulty of getting them across the desert, and of guarding them afterwards from the Pa-utah Indians, who inhabit the Sierra, at the head of the ***Rio Virgen***, (river of the Virgin.)

He informed us that, a short distance below, this river finally disappeared. The two different portions in which water is found had received from the priests two different names; and subsequently I heard it called by the Spaniards the ***Rio de las Animas***, but on the map we have called it the ***Mohahve*** river.

24th.--We continued down the stream (or rather its bed) for about eight miles, where there was water still in several holes, and encamped. The caravans sometimes continued below, to the end of the river, from which there is a very long ***jornada*** of perhaps 60 miles, without water. Here a singular and new species of acacia, with spiral pods or seed- vessels, made its first appearance; becoming henceforward, for a considerable distance, the characteristic tree. It was here comparatively large, being about 20 feet in height, with a full and spreading top, the lower branches declining towards the ground. It afterwards occurred of smaller size, frequently in groves, and is very fragrant. It has been called by Dr. Torrey, ***spirolobium odoratum***. The zygophyllaceous shrub had been constantly characteristic of the plains along the river; and here, among many new plants, a new and very remarkable species of eriogonum (***eriogonum inflatum***, Tor. & Frem.) made its first appearance.

Our cattle had become so tired and poor by this fatiguing traveling, that three of them were killed here, and the meat dried. The Indians had now an occasion for a great feast and were occupied the remainder of the day and all night in cooking and eating. There was no part of the animal for which they did not find some use, except the bones. In the afternoon we were surprised by the sudden appearance in the camp of two Mexicans--a man and a boy. The name of the man was ***Andreas Fuentes***; and that of the boy, (a handsome lad, 11 years old,) ***Pablo Hernandez***. They belonged to a party consisting of six persons, the remaining four being the wife of Fuentes, and the father and mother of Pablo, and Santiago Giacome, a resident of New Mexico. With a cavalcade of about thirty horses, they had come out from Puebla de los Angeles, near the coast, under the guidance of Giacome, in advance of the great caravan, in order to travel more at leisure, and obtain better grass. Having advanced as far into the desert as was considered consistent with their safety, they halted at the ***Archilette***, one of the customary camping-grounds, about

80 miles from our encampment, where there is a spring of good water, with sufficient grass; and concluded to await there the arrival of the great caravan. Several Indians were soon discovered lurking about the camp, who, in a day or two after, came in, and, after behaving in a very friendly manner, took their leave, without awakening any suspicions. Their deportment begat a security which proved fatal. In a few days afterwards, suddenly a party of about one hundred Indians appeared in sight, advancing towards the camp. It was too late, or they seemed not to have presence of mind to take proper measures of safety; and the Indians charged down into their camp, shouting as they advanced, and discharging flights of arrows. Pablo and Fuentes were on horse-guard at the time, and mounted according to the custom of the country. One of the principal objects of the Indians was to get possession of the horses, and part of them immediately surrounded the band; but, in obedience to the shouts of Giacome, Fuentes drove the animals over and through the assailants, in spite of their arrows; and, abandoning the rest to their fate, carried them off at speed across the plain. Knowing that they would be pursued by the Indians, without making any halt except to shift their saddles to other horses, they drove them on for about sixty miles, and this morning left them at a watering-place on the trail, called Agua de Tomaso. Without giving themselves any time for rest, they hurried on, hoping to meet the Spanish caravan, when they discovered my camp. I received them kindly, taking them into my own mess, and promised them such aid as circumstances might put it in my power to give.

25th.--We left the river abruptly, and, turning to the north, regained in a few miles the main trail, (which had left the river sooner than ourselves,) and continued our way across a lower ridge of the mountain, through a miserable tract of sand and gravel. We crossed at intervals the broad beds of dry gullies, where in the seasons of rains and melting snows there would be brooks or rivulets: and at one of these, where there was no indication of water, were several freshly-dug holes, in which there was water at the depth of two feet. These holes had been dug by the wolves, whose keen sense of smell had scented the water under the dry sand. They were nice little wells, narrow, and dug straight down; and we got pleasant water out of them.

The country had now assumed the character of an elevated and mountainous desert; its general features being black, rocky ridges, bald, and destitute of timber, with sandy basins between. Where the sides of these ridges are washed by gullies, the plains below are strewed with beds of large pebbles or rolled stones, destructive to our soft-footed animals, accustomed to the soft plains of the Sacramento valley. Through these sandy basins sometimes struggled a scanty stream, or occurred a hole of water, which furnished camping-grounds for travelers. Frequently in our journey across, snow was visible on the surrounding mountains; but their waters rarely reached the sandy plain below, where we toiled along, oppressed with thirst and a burning sun. But, throughout this nakedness of sand and gravel, were many beautiful plants and flowering shrubs, which occurred in many new species, and with greater variety than we had been accustomed to see in the most luxuriant prairie countries; this was a peculiarity of this desert. Even where no grass would take root, the naked sand would bloom with some rich and rare flower, which found its appropriate home in the arid and barren spot.

Scattered over the plain, and tolerably abundant, was a handsome leguminous shrub, three or four feet high, with fine bright purple flowers. It is a new ***psoralea***, and occurred frequently henceforward along our road.

Beyond the first ridge, our road bore a little to the east of north, towards a gap in a higher line of mountains; and, after traveling about 25 miles, we arrived at the ***Agua de Tomaso***--the spring where the horses had been left; but, as we expected, they were gone. A brief examination of the ground convinced us that they had been driven off by the Indians. Carson and Godey volunteered, with the Mexican, to pursue them; and, well mounted, the three set off on the trail. At this stopping- place there are a few bushes, and a very little grass. Its water was a pool; but near by was a spring, which had been dug out by Indians or travelers. Its water was cool--a great refreshment to us under a burning sun.

In the evening Fuentes returned, his horse having failed; but Carson and Godey had continued the pursuit.

I observed to-night an occultation of ***a2 Cancri***, at the dark limb of the moon, which gives for the longitude of the place 116 deg. 23' 28"; the latitude, by observation, is 35 deg. 13' 08". From Helvetia to this place, the positions along the intervening line are laid down, with the longitudes obtained from the chronometer, which appears to have retained its rate remarkably well; but henceforward, to the end of our journey, the few longitudes given are absolute, depending upon a subsequent occultation and eclipses of the satellites.

   In the afternoon of the next day, a war-whoop was heard, such as Indians make when returning from a victorious enterprise; and soon Carson and Godey appeared, driving before them a band of horses, recognised by Fuentes to be part of those they had lost. Two bloody scalps, dangling from the end of Godey's gun, announced that they had overtaken the Indians as well as the horses. They informed us, that after Fuentes left them, from the failure of his horse, they continued the pursuit alone, and towards night-fall entered the mountains, into which the trail led. After sunset the moon gave light, and they followed the trail by moonshine until late in the night, when it entered a narrow defile, and was difficult to follow. Afraid of losing it in the darkness of the defile, they tied up their horses, struck no fire, and lay down to sleep, in silence and in darkness. Here they lay from midnight until morning. At daylight they resumed the pursuit, and about sunrise discovered the horses; and, immediately dismounting and tying up their own, they crept cautiously to a rising ground which intervened, from the crest of which they perceived the encampment of four lodges close by. They proceeded quietly, and had got within 30 or 40 yards of their object, when a movement among the horses discovered them to the Indians. Giving the war-shout, they instantly charged into the camp, regardless of the number which the *four* lodges would imply. The Indians received them with a flight of arrows shot from their long-bows, one of which passed through Godey's shirt-collar, barely missing the neck: our men fired their rifles upon a steady aim, and rushed in. Two Indians were stretched upon the ground, fatally pierced with bullets: the rest fled, except a little lad that was captured. The scalps of the fallen were instantly stripped off; but in the process, one of them, who had two balls through his body, sprang to his feet, the blood streaming from his skinned head, and uttering a hideous howl. An old squaw, possibly his mother, stopped and looked back from the mountainsides she was climbing, threatening and lamenting. The frightful spectacle appalled the stout hearts of our men; but they did what humanity required, and quickly terminated the agonies of the gory savage. They were now masters of the camp, which was a pretty little recess in the mountain, with a fine spring, and apparently safe from all invasion. Great preparations had been made to feast a large party, for it was a very proper place to rendezvous, and for the celebration of such orgies as robbers of the desert would delight in. Several of the best horses had been killed, skinned, and cut up; for the Indians living in mountains, and only coming into the plains to rob and murder, make no other use of horses than to eat them. Large earthen vessels were on the fire, boiling and stewing the horse-beef; and several baskets, containing 50 or 60 pairs of moccasins, indicated the presence, or expectation, of a considerable party. They released the boy, who had given strong evidence of the stoicism, or something else, of the savage character, in commencing his breakfast upon a horse's head, as soon as he found he was not to be killed, but only tied as a prisoner. Their object accomplished, our men gathered up all the surviving horses, fifteen in number, returned upon their trail, and rejoined us, at our camp, in the afternoon of the same day. They had rode about 100 miles, in the pursuit and return, and all in 30 hours. The time, place, object, and numbers considered, this expedition of Carson and Godey may be considered among the boldest and most disinterested which the annals of western adventure, so full of daring deeds, can present. Two men, in a savage desert, pursue day and night an unknown body of Indians, into the defile of an unknown mountain--attack them on sight, without counting numbers--and defeat them in an instant-- and for what? To punish the robbers of the desert, and to avenge the wrongs of Mexicans whom they did not know. I repeat: it was Carson and Godey who did this--the former an **American**, born in the Boonslick county of Missouri; the latter a Frenchman, born in St. Louis,--and both trained to western enterprise from early life.

By the information of Fuentes, we had now to make a long stretch of 40 or 50 miles across a plain which lay between us and the next possible camp; and we resumed our journey late in the afternoon, with the intention of traveling through the night, and avoiding the excessive heat of the day, which was oppressive to our animals. For several hours we traveled across a high plain, passing, at the opposite side, through a canon by the bed of a creek, running northwardly into a small lake beyond, and both of them being dry. We had a warm, moonshiny night; and, traveling directly towards the north-star, we journeyed now across an open plain, between mountain- ridges--that on the left being broken, rocky, and bald, according to Carson and Godey, who had entered here in pursuit of the horses. The plain appeared covered principally with the *zygophyllum Californicum*, already mentioned; and the line of our road was marked by the skeletons of horses, which were strewed to considerable breadth over the plain. We were always warned on entering one of these long stretches, by the bones of these animals, which had perished before they could reach the water. About midnight we reached a considerable stream-bed, now dry--the discharge of the waters of this basin, (when it collected any)--down which we descended, in a northwesterly direction. The creek-bed was overgrown with shrubbery, and several hours before day it brought us to the entrance of a canon, where we found water, and encamped. This word *canon* is used by the Spaniards to signify a defile or gorge in a creek or river, where high rocks press in close, and make a narrow way, usually difficult, and often impossible to be passed.

In the morning we found that we had a very poor camping-ground--a swampy, salty spot, with a little long, unwholesome grass; and the water, which rose in springs, being useful only to wet the mouth, but entirely too salt to drink. All around was sand and rocks, and skeletons of horses which had not been able to find support for their lives. As we were about to start, we found, at the distance of a few hundred yards, among the hills to the southward, a spring of tolerably good water, which was a relief to ourselves; but the place was too poor to remain long, and therefore we continued on this morning. On the creek were thickets of *spirolobium odoratum* (acacia) in bloom, and very fragrant.

Passing through the canon, we entered another sandy basin, through which the dry stream-bed continued its north-westerly course, in which direction appeared a high snowy mountain.

We traveled through a barren district, where a heavy gale was blowing about the loose sand, and, after a ride of eight miles, reached a large creek of salt and bitter water, running in a westerly direction, to receive the stream-bed we had left. It is called by the Spaniards *Amargosa*--the bitter-water of the desert. Where we struck it, the stream bends; and we continued in a northerly course up the ravine of its valley, passing on the way a fork from the right, near which occurred a bed of plants, consisting of a remarkable new genus of *cruciferae*.

Gradually ascending, the ravine opened into a green valley, where, at the foot of the mountain, were springs of excellent water. We encamped among groves of the new *acacia*, and there was an abundance of good grass for the animals.

This was the best camping-ground we had seen since we struck the Spanish trail. The day's journey was about twelve miles.

29th.--To-day we had to reach the *Archilette*, distant seven miles, where the

Mexican party had been attacked, and, leaving our encampment early, we traversed a part of the desert the most sterile and repulsive we had yet seen. Its prominent features were dark *sierras*, naked and dry; on the plains a few straggling shrubs--among them, cactus of several varieties. Fuentes pointed out one called by the Spaniards ***bisnada***, which has a juicy pulp, slightly acid, and is eaten by the traveler to allay thirst. Our course was generally north; and, after crossing an intervening ridge, we descended into a sandy plain, or basin, in the middle of which was the grassy spot, with its springs and willow bushes, which constitutes a camping-place in the desert, and is called the ***Archilette***. The dead silence of the place was ominous; and, galloping rapidly up, we found only the corpses of the two men: every thing else was gone. They were naked, mutilated, and pierced with arrows. Hernandez had evidently fought, and with desperation. He lay in advance of the willow half-faced tent, which sheltered his family, as if he had come out to meet danger, and to repulse it from that asylum. One of his hands, and both his legs, had been cut off. Giacome, who was a large and strong- looking man, was lying in one of the willow shelters, pierced with arrows.

Of the women no trace could be found, and it was evident they had been carried off captive. A little lap-dog, which had belonged to Pablo's mother, remained with the dead bodies, and was frantic with joy at seeing Pablo; he, poor child, was frantic with grief, and filled the air with lamentations for his father and mother. ***Mi Padre! Mi Madre!***--was his incessant cry. When we beheld this pitiable sight, and pictured to ourselves the fate of the two women, carried off by savages so brutal and so loathsome, all compunction for the scalped-alive Indian ceased; and we rejoiced that Carson and Godey had been able to give so useful a lesson to these American Arabs who lie in wait to murder and plunder the innocent traveler.

We were all too much affected by the sad feelings which the place inspired, to remain an unnecessary moment. The night we were obliged to pass there. Early in the morning we left it, having first written a brief account of what had happened, and put it in the cleft of a pole planted at the spring, that the approaching caravan might learn the fate of their friends. In commemoration of the event, we called the place ***Ague de Hernandez***--Hernandez's spring. By observation, its latitude was 35 deg. 51' 21".

30th.--We continued our journey over a district similar to that of the day before. From the sandy basin, in which was the spring, we entered another basin of the same character, surrounded everywhere by mountains. Before us stretched a high range, rising still higher to the left, and terminating in a snowy mountain.

After a day's march of 24 miles, we reached at evening the bed of a stream from which the water had disappeared, a little only remaining in holes, which we increased by digging; and about a mile above, the stream, not yet entirely sunk, was spread out over the sands, affording a little water for the animals. The stream came out of the mountains on the left, very slightly wooded with cottonwood, willow, and acacia, and a few dwarf-oaks; and grass was nearly as scarce as water. A plant with showy yellow flowers (*Stanleya integrifolia*) occurred abundantly at intervals for the last two days, and *eriogonum inflatum* was among the characteristic plants.

MAY.

1st.--The air is rough, and overcoats pleasant. The sky is blue, and the day bright. Our road was over a plain, towards the foot of the mountain; *zygophyllum Californicum*, now in bloom, with a small yellow flower, is characteristic of the country; and *cacti* were very abundant, and in rich fresh bloom, which wonderfully ornaments this poor country. We encamped at a spring in the pass, which had been the site of an old village. Here we found excellent grass, but very little water. We dug out the old spring, and watered some of our animals. The mountain here was wooded very slightly with the nut-pine, cedars, and a dwarf species of oak; and among the shrubs were *Purshia tridentata, artemisia*, and *ephedra occidentalis*. The numerous shrubs which constitute the vegetation of the plains are now in bloom, with flowers of white, yellow, red, and purple. The continual rocks, and want of water and grass, began to be very hard on our mules and horses; but the principal loss is occasioned by their crippled feet, the greater part of those left being in excellent order, and scarcely a day passes without some loss; and, one by one, Fuentes' horses are constantly dropping behind. Whenever they give out, he dismounts and cuts off their tails and manes, to make saddle-girths--the last advantage one can gain from them.

The next day, in a short but rough ride of 12 miles, we crossed the mountain; and, descending to a small valley plain, encamped at the foot of the ridge, on the bed of a creek, and found good grass in sufficient quantity, and abundance of water in holes. The ridge is extremely rugged and broken, presenting on this side a continued precipice, and probably affords very few passes. Many *digger* tracks were seen around us, but no Indians were visible.

3d.--After a day's journey of 18 miles, in a northeasterly direction, we encamped in the midst of another very large basin, at a camping ground called *las Vegas*--a term which the Spaniards use to signify fertile or marshy plains, in contradistinction to *llanos*, which they apply to dry and sterile plains. Two narrow streams of clear water, four or five feet deep, gush suddenly, with a quick current, from two singularly large springs; these, and other waters of the basin, pass out in a gap to the eastward. The taste of the water is good, but rather too warm to be agreeable; the temperature being 71 deg. in the one, and 73 deg. in the other. They, however, afford a delightful bathing-place.

4th.--We started this morning earlier than usual, traveling in a northeasterly direction across the plain. The new acacia (*spirolobium odoratum*) has now become the characteristic tree of the country; it is in bloom, and its blossoms are very fragrant. The day was still, and the heat, which soon became very oppressive, appeared to bring out strongly the refreshing scent of the zygophyllaceous shrubs and the sweet perfume of the acacia. The snowy ridge we had just crossed looked out conspicuously in the northwest. In about five hours' ride, we crossed a gap in the surrounding ridge, and the appearance of skeletons of horses very soon warned us that we were engaged in another dry *jornada*, which proved the longest we had made in all our journey--between fifty and sixty miles without a drop of water.

Travelers through countries affording water and timber can have no conception of our intolerable thirst while journeying over the hot yellow sands of this elevated country, where the heated air seems to be entirely deprived of moisture. We ate occasionally the *bisnada*, and moistened our mouths with the acid of the sour dock, (*rumex venosus*.) Hourly expecting to find water, we continued to press on until towards midnight, when, after a hard and uninterrupted march of 16 hours, our wild mules began running ahead; and in a mile or two we came to a bold running stream--so keen is the sense of that animal, in these desert regions, in scenting at a distance this necessary of life.

According to the information we had received, Sevier river was a tributary of the Colorado; and this, accordingly, should have been one of its affluents. It proved to be the ***Rio de los Angeles***, (river of the Angels)--a branch of the ***Rio Virgen***. (river of the Virgin.)

5th.--On account of our animals, it was necessary to remain to-day at this place. Indians crowded numerously around us in the morning; and we were obliged to keep arms in hand all day, to keep them out of the camp. They began to surround the horses, which, for the convenience of grass, we were guarding a little above, on the river. These were immediately driven in, and kept close to the camp.

In the darkness of the night we had made a very bad encampment, our fires being commanded by a rocky bluff within 50 yards; but, notwithstanding, we had the river and small thickets of willows on the other side. Several times during the day the camp was insulted by the Indians; but, peace being our object, I kept simply on the defensive. Some of the Indians were on the bottoms, and others haranguing us from the bluffs; and they were scattered in every direction over the hills. Their language being probably a dialect of the ***Utah***, with the aid of signs some of our people could comprehend them very well. They were the same people who had murdered the Mexicans; and towards us their disposition was evidently hostile, nor were we well disposed towards them. They were barefooted, and nearly naked; their hair gathered up into a knot behind; and with his bow, each man carried a quiver with thirty or forty arrows partially drawn out. Besides these, each held in his hand two or three arrows for instant service. Their arrows are barbed with a very clear translucent stone, a species of opal, nearly as hard as the diamond; and, shot from their long bow, are almost as effective as a gunshot. In these Indians, I was forcibly struck by an expression of countenance resembling that in a beast of prey; and all their actions are those of wild animals. Joined to the restless motion of the eye, there is a want of mind--an absence of thought--and an action wholly by impulse, strongly expressed, and which constantly recalls the similarity.

A man who appeared to be a chief, with two or three others forced himself into the camp, bringing with him his arms, in spite of my orders to the contrary. When shown our weapons, he bored his ear with his fingers, and said he could not hear. "Why," said he, "there are none of you." Counting the people around the camp, and including in the number a mule that was being shod, he made out 22. "So many," said he, showing the number, "and we--we are a great many;" and he pointed to the hills and mountains round about. "If you have your arms," said he, twanging his bow, "we have these." I had some difficulty in restraining the people, particularly Carson, who felt an insult of this kind as much as if it had been given by a more responsible being. "Don't say that, old man," said he; "don't you say that--your life's in danger"--speaking in good English; and probably the old man was nearer to his end than he will be before he meets it.

Several animals had been necessarily left behind near the camp last night; and early in the morning, before me Indians made their appearance, several men were sent to bring them in. When I was beginning to be uneasy at their absence, they returned with information that they had been driven off from the trail by Indians; and, having followed the tracks in a short distance, they found the animals cut up and spread out upon bushes. In the evening I gave a fatigued horse to some of the Indians for a feast; and the village which carried him off refused to share with the others, who made loud complaints from the rocks of the partial distribution. Many of these Indians had long sticks, hooked at the end, which they use in hauling out lizards, and other small animals, from their holes. During the day they occasionally roasted and ate lizards at our fires. These belong to the people who are generally known under the name of ***Diggers***; and to these I have more particularly had reference when occasionally speaking of a people whose sole occupation is to procure food sufficient to support existence. The formation here consists of fine yellow sandstone, alternating with a coarse conglomerate, in which the stones are from the size of ordinary gravel to six or eight inches in diameter. This is the formation which renders the surface of the country so rocky, and gives us now a road alternately of loose heavy sands and rolled stones, which cripple the animals in a most extraordinary manner.

On the following morning we left the ***Rio de los Angeles***, and continued our way through the same desolate and revolting country, where lizards were the only animal, and the tracks of the lizard eaters the principal sign of human beings. After twenty miles' march through a road of hills and heavy sands, we reached the most dreary river I have ever seen--a deep rapid stream, almost a torrent, passing swiftly by, and roaring against obstructions. The banks were wooded with willow, acacia, and a frequent plant of the country already mentioned, (***Garrya elliptica***,) growing in thickets, resembling willow, and bearing a small pink flower. Crossing it we encamped on the left bank, where we found a very little grass. Our three remaining steers, being entirely given out, were killed here. By the boiling point, the elevation of the river here is 4,060 feet; and latitude, by observation, 36 deg.41' 33". The stream was running towards the southwest, and appeared to come from a snowy mountain in the north. It proved to be the **Rio Virgen**--a tributary to the Colorado. Indians appeared in bands on the hills, but did not come into camp. For several days we continued our journey up the river, the bottoms of which were thickly overgrown with various kinds of brush; and the sandy soil was absolutely covered with the tracks of **Diggers**, who followed us stealthily, like a band of wolves; and we had no opportunity to leave behind, even for a few hours, the tired animals, in order that they might be brought into camp after a little repose. A horse or mule, left behind, was taken off in a moment. On the evening of the 8th, having traveled 28 miles up the river from our first encampment on it, we encamped at a little grass-plat, where a spring of cool water issued from the bluff. On the opposite side was a grove of cottonwoods at the mouth of a fork, which here enters the river. On either side the valley is bounded by ranges of mountains, everywhere high, rocky, and broken. The caravan road was lost and scattered in the sandy country, and we had been following an Indian trail up the river. The hunters the next day were sent out to reconnoitre, and in the mean time we moved about a mile farther up, where we found a good little patch of grass. There being only sufficient grass for the night, the horses were sent with a strong guard in charge of Tabeau to a neighboring hollow, where they might pasture during the day; and, to be ready in case the Indians should make any attempt on the animals, several of the best horses were picketed at the camp. In a few hours the hunters returned, having found a convenient ford in the river, and discovered the Spanish trail on the other side.

    I had been engaged in arranging plants; and, fatigued with the heat of the day, I fell asleep in the afternoon, and did not awake until sundown. Presently Carson came to me, and reported that Tabeau, who early in the day had left his post, and, without my knowledge, rode back to the camp we had left, in search of a lame mule, had not returned. While we were speaking, a smoke rose suddenly from the cottonwood grove below, which plainly told us what had befallen him; it was raised to inform the surrounding Indians that a blow had been struck, and to tell them to be on their guard. Carson, with several men well mounted, was instantly sent down the river, but returned in the night without tidings of the missing man. They went to the camp we had left, but neither he nor the mule was there. Searching down the river, they found the tracks of the mule, evidently driven along by Indians, whose tracks were on each side of those made by the animal. After going several miles, they came to the mule itself, standing in some bushes, mortally wounded in the side by an arrow, and left to die, that it might be afterwards butchered for food. They also found, in another place, as they were hunting about on the ground for Tabeau's tracks, something that looked like a little puddle of blood, but which the darkness prevented them from verifying. With these details they returned to our camp, and their report saddened all our hearts.

10th.--This morning, as soon as there was light enough to follow tracks, I set out myself, with Mr. Fitzpatrick and several men, in search of Tabeau. We went to the spot where the appearance of puddled blood had been seen; and this, we saw at once, had been the place where he fell and died. Blood upon the leaves, and beaten-down bushes, showed that he had got his wound about twenty paces from where he fell, and that he had struggled for his life. He had probably been shot through the lungs with an arrow. From the place where he lay and bled, it could be seen that he had been dragged to the river bank, and thrown into it. No vestige of what had belonged to him could be found, except a fragment of his horse equipment. Horse, gun, clothes--all became the prey of these Arabs of the New World.

Tabeau had been one of our best men, and his unhappy death spread a gloom over our party. Men, who have gone through such dangers and sufferings as we had seen, become like brothers, and feel each other's loss. To defend and avenge each other, is the deep feeling of all. We wished to avenge his death; but the condition of our horses, languishing for grass and repose, forbade an expedition into unknown mountains. We knew the tribe who had done the mischief--the same which had been insulting our camp. They knew what they deserved, and had the discretion to show themselves to us no more. The day before, they infested our camp; now, not one appeared; nor did we ever afterwards see but one who even belonged to the same tribe, and he at a distance.

Our camp was in a basin below a deep canon--a gap of two thousand feet deep in the mountain--through which the *Rio Virgen* passes, and where no man or beast could follow it. The Spanish trail, which we had lost in the sands of the basin, was on the opposite side of the river. We crossed over to it, and followed it northwardly towards a gap which was visible in the mountain. We approached it by a defile, rendered difficult for our barefooted animals by the rocks strewed along it; and here the country changed its character. From the time we entered the desert, the mountains had been bald and rocky; here they began to be wooded with cedar and pine, and clusters of trees gave shelter to birds--a new and welcome sight--which could not have lived in the desert we had passed.

Descending a long hollow, towards the narrow valley of a stream, we saw before us a snowy mountain, far beyond which appeared another more lofty still. Good bunch-grass began to appear on the hill-sides, and here we found a singular variety of interesting shrubs. The changed appearance of the country infused among our people a more lively spirit, which was heightened by finding at evening a halting-place of very good grass on the clear waters of the **Santa Clara** fork of the **Rio Virgen**.

11th.--The morning was cloudy and quite cool, with a shower of rain--the first we have had since entering the desert, a period of 27 days--and we seem to have entered a different climate, with the usual weather of the Rocky mountains. Our march to-day was very laborious, over very broken ground, along the Santa Clara river; but then the country is no longer so distressingly desolate. The stream is prettily wooded with sweet cottonwood trees--some of them of large size; and on the hills, where the nut-pine is often seen, a good and wholesome grass occurs frequently. This cottonwood, which is now in fruit, is of a different species from any in Michaux's Sylva. Heavy dark clouds covered the sky in the evening and a cold wind sprang up, making fires and overcoats comfortable.

12th.--A little above our encampment the river forked, and we continued up the right-hand branch, gradually ascending towards the summit of the mountain. As we rose towards the head of the creek, the snowy mountains on our right showed out handsomely--high and rugged, with precipices, and covered with snow for about two thousand feet from their summits down. Our animals were somewhat repaid for their hard marches by an excellent camping-ground on the summit of the ridge, which forms here the dividing chain between the waters of the **Rio Virgen**, which goes south to the Colorado, and those of Sevier river, flowing northwardly, and belonging to the Great Basin. We considered ourselves as crossing the rim of the basin; and, entering it at this point, we found here an extensive mountain meadow, rich in bunch-grass, and fresh with numerous springs of clear water, all refreshing and delightful to look upon. It was, in fact, that *las Vegas de Santa Clara*, which had been so long presented to us as the terminating point of the desert, and where the annual caravan from California to New Mexico halted and recruited for some weeks. It was a very suitable place to recover from the fatigue and exhaustion of a month's suffering in the hot and sterile desert. The meadow was about a mile wide, some ten miles long, bordered by grassy hills and mountains-- some of the latter rising two thousand feet, and white with snow down to the level of the *vegas*. Its elevation above the sea was 5,280 feet; latitude, by observation, 37 deg. 28' 28", and its distance from where we first struck the Spanish trail about 400 miles. Counting from the time we reached the desert, and began to skirt, at our descent from Walker's Pass in the Sierra Nevada, we had traveled 550 miles, occupying 27 days, in that inhospitable region. In passing before the Great Caravan, we had the advantage of finding more grass, but the disadvantage of finding also the marauding savages, who had gathered down upon the trail, waiting the approach of that prey. This greatly increased our labors, besides costing us the life of an excellent man. We had to move all day in a state of watch, and prepared for combat--scouts and flankers out, a front and rear division of our men, and baggage-animals in the centre. At night, camp duty was severe. Those who had toiled all day, had to guard, by turns, the camp and the horses, all night. Frequently one-third of the whole party were on guard at once; and nothing but this vigilance saved us from attack. We were constantly dogged by bands, and even whole tribes of marauders; and although Tabeau was killed, and our camp infested and insulted by some, while swarms of them remained on the hills and mountain- sides, there was manifestly a consultation and calculation going on, to decide the question of attacking us. Having reached the resting-place of the *Vegas de Santa Clara*, we had complete relief from the heat and privations of the desert, and some relaxation from the severity of camp duty. Some relaxation, and relaxation only--for camp-guards, horse-guards, and scouts, are indispensable from the time of leaving the frontiers of Missouri until we return to them.

After we left the *Vegas*, we had the gratification to be joined by the famous hunter and trapper, Mr. Joseph Walker, whom I have before mentioned, and who now became our guide. He had left California with the great caravan; and perceiving, from the signs along the trail, that there was a party of whites ahead, which he judged to be mine, he detached himself from the caravan, with eight men, (Americans,) and ran the gauntlet of the desert robbers, killing two, and getting some of the horses wounded, and succeeded in overtaking us. Nothing but his great knowledge of the country, great courage and presence of mind, and good rifles, could have brought him safe from such a perilous enterprise.

13th.--We remained one day at this noted place of rest and refreshment; and, resuming our progress in a northwestwardly direction, we descended into a broad valley, the water of which is tributary to Sevier lake. The next day we came in sight of the Wahsatch range of mountains on the right, white with snow, and here forming the southeast part of the Great Basin. Sevier lake, upon the waters of which we now were, belonged to the system of lakes in the eastern part of the Basin--of which, the Great Salt lake, and its southern limb, the Utah lake, were the principal--towards the region of which we were now approaching. We traveled for several days in this direction, within the rim of the Great Basin, crossing little streams which bore to the left for Sevier lake; and plainly seeing, by the changed aspect of the country, that we were entirely clear of the desert, and approaching the regions which appertained to the system of the Rocky mountains. We met, in this traverse, a few mounted Utah Indians, in advance of their main body, watching the approach of the great caravan.

16th.--We reached a small salt lake, about seven miles long and one broad, at the northern extremity of which we encamped for the night. This little lake, which well merits its characteristic name, lies immediately at the base of the Wah-satch range, and nearly opposite a gap in that chain of mountains through which the Spanish trail passes; and which, again falling upon the waters of the Colorado, and crossing that river, proceeds over a mountainous country to Santa Fe.

17th.--After 440 miles of traveling on a trail, which served for a road, we again found ourselves under the necessity of exploring a track through the wilderness. The Spanish trail had borne off to the southeast, crossing the Wah-satch range. Our course led to the northeast, along the foot of that range, and leaving it on the right. The mountain presented itself to us under the form of several ridges, rising one above the other, rocky, and wooded with pine and cedar; the last ridge covered with snow. Sevier river, flowing northwardly to the lake of the same name, collects its principal waters from this section of the Wah-satch chain. We had now entered a region of great pastoral promise, abounding with fine streams, the rich bunch-grass, soil that would produce wheat, and indigenous flax growing as if it had been sown. Consistent with the general character of its bordering mountains, this fertility of soil and vegetation does not extend far into the Great Basin. Mr. Joseph Walker, our guide, and who has more knowledge of these parts than any man I know, informed me that all the country to the left was unknown to him, and that even the ***Digger*** tribes, which frequented Lake Sevier, could tell him nothing about it.

20th.--We met a band of Utah Indians, headed by a well-known chief, who had obtained the American or English name of Walker, by which he is quoted and well known. They were all mounted, armed with rifles, and used their rifles well. The chief had a fusee, which he carried slung, in addition to his rifle. They were journeying slowly towards the Spanish trail, to levy their usual tribute upon the great California caravan. They were robbers of a higher order than those of the desert. They conducted their depredations with form, and under the color of trade and toll, for passing through their country. Instead of attacking and killing, they affect to purchase--taking the horses they like, and giving something nominal in return. The chief was quite civil to me. He was personally acquainted with his namesake, our guide, who made my name known to him. He knew of my expedition of 1842; and, as tokens of friendship, and proof that we had met, proposed an interchange of presents. We had no great store to choose out of; so he gave me a Mexican blanket, and I gave him a very fine one which I had obtained at Vancouver.

23d.--We reached Sevier river--the main tributary of the lake of the same name--which, deflecting from its northern course, here breaks from the mountains to enter the lake. It was really a fine river, from eight to twelve feet deep; and after searching in vain for a fordable place, we made little boats (or rather rafts) out of bulrushes, and ferried across. These rafts are readily made, and give a good conveyance across a river. The rushes are bound in bundles, and tied hard; the bundles are tied down upon poles, as close as they can be pressed, and fashioned like a boat, in being broader in the middle and pointed at the ends. The rushes, being tubular and jointed, are light and strong. The raft swims well, and is shoved along by poles, or paddled, or pushed and pulled by swimmers, or drawn by ropes. On this occasion, we used ropes--one at each end--and rapidly drew our little float backwards and forwards from shore to shore. The horses swam. At our place of crossing, which was the most northern point of its bend, the latitude was 39 deg. 22' 19". The banks sustained the character for fertility and vegetation which we had seen for some days. The name of this river and lake was an indication of our approach to regions of which our people had been the explorers. It was probably named after some American trapper or hunter, and was the first American name we had met with since leaving the Columbia river. From the Dalles to the point where we turned across the Sierra Nevada, near 1,000 miles, we heard Indian names, and the greater part of the distance none; from Nueva Helvetia (Sacramento) to *las Vegas de Santa Clara*, about 1,000 more, all were Spanish; from the Mississippi to the Pacific, French and American or English were intermixed; and this prevalence of names indicates the national character of the first explorers.

We had here the misfortune to lose one of our people, Francois Badeau, who had been with me on both expeditions; during which he had always been one of my most faithful and efficient men. He was killed in drawing towards him a gun by the muzzle; the hammer being caught, discharged the gun, driving the ball through his head. We buried him on the banks of the river.

Crossing the next day a slight ridge along the river, we entered a handsome mountain valley covered with fine grass, and directed our course towards a high snowy peak, at the foot of which lay the Utah lake. On our right was a bed of high mountains, their summits covered with snow, constituting the dividing ridge between the Basin waters and those of the Colorado. At noon we fell in with a party of Utah Indians coming out of the mountain, and in the afternoon encamped on a tributary to the lake, which is separated from the waters of the Sevier by very slight dividing grounds.

Early the next day we came in sight of the lake; and, as we descended to the broad bottoms of the Spanish fork, three horsemen were seen galloping towards us, who proved to be Utah Indians--scouts from a village, which was encamped near the mouth of the river. They were armed with rifles, and their horses were in good condition. We encamped near them, on the Spanish fork, which is one of the principal tributaries to the lake. Finding the Indians troublesome, and desirous to remain here a day, we removed the next morning farther down the lake and encamped on a fertile bottom near the foot of the same mountainous ridge which borders the Great Salt lake, and along which we had journeyed the previous September. Here the principal plants in bloom were two, which were remarkable as affording to the Snake Indians--the one an abundant supply of food, and the other the most useful among the applications which they use for wounds. These were the kooyah plant, growing in fields of extraordinary luxuriance, and ***convollaria stellata***, which, from the experience of Mr. Walker, is the best remedial plant known among these Indians. A few miles below us was another village of Indians, from which we obtained some fish--among them a few salmon trout, which were very much inferior in size to those along the Californian mountains. The season for taking them had not yet arrived; but the Indians were daily expecting them to come up out of the lake.

We had now accomplished an object we had in view when leaving the Dalles of the Columbia in November last: we had reached the Utah lake; but by a route very different from the one we had intended, and without sufficient time remaining to make the examinations which we desired. It is a lake of note in this country, under the dominion of the Utahs, who resort to it for fish. Its greatest breadth is about fifteen miles, stretching far to the north, narrowing as it goes, and connecting with the Great Salt lake. This is the report, which I believe to be correct; but it is fresh water, while the other is not only salt, but a saturated solution of salt; and here is a problem which requires to be solved. It is almost entirely surrounded by mountains, walled on the north and east by a high and snowy range, which supplies to it a fan of tributary streams. Among these, the principal river is the ***Timpan-ogo***--signifying Rock river--a name which the rocky grandeur of its scenery, remarkable even in this country of rugged mountains, has obtained for it from the Indians. In the Utah language, ***og-wah-be***, the term for river, when coupled with other words in common conversation, is usually abbreviated to ***ogo; timpan*** signifying rock. It is probable that this river furnished the name which on the older maps has been generally applied to the Great Salt lake; but for this I have preferred a name which will be regarded as highly characteristic, restricting to the river the descriptive term Timpan-ogo, and leaving for the lake into which it flows the name of the people who reside on its shores, and by which it is known throughout the country.

The volume of water afforded by the Timpan-ogo is probably equal to that of the Sevier river; and, at the time of our visit, there was only one place in the lake-valley at which the Spanish fork was fordable. In the cove of the mountains along its eastern shore, the lake is bordered by a plain, where the soil is generally good, and in greater part fertile; watered by a delta of prettily timbered streams. This would be an excellent locality for stock-farms; it is generally covered with good bunch-grass, and would abundantly produce the ordinary grains.

In arriving at the Utah lake, we had completed an immense circuit of twelve degrees diameter north and south, and ten degrees east and west; and found ourselves, in May, 1844, on the same sheet of water which we had left in September, 1843. The Utah is the southern limb of the Great Salt lake; and thus we had seen that remarkable sheet of water both at its northern and southern extremity, and were able to fix its position at these two points. The circuit which we had made, and which had cost us eight months of time, and 3,500 miles of traveling, had given us a view of Oregon and of North California from the Rocky mountains to the Pacific ocean, and of the two principal streams which form bays or harbors on the coast of that sea. Having completed this circuit, and being now about to turn the back upon the Pacific slope of our continent, and to recross the Rocky mountains, it is natural to look back upon our footsteps, and take some brief view of the leading features and general structure of the country we had traversed. These are peculiar and striking, and differ essentially from the Atlantic side of the country. The mountains all are higher, more numerous, and more distinctly defined in their ranges and directions; and, what is so contrary to the natural order of formations, one of these ranges, which is near the coast, (the Sierra Nevada and the Coast Range,) presents higher elevations and peaks than any which are to be found in the Rocky mountains themselves. In our eight months' circuit, we were never out of sight of snow; and the Sierra Nevada, where we crossed it, was near 2,000 feet higher than the South Pass in the Rocky mountains. In height, these mountains greatly exceed those of the Atlantic side, constantly presenting peaks which enter the region of eternal snow; and some of them volcanic, and in a frequent state of activity. They are seen at great distances, and guide the traveler in his course.

The course and elevation of these ranges give direction to the rivers and character to the coast. No great river does, or can, take its rise below the Cascade and Sierra Nevada range; the distance to the sea is too short to admit of it. The rivers of the San Francisco bay, which are the largest after the Columbia, are local to that bay, and lateral to the coast, having their sources about on a line with the Dalles of the Columbia, and running each in a valley of its own, between the Coast range and the Cascade and Sierra Nevada range. The Columbia is the only river which traverses the whole breadth of the country, breaking through all the ranges, and entering the sea. Drawing its waters from a section of ten degrees of latitude in the Rocky mountains, which are collected into one stream by three main forks (Lewis's, Clark's, and the North fork) near the centre of the Oregon valley, this great river thence proceeds by a single channel to the sea, while its three forks lead each to a pass in the mountains, which opens the way into the interior of the continent. This fact in relation to the rivers of this region, gives an immense value to the Columbia. Its mouth is the only inlet and outlet to and from the sea: its three forks lead to the passes in the mountains: it is, therefore, the only line of communication between the Pacific and the interior of North America; and all operations of war or commerce, of national or social intercourse, must be conducted upon it. This gives it a value beyond estimation, and would involve irreparable injury if lost. In this unity and concentration of its waters, the Pacific side of our continent differs entirely from the Atlantic side, where the waters of the Alleghany mountains are dispersed into many rivers, having their different entrances into the sea, and opening many lines of communication with the interior.

The Pacific coast is equally different from that of the Atlantic. The coast of the Atlantic is low and open, indented with numerous bays, sounds, and river estuaries, accessible everywhere, and opening by many channels into the heart of the country. The Pacific coast, on the contrary, is high and compact, with few bays, and but one that opens into the heart of the country. The immediate coast is what the seamen call ***iron-bound***. A little within, it is skirted by two successive ranges of mountains, standing as ramparts between the sea and the interior of the country; and to get through which there is but one gate, and that narrow and easily defended. This structure of the coast, backed by these two ranges of mountains, with its concentration and unity of waters, gives to the country an immense military strength, and will probably render Oregon the most impregnable country in the world.

Differing so much from the Atlantic side of our continent, in coast, mountains, and rivers, the Pacific side differs from it in another most rare and singular feature--that of the Great Interior Basin, of which I have so often spoken, and the whole form and character of which I was so anxious to ascertain. Its existence is vouched for by such of the American traders and hunters as have some knowledge of that region; the structure of the Sierra Nevada range of mountains requires it to be there; and my own observations confirm it. Mr. Joseph Walker, who is so well acquainted in these parts, informed me that, from the Great Salt lake west, there was a succession of lakes and rivers which have no outlet to the sea, nor any connection with the Columbia, or with the Colorado of the Gulf of California. He described some of these lakes as being large, with numerous streams, and even considerable rivers falling into them. In fact, all concur in the general report of these interior rivers and lakes; and, for want of understanding the force and power of evaporation, which so soon establishes an equilibrium between the loss and supply of waters, the fable of whirlpools and subterraneous outlets has gained belief, as the only imaginable way of carrying off the waters which have no visible discharge. The structure of the country would require this formation of interior lakes; for the waters which would collect between the Rocky mountains and the Sierra Nevada, not being able to cross this formidable barrier, nor to get to the Columbia or the Colorado, must naturally collect into reservoirs, each of which would have its little system of streams and rivers to supply it. This would be the natural effect; and what I saw went to confirm it. The Great Salt lake is a formation of this kind, and quite a large one; and having many streams, and one considerable river, 400 or 500 miles long, falling into it. This lake and river I saw and examined myself; and also saw the Wah-satch and Bear River mountains, which enclose the waters of the lake on the east, and constitute, in that quarter, the rim of the Great Basin. Afterwards, along the eastern base of the Sierra Nevada, where we traveled for 42 days, I saw the line of lakes and rivers which lie at the foot of that Sierra; and which Sierra is the western rim of the Basin. In going down Lewis's fork and the main Columbia, I crossed only inferior streams coming in from the left, such as could draw their water from a short distance only; and I often saw the mountains at their heads white with snow,--which, all accounts said, divided the waters of the *desert* from those of the Columbia, and which could be no other than the range of mountains which form the rim of the Basin on its northern side. And in returning from California along the Spanish trail, as far as the head of the Santa Clara fork of the Rio Virgen, I crossed only small streams making their way south to the Colorado, or lost in sand, (as the Mo-hah-ve;) while to the left, lofty mountains, their summits white with snow, were often visible, and which must have turned water to the north as well as to the south, and thus constituted, on this part, the southern rim of the Basin. At the head of the Santa Clara fork, and in the Vegas de Santa Clara, we crossed the ridge which parted the two systems of waters. We entered the Basin at that point, and have traveled in it ever since; having its southeastern rim (the Wah-satch mountain) on the right, and crossing the streams which flow down into it. The existence of the Basin is, therefore, an established fact in my mind: its extent and contents are yet to be better ascertained. It cannot be less than 400 or 500 miles each way, and must lie principally in the Alta California; the demarcation latitude of 42 deg. probably cutting a segment from the north part of the rim. Of its interior, but little is known. It is called a **desert**, and, from what I saw of it, sterility may be its prominent characteristic; but where there is so much water, there must be some **oasis**. The great river, and the great lake, reported, may not be equal to the report; but where there is so much snow, there must be streams; and where there is no outlet, there must be lakes to hold the accumulated waters, or sands to swallow them up. In this eastern part of the Basin, containing Sevier, Utah, and the Great Salt lakes, and the rivers and creeks falling into them, we know there is good soil and good grass, adapted to civilized settlements. In the western part, on Salmon Trout river, and some other streams, the same remark may be made.

    The contents of this great Basin are yet to be examined. That it is peopled, we know; but miserably and sparsely. From all that I heard and saw, I should say that humanity here appeared in its lowest form, and in its most elementary state. Dispersed in single families; without fire- arms; eating seeds and insects; digging roots, (and hence their name,)-- such is the condition of the greater part. Others are a degree higher, and live in communities upon some lake or river that supplies fish, and from which they repulse the miserable **Digger**. The rabbit is the largest animal known in this desert; its flesh affords a little meat; and their bag-like covering is made of its skins. The wild sage is their only wood, and here it is of extraordinary size--sometimes a foot in diameter, and six or eight feet high. It serves for fuel, for building material, for shelter to the rabbits, and for some sort of covering for the feet and legs in cold weather. Such are the accounts of the inhabitants and productions of the Great Basin; and which, though imperfect, must have some foundation, and excite our desire to know the whole.

The whole idea of such a desert, and such a people, is a novelty in our country, and excites Asiatic, not American ideas. Interior basins, with their own systems of lakes and rivers, and often sterile, are common enough in Asia; people still in the elementary state of families, living in deserts, with no other occupation than the mere animal search for food, may still be seen in that ancient quarter of the globe; but in America such things are new and strange, unknown and unsuspected, and discredited when related. But I flatter myself that what is discovered, though not enough to satisfy curiosity, is sufficient to excite it, and that subsequent explorations will complete what has been commenced.

This account of the Great Basin, it will be remembered, belongs to the Alta California, and has no application to Oregon, whose capabilities may justify a separate remark. Referring to my journal for particular descriptions, and for sectional boundaries between good and bad districts, I can only say, in general and comparative terms, that, in that branch of agriculture which implies the cultivation of grains and staple crops, it would be inferior to the Atlantic States, though many parts are superior for wheat; while in the rearing of flocks and herds it would claim a high place. Its grazing capabilities are great; and even in the indigenous grass now there, an element of individual and national wealth may be found. In fact, the valuable grasses begin within one hundred and fifty miles of the Missouri frontier, and extend to the Pacific ocean. East of the Rocky mountains, it is the short curly grass, on which the buffalo delights to feed, (whence its name of buffalo,) and which is still good when dry and apparently dead. West of those mountains it is a larger growth, in clusters, and hence called bunch-grass, and which has a second or fall growth. Plains and mountains both exhibit them; and I have seen good pasturage at an elevation of ten thousand feet. In this spontaneous product the trading or traveling caravans can find subsistence for their animals; and in military operations any number of cavalry may be moved, and any number of cattle may be driven; and thus men and horses be supported on long expeditions, and even in winter, in the sheltered situations.

Commercially, the value of the Oregon country must be great, washed as it is by the North Pacific ocean--fronting Asia--producing many of the elements of commerce--mild and healthy in its climate--and becoming, as it naturally will, a thoroughfare for the East India and China trade.

Turning our faces once more eastward, on the morning of the 27th we left the Utah lake, and continued for two days to ascend the Spanish fork, which is dispersed in numerous branches among very rugged mountains, which afford few passes, and render a familiar acquaintance with them necessary to the traveler. The stream can scarcely be said to have a valley, the mountains rising often abruptly from the water's edge; but a good trail facilitated our traveling, and there were frequent bottoms, covered with excellent grass. The streams are prettily and variously wooded; and everywhere the mountain shows grass and timber.

At our encampment on the evening of the 28th, near the head of one of the branches we had ascended, strata of bituminous limestone were displayed in an escarpment on the river bluffs, in which were contained a variety of fossil shells of new species.

It will be remembered, that in crossing this ridge about 120 miles to the northward in August last, strata of fossiliferous rock were discovered, which have been referred to the oolitic period; it is probable that these rocks also belong to the same formation.

A few miles from this encampment we reached the bed of the stream, and crossing, by an open and easy pass, the dividing ridge which separates the waters of the Great Basin from those of the Colorado, we reached the head branches of one of its larger tributaries, which, from the decided color of its waters, has received the name of White river. The snows of the mountains were now beginning to melt, and all the little rivulets were running by in rivers, and rapidly becoming difficult to ford. Continuing a few miles up a branch of White river, we crossed a dividing ridge between its waters and those of ***Uintah***. The approach to the pass, which is the best known to Mr. Walker, was somewhat difficult for packs, and impracticable for wagons--all the streams being shut in by narrow ravines, and the narrow trail along the steep hill-sides allowing the passage of only one animal at a time. From the summit we had a fine view of the snowy Bear River range, and there were still remaining beds of snow on the cold sides of the hills near the pass. We descended by a narrow ravine, in which was rapidly gathered a little branch of the Uintah, and halted to noon about 1,500 feet below the pass, at an elevation, by the boiling point, of 6,900 feet above the sea.

The next day we descended along the river, and about noon reached a point where three forks come together. Fording one of these with some difficulty, we continued up the middle branch, which, from the color of its waters, is named the Red river. The few passes, and extremely rugged nature of the country, give to it great strength, and secure the Utahs from the intrusion of their enemies. Crossing in the afternoon a somewhat broken highland, covered in places with fine grasses, and with cedar on the hill-sides, we encamped at evening on another tributary to the *Uintah*, called the *Duchesne* fork. The water was very clear, the stream not being yet swollen by the melting snows, and we forded it without any difficulty. It is a considerable branch, being spread out by islands, the largest arm being about a hundred feet wide, and the name it bears is probably that of some old French trapper.

The next day we continued down the river, which we were twice obliged to cross; and, the water having risen during the night, it was almost everywhere too deep to be forded. After traveling about sixteen miles, we encamped again on the left bank.

I obtained here an occultation of *Scorpii* at the dark limb of the moon, which gives for the longitude of the place 112 deg. 18' 30", and the latitude 40 deg. 18' 53".

JUNE.

1st.--We left to-day the Duchesne fork, and, after traversing a broken country for about sixteen miles, arrived at noon at another considerable branch, a river of great velocity, to which the trappers have improperly given the name of Lake fork. The name applied to it by the Indians signifies great swiftness, and is the same which they use to express the speed of a racehorse. It is spread out in various channels over several hundred yards, and is everywhere too deep and swift to be forded. At this season of the year, there is an uninterrupted noise from the large rocks which are rolled along the bed. After infinite difficulty, and the delay of a day, we succeeded in getting the stream bridged, and got over with the loss of one of our animals. Continuing our route across a broken country, of which the higher parts were rocky and timbered with cedar, and the lower parts covered with good grass, we reached, on the afternoon of the 3d, the Uintah fort, a trading-post belonging to Mr. A. Roubideau, on the principal fork of the Uintah river. We found the stream nearly as rapid and difficult as the Lake fork, divided into several channels, which were too broad to be bridged. With the aid of guides from the fort, we succeeded, with very great difficulty, in fording it, and encamped near the fort, which is situated a short distance above the junction of two branches which make the river.

By an immersion of the first satellite, (agreeing well with the result of the occultation observed at the Duchesne fork,) the longitude of the post is 109 deg. 56' 42", the latitude 40 deg. 27' 45".

It has a motley garrison of Canadian and Spanish *engages* and hunters, with the usual number of Indian women. We obtained a small supply of sugar and coffee, with some dried meat and a cow, which was a very acceptable change from the *pinoli* on which we had subsisted for some weeks past. I strengthened my party at this place by the addition of Auguste Archambeau, an excellent voyageur and hunter, belonging to the class of Carson and Godey.

On the morning of the 5th we left the fort [Footnote: This fort was attacked and taken by a band of the Utah Indians since we passed it, and the men of the garrison killed--the women carried off. Mr. Roubideau, a trader of St. Louis, was absent, and so escaped the fate of the rest.] and the Uintah river, and continued our road over a broken country, which afforded, however, a rich addition to our botanical collection; and, after a march of 25 miles, were again checked by another stream, called Ashley's fork, where we were detained until noon of the next day.

An immersion of the second satellite gave for this place a longitude of 109 deg. 27' 07", the latitude, by observation, being 40 deg. 28' 07".

In the afternoon of the next day we succeeded in finding a ford; and, after traveling 15 miles, encamped high up on the mountain-side, where we found excellent and abundant grass, which we had not hitherto seen. A new species of *elymus*, which had a purgative and weakening effect upon the animals, had occurred abundantly since leaving the fort. From this point, by observation 7,300 feet above the sea, we had a view of Colorado below, shut up amongst rugged mountains, and which is the recipient of all the streams we had been crossing since we passed the rim of the Great Basin at the head of the Spanish fork.

On the 7th we had a pleasant but long day's journey, through beautiful little valleys and a high mountain country, arriving about evening at the verge of a steep and rocky ravine, by which we descended to "*Brown's hole*." This is a place well known to trappers in the country, where the canons through which the Colorado runs expand into a narrow but pretty valley, about 16 miles in length. The river was several hundred yards in breadth, swollen to the top of its banks, near to which it was in many places 15 to 20 feet deep. We repaired a skin-boat which had been purchased at the fort, and, after a delay of a day, reached the opposite banks with much less delay than had been encountered on the Uintah waters. According to information, the lower end of the valley is the most eastern part of the Colorado; and the latitude of our encampment, which was opposite to the remains of an old fort on the left bank of the river, was 40 deg. 46' 27", and, by observation, the elevation above the sea 5,150 feet. The bearing to the entrance of the canon below was south 20 deg. east. Here the river enters between lofty precipices of red rock, and the country below is said to assume a very rugged character, the river and its affluents passing through canons which forbid all access to the water. This sheltered little valley was formerly a favorite wintering ground for the trappers, as it afforded them sufficient pasturage for their animals, and the surrounding mountains are well stocked with game.

We surprised a flock of mountain sheep as we descended to the river, and our hunters killed several. The bottoms of a small stream called Vermilion creek, which enters the left bank of the river a short distance below our encampment, were covered abundantly with **F. vermicularis**, and other chenopodiaceous shrubs. From the lower end of Brown's hole we issued by a remarkably dry canon, fifty or sixty yards wide, and rising, as we advanced, to the height of six or eight hundred feet. Issuing from this, and crossing a small green valley, we entered another rent of the same nature, still narrower than the other, the rocks on either side rising in nearly vertical precipices perhaps 1,500 feet in height. These places are mentioned, to give some idea of the country lower down on the Colorado, to which the trappers usually apply the name of a canon country. The canon opened upon a pond of water, where we halted to noon. Several flocks of mountain sheep were here among the rocks, which rung with volleys of small-arms. In the afternoon we entered upon an ugly, barren, and broken country, corresponding well with that we had traversed a few degrees north, on the same side of the Colorado. The Vermilion creek afforded us brackish water and indifferent grass for the night.

A few scattered cedar-trees were the only improvement of the country on the following day; and at a little spring of bad water, where we halted at noon, we had not even the shelter of these from the hot rays of the sun. At night we encamped in a fine grove of cottonwood-trees, on the banks of the Elk Head river, the principal fork of the Yampah river, commonly called by the trappers the Bear river. We made here a very strong fort, and formed the camp into vigilant guards. The country we were now entering was constantly infested by war parties of the Sioux and other Indians, and is among the most dangerous war-grounds in the Rocky mountains; parties of whites having been repeatedly defeated on this river.

On the 11th we continued up the river, which is a considerable stream, fifty to a hundred yards in width, handsomely and continuously wooded with groves of the narrow-leaved cottonwood, ***populus angustifolia***; with these were thickets of willow, and ***grain du boeuf***. The characteristic plant along the river is **F. vermicularis**, which generally covers the bottoms; mingled with this are saline shrubs and artemisia. The new variety of grass which we had seen on leaving the Uintah fort had now disappeared. The country on either side was sandy and poor, scantily wooded with cedars, but the river bottoms afforded good pasture. Three antelopes were killed in the afternoon, and we encamped a little below a branch of the river, called St. Vrain's fork. A few miles above was the fort at which Frapp's party had been defeated two years since; and we passed during the day a place where Carson had been fired upon so close that one of the men had five bullets through his body. Leaving this river the next morning, we took our way across the hills, where every hollow had a spring of running water with good grass.

Yesterday and to-day we had before our eyes the high mountains which divide the Pacific from the Mississippi waters; and entering here among the lower spurs or foot-hills of the range, the face of the country began to improve with a magical rapidity. Not only the river bottoms, but the hills were covered with grass; and among the usual varied flora of the mountain region, these were occasionally blue with the showy bloom of a ***lupinus***. In the course of the morning we had the first glad view of buffalo, and welcomed the appearance of two old bulls with as much joy as if they had been messengers from home; and when we descended to noon on St. Vrain's fork, an affluent of Green river, the hunters brought in mountain sheep and the meat of two fat bulls. Fresh entrails in the river showed us that there were Indians above, and at evening, judging it unsafe to encamp in the bottoms, which were wooded only with willow thickets, we ascended to the spurs above, and forted strongly in a small aspen grove, near to which was a spring of cold water. The hunters killed two fine cows near the camp. A band of elk broke out of a neighboring grove; antelopes were running over the hills; and on the opposite river-plains herds of buffalo were raising clouds of dust. The country here appeared more variously stocked with game than any part of the Rocky mountains we had visited; and its abundance is owing to the excellent pasturage, and its dangerous character as a war-ground.

13th.--There was snow here near our mountain camp, and the morning was beautiful and cool. Leaving St. Vrain's fork, we took our way directly towards the summit of the dividing ridge. The bottoms of the streams and level places were wooded with aspens; and as we neared the summit, we entered again the piny region. We had a delightful morning's ride, the ground affording us an excellent bridle-path, and reached the summit towards mid-day, at an elevation of 8,000 feet. With joy and exultation we saw ourselves once more on the top of the Rocky mountains, and beheld a little stream taking its course towards the rising sun. It was an affluent of the Platte, called Pullam's fork, and we descended to noon upon it. It is a pretty stream, twenty yards broad, and bears the name of a trapper who, some years since, was killed here by the **Gros Ventre** Indians.

Issuing from the pines in the afternoon we saw spread out before us the valley of the Platte, with the pass of the Medicine Butte beyond, and some of the Sweet Water mountains; but a smoky haziness in the air entirely obscured the Wind River chain.

We were now about two degrees south of the South Pass, and our course home would have been eastwardly; but that would have taken us over ground already examined, and therefore without the interest that would excite curiosity. Southwardly there were objects worthy to be explored, to wit: the approximation of the head-waters of three different rivers--the Platte, the Arkansas, and the Grand River fork of the Rio Colorado of the Gulf of California; the passages at the heads of these rivers; and the three remarkable mountain coves, called Parks, in which they took their rise. One of these Parks was, of course, on the western side of the dividing ridge; and a visit to it would once more require us to cross the summit of the Rocky mountains to the west, and then to recross to the east, making in all, with the transit we had just accomplished, three crossings of that mountain in this section of its course. But no matter. The coves, the heads of the rivers, the approximation of their waters, the practicability of the mountain passes, and the locality of the three Parks, were all objects of interest, and, although well known to hunters and trappers, were unknown to science and to history. We therefore changed our course, and turned up the valley of the Platte instead of going down it.

We crossed several small affluents, and again made a fortified camp in a grove. The country had now became very beautiful--rich in water, grass, and game; and to these were added the charm of scenery and pleasant weather.

14th.--Our route this morning lay along the foot of the mountain, over the long low spurs which sloped gradually down to the river, forming the broad valley of the Platte. The country is beautifully watered. In almost every hollow ran a clear, cool, mountain stream; and in the course of the morning we crossed seventeen, several of them being large creeks, forty to fifty feet wide, with a swift current, and tolerably deep. These were variously wooded with groves of aspen and cottonwood, with willow, cherry, and other shrubby trees. Buffalo, antelope, and elk, were frequent during the day; and, in their abundance; the latter sometimes reminded us slightly of the Sacramento valley.

We halted at noon on Potter's fork--a clear and swift stream, forty yards wide, and in many places deep enough to swim our animals; and in the evening encamped on a pretty stream, where there were several beaver dams, and many trees recently cut down by the beaver. We gave to this the name of Beaver Dam creek, as now they are becoming sufficiently rare to distinguish by their names the streams on which they are found. In this mountain they occurred more abundantly than elsewhere in all our journey, in which their vestiges had been scarcely seen.

The next day we continued our journey up the valley, the country presenting much the same appearance, except that the grass was more scanty on the ridges, over which was spread a scrubby growth of sage; but still the bottoms of the creeks were broad, and afforded good pasture-grounds. We had an animated chase after a grizzly bear this morning, which we tried to lasso. Fuentes threw the lasso upon his neck, but it slipped off, and he escaped into the dense thickets of the creek, into which we did not like to venture. Our course in the afternoon brought us to the main Platte river, here a handsome stream, with a uniform breadth of seventy yards, except where widened by frequent islands. It was apparently deep, with a moderate current, and wooded with groves of large willow.

The valley narrowed as we ascended, and presently degenerated into a gorge, through which the river passed as through a gate. We entered it, and found ourselves in the New Park--a beautiful circular valley of thirty miles diameter, walled in all round with snowy mountains, rich with water and with grass, fringed with pine on the mountain sides below the snow line, and a paradise to all grazing animals. The Indian name for it signifies "cow lodge," of which our own may be considered a translation; the enclosure, the grass, the water, and the herds of buffalo roaming over it, naturally presenting the idea of a park. We halted for the night just within the gate, and expected, as usual, to see herds of buffalo; but an Arapahoe village had been before us, and not one was to be seen. Latitude of the encampment 40 deg. 52' 44". Elevation by the boiling point 7,720 feet.

It is from this elevated cove, and from the gorges of the surrounding mountains, and some lakes within their bosoms, that the Great Platte river collects its first waters, and assumes its first form; and certainly no river could ask a more beautiful origin.

16th.--In the morning we pursued our way through the Park, following a principal branch of the Platte, and crossing, among many smaller ones, a bold stream, scarcely fordable, called Lodge Pole fork, and which issues from a lake in the mountains on the right, ten miles long. In the evening we encamped on a small stream near the upper end of the Park. Latitude of the camp 40 deg. 33' 22".

17th.--We continued our way among the waters of the Park over the foot- hills of the bordering mountains, where we found good pasturage, and surprised and killed some buffalo. We fell into a broad and excellent trail, made by buffalo, where a wagon would pass with ease; and, in the course of the morning we crossed the summit of the Rocky mountains, through a pass which was one of the most beautiful we had ever seen. The trail led among the aspens, through open grounds, richly covered with grass, and carried us over an elevation of about 9,000 feet above the level of the sea.

The country appeared to great advantage in the delightful summer weather of the mountains, which we still continued to enjoy. Descending from the pass, we found ourselves again on the western waters; and halted to noon on the edge of another mountain valley, called the Old Park, in which is formed Grand river, one of the principal branches of the Colorado of California. We were now moving with some caution, as, from the trail, we found the Arapahoe village had also passed this way; as we were coming out of their enemy's country, and this was a war-ground, we were desirous to avoid them. After a long afternoon's march, we halted at night on a small creek, tributary to a main fork of Grand river, which ran through this portion of the valley. The appearance of the country in the Old Park is interesting, though of a different character from the New; instead of being a comparative plain, it is more or less broken into hills, and surrounded by the high mountains, timbered on the lower parts with quaking asp and pines.

18th.--Our scouts, who were as usual ahead, made from a ***butte*** this morning the signal of Indians, and we rode up in time to meet a party of about 30 Arapahoes. They were men and women going into the hills--the men for game, the women for roots--and informed us that the village was encamped a few miles above, on the main fork of Grand river, which passes through the midst of the valley. I made them the usual presents; but they appeared disposed to be unfriendly, and galloped back at speed to the village. Knowing that we had trouble to expect, I descended immediately into the bottoms of Grand river, which were overflowed in places, the river being up, and made the best encampment the ground afforded. We had no time to build a fort, but found an open place among the willows, which was defended by the river on one side and the overflowed bottoms on the other. We had scarcely made our few preparations, when about 200 of them appeared on the verge of the bottom, mounted, painted, and armed for war. We planted the American flag between us; and a short parley ended in a truce, with something more than the usual amount of presents. About 20 Sioux were with them--one of them an old chief, who had always been friendly to the whites. He informed me that, before coming down, a council had been held at the village, in which the greater part had declared for attacking us--we had come from their enemies, to whom we had doubtless been carrying assistance in arms and ammunition; but his own party, with some few of the Arapahoes who had seen us the previous year in the plains, opposed it. It will be remembered that it is customary for this people to attack the trading parties which they meet in this region, considering all whom they meet on the western side of the mountains to be their enemies. They deceived me into the belief that I should find a ford at their village, and I could not avoid accompanying them; but put several sloughs between us and their village, and forted strongly on the banks of the river, which was everywhere rapid and deep, and over a hundred yards in breadth. The camp was generally crowded with Indians; and though the baggage was carefully watched and covered, a number of things were stolen.

The next morning we descended the river for about eight miles, and halted a short distance above a canon, through which Grand river issues from the Park. Here it was smooth and deep, 150 yards in breadth, and its elevation at this point 6,700 feet. A frame for the boat being very soon made, our baggage was ferried across; the horses, in the mean time, swimming over. A southern fork of Grand river here makes its junction, nearly opposite to the branch by which we had entered the valley, and up this we continued for about eight miles in the afternoon and encamped in a bottom on the left bank, which afforded good grass. At our encampment it was 70 to 90 yards in breadth, sometimes widened by islands, and separated into several channels, with a very swift current and bed of rolled rocks.

On the 20th we traveled up the left bank, with the prospect of a bad road, the trail here taking the opposite side; but the stream was up, and nowhere fordable. A piny ridge of mountains, with bare rocky peaks, was on our right all the day, and a snowy mountain appeared ahead. We crossed many foaming torrents with rocky beds, rushing down the river; and in the evening made a strong fort in an aspen grove. The valley had already become very narrow, shut up more closely in densely timbered mountains, the pines sweeping down the verge of the bottoms. The coq de prairie (tetrao europhasianus) was occasionally seen among the sage.

We saw to-day the returning trail of an Arapahoe party which had been sent from the village to look for Utahs in the Bayou Salade, (South Park;) and it being probable that they would visit our camp with the desire to return on horseback, we were more than usually on the alert.

Here the river diminished to 35 yards, and, notwithstanding the number of affluents we had crossed, was still a large stream, dashing swiftly by, with a great continuous fall, and not yet fordable. We had a delightful ride along a good trail among the fragrant pines; and the appearance of buffalo in great numbers indicated that there were Indians in the Bayou Salade, (South Park,) by whom they were driven out. We halted to noon under the shade of the pines, and the weather was most delightful. The country was literally alive with buffalo; and the continued echo of the hunters' rifles on the other side of the river for a moment made me uneasy, thinking perhaps they were engaged with Indians; but in a short time they came into camp with the meat of seven fat cows.

During the earlier part of the day's ride, the river had been merely a narrow ravine between high piny mountains, backed on both sides, but particularly on the west, by a line of snowy ridges; but, after several hours' ride, the stream opened out into a valley with pleasant bottoms. In the afternoon the river forked into three apparently equal streams; broad buffalo trails leading up the left hand, and the middle branch, indicating good passes over the mountains; but up the right-hand branch, (which, in the object of descending from the mountain by the main head of the Arkansas, I was most desirous to follow,) there was no sign of a buffalo trace. Apprehending from this reason, and the character of the mountains, which are known to be extremely rugged, that the right-hand branch led to no pass, I proceeded up the middle branch, which formed a flat valley- bottom between timbered ridges on the left and snowy mountains on the right, terminating in large **buttes** of naked rock. The trail was good, and the country interesting; and at nightfall we encamped in an open place among the pines, where we built a strong fort. The mountains exhibit their usual varied growth of flowers, and at this place I noticed, among others, ***thermopsis montana***, whose bright yellow color makes it a showy plant. This has been a characteristic in many parts of the country since reaching the Uintah waters. With fields of iris were ***aquilegia coerulea***, violets, esparcette, and strawberries.

At dark we perceived a fire in the edge of the pines, on the opposite side of the valley. We had evidently not been discovered, and, at the report of a gun, and the blaze of fresh fuel which was heaped on our fires, those of the strangers were instantly extinguished. In the morning, they were found to be a party of six trappers, who had ventured out among the mountains after beaver. They informed us that two of the number with which they had started had been already killed by the Indians--one of them but a few days since--by the Arapahoes we had lately seen, who had found him alone at a camp on this river, and carried off his traps and animals. As they were desirous to join us, the hunters returned with them to the encampment, and we continued up the valley, in which the stream rapidly diminished, breaking into small tributaries--every hollow affording water. At our noon halt, the hunters joined us with the trappers. While preparing to start from their encampment, they found themselves suddenly surrounded by a party of Arapahoes, who informed them that their scouts had discovered a large Utah village in the Bayou Salade, (South Park,) and that a large war-party, consisting of almost every man in the village, except those who were too old to go to war, were going over to attack them. The main body had ascended the left fork of the river, which afforded a better pass than the branch we were on, and this party had followed our trail, in order that we might add our force to theirs. Carson informed them that we were too far ahead to turn back, but would join them in the bayou; and the Indians went off apparently satisfied. By the temperature of boiling water, our elevation here was 10,430 feet, and still the pine forest continued, and grass was good.

 In the afternoon we continued our road occasionally through open pines, with a very gradual ascent. We surprised a herd of buffalo, enjoying the shade at a small lake among the pines, and they made the dry branches crack, as they broke through the woods. In a ride of about three-quarters of an hour, and having ascended perhaps 800 feet, we reached the ***summit of the dividing ridge***, which would thus have an estimated height of 11,200 feet. Here the river spreads itself into small branches and springs, heading nearly in the summit of the ridge, which is very narrow. Immediately below us was a green valley, through which ran a stream; and a short distance opposite rose snowy mountains, whose summits were formed into peaks of naked rock. We soon afterwards satisfied ourselves that immediately beyond these mountains was the main branch of the Arkansas river--most probably heading directly with the little stream below us, which gathered its waters in the snowy mountains near by. Descriptions of the rugged character of the mountains around the head of the Arkansas, which their appearance amply justified, deterred me from making any attempt to reach it, which would have involved a greater length of time than now remained at my disposal.

 In about a quarter of an hour, we descended from the summit of the Pass into the creek below, our road having been very much controlled and interrupted by the pines and springs on the mountain-side. Turning up the stream, we encamped on a bottom of good grass near its head, which gathers its waters in the dividing crest of the Rocky mountains, and, according to the best information we could obtain, separated only by the rocky wall of the ridge from the head of the main Arkansas river. By the observations of the evening, the latitude of our encampment was 39 deg. 20'

24", and south of which; therefore, is the head of the Arkansas river. The stream on which we had encamped is the head of either the ***Fontaine-qui-bouit***, a branch of the Arkansas, or the remotest head of the south fork of the Platte, as which you will find it laid down on the map. But descending it only through a portion of its course, we have not been able to settle this point satisfactorily. In the evening a band of buffalo furnished a little excitement, by charging through the camp.

On the following day we descended the stream by an excellent buffalo-trail, along the open grassy bottom of the river. On our right, the bayou was bordered by a mountainous range, crested with rocky and naked peaks; and below, it had a beautiful park-like character of pretty level prairies, interspersed among low spurs, wooded openly with pine and quaking asp, contrasting well with the denser pines which swept around on the mountain sides. Descending always the valley of the stream, towards noon we descried a mounted party descending the point of a spur, and, judging them to be Arapahoes--who, defeated or victorious, were equally dangerous to us, and with whom a fight would be inevitable--we hurried to post ourselves as strongly as possible on some willow islands in the river. We had scarcely halted when they arrived, proving to be a party of Utah women, who told us that on the other side of the ridge their village was fighting with the Arapahoes. As soon as they had given us this information, they filled the air with cries and lamentations, which made us understand that some of their chiefs had been killed.

Extending along the river, directly ahead of us, was a low piny ridge, leaving between it and the stream a small open bottom, on which the Utahs had very injudiciously placed their village, which, according to the women, numbered about 300 warriors. Advancing in the cover of the pines, the Arapahoes, about daylight, charged into the village, driving off a great number of their horses, and killing four men; among them, the principal chief of the village. They drove the horses perhaps a mile beyond the village, to the end of a hollow, where they had previously forted, at the edge of the pines. Here the Utahs had instantly attacked them in turn, and, according to the report of the women, were getting rather the best of the day. The women pressed us eagerly to join with their people, and would immediately have provided us with the best horses at the village; but it was not for us to interfere in such a conflict. Neither party were our friends, or under our protection; and each was ready to prey upon us that could. But we could not help feeling an unusual excitement at being within a few hundred yards of a fight, in which 500 men were closely engaged, and hearing the sharp cracks of their rifles. We were in a bad position, and subject to be attacked in it. Either party which we might meet, victorious or defeated, was certain to fall upon us; and, gearing up immediately, we kept close along the pines of the ridge, having it between us and the village, and keeping the scouts on the summit, to give us notice of the approach of Indians. As we passed by the village, which was immediately below us, horsemen were galloping to and fro, and groups of people were gathered around those who were wounded and dead, and who were being brought in from the field. We continued to press on, and, crossing another fork, which came in from the right, after having made fifteen miles from the village, fortified ourselves strongly in the pines, a short distance from the river.

During the afternoon, Pike's Peak had been plainly in view before us, and, from our encampment, bore N. 87 deg. E. by compass. This was a familiar object, and it had for us the face of an old friend. At its foot were the springs, where we had spent a pleasant day in coming out. Near it were the habitations of civilized men; and it overlooked the broad smooth plains, which promised us an easy journey to our home.

The next day we left the river, which continued its course towards Pike's Peak; and taking a southeasterly direction, in about ten miles we crossed a gentle ridge, and, issuing from the South Park, found ourselves involved among the broken spurs of the mountains which border the great prairie plains. Although broken and extremely rugged, the country was very interesting, being well watered by numerous affluents to the Arkansas river, and covered with grass and a variety of trees. The streams, which, in the upper part of their course, ran through grassy and open hollows, after a few miles all descended into deep and impracticable canons, through which they found their way to the Arkansas valley. Here the buffalo trails we had followed were dispersed among the hills, or crossed over into the more open valleys of other streams.

During the day our road was fatiguing and difficult, reminding us much, by its steep and rocky character, of our traveling the year before among the Wind River mountains; but always at night we found some grassy bottom, which afforded us a pleasant camp. In the deep seclusion of these little streams, we found always an abundant pasturage, and a wild luxuriance of plants and trees. Aspens and pines were the prevailing timber: on the creeks oak was frequent; but the narrow-leaved cottonwood, (*populus angustifolia*,) of unusually large size, and seven or eight feet in circumference, was the principal tree. With these were mingled a variety of shrubby trees, which aided to make the ravines almost impenetrable.

After several days' laborious traveling, we succeeded in extricating ourselves from the mountains, and on the morning of the 28th encamped immediately at their foot, on a handsome tributary to the Arkansas river. In the afternoon we descended the stream, winding our way along the bottoms, which were densely wooded with oak, and in the evening encamped near the main river. Continuing the next day our road along the Arkansas, and meeting on the way a war-party of Arapahoe Indians, (who had recently been committing some outrages at Bent's fort, killing stock and driving off horses,) we arrived before sunset at the Pueblo, near the mouth of the *Fontaine-qui-bouit* river, where we had the pleasure to find a number of our old acquaintances. The little settlement appeared in a thriving condition; and in the interval of our absence another had been established on the river, some thirty miles above.

On the 30th of June our cavalcade moved rapidly down the Arkansas, along the broad road which follows the river.

JULY.

On the 1st of July we arrived at Bent's fort, about 70 miles below the mouth of the *Fontaine-qui-bouit*. As we emerged into view from the groves on the river, we were saluted with a display of the national flag, and repeated discharges from the guns of the fort, where we were received by Mr. George Bent with a cordial welcome and a friendly hospitality, in the enjoyment of which we spent several very agreeable days. We were now in the region where our mountaineers were accustomed to live; and all the dangers and difficulties of the road being considered past, four of them, including Carson and Walker, remained at the fort.

On the 5th we resumed our journey down the Arkansas, traveling along a broad wagon-road, and encamped about 20 miles below the fort. On the way we met a very large village of Sioux and Cheyenne Indians, who, with the Arapahoes were returning from the crossing of the Arkansas, where they had been to meet the Kioway and Camanche Indians. A few days previous they had massacred a party of fifteen Delawares, whom they had discovered in a fort on the Smoky Hill river, losing in the affair several of their own people. They were desirous that we should bear a pacific message to the Delawares on the frontier, from whom they expected retaliation; and we passed through them without any difficulty or delay. Dispersed over the plain in scattered bodies of horsemen, and family groups of women and children, with dog-trains carrying baggage, and long lines of pack-horses, their appearance was picturesque and imposing.

Agreeably to your instructions, which required me to complete, as far as practicable, our examinations of the Kansas, I left at this encampment the Arkansas river, taking a northeasterly direction across the elevated dividing grounds which separate that river from the waters of the Platte. On the 7th we crossed a large stream, about forty yards wide, and one or two feet deep, flowing with a lively current on a sandy bed. The discolored and muddy appearance of the water indicated that it proceeded from recent rains; and we are inclined to consider this a branch of the Smoky Hill river, although, possibly, it may be the Pawnee fork of the Arkansas. Beyond this stream we traveled over high and level prairies, halting at small ponds and holes of water, and using for our fires the ***bois de vache***, the country being without timber. On the evening of the 8th we encamped in a cottonwood grove on the banks of a sandy stream- bed, where there was water in holes sufficient for the camp. Here several hollows, or dry creeks with sandy beds, met together, forming the head of a stream which afterwards proved to be the Smoky Hill fork of the Kansas river.

The next morning, as we were leaving our encampment, a number of Arapahoe Indians were discovered. They belonged to a war-party which had scattered over the prairie in returning from an expedition against the Pawnees.

As we traveled down the valley, water gathered rapidly in the sandy bed from many little tributaries; and at evening it had become a handsome stream, fifty to eighty feet in width, with a lively current in small channels, the water being principally dispersed among quicksands.

Gradually enlarging, in a few days' march it became a river eighty yards in breadth, wooded with occasional groves of cottonwood. Our road was generally over level uplands bordering the river, which were closely covered with a sward of buffalo-grass.

On the 10th we entered again the buffalo range, where we had found these animals so abundant on our outward journey, and halted for a day among numerous herds, in order to make a provision of meat sufficient to carry us to the frontier.

A few days afterwards, we encamped, in a pleasant evening, on a high river prairie, the stream being less than a hundred yards broad. During the night we had a succession of thunder-storms, with heavy and continuous rain, and towards morning the water suddenly burst over the bank, flooding the bottoms and becoming a large river, five or six hundred yards in breadth. The darkness of the night and incessant rain had concealed from the guard the rise of the water; and the river broke into the camp so suddenly, that the baggage was instantly covered, and all our perishable collections almost entirely ruined, and the hard labor of many months destroyed in a moment.

On the 17th we discovered a large village of Indians encamped at the mouth of a handsomely wooded stream on the right bank of the river. Readily inferring, from the nature of the encampment, that they were Pawnee Indians, and confidently expecting good treatment from a people who receive regularly an annuity from the government, we proceeded directly to the village, where we found assembled nearly all the Pawnee tribe, who were now returning from the crossing of the Arkansas, where they had met the Kioway and Camanche Indians. We were received by them with the unfriendly rudeness and characteristic insolence which they never fail to display whenever they find an occasion for doing so with impunity. The little that remained of our goods was distributed among them, but proved entirely insufficient to satisfy their greedy rapacity; and, after some delay, and considerable difficulty, we succeeded in extricating ourselves from the village, and encamped on the river about 15 miles below.

[Footnote: In a recent report to the department, from Major Wharton, who visited the Pawnee villages with a military force some months afterwards, it is stated that the Indians had intended to attack our party during the night we remained at this encampment, but were prevented by the interposition of the Pawnee Loups.]

The country through which we had been traveling since leaving the Arkansas river, for a distance of 260 miles, presented to the eye only a succession of far-stretching green prairies, covered with the unbroken verdure of the buffalo-grass, and sparingly wooded along the streams with straggling trees and occasional groves of cottonwood; but here the country began perceptibly to change its character, becoming a more fertile, wooded, and beautiful region, covered with a profusion of grasses, and watered with innumerable little streams, which were wooded with oak, large elms, and the usual varieties of timber common to the lower course of the Kansas river.

As we advanced, the country steadily improved, gradually assimilating itself in appearance to the northwestern part of the state of Missouri. The beautiful sward of the buffalo-grass, which is regarded as the best and most nutritious found on the prairies, appeared now only in patches, being replaced by a longer and coarser grass, which covered the face of the country luxuriantly. The difference in the character of the grasses became suddenly evident in the weakened condition of our animals, which began sensibly to fail as soon as we quitted the buffalo-grass.

The river preserved a uniform breadth of eighty or a hundred yards, with broad bottoms continuously timbered with large cottonwood-trees, among which were interspersed a few other varieties.

While engaged in crossing one of the numerous creeks which frequently impeded and checked our way, sometimes obliging us to ascend them for several miles, one of the people (Alexis Ayot) was shot through the leg by the accidental discharge of a rifle--a mortifying and painful mischance, to be crippled for life by an accident, after having nearly accomplished in safety a long and eventful journey. He was a young man of remarkably good and cheerful temper, and had been among the useful and efficient men of the party.

After having traveled directly along its banks for 290 miles, we left the river, where it bore suddenly off in a northwesterly direction, towards its junction with the Republican fork of the Kansas, distant about 60 miles; and, continuing our easterly course, in about 20 miles we entered the wagon-road from Santa Fe to Independence, and on the last day of July encamped again at the little town of Kansas, on the banks of the Missouri river.

During our protracted absence of 14 months, in the course of which we had necessarily been exposed to great varieties of weather and of climate, not one case of sickness had ever occurred among us.

Here ended our land journey; and the day following our arrival, we found ourselves on board a steamboat rapidly gliding down the broad Missouri. Our travel-worn animals had not been sold and dispersed over the country to renewed labor, but were placed at good pasturage on the frontier, and are now ready to do their part in the coming expedition.

On the 6th of August we arrived at St. Louis, where the party was finally disbanded, a great number of the men having their homes in the neighborhood.

Andreas Fuentes also remained here, having readily found employment for the winter, and is one of the men engaged to accompany me the present year.

Pablo Hernandez remains in the family of Senator Benton, where he is well taken care of, and conciliates good-will by his docility, intelligence, and amiability. General Almonte, the Mexican minister at Washington, to whom he was of course made known, kindly offered to take charge of him, and to carry him back to Mexico; but the boy preferred to remain where he was until he got an education, for which he shows equal ardor and aptitude.

Our Chinook Indian had his wish to see the whites fully gratified. He accompanied me to Washington, and, after remaining several months at the Columbia College, was sent by the Indian department to Philadelphia, where, among other things, he learned to read and write well, and speak the English language with some fluency. He will accompany me in a few days to the frontier of Missouri, where he will be sent with some one of the emigrant companies to the village at the Dalles of the Columbia.

Very respectfully, your obedient servant, J. C. FREMONT, **Bt. Capt. Topl. Engineers**.

* * * * *

GOLD REGIONS OF CALIFORNIA.

The "placers" or Gold Mines of California, are located in the valley of the Sacramento, in the northern part of that new territory. They are all on the public lands, with the exception of the portion belonging to Messrs. Forbes and Sutter. The region which they embrace and which lies, according to authentic reports, on both sides of the Sierra Nevada, must be "larger than the State of New York." The mines, it is estimated, are worth a thousand millions of dollars. The most reliable information in regard to them may be found in the official reports communicated to the authorities at Washington, by some of the American officers who have visited the region. The following document is of this nature. The author of it, Col. Mason, the military commander in California, speaks, as will be seen, from observation, and the fullest confidence may be placed in his account:--

HEADQUARTERS 10TH MILITARY DEPOT, Monterey, California, Aug. 17, 1848.

SIR:--I have the honor to inform you that, accompanied by Lieut. W. T. Sherman, 3d artillery, A. A. A. General, I started on the 12th of June last to make a tour through the northern part of California. My principal purpose, however, was to visit the newly-discovered gold "placer," in the Valley of the Sacramento. I had proceeded about forty miles, when I was overtaken by an express, bringing me intelligence of the arrival at Monterey of the U. S. ship Southampton, with important letters from Com. Shubrick and Lieut. Col. Barton. I returned at once to Monterey, and dispatched what business was most important, and on the 17th resumed my journey. We reached San Francisco on the 20th, and found that all, or nearly all, its male inhabitants had gone to the mines. The town, which a few months before was so busy and thriving, was then almost deserted.

On the evening of the 25th, the horses of the escort were crossed to Sousoleto in a launch, and on the following day we resumed the journey by way of Bodega and Sonoma to Sutter's fort, where we arrived on the morning of the 2d of July. Along the whole route mills were lying idle, fields of wheat were open to cattle and horses, houses vacant, and farms going to waste. At Sutter's there was more life and business. Launches were discharging their cargoes at the river, and carts were hauling goods to the fort, where already were established several stores, a hotel, &c. Captain Sutter had only two mechanics in his employ, (a wagon-maker and a blacksmith,) whom he was then paying ten dollars a day. Merchants pay him a monthly rent of $100 per room; and while I was there, a two-story house in the fort was rented as a hotel for $500 a month.

At the urgent solicitation of many gentlemen, I delayed there to participate in the first public celebration of our national anniversary at that fort, but on the 5th resumed the journey and proceeded twenty-five miles up the American fork to a point on it now known as the Lower Mines, or Mormon Diggings: The hill-sides were thickly strewn with canvas tents and bush arbors; a store was erected, and several boarding shanties in operation. The day was intensely hot, yet about two hundred men were at work in the full glare of the sun, washing for gold--some with tin pans, some with close-woven Indian baskets, but the greater part had a rude machine, known as the cradle. This is on rockers, six or eight feet long, open at the foot, and at its head has a coarse grate, or sieve; the bottom is rounded, with small cleets nailed across. Four men are required to work this machine: one digs the ground in the bank close by the stream; another carries it to the cradle and empties it on the grate; a third gives a violent rocking motion to the machine; while a fourth dashes on water from the stream itself.

The sieve keeps the coarse stones from entering the cradle, the current of water washes off the earthy matter, and the gravel is gradually carried out at the foot of the machine, leaving the gold mixed with a heavy fine black sand above the first cleets. The sand and gold mixed together are then drawn off through auger holes into a pan below, are dried in the sun, and afterwards separated by blowing off the sand. A party of four men thus employed at the lower mines averaged $100 a day. The Indians, and those who have nothing but pans or willow baskets, gradually wash out the earth and separate the gravel by hand, leaving nothing but the gold mixed with sand, which is separated in the manner before described. The gold in the lower mines is in fine bright scales, of which I send several specimens.

As we ascended the north branch of the American fork, the country became more broken and mountainous, and at the saw-mill, 25 miles above the lower washings, or 50 miles from Sutter's, the hills rise to about a thousand feet above the level of the Sacramento plain. Here a species of pine occurs which led to the discovery of the gold. Capt Sutter, feeling the great want of lumber, contracted in September last with a Mr. Marshall to build a saw-mill at that place. It was erected in the course of the past winter and spring--a dam and race constructed; but when the water was let on the wheel, the tail-race was found to be too narrow to permit the water to escape with sufficient rapidity. Mr. Marshall, to save labor, let the water directly into the race with a strong current, so as to wash it wider and deeper. He effected his purpose, and a large bed of mud and gravel was carried to the foot of the race.

One day Mr. Marshall, as he was walking down the race to this deposit of mud, observed some glittering particles at its upper edge; he gathered a few, examined them, and became satisfied of their value. He then went to the fort, told Capt. Sutter of his discovery, and they agreed to keep it secret until a certain grist-mill of Sutter's was finished. It, however, got out, and spread like magic. Remarkable success attended the labors of the first explorers, and in a few weeks hundreds of men were drawn thither. At the time of my visit, but little over three months after the first discovery, it was estimated that upwards of four thousand people were employed. At the mill there is a fine deposit or bank of gravel, which the people respect as the property of Captain Sutter, although he pretends to no right to it, and would be perfectly satisfied with the simple promise of a pre-emption, on account of the mill which he has built there at considerable cost. Mr. Marshall was living near the mill, and informed me that many persons were employed above and below him; that they used the same machines at the lower washings, and that their success was about the same--ranging from one to three ounces of gold per man daily. This gold, too, is in scales a little coarser than those of the lower mines.

From the mill Mr. Marshall guided me up the mountain on the opposite or north bank of the south fork, where, in the bed of small streams or ravines, now dry, a great deal of coarse gold has been found. I there saw several parties at work, all of whom were doing very well; a great many specimens were shown me, some as heavy as four or five ounces in weight, and I send three pieces labelled No. 5, presented by a Mr. Spence. You will perceive that some of the specimens accompanying this, hold mechanically pieces of quartz; that the surface is rough and evidently moulded in the crevice of a rock. This gold cannot have been carried far by water, but must have remained near where it was first deposited from the rock that once bound it. I inquired of many people if they had encountered the metal in its matrix, but in every instance they said they had not, but that the gold was invariably mixed with washed gravel or lodged in the crevices of other rocks. All bore testimony that they had found gold in greater or less quantities in the numerous small gullies or ravines that occur in that mountainous region.

On the 7th of July I left the mill, and crossed to a stream emptying into the American fork, three or four miles below the saw mill. I struck this stream (now known as Weber's creek) at the washings of Sunol & Co. They had about thirty Indians employed, whom they payed in merchandise. They were getting gold of a character similar to that found on the main fork, and doubtless in sufficient quantities to satisfy them. I send you a small specimen, presented by this company, of their gold. From this point we proceeded up the stream about eight miles, where we found a great many people and Indians--some engaged in the bed of the stream, and others in the small side valleys that put into it. These latter are exceedingly rich, and two ounces were considered an ordinary yield for a day's work. A small gutter, not more than a hundred yards long by four feet wide and two or three feet deep, was pointed out to me as the one where two men-- William Daly and Parry McCoon--had, a short time before, obtained 17,000 dollars worth of gold. Capt. Weber informed me that he knew that these two men had employed four white men and about a hundred Indians, and that at the end of one week's work, they paid off their party, and had left $10,000 worth of this gold. Another small ravine was shown me, from which had been taken upwards of $12,000 worth of gold. Hundreds of similar ravines to all appearances are as yet untouched. I could not have credited these reports had I not seen, in the abundance of the precious metal, evidence of their truth.

Mr. Neligh, an agent of Commodore Stockton, had been at work about three weeks in the neighborhood, and showed me in bags and bottles over $2,000 worth of gold; and Mr. Lyman, a gentleman of education and worthy of every credit, said he had been engaged with four others, with a machine, on the American fork, just below Sutter's mill; that they worked eight days, and that his share was at the rate of $50 a day; but hearing that others were doing better at Weber's place they had removed there, and were then on the point of resuming operations. I might tell of hundreds of similar instances; but to illustrate how plentiful the gold was in the pockets of common laborers, I will mention a simple occurrence which took place in my presence when I was at Weber's store. This store was nothing but an arbor of bushes, under which he had exposed for sale goods and groceries suited to his customers. A man came in, picked up a box of Seidlitz powders and asked the price. Captain Weber told him it was not for sale. The man offered an ounce of gold, but Capt. Weber told it only cost fifty cents, and he did not wish to sell it. The man then offered an ounce and a half, when Capt. Weber *had* to take it. The prices of all things are high, and yet Indians, who before hardly knew what a breech cloth was, can now afford to buy the most gaudy dresses.

The country on either side of Weber's creek is much broken up by hills, and is intersected in every direction by small streams or ravines, which contain more or less gold. Those that have been worked are barely scratched; and although thousands of ounces have been carried away, I do not consider that a serious impression has been made upon the whole. Every day was developing new and richer deposits; and the only impression seemed to be, that the metal would be found in such abundance as seriously to depreciate in value.

On the 8th of July I returned to the lower mines, and on the following day to Sutter's, where, on the 19th. I was making preparations for a visit to the Feather, Yubah, and Bear rivers, when I received a letter from Commander A. R. Long, United States Navy, who had just arrived at San Francisco from Mazatlan, with a crew for the sloop-of-war Warren, with orders to take that vessel to the squadron at La Paz. Capt. Long wrote to me that the Mexican Congress had adjourned without ratifying the treaty of peace, that he had letters from Commodore Jones, and that his orders were to sail with the Warren on or before the 20th of July. In consequence of this I determined to return to Monterey, and accordingly arrived here on the 17th of July. Before leaving Sutter's I satisfied myself that gold existed in the bed of the Feather river, in the Yubah and Bear, and in many of the smaller streams that lie between the latter and the American fork; also that it had been found in the Cosummes to the south of the American fork. In each of these streams, the gold is found in small scales, whereas in the intervening mountains it occurs in coarser lumps.

Mr. Sinclair, whose rancho is three miles above Sutter's on the north side of the American, employs about fifty Indians on the north fork, not far from its junction with the main stream. He had been engaged about five weeks when I saw him, and up to that time his Indians had used simply closely woven willow baskets. His nett proceeds (which I saw) were about $16,000 worth of gold. He showed me the proceeds of his last week's work-- fourteen pounds avoirdupois of clean-washed gold.

The principal store at Sutter's Fort, that of Brannan & Co., had received in payment for goods $36,000 (worth of this gold) from the 1st of May to the 10th of July. Other merchants had also made extensive sales. Large quantities of goods were daily sent forward to the mines, as the Indians, heretofore so poor and degraded, have suddenly become consumers of the luxuries of life. I before mentioned that the greater part of the farmers and rancheros had abandoned their fields to go to the mines. This is not the case with Capt. Sutter, who was carefully gathering his wheat, estimated at 40,000 bushels. Flour is already worth at Sutter's $36 a barrel, and soon will be fifty. Unless large quantities of breadstuffs reach the country, much suffering will occur; but as each man is now able to pay a large price, it is believed the merchants will bring from Chili and Oregon a plentiful supply for the coming winter.

The most moderate estimate I could obtain from men acquainted with the subject, was, that upwards of four thousand men were working in the gold district, of whom more than one-half were Indians; and that from $30,000 to $50,000 worth of gold, if not more, was daily obtained. The entire gold district, with very few exceptions of grants made some years ago by the Mexican authorities, is on land belonging to the United States. It was a matter of serious reflection with me, how I could secure to the Government certain rents and fees for the privilege of procuring this gold; but upon considering the large extent of country, the character of the people engaged, and the small scattered force at my command, I resolved not to interfere but to permit all to work freely, unless broils and crimes should call for interferance. I was surprised to learn that crime of any kind was very unfrequent, and that no thefts or robberies had been committed in the gold district.

All live in tents, in bush arbors, or in the open air; and men have frequently about their persons thousands of dollars worth of this gold, and it was to me a matter of surprise that so peaceful and quiet state of things should continue to exist. Conflicting claims to particular spots of ground may cause collisions, but they will be rare, as the extent of country is so great, and the gold so abundant, that for the present there is room enough for all. Still the Government is entitled to rents for this land, and immediate steps should be devised to collect them, for the longer it is delayed the more difficult it will become. One plan I would suggest is, to send out from the United States surveyors with high salaries, bound to serve specified periods.

A superintendent to be appointed at Sutter's Fort, with power to grant licenses to work a spot of ground--say 100 yards square--for one year, at a rent of from 100 to 1,000 dollars, at his discretion; the surveyors to measure the ground, and place the rentor in possession.

A better plan, however, will be to have the district surveyed and sold at public auction to the highest bidder, in small parcels--say from 20 to 40 acres. In either case, there will be many intruders, whom for years it will be almost impossible to exclude.

The discovery of these vast deposits of gold has entirely changed the character of Upper California. Its people, before engaged in cultivating their small patches of ground, and guarding their herds of cattle and, horses, have all gone to the mines, or are on their way thither. Laborers of every trade have left their work benches, and tradesmen their shops. Sailors desert their ships as fast as they arrive on the coast, and several vessels have gone to sea with hardly enough hands to spread a sail. Two or three are now at anchor in San Francisco with no crew on board. Many desertions, too, have taken place from the garrisons within the influence of these mines; twenty-six soldiers have deserted from the post of Sonoma, twenty-four from that of San Francisco, and twenty-four from Monterey. For a few days the evil appeared so threatening, that great danger existed that the garrisons would leave in a body; and I refer you to my orders of the 25th of July, to show the steps adopted to met this contingency. I shall spare no exertions to apprehend and punish deserters, but I believe no time in the history of our country has presented such temptations to desert as now exist in California.

The danger of apprehension is small, and the prospect of high wages certain; pay and bounties are trifles, as laboring men at the mines can now earn in **one day** more than double a soldier's pay and allowances for a month, and even the pay of a lieutenant or captain cannot hire a servant. A carpenter or mechanic would not listen to an offer of less than fifteen or twenty dollars a day. Could any combination of affairs try a man's fidelity more than this? I really think some extraordinary mark of favor should be given to those soldiers who remain faithful to their flag throughout this tempting crisis. No officer can now live in California on his pay, money has so little value; the prices of necessary articles of clothing and subsistence are so exorbitant and labor so high, that to hire a cook or servant has become an impossibility, save to those who are earning from thirty to fifty dollars a day. This state of things cannot last for ever. Yet from the geographical position of California, and the new character it has assumed as a mining country, prices of labor will always be high, and will hold out temptations to desert. I therefore have to report, if the Government wish to prevent desertions here on the part of men, and to secure zeal on the part of officers, their pay must be increased very materially. Soldiers, both of the volunteers and regular service, discharged in this country, should be permitted at once to locate their land warrants in the gold district.

Many private letters have gone to the United States giving accounts of the vast quantity of gold recently discovered, and it may be a matter of surprise why I have made no report on this subject at an earlier date. The reason is, that I could not bring myself to believe the reports that I heard of the wealth of the gold district until I visited it myself. I have no hesitation now in saying that there is more gold in the country drained by the Sacramento and San Joaquin rivers than will pay the cost of the present war with Mexico a hundred times over. No capital is required to obtain this gold, as the laboring man wants nothing but his pick and shovel and tin pan, with which to dig and wash the gravel; and many frequently pick gold out of the crevices of rocks with their butcher knives in pieces from one to six ounces.

Mr. Dye, a gentleman residing in Monterey, and worthy of every credit, has just returned from Feather river. He tells me that the company to which he belonged worked seven weeks and two days, with an average of fifty Indians (washers) and that their gross product was 273 pounds of gold. His share (one seventh,) after paying all expenses, is about thirty-seven pounds, which he brought with him and exhibited in Monterey. I see no laboring man from the mines who does not show his two, three, or four pounds of gold. A soldier of the artillery company returned here a few days ago from the mines, having been absent on furlough twenty days. He made by trading and working during that time $1500. During these twenty days he was traveling ten or eleven days, leaving but a week, in which he made a sum of money greater than he receives in pay, clothes, and rations during a whole enlistment of five years. These statements appear incredible, but they are true.

Gold is also believed to exist on the eastern slope of the Sierra Nevada; and when at the mines, I was informed by an intelligent Mormon, that it had been found near the Great Salt lake by some of his fraternity. Nearly all the Mormons are leaving California to go to the Salt lake, and this they surely would not do unless they were sure of finding gold there in the same abundance as they now do on the Sacramento.

The gold "placer" near the mission of San Fernando has long been known, but has been little wrought for want of water. This is a spur which puts off from the Sierra Nevada, (see Fremont's map,) the same in which the present mines occur. There is, therefore, every reason to believe, that in the intervening spaces of 500 miles, (entirely unexplored,) there must be many hidden and rich deposits. The "placer" gold is now substituted as the currency of this country; in trade it passes freely at $16 per ounce; as an article of commerce its value is not yet fixed. The only purchase I made was of the specimen No. 7, which I got of Mr. Neligh at $12 the ounce. That is about the present cash value in the country, although it has been sold for less. The great demand for goods and provisions made by sudden development of wealth, has increased the amount of commerce at San Francisco very much, and it will continue to increase.

I would recommend that a mint be established at some eligible point of the Bay of San Francisco; and that machinery, and all the necessary apparatus and workmen, be sent out by sea. These workmen must be bound by high wages, and even bonds, to secure their faithful services, else the whole plan may be frustrated by their going to the mines as soon as they arrive in California. If this course be not adopted, gold to the amount of many millions of dollars will pass yearly to other countries, to enrich their merchants and capitalists. Before leaving the subject of mines, I will mention that on my return from the Sacramento, I touched at New Almoder, the quicksilver mine of Mr. Alexander Forbes, Consul of Her Britannic Majesty at Tepic. This mine is in a spur of the mountains, 1000 feet above the level of the Bay of San Francisco, and is distant in a southern direction from the Puebla de San Jose about twelve miles. The ore (cinnabar) occurs in a large vein dipping at a strong angle to the horizon. Mexican miners are employed in working it, by driving shafts and galleries about six feet by seven, following the vein.

The fragments of rock and ore are removed on the backs of Indians, in rawhide sacks. The ore is then hauled in an ox wagon, from the mouth of the mine down to a valley well supplied with wood and water, in which the furnaces are situated. The furnaces are of the simplest construction-- exactly like a common bake-oven, in the crown of which is inserted a whaler's frying-kettle; another inverted kettle forms the lid. From a hole in the lid a small brick channel leads to an apartment or chamber, in the bottom of which is inserted a small iron kettle. The chamber has a chimney.

In the morning of each day the kettles are filled with the mineral (broken in small pieces) mixed with lime; fire is then applied and kept up all day. The mercury is volatilized, passes into the chamber, is condensed on the sides and bottom of the chamber, and flows into the pot prepared for it. No water is used to condense the mercury.

During a visit I made last spring, four such ovens were in operation, and yielded in the two days I was there 656 pounds of quicksilver, worth at Mazatlan $180 per pound. Mr. Walkinshaw, the gentleman now in charge of this mine, tells me that the vein is improving, and that he can afford to keep his people employed even in these extraordinary times. The mine is very valuable of itself, and will become the more so as mercury is extensively used in obtaining gold. It is not at present used in California for that purpose, but will be at some future time. When I was at this mine last spring, other parties were engaged in searching for veins, but none have been discovered worth following up, although the earth in that whole range of hills is highly discolored, indicating the presence of this ore. I send several beautiful specimens, properly labelled. The amount of quicksilver in Mr. Forbes' vats on the 15th of July was about 2,500 pounds.

I inclose you herewith sketches of the country through which I passed, indicating the position of the mines and the topography of the country in the vicinity of those I visited.

Some of the specimens of gold accompanying this were presented for transmission to the Department by the gentlemen named below. The numbers on the topographical sketch corresponding to the labels of the respective specimens, show from what part of the gold region they are obtained.

1. Captain J. A. Sutter. 2. John Sinclair. 3. Wm. Glover, R. C. Kirby, Ira Blanchard, Levi Fifield, Franklin H. Arynes, Mormon diggings. 4. Charles Weber. 5. Robert Spence. 6. Sunol & Co. 7. Robert D. Neligh. 8. C. E. Picket, American Fort Columa. 9. E. C. Kemble. 10. T. H. Green, from San Fernando, near Los Angelos.

A. 2 oz. purchased from Mr. Neligh.

B. Sand found in washing gold, which contains small particles. 11. Captain Frisbie, Dry Diggings, Weber's Creek. 12. Consumnes. 13. Consumnes, Hartwell's Ranch.

I have the honor to be your most ob't ser't, R. B. MASON, Col. 1st Dragoons, Commanding. Brig. Gen. R. JONES, Adj. Gen. U. S. A., Washington, D. C.

[NOTE.--The original letter, of which this is a copy, was sent to its address, in charge of Lieut. L. Loeser, 3d Artillery, bearer of dispatches, who sailed in the schooner Lambayecana, from Monterey, Aug. 30, 1848, bound for Payta, Peru. Lieut. Loeser bears, in addition to the specimens mentioned in the foregoing letter, a tea-caddy containing two hundred and thirty ounces fifteen pennyweights and nine grains of gold. This was purchased at San Francisco by my order, and is sent to you as a fair sample of the gold obtained from the mines of the Sacramento. It is a mixture, coming from the various parts of the gold district.

R. B. MASON, Col. 1st Drag. Comd'g. HEADQUARTERS 10TH MIL. DEPARTMENT, Monterey, (Cal.,) Sept. 10th, 1848.]

* * * * *

PURITY OF CALIFORNIA GOLD DUST.

The numerous analyses which have been made show that the gold dust of California is remarkably pure. The editor of the Buffalo Commercial Advertiser, under date of December 20th, 1848, says:-- "A small quantity of California gold was shown us this morning. It was in grains, about the size and shape of flax seed. Altogether there was half an ounce. It was received by a gentleman of this city, who, last year, left a quantity of goods in California for sale on commission. A few days ago he received advices that his goods had been sold, and the proceeds remitted in gold dust to New York. The receipts from the mint show its great purity. The weight before melting was 428 ounces; after melting 417. Nett value, $7,685.49."

Gold is seldom found, in any parts of the earth, more than 22 carats fine: and it will be seen by the following report lately made by an experienced smelter and refiner, Mr. John Warwick, of New York city, that the gold dust of California is as pure as that found in any part of this country. Probably there is none in Europe purer:

"I have assayed the portion of gold dust, or metal, from California, sent me, and the result shows that it is fully equal to any found in our Southern gold mines.

I return you 10 3/4 grains out of the 12 which I have tested--the value of which is 45 cents. It is 21 1/2 carats fine--within half a carat of the quality of English sovereigns or American Eagles, and is almost ready to go to the mint.

The finest gold metal we get is from Africa, which is 22 1/2 to 23 carats fine. In Virginia we have mines where the quality of the gold is much inferior--some of it as low as 19 carats, and in Georgia the mines produce it nearly 22 carats fine.

The gold of California which I have now assayed, is fully equal to that of any, and much superior to some produced from the mines in our Southern States."

PHYSICAL GEOGRAPHY OF CALIFORNIA.

Whatever appertains to California, the new El Dorado of the southwest, is interesting to Americans and indeed to the whole civilized world. The following brief account, therefore, of its physical geography, compiled from authentic sources and carefully condensed, will readily receive the attention of the inquiring mind:

"Upper California extends, upon the Pacific, from the 32d parallel of latitude, about seven hundred miles north-westward to Oregon, from which it is divided, nearly in the course of the 42d parallel--that is in the latitude of Boston--by a chain of highlands called the Snowy Mountains; the Sierra Nevada of the Spaniards. Its boundaries on the west are not, as yet, politically determined by the Mexican government; nor do geographers agree with regard to natural limits in that direction. By some, it is considered as embracing only the territory between the Pacific and the summit of the mountains which border the western side of the continent: others extend its limits to the Colorado; while others include in it, and others again exclude from it, the entire regions drained by that river. The only portion occupied by Mexicans, or of which any distinct accounts have been obtained, is that between the great chain of mountains and the ocean; the country east of that ridge to the Colorado appears to be an uninhabitable desert.

"Northward from the Peninsula, or Lower California, the great western-most chain of mountains continues nearly parallel with the Pacific coast, to the 34th degree of latitude, under which rises Mount San Bernardin, one of the highest peaks in California, about forty miles from the ocean. Further north the coast turns more to the west, and the space between it and the summit line of the mountains becomes wider, so as to exceed eighty miles in some places; the intermediate region being traversed by lines of hills, or smaller mountains, connected with the main range. The principal of these inferior ridges extends from Mount San Bernardin north-westward to its termination on the south side of the entrance of the Bay of San Franciso, near the 38th degree of latitude, where it is called the San Bruno Mountains. Between this range and the coast run the San Barbara Mountains, terminating on the north at the Cape of Pines, on the south-west side of the Bay of Monterey, near the latitude 361/2 degrees. North of the San Bruno mountains is the Bolbones ridge, bordering the Bay of San Francisco on the east; and still further in the same direction are other and much higher lines of highlands, stretching from the great chain and terminating in capes on the Pacific.

"The southern part of Upper California, between the Pacific and the great westernmost chain of mountains, is very hot and dry, except during a short time in winter. Further north the wet season increases in length, and about the Bay of San Francisco the rains are almost constant from November to April, the earth being moistened during the remainder of the year by heavy dews and fogs. Snow and ice are sometimes seen in the winter on the shores of the bay, but never further south, except on the mountain tops. The whole of California is, however, subject to long droughts." Heavy rains are of rare occurrence, and two years without any is not unusual; notwithstanding which, vegetation does not suffer to the extent that might be inferred, because, in the first place, many small streams descend from the mountain ranges, supplying the means of both natural and artificial irrigation; and, next, that the country near the coast is favored with a diurnal land and sea breeze; and, from the comparatively low temperature of the sea, the latter is always in summer accompanied with fogs, in the latter part of the night, and which are dissipated by the morning's sun, but serve to moisten the pastures and nourish a somewhat peculiar vegetation abounding in beautiful flowers.

"Among the valleys of Upper California are many streams, some of which discharge large quantities of water in the rainy season; but no river is known to flow through the maritime ridge of mountains from the interior to the Pacific, except perhaps the Sacramento, falling into the Bay of San Francisco, though several are thus represented on the maps. The valleys thus watered afford abundant pasturage for cattle, with which they are covered; California, however, contains but two tracts of country capable of supporting large numbers of inhabitants, which are that west of Mt. San Bernardin, about the 34th degree of latitude, and that surrounding the Bay of San Francisco, and the lower part of the Sacramento; and even in these, irrigation would be indispensable to insure success in agriculture."

"The provincial terms of New Mexico, and of Upper and Lower California, have been, and are yet, rather designations of indefinite tracts than of real defined political sections. The Pacific ocean limits on the west, and by treaty, N. lat. 42 deg. on the north; but inland and southward, it is in vain to seek any definite boundary. In order, however, to give as distinct a view as the nature of the case will admit, let us adopt the mouth of the Colorado and Gila, or the head of the Gulf of California, as a point on the southern boundary of Upper California. The point assumed coincides very nearly with N. lat. 32 deg. and, if adopted, would give to that country a breadth of ten degrees of latitude or in round numbers 800 statute miles from south to north. As already, stated, the Pacific Ocean bounds this country on the west, and lat. 42 deg. on the north. To separate it on the east from New Mexico, we must assume the mountain chain of Sierra Madre, or Anahuac, which, in this region, inclines but little from north to south: whilst the Pacific coast extends in general course north-west and south- east. These opposite outlines contract the southern side to about 500 miles, and open the northern side to rather above 800 miles; giving a mean breadth of 650 miles. The area, for all general purposes, may be safely taken at 500,000 square miles. The general slope or declination of this great region is westward, towards the Pacific and Gulf of California."

"The climate of the western slope of North America has a warmth ten degrees at least higher than the eastern, upon similar latitude. The cause of this difference is the course of prevailing winds in the temperate zones of the earth, from the western points. Thus the winds on the western side of the continent are from the ocean, and on the eastern from the land.

"The soil is as variable as the face of the country. On the coast range of hills there is little to invite the agriculturist, except in some vales of no great extent. The hills are, however, admirably adapted for raising herds and flocks, and are at present the feeding-grounds of numerous deer, elk, &c., to which the short, sweet grass and wild oats that are spread over them afford a plentiful supply of food. The valley of the Sacramento, and that of San Juan, are the most fruitful parts of California, particularly the latter, which is capable of producing wheat, Indian corn, rye, oats, &c., with all the fruits of the temperate, and many of the tropical climates. It likewise offers pasture grounds for cattle. This region comprises a level plain, from fifteen to twenty miles in width, extending from the Bay of San Francisco, beyond the mission of that name, north and south. This may be termed the garden of California; but although several small streams and lakes serve to water it, yet in dry seasons or droughts, not only the crops but the herbage also suffers extremely, and the cattle are deprived of food." The most extensive portion of Upper California--the inland plain between the California and the Colorado range of mountains--is an arid waste, destitute of the requisites for supplying the wants of man. This plain is a waste of sand, with a few detached mountains (some of which rise to the region of perpetual snow,) whose positions are unknown; from these flow small streams that are soon lost in the sand. A few Indians are scattered over the plain, the most miserable objects in creation."

The climate is very peculiar, the thermometer on the coast ranging as high, on the average, in winter as in summer. Indeed, summer is really the coldest and most disagreeable part of the year, owing to the north-west winds which frequently prevail during that season. As you recede from the coast, however, the climate undergoes a great change for the better. At San Juan, thirty miles from the coast, is one of the most delightful climates in the world. The two principal rivers in Upper California are the Sacramento and the San Joaquim. There are, however, many smaller streams flowing through the different valleys, which serve, during the dry season, to irrigate the land. The only navigable stream is the Sacramento.

Beside the bays and harbors of Monterey, Santa Barbara and San Pedro, Upper California possesses the harbor of San Francisco, within a few miles of the Gold Mines, and one of the largest and most magnificent harbors in the world.

The yield of wheat, small grain, and vegetables, is said to be great, and very remarkable, but, as agriculture cannot succeed in Upper California, but by irrigation, it has hitherto happened that it has been principally occupied as a pastoral country--as costing less labor to rear cattle, for which it is only necessary to provide keepers, and have them marked. The numerous animals which are there slaughtered for little more than their hides and tallow, do not putrify and become offensive as they would in other climates, but, as wood is not everywhere as abundant as their bones, the last are sometimes used to supply the place of the former, in the construction of garden fences &c.

"The area of Upper California is about 500,000 square miles, and the population, exclusive of Indians scattered over this extent, as follows:

Californians descended from Spain,	4000
Americans from United States,	360
English, Scotch, and Irish,	300
European Spaniards,	80
French and Canadians,	80
Germans, Italians, Portugese, and Sandwich Islanders,	90
Mexicans,	90
Total	5000

"Upper California is, on the whole, admirably fitted for colonization. This province presents the greatest facilities for raising cattle, for cultivating corn, plants, and for the grape; it might contain twenty millions of inhabitants; and its ports are a point of necessary communication for vessels going from China and Asia to the western coasts of North America.

"It is beyond doubt, that so soon as an intelligent and laborious population is established there, this country will occupy an elevated rank in the commercial scale; it would form the ***entrepot*** where the coasts of the great ocean would send their products, and would furnish the greatest part of their subsistence in grains to the north-west, to Mexico, to Central America, to Ecuador, to Peru, to the north coast of Asia, and to many groups of Polynesia--such as the Sandwich isles, the Marquesas, and Tahiti."

"The peninsula of Lower California, extending from Cape San Lucas to the Bay of Todos Santos, in lat. 32 deg. N., on the Pacific, and to the mouth of the Colorado on the Gulf side, is a pile of volcanic debris and scoriae. Much of the surface is still heated by subterranean fires. No craters are in action; but hot springs of water and bitumen, and frequent earthquakes, and the scorched face of the whole region, demonstrate it to be a mere mass upheaved from the sea, and burned to cinders. The range of mountains that comes up through Lower California, runs on northwardly into Upper California, at an average distance of sixty or seventy miles from the sea, till it falls away into low hills south of the bay of San Francisco. This, also, is a volcanic range; though not so strongly marked to that effect in the Upper as in the Lower Province.

"Some portions of this range are lofty. That part lying east and southeast of El Pueblo de los Angelos, is tipped with perpetual snows. But the greater part of it presents a base covered up to more than half of the whole elevation with pine and cedar forests; the remaining height being composed of bare, dark, glistening rocks, lying in confused masses, or turreted in the manner observed on the Black Hills in the Great Prairie Wilderness---spires, towers, and battlements, lifted up to heaven, among which the white feathery clouds of beautiful days rest shining in the mellow sun.

"The Snowy Mountain range is perhaps the boldest and most peculiar of the California highlands. Its western terminus is Cape Mendocino, a bold snow-capped headland, bending over the Pacific in 40 deg. north latitude. Its western terminus is in the Wind River Mountains, latitude 42 deg. N., about seven hundred miles from the sea. Its peculiarity consists in what may be termed its confused geological character. Near the sea its rocks are primitive, its strata regular. A hundred miles from the sea where the President's range crosses it, everything is fused--burned; and at the distance of seventy miles northeastwardly from the Bay of San Francisco, a spur comes off with a lofty peak, which pours out immense quantities of lava, and shoots up a flame so broad and bright as to be seen at sea, and to produce distinct shadows at eighty miles' distance. Here is an extensive tract of this range which has been burned, and whose strata have been torn from their natural positions; displaying an amalgamated mass of primitive rock *ex loco*, mingled with various descriptions of volcanic remains. From this point eastward, it is a broken irregular chain of peaks and rifted collateral ranges, and spurs running off northwardly and southwardly, some of which are primitive and others volcanic.

"Another range of mountains which deserves notice in this place, is that which bounds the valley of the San Joaquim on the east. This is a wide and towering range. It is in fact a continuation of the President's range, and partakes very strongly of its volcanic character. That part of it which lies eastwardly from the Bay of San Francisco, is very broad and lofty. One of its peaks, Mount Jackson, as it is called, is the highest in all the President's range. Mountains of great size are piled around it, but they appear like molehills beside that veteran mount. Its vast peak towers over them all several thousand feet, a glittering cone of ice.

"All over the Californias, the traveler finds evidences of volcanic action. Far in the interior, among the deserts; in the streams; in the heights; in the plains; everywhere, are manifestations of the fact, that the current of subterranean fire which crossed the Pacific, throwing up that line of islands lying on the south of the Sea of Kamschatka, and passed down the continent, upheaving the Oregon territory, did also bring up from the bed of the ocean the Californias.

"The peninsula, or lower California, which extends from Cape San Lucas in N. lat. 22 deg. 48', to the Bay of Todos Santos in lat. 32 deg. N., is a pile of barren, volcanic mountains, with very few streams, and still fewer spots of ground capable of sustaining vegetation. The territory lying north and south of the Colorado of the west, and within the boundaries of the Californias, is a howling desolation.

"From the highlands near the mouth of the Rio Colorado, a wild and somewhat interesting scene opens. In the east appears a line of mountains of a dark hue, stretching down the coast of the Gulf as far as the eye can reach. These heights are generally destitute of trees; but timber grows in some of the ravines. The general aspect, however, is far from pleasing. There is such a vastness of monotonous desolation; so dry, so blistered with volcanic fires; so forbidding to the wants of thirsting and hungering men, that one gladly turns his eye upon the water, the **Mar de Cortez**, the Gulf of California. The Colorado, two and a half miles in width, rushes into this Gulf with great force, lashing as it goes the small islands lying at its mouth, and for many leagues around the waters of the Gulf are discolored by its turbulent flood. On the west, sweep away the mountains of Lower California. These also are a thirsty mass of burned rocks, so dry that vegetation finds no resting-place among them.

"That province of Lower California varies from thirty to one hundred and fifty miles in width, a superficial extent almost equal to that of Great Britain; and yet on account of its barrenness, never will, from the products of the soil, maintain five hundred thousand people in a state of comfort, ordinarily found in the civilized condition. Every few years tornadoes sweep over the country with such violence, and bearing with them such floods of rain, that whatever of soil has been in any manner previously formed, is swept into the sea. So that even those little nooks among the mountains, where the inhabitants from time to time make their fields, and task the vexed earth for a scanty subsistence, are liable to be laid bare by the torrents. In case the soil chance to be lodged in some other dell, before it reach the Ocean or the Gulf, and the people follow it to its new location, they find perhaps no water there and cannot cultivate it. Consequently they are often driven by dreadful want to some other point in quest of sustenance, where they may not find it, and perish among the parched highlands. The mean range of temperature in the whole country in the summer season is from 60 deg. to 74 deg. Fahrenheit. The rains fall in the winter months; are very severe, and of short duration. During the remainder of the year the air is dry and clear; and the sky more beautiful than the imagination can conceive.

"The range of mountains occupying the whole interior of this country, vary in height from one to five thousand feet above the level of the sea. They are almost bare of all verdure, mere brown piles of barrenness, sprinkled here and there with a cluster of briars, small shrubs, or dwarf trees. Among the ridges are a few spots to which the sweeping rains have spared a little soil. These, if watered by springs or streams, are beautiful and productive. There are also a few places near the coast which are well adapted to tillage and pasturage.

"But the principal difficulty with this region, is one common to all countries of volcanic, origin,--a scarcity of water. The porousness of the rocks allows it to pass under ground to the sea. Consequently one finds few streams and springs in Lower California. From the Cape San Lucas to the mouth of the Colorado, six hundred miles, there are only two streams emptying into the Gulf. One of these is called San Josef del Cabo. It passes through the plantations of the Mission bearing the same name, and discharges itself into the bay of San Barnabas. The other is the Mulege, which waters the Mission of Santa Rosalia, and enters the Gulf in latitude 27 deg. N. These are not navigable. The streams on the ocean coast, also, are few and small. Some of them are large enough to propel light machinery, or irrigate considerable tracts of land, but none of them are navigable. In the interior are several large springs, which send out abundant currents along the rocky beds of their upper courses; but when they reach the loose sands and porous rocks of the lower country, they sink and enter the sea through subterranean channels. A great misfortune it is too, that the lands which border those portions of these streams which run above the ground, consist of barren rocks. Where springs, however, and arable land occur together, immense fertility is the consequence. There is some variety of climate on the coasts, which it may be well to mention. On the Pacific shore the temperature is rendered delightfully balmy by the sea breezes, and the humidity which they bring along with them. Fahrenheit's thermometer ranges on this coast, during the summer, between fifty-eight and seventy-one degrees. In the winter months, while the rains are falling, it sinks as low as fifty degrees above zero. On the Gulf coast there is a still greater variation. While at the Cape, the mercury stands between sixty and seventy degrees, near the head of the Gulf it is down to the freezing point.

"These isolated facts, in regard to the great territory under consideration, will give the reader as perfect an idea of the surface and agricultural capacities of Lower California as will be here needed.

* * * *

DIFFERENT ROUTES TO CALIFORNIA.

There are four different routes to California from the United States. One is from New York to Vera Cruz, thence across Mexico by the *Diligencia*, to Acapulco on the Pacific, where all the northern bound vessels touch. This route would be preferable to all others, were it not for the fact that the road from Vera Cruz to Acapulco is infested with robbers.

Another route is by steam around Cape Horn--a long voyage, though perhaps the cheapest route. It should be performed in our winter, when it is summer in the Southern Hemisphere and consequently warmer at Cape Horn than at any other season of the year. The fare on this route by steam is about $350. The time of performing the voyage is about 130 days.

From New York to Chagres (by steam)---------- $150
From Chagres to Panama, across the Isthmus---   20
From Panama to San Francisco----------------- 250
From New York to Chagres (by sailing vessel)- 80

The time of the voyage is as follows:--

From New York to Chagres----- 12 to 15 days.
From Chagres to Panama-------   2 "
From Panama to San Francisco-   20 "

The following description of Chagres and Panama, will be found both interesting and valuable to the traveler on this route.

THE TOWN OF CHAGRES,

as it is usually called, but in reality village, or collection of huts, is, as is well known, situated at the mouth of the river Chagres, where it empties itself into the Atlantic ocean.

It is but a small village, and the harbor is likewise small, though secure. It is formed by the jutting out of a narrow neck of land, and is defended by the castle, which is built on a high bluff on the other side. The village itself, as I have before said, is merely a collection of huts, and is situated in the midst of a swamp--at least the ground is low, and the continual rains which prevail at Chagres, keep it in a swampy condition. Chagres is inhabited by colored people, entirely, with the exception of some few officials at the castle and in the custom-house. Its population, (I speak, of course, of it previous to the influx,) was probably not more than 500 in all, if so much.

ITS CLIMATE

is, without doubt, the most pestiferous for whites in the whole world. The coast of Africa, which enjoys a dreadful reputation in this way, is not so deadly in its climate as is Chagres. The thermometer ranges from 78 deg. to 85 deg. all the year, and it rains every day. Many a traveler who has incautiously remained there for a few days and nights, has had cause to remember Chagres; and many a gallant crew, who have entered the harbor in full health, have, ere many days, found their final resting place on the dank and malarious banks of the river. Bilious, remittent, and congestive fever, in their most malignant forms, seem to hover over Chagres, ever ready to pounce down on the stranger. Even the acclimated resident of the tropics runs a great risk in staying any time in Chagres; but the stranger fresh from the North and its invigorating breezes, runs a most fearful one.

THE RIVER JOURNEY

is performed in canoes, propelled up the stream by means of poles. There are two points at which one may land, viz: the villages of Gorgona and Cruces. The distance from Chagres to the first named, is about 45 or 50 miles--to the latter, some 50 or 55 miles. The traveler, who for the first time in his life embarks on a South American river like the Chagres, cannot fail to experience a singular depression of spirits at the dark and sombre aspect of the scene. In the first place, he finds himself in a canoe, so small that he is forced to lay quietly in the very centre of the stern portion, in order to prevent it upsetting. The palm leaf thatch (or *toldo*, as it is termed on the river) over his portion of the boat, shuts out much of the view, while his baggage, piled carefully amidships, and covered with oil cloths, *encerrados* as they are termed, is under the charge of his active boatman, who, stripped to the buff, with long pole in hand, expertly propels the boat up stream, with many a cry and strange exclamation. The river itself is a dark, muddy, and rapid stream; in some parts quite narrow, and again at other points it is from 300 to 500 yards wide. Let no one fancy that it resembles the bright and cheerful rivers which are met with here at the North. No pleasant villages adorn its banks--no signs of civilization are seen on them, nothing but the sombre primeval forest, which grows with all the luxury of the tropics down to the very margin of its swampy banks.

A light canoe with two active boatmen and but one passenger in it, will reach Cruces in ten or twelve hours, whilst a heavier one might require thirty-six hours to accomplish the passage. The passenger must take his provisions with him, as none are to be had on the river.

A doubloon ($16) was the lowest charge for a single passenger, and from that up to two, three, and even four doubloons. As for taking our boats from here, and rowing them up the river, I should think it would be a hopeless attempt. Hardy boatmen from our southwestern States, who are accustomed to a much similar mode of travel on their rivers, would probably be able to accomplish it; but in that burning and unhealthy climate, for young men fresh from the North, unacquainted with the dangers of such navigation, and all unacclimated, to attempt such a feat would be madness indeed.

Let us, however, suppose the journey completed, and our adventurer safely arrived at

CRUCES

He may now congratulate himself on having achieved the most toilsome part of his journey, and but twenty-one miles of land route intervene between him and the glorious Pacific Ocean. Cruces is a small village, situated on a plain, immediately on the banks of the river, which here are high and sandy. Gorgona, the other landing place, is a few miles below Cruces, and is likewise a small village, very similar to Cruces--in fact, all South American villages resemble one another very much. From these two points, both about the same distance from Panama, there are roads to that city, which roads unite about nine miles from it. Starting from either point he commences his

JOURNEY ACROSS THE ISTHMUS.

The usual method of performing it, is on horse or on mule-back, with another mule to carry the baggage and a muleteer who acts as guide. The road is a mere bridle path, and as the rains on the Isthmus are very heavy, and there is more or less of them all the year round, the mud-holes and swampy places to be crossed are very numerous. Those who, at the North, talk gaily of a walk across the Isthmus, as if the road were as plain and easy as some of our macadamized turnpikes, would alter their tone a little, could they see the road as it is. As for walking from Cruces to Panama, in case mules are scarce, the feat is by no means impossible, provided the traveler arrives in Cruces in good health, and has but little baggage. It might easily be done with the assistance of a guide; but let no stranger, unacquainted with the language and new to such countries, attempt it without a guide. Having, then, fairly started from Cruces, either on horse or on foot, after a toilsome journey of some eight or ten hours, the Savanna of Panama is at last reached, and the sight of the broad and glittering Pacific Ocean, and the white towers of the Cathedral of Panama, which are seen at the distance of about four miles from the city, give the now weary traveler assurance that his journey will shortly end; and another hour's toil brings him to the suburbs of the famed

CITY OF PANAMA.

We will find, however, that with this, as with most other South American cities,

"'Tis distance lends enchantment to the view, And clothes the mountain with its azure hue."

The city of Panama is situated on the shores of the bay of that name, and a most beautiful bay it is, too. What is the number of the present population, I cannot say, as it is doubtless filled with strangers--it formerly contained from 5000 to 7000 inhabitants, and was a quiet, still city, where, during the day, nought but the sounds of the convent bell and church bells disturbed the horses of the citizens in their grazings in the public squares, which were all overgrown with grass. The trade carried on consisted in importing dry goods from Jamaica, for the supply of the Isthmenians, the neighboring produce of Veragua, the Pearl Islands, the towns of Chiriqui, David, and their vicinities, and the various little inland towns. Goods also were sent down to the ports of Payta, in Peru, and Guayaquil, in the Ecuador. The returns made for these goods, consisted in the produce of the Isthmus: such as gold dust, hides, India rubber, pearl oyster shells, (from which the mother of pearl of commerce is made,) sarsaparilla, &c. The climate is warm, say from 80 to 85 degrees all the year round--the rainy season long and severe. The nights in Panama, however, are much cooler than usual in tropical climate.

The other route is the overland, by Independence. The details of this route are given below by Mr. Edwin Bryant, the author of "What I saw in California." They were communicated to the Louisville Courier in answer to questions but to Mr. B. by the editor:

First--Which route by land is the best for the emigrant?

Answer--The route via Independence or St. Joseph, Missouri, to Fort Daramie, South Pass, Fort Hall, the Sink of Mary's River, &c. &c. the old route. Let no emigrant, carrying his family with him, deviate from it, or imagine to himself that he can find a better road. This road is the best that has yet been discovered, and to the Bay of San Francisco and the gold regions it is much the shortest. The Indians, moreover, on this route, have, up to the present time been so friendly as to commit no acts of hostility on the emigrants. The trail is plain and good, where there are no physical obstructions and the emigrant, by taking this route, will certainly reach his destination in good season, and without disaster. From our information we would most earnestly advise all emigrants to take this trail, without deviation, if they would avoid the fatal calamities which almost invariably have attended those who have undertaken to explore new routes.

Second--What kind of wagon and team is preferable?

Answer--The lightest wagon that can be constructed of sufficient strength to carry 2,500 pounds weight, as the vehicle most desirable. No wagon should be loaded over this weight, for if it is, it will be certain to stall in the muddy sloughs and crossings on the prairie in the first part of the journey. This wagon can be hauled by three or four yokes of oxen or six mules. Oxen are usually employed by the immigrants for hauling their wagons. They travel about fifteen miles per day, and all things considered, are perhaps equal to mules for this service, although they cannot travel so fast. They are, however, less expensive, and there is not so much danger of their starving and of being stolen by the Indians.

Pack-mules can only be employed by parties of men. It would be very difficult to transport a party of women and children on pack-mules with the provisions, clothing and baggage necessary to their comfort. A party of men, however, with pack-mules, can make the journey in less time by one month than it can be done in wagons, carrying with them, however, nothing more than their provisions clothing and ammunition.

For parties of men going out, it would be well to haul their wagons, provisions, &c., as far as Fort Laramie or Fort Hall by mules, carrying with them pack-saddles and *alforgases*, or large saddle-bags, adapted to the pack saddle, with ropes for packing, &c., when, if they saw proper, they could dispose of their wagons for Indian ponies, and pack into California, gaining perhaps two or three weeks' time.

Third--What provisions are necessary to a man?

Answer-- The provisions actually necessary per man are as follows.

Of Flour, ...150 lbs.	Of Bacon, ... 150 lbs.
Coffee,..... 25 "	Sugar, ... 30 "

Added to these, the main items, there should be a small quantity of rice, fifty or seventy-five pounds of crackers, dried peaches, &c., and a keg of lard, with salt, pepper, &c., with such other luxuries of light weight as the person out-fitting chooses to purchase. He will think of them before he starts.

Fourth--What arms and ammunition are necessary?

Answer--Every man should be provided with a good rifle, and if convenient with a pair of pistols, five pounds of powder and ten pounds of lead. A revolving belt pistol may be found useful.

With the wagon there should be carried such carpenter's tools as a hand- saw, auger, gimblet, chisel, shaving-knife, &c., an axe, hammer, and hatchet. The last weapon every man should have in his belt, with a hunter's or a bowie knife.

Fifth--What is the length of the journey?

Answer--From Independence to the first settlement in California, which is near the gold region, is about 2050 miles--to San Francisco, 2290 miles.

Sixth--What is the time for starting?

Answer--Emigrants should be at Independence, St. Joseph, Mo., or the point of starting, by the 20th of April, and start as soon thereafter as the grass on the prairies will permit. This is sometimes by the first of May, and sometimes ten days later, according to the season.

* * * * *

THE GOLD REGIONS--MISCELLANEOUS MATTER.

The following extract is from a letter written by Thomas O. Larkin to Mr. Buchanan, the Secretary of State. It is dated at Monterey, June 28, 1848. I am of the opinion that on the American fork, Feather River, and Copimes River, there are near two thousand people, nine-tenths of them foreigners. Perhaps there are one hundred families, who have their teams, wagons and tents. Many persons are waiting to see whether the months of July and August will be sickly, before they leave their present business to go to the "Placer." The discovery of this gold was made by some Mormons, in January or February, who for a time kept it a secret; the majority of those who are working there began in May. In most every instance the men, after digging a few days, have been compelled to leave for the purpose of returning home to see their families, arrange their business and purchase provisions. I feel confident in saying there are fifty men in this "placer" who have on an average $1000 each, obtained in May and June. I have not met with any person who had been fully employed in washing gold one month; most, however, appear to have averaged an ounce per day. I think there must, by, this time, be over 1000 men at work upon the different branches of the Sacramento; putting their gains at $10,000 per day, for six days in the week, appears to me not overrated.

Should this news reach the emigration of California and Oregon, now on the road, connected with the Indian wars, now impoverishing the latter country, we should have a large addition to our population; and should the richness of the gold region continue, our emigrants in 1849 will be many thousand, and in 1850 still more. If our countrymen in California as clerks, mechanics and workmen will forsake employment at from $2 to $6 per day, how many more of the same class in the Atlantic States, earning much less, will leave for this country under such prospects? It is the opinion of many who have visited the gold regions the past and present months, that the ground will afford gold for many years, perhaps for a century. From my own examination of the rivers and their banks, I am of opinion that, at least for a few years, the golden products will equal the present year. However, as neither men of science, nor the laborers now at work, have made any explorations of consequence, it is a matter of impossibility to give any opinion as to the extent and richness of this part of California. Every Mexican who has seen the place says throughout their Republic there has never been any "placer like this one."

Could Mr. Polk and yourself see California as we now see it, you would think that a few thousand people, on 100 miles square of the Sacramento valley, would yearly turn out of this river the whole price our country pays for the acquired territory. When I finished my first letter I doubted my own writing, and, to be better satisfied, showed it to one of the principal merchants of San Francisco, and to Capt. Folsom, of the Quartermaster's Department, who decided at once I was far below the reality. You certainly will suppose, from my two letters, that I am, like others, led away by the excitement of the day. I think I am not. In my last I inclosed a small sample of the gold dust, and I find my only error was in putting a value to the sand. At that time I was not aware how the gold was found; I now can describe the mode of collecting it.

A person without a machine, after digging off one or two feet of the upper ground, near the water (in some cases they take the top earth,) throws into a tin pan or wooden bowl a shovel full of loose dirt and stones; then placing the basin an inch or two under water, continues to stir up the dirt with his hand in such a manner that the running water will carry off the light earths, occasionally, with his hand, throwing out the stones; after an operation of this kind for twenty or thirty minutes, a spoonful of small black sand remains; this is, on a handkerchief or cloth, dried in the sun, the emerge is blown off, leaving the pure gold. I have the pleasure of inclosing a paper of this sand and gold, which I, from a bucket of dirt and stones, in half an hour, standing at the edge of the water, washed out myself. The value of it may be $2 or $3.

The size of the gold depends in some measure upon the river from which it is taken, the banks of one river having larger grains of gold than another. I presume more than one-half of the gold put into pans or machines is washed out and goes down the stream; this is of no consequence to the washers, who care only for the present time. Some have formed companies of four or five men, and have a rough-made machine put together in a day, which worked to much advantage, yet many prefer to work alone, with a wooden bowl or tin pan, worth fifteen or twenty cents in the States, but eight to sixteen dollars at the gold region. As the workmen continue, and materials can be obtained, improvements will take place in the mode of obtaining gold; at present it is obtained by standing in the water, and with much severe labor, or such as is called here severe labor.

How long this gathering of gold by the handful will continue here, or the future effect it will have on California, I cannot say. Three-fourths of the houses in the town on the Bay of San Francisco are deserted. Houses are sold at the price of the ground lots. The effects are this week showing themselves in Monterey. Almost every house I had hired out is given up. Every blacksmith, carpenter and lawyer is leaving; brick yards, saw mills and ranches are left perfectly alone. A large number of the volunteers at San Francisco and Sonoma have deserted; some have been retaken and brought back; public and private vessels are losing their crews: my clerks have had 100 per cent advance offered them on their wages to accept employment. A complete revolution in the ordinary state of affairs is taking place; both of our newspapers are discontinued from want of workmen and the loss of their agencies; the Alcaldes have left San Francisco, and I believe Sonoma likewise; the former place has not a Justice of the Peace left.

The second Alcalde of Monterey to-day joins the keepers of our principal hotel, who have closed their office and house, and will leave tomorrow for the golden rivers. I saw on the ground a lawyer who was last year Attorney General of the King of the Sandwich Islands, digging and washing out his ounce and a half per day; near him can be found most all his brethren of the long robe, working in the same occupation.

To conclude; my letter is long, but I could not well describe what I have seen in less words, and I now can believe that my account may be doubted; if the affair proves a bubble, a mere excitement, I know not how we can all be deceived, as we are situated. Gov. Mason and his staff have left Monterey to visit the place in question, and will, I suppose, soon forward to his department his views and opinions on this subject. Most of the land where gold has been discovered, is public land; there are, on different rivers, some private grants. I have three such, purchased in 1846 and '47, but have not learned that any private lands have produced gold, though they may hereafter do so.

* * * *

Here is a letter of great sprightliness, beauty and interest, prepared by that finished scholar and noted writer, the Rev. Walter Colton, Alcalde of Monterey.

MONTEREY, California, Aug. 29, 1848.

The gold discoveries still continue--every day brings some new deposit to light. It has been found in large quantities on the Sacramento, Feather River, Yerba River, the American fork--North and South branches--the Cosamer, and in many dry ravines, and indeed on the tops of high hills The tract of country in which it is ascertained to exist, extends some two hundred miles North and South, and some sixty East and West; and these limits are every day enlarging by new discoveries. On the streams where the gold has been subjected to the action of water and sand, it exists in fine grains; on the hills and among the clefts of the rocks it is found in rough, jagged pieces of a quarter or half an ounce in weight, and sometimes two or three ounces.

The gold is obtained in a variety of ways; some wash it out of the sand with bowls, some with a machine made like a cradle, only longer and open at the foot, while at the other end, instead of a squalling infant, there is a grating upon which the earth is thrown, and then water; both pass through the grating,--the cradle is rocked, and being on an inclined plane, the water carries off the earth, and the gold is deposited in the bottom of the cradle. So the two things most prized in this world, gold and infant beauty, are both rocked out of their primitive stage, one to pamper pride, and the other to pamper the worm. Some forego cradles and bowls as too tame an occupation, and mounted on horses, half wild, dash up the mountain gorges and over the steep hills, picking the gold from the clefts of the rocks with their bowie knives,--a much better use to make of these instruments than picking the life out of men's bodies; for what is a man with that article picked out of him?

A larger party, well mounted, are following up the channel of the Sacramento, to discover where this gold, found in its banks, comes from; and imagine that near the river's fount they will find the great yellow mass itself. But they might as well hunt the fleeting rainbow. The gold was thrown up from the bed of the ocean with the rocks and sands in which it is found; and still bears, where it has escaped the action of the element, vivid traces of volcanic fire. It often encases a crystal of quartz, in which the pebble lies as if it had slumbered there from eternity; its beautiful repose sets human artifice at defiance. How strange that this ore should have lain here, scattered about in all directions, peeping everywhere out of the earth, and sparkling in the sun, and been trod upon for ages by white men and savages, and by the emissaries of every scientific association in the world, and never till now have been discovered! What an ass man is, with all his learning! He stupidly stumbles over hills of gold to reach a rare pepper pod, or rifle a bird's nest!

The whole country is now moving on the mines. Monterey, San Francisco, Sonoma, San Jose, and Santa Cruz, are emptied of their male population. A stranger coming here would suppose he had arrived among a race of women, who, by some anomalous provision of nature, multiplied their images without the presence of the other sex. But not a few of the women have gone too, especially those who had got out of tea--for what is women without her tea pot--a pythoness without her shaking trypod--an angel that has lost his lyre. Every bowl, tray, warming-pan, and piggin has gone to the mines. Everything in short, that has a scoop in it that will hold sand and water. All the iron has been worked up into crow-bars, pick-axes and spades. And all these roll back upon us in the shape of gold. We have, therefore, plenty of gold, but little to eat, and still less to wear. Our supplies must come from Oregon, Chili and the United States. Our grain gold, in exchange for coin, sells for nine and ten dollars the ounce, though it is well known to be worth at the mint in Philadelphia eighteen dollars the ounce at least. Such is the scarcity of coin here.

We want a mint. Let Congress send us one at once over the Isthmus; else this grain gold goes to Mazatlan, to Chili and Peru--where it is lost to our national currency. Over a million of gold, at the lowest computation, is taken from these mines every month---and this quantity will be more than doubled when the emigration from they States, from Oregon, the Sandwich Islands, and the Southern republics arrives. Send us a mint! I could give you forty more illustrations of the extent and productiveness of these mines, but no one will believe what I ***have*** said without my name, and perhaps but few with it.

* * * * *

LETTER FROM CAPT. FOLSOM.

The latest and most authentic intelligence from the Gold Regions of California, is the most interesting and the best. The following letter from Capt. Folsom, it will be seen, is of recent date; and on perusal the reader will find it is pregnant with valuable facts:

SAN FRANCISCO, CALIFORNIA, Oct. 8th, 1848.

MY DEAR SIR:--The prices of labor here will create surprise in the United States. Kannakas, or Sandwich Islanders, the worst of laborers, are now employed constantly about town in storing and landing merchandise at a dollar an hour each; and the most indifferent laborers are hired by the week together at six or eight dollars per day. Mechanics obtain, when employed by the day, eight or ten dollars per day, and by the month about six. In a few days, as the sickly season is over, I presume wages will advance, for most of the laboring classes are returning to the mines.

I have just completed the repairs upon a government lighter, preparatory to discharging the cargo of the transport ship Huntress. I attempted to hire a lighter to effect this, but could not get one capable of containing one hundred and twenty barrels manned by two men, short of fifty dollars per day. I have had the master of the government lighter employed for several days in getting a crew for her; and when he offers $80 per month for sailors, he is laughed at, and told that a man can get that amount at the mines in one day.

A few days since, I sent a wagon-master to employ some men to handle stores in the public warehouse. After searching about the town in vain, for several hours, he saw a man on the dock whom he felt sure of getting, for the individual in question did not seem to be blessed with a redundancy of this world's gear. He was wearing a slouched hat without a crown, a dilapidated buckskin hunting shirt or frock, a very uncleanly red woolen shirt, with pantaloons hanging in tatters, and his feet had an apology for a covering in one old shoe, and one buckskin moccasin, sadly the worse for wear and age. When asked if he wanted employment, he replied in the affirmative; and as the young man was proceeding to tell him what he wished to have him do, he was interrupted with "It is not that kind of work, sir, that I want; (at the same time taking a bag containing about *two quarts* of gold dust from his buckskin shirt,) I want to work in the mines, sir. Look here, stranger, do you see this? This bag contains gold dust; and do you suppose I am to make a d----d nigger of myself, handling boxes and barrels for *eight or ten dollars per day?* I should think not, stranger!" And our friend left in a most contemptuous manner. Nor was this a solitary instance of like conduct; they occur daily and hourly in this village.

All sorts of labor is got at enormous rates of compensation. Common clerks and salesmen in the stores about town often receive as high as $2500 and their board. The clerk now in my office is a young boy, who, until a few weeks since, was a *private of volunteers*, and I am now paying him $1500 per annum. This will not appear high, when I tell you that I have just seen upon his table a wash bill, made out and paid, at the rate of eight dollars per dozen; and that almost every thing else is at corresponding prices. The principal waiter in the hotel where I board is paid $1,700 per year, and several others from $1,200 to $1,500. I fortunately have an Indian boy, or I should be forced to clean my own boots, for I could not employ a good body servant for the full amount of my salary as a government officer. It will be impossible for any army officer to live here upon his pay without becoming rapidly impoverished, for his time is not his own to enter upon business; and although he might have money, his opportunities for making it useful to him are few, unless he invests it in real estate. Unless something is done, I am unable to see how it is possible for officers, living upon the salaries granted by law to military men, to support themselves in this country.

I believe every army officer in California, with one or two exceptions, would have resigned last summer, could they have done it and been free at once to commence for themselves. But the war was not then terminated, and no one could hope to communicate with Washington correspondents, to get an answer in less than six, and perhaps ten months. For some time last summer, (August and July,) the officers at Monterey were entirely without servants; and the Governor (Col. Mason,) actually took his turn in cooking for his mess. Unless some prompt action is taken to pay both officers and men serving in this country, in proportion to the unavoidable expenses to be incurred, the former will resign and the latter will desert, and it will be impossible to maintain a military force in California.

I look upon California as perhaps the richest mineral country on the globe. I have written you at great length as to the gold, and since the date of that letter other and richer mines have been discovered. Rich silver mines are known to exist in various parts of the country, but they are not worked. Quicksilver mines are found at innumerable places, and many of them afford the richest ores. The new Almadin mine at Santa Clara gives the richest ore of which we have any accounts. With very imperfect machinery, it yields upward of fifty per cent, and the proprietors are now working it, and are preparing to quadruple their force. Iron, copper, lead, tin, sulphur, zinc, platinum, cobalt, &c. are said to be found in abundance, and most of them are known to exist in various sections of the country.

As an agricultural territory, its great disadvantage is a want of rain; but this is by no means so great as has been represented. I believe California can be made to produce as fine wheat, rye, oats, buckwheat, barley, vegetables, and fruits, especially grapes, as any portion of the world. Nothing that has been fairly tried has failed, and nearly every thing has produced wonderfully. The portions of the soil which are capable of cultivation are inconsiderable in comparison with the whole area of the country; but the soil about this bay, and in many of the large valleys, is equal to the wants of a dense population. It is proverbially healthy, and with the exception of portions of the Sacramento and San Joaquin valleys, no country ever had, at the same period of its settlement, a more salubrious climate.

I think California affords means for the investment of capital such as few other countries offer. Any person who could come in here now with ready cash would be certain of doubling his money in a few months. Large fortunes will be made here within the ensuing year, and I am told that there are some hundreds of persons who have already made on an average $25,000 each. Whole cargoes of goods are sold at an average of about 150 per cent. clear profit, and ready pay in gold dust.

When I came to this place I expended a few hundred dollars in waste lots, covered with bushes and sand hills. The chapter of events which has followed is likely to make this property quite valuable, if I am able to look after it. What cost me less than $800, I suppose I could now sell for $8,000 or perhaps $10,000. It is this consideration which makes me willing to return to a country where my salary is insufficient for my support. If Congress does not increase the pay of officers serving here, I should still be willing to return, in the expectation that my private interests would justify a measure which would otherwise be certain to impoverish me.

Something should be done here at once for the establishment of peace and good order in the country. All law, both civil and military, is at an end. Among the mines, and indeed in most parts of the country out of the villages, no authority but that of the strongest exists, and outrages of the most disgraceful nature are constantly occurring, and the offenders go unpunished. There are now about twenty-five vessels in this port, and I believe there is not one of them that has a crew to go to sea. Frequently the sailors arm themselves, take the ship's boats, and leave in the most open manner, defying both their officers and the civil magistrates. These things are disgraceful to the country and the flag, and while vessels have to pay port charges, duties, &c., their owners ought to be protected. The tariff law of 1846 is now in force in California.

We have not had an American man-of-war in this port for more than a year, and all the naval resources of the United States on this coast are concentrated at Monterey, which is not a harbor but an open roadstead, and which has not one-tenth of the business on its waters which is done in this bay. During the whole year that I was collector of this port, there was not a gun mounted for commanding the entrance of the port, and there was not a United States man-of-war in the harbor. We were exacting a "military contribution," and we possessed not the slightest means of preventing vessels from leaving in defiance of our authority.

In a few months the line of ocean mail steamers will be in operation from Panama to Oregon, and this port is to be a depot for coal, and of course a stopping point in passing both ways. The starting of the line of steamers on this coast is likely to be an undertaking of very great difficulty, and at this time, such is its importance, with reference to both Oregon and California, that its failure might be looked upon as a national calamity. Still, unless some kind of protection is extended to the shipping of this port, it is not at all improbable that it may fail for want of the necessary laborers, as soon as the boats reach this harbor. Indeed, it is altogether probable, unless some competent authority is found here at the time to preserve order, that the crew will quit in a body as soon as the first vessel arrives.

Every possible assistance should be extended to insure the success of this company, and every reasonable latitude should be granted in the execution of their contract. It is now uncertain if the steamers can enter Columbia river at all times in the winter; and they may find it necessary to run up to Paget's Sound. This would be a small inconvenience in comparison to the loss of one of these vessels upon the very dangerous bar at the mouth of the Columbia--an event not at all improbable, if they enter that river in the winter.

* * * * *

NEWSPAPER CORRESPONDENCE.

The following letters were communicated to the "Californian" newspaper, and exhibit very graphically the state of excitement and the actual state of things in the Gold Regions during last summer.

NEW HELVETIA, June 30, 1848.

I have just returned from Fort Sacramento, from the gold region, from whence I write this; and in compliance with my promise, on leaving the sea coast, I send you such items as I have gathered.

Our trip after leaving your city, by way of Pueblo, San Jose, and the San Joaquin river, we found very agreeable. Passing over a lovely country, with its valleys and hills covered with the richest verdure, intertwined with flowers of every hue. The country from the San Joaquin river to this place, is rich beyond comparison, and will admit of a dense population.

We found the fort a miniature Manchester, a young Lowell. The blacksmith's hammer, the tinner, the carpenter, and the weaver's shuttle, plying by the ingenuity of Indians, at which place there are several hundred in the employ of Capt. J.A. Sutter. I was much pleased with a walk in a large and beautiful garden attached to the fort. It contains about eight or ten acres, laid out with great taste, under the supervision of a young Swiss. Among the fruit trees I noticed the almond, fig, olive, pear, apple, and peach. The grape vines are in the highest state of cultivation, and for vegetables, I would refer you to a seedman's catalogue.

About three miles from the fort, on the east bank of the Sacramento, the town of Suttersville is laid out. The location is one of the best in the country, situated in the largest and most fertile district in California, and being the depot for the extensive, gold, silver, platina, quicksilver, and iron mines. A hotel is now building for the accomodation of the travelling public, who are now obliged to impose on the kind hospitalities of Capt. Sutter. A party of men who have been exploring a route to cross the Sierra Nevada mountains, have just returned, and report that they have found a good wagon road on the declivity ridge between the American fork and the McCossamy rivers, the distance being much less than by the old route. The road will pass through the gold district, and enter the valley near the American fork.

A ferry is to be established at Suttersville, on the Sacramento, and the road across the *tularie* improved soon, which will shorten the distance from this place to Sonoma and your city, about 60 miles.

After leaving the fort we passed up on the south bank of the American fork, about twelve miles. This is a beautiful river, about three fathoms deep the water being very cold and clear; and after leaving the river we passed through a country rolling and timbered with oak. We soon commenced ascending the hills at the base of the Sierra Nevada, which are thickly set with oak and pine timber, and soon arrived at a small rivulet. One of our party dipped up a cupful of sand from the bed of the creek, washed it, and found five pieces of gold. This was our first attempt at gold digging. About dark we arrived at the saw-mill of Captain Sutter, having ridden over gold, silver, platina and iron mines, some twenty or thirty miles. The past three days I have spent in exploring the mountains in this district, and conversing with many men who have been at work here for some weeks past. Should I attempt to relate to you all that I have seen, and have been told, concerning the extent and productions of the mines, I am fearful your readers would think me exaggerating too much, therefore I will keep within bounds. I could fill your columns with the most astonishing tales concerning the mines here, far excelling the Arabian Nights, and all true to the letter.

As near as I can ascertain, there are now about 2,000 persons engaged, and the roads leading to the mines are thronged with people and wagons. From one to nine ounces of pure virgin gold per day is gathered by every man who performs the requisite labor. The mountains have been explored for about forty miles, and gold has been found in great abundance in almost every part of them. A gentleman informed me that he had spent some time in exploring the country, and had dug fifty-two holes with his butcher's knife in different places, and found gold in every one.

Several extensive silver mines have been discovered, but very little attention is paid to them now. Immense beds of iron ore, of superior quality, yielding 85 to 90 per cent., have also been found near the American Fork.

A grist mill is to be attached to the saw mill, for the purpose of convenience of families and others settling at the mines. The water power of the American Fork is equal to any upon this continent, and in a few years large iron founderies, rolling, splitting and nail mills will be erected.

The granite of the mountains is superior to the celebrated Quincy. A quarry of beautiful marble has been discovered near the McCossanny river, specimens of which you will see in a few years in the front of the Custom House, Merchants' Exchange, City Hall, and other edifices in your flourishing city.

P. S.-"The cry is still, they come." Two men have just arrived for provisions from the Abjuba river, who state that they have worked five days, and gathered $950 in gold, the largest piece weighing nearly one ounce. They report the quantity on that river to be immense, and in much larger pieces than that taken in other parts.

SONOMA. Aug. 5, 1848.

The mining fever is raging here, as well as elsewhere. Not a mechanic or laboring man can be obtained in town, and most of our male citizens have "gone up" to the Sierra Nevada, and are now enjoying "golden moments." Spades, shovels, pickaxes, hoes, bottles, vials, snuff-boxes, brass tubes, earthern jars, and even barrels, have been put in requisition, and have also abruptly left town.

I have heard from one of our citizens who has been at the Gold Placer a few weeks, and he had collected $1,500 worth of the "root of evil," and was still averaging $100 per day. Another gent, wife and boy collected $500 worth in one day. Another still, who shut up his hotel here some five or six weeks since, has returned with $2,200 in pure virgin gold, collected by his own exertions, with no other aid than a spade, pick and Indian basket.

Three new and valuable lead mines have recently been discovered in this vicinity, and one of our citizens, Mr. John Bowles, of Galena, Ill.--a gent, who has been reported by the Boston press as having been murdered by the Indians, on the Southern route to Oregon, from the States--informed me that the ore would yield 90 per cent., and that it was his intention to erect, as soon as practicable, six large smelting furnaces.

The Colonnade Theatre, at this place, has closed for the season; it was well attended, however, from the time the Thespians made their debut till they made their exit. The "Golden Farmer," the "Omnibus," and a Russian comedy called "Feodora,' (translated from the German of Kotzebue, by Mr. F. Linz, of Sonoma,) were their last attractions.

The military company under command of Capt. J. E. Brackett, are today exchanging posts with Company H., under command of Captain Frisbie, both of the New York Volunteers. Company C. has been stationed with us more than a year, and much praise is due its members, not only for the military and soldier-like manner in which they have acquitted themselves as a corps, but for their gentlemanly and orderly deportment individually and collectively. We regret to part with them, and cannot let them go without expressing a hope that when peace shall have been declared, their regiment disbanded, and their country no longer needs their services, they may have fallen sufficiently in love with our healthy climate and our beautiful valley to come back and settle.

* * * * *

GOLD.

The New York *Evening Post* has an article upon this subject, from which we take the following:

The places where it is found are much more numerous than we might at first suppose. The mines of America, however, surpass those of all other countries. Though of comparative newness, they have furnished three times and a half more gold and twelve times more silver than those of the old world. Silver and gold were, before the discovery of America, supposed to bear to each other the relation of 55 to 1. In Europe the proportion is now about 15 to 1.

The gold of Mexico is chiefly found in argentiferous veins, as at Guanaxuato, where it is obtained one ounce in 360. The only auriferous veins, worked as such, are at Oaxaca. The rivers in Caraccas flow over auriferous sands. Peru is not reported rich in gold at present. The gold of New Grenada is found in alluvial soil, and is washed out in the shape of spangles and grains. The gold of Chili, is found under similar circumstances. Brazil formerly brought the most gold to market, not even excepting Russia, which now, however, surpasses her. All the rivers running from the Brazilian mountains have gold, and the annual product of fine metal is now rated at $5,000,000.

There are no very late tables of the products of the American mines. We have ascertained, by accident purely, how the estimate is made at present.

From 1790 to 1830, forty years, the product of Mexico was:--
Gold   L6,436,453 Silver 139,818,032
Chili--
Gold   L2,768,488 Silver 1,822,924
Buenos Ayres--
Gold   L4,024,895 Silver 27,182,673
Add to this Russia--
Gold   L2,703,743 Silver 1,502,981

And we have from four countries alone 1880 millions of pounds sterling, or forty-seven millions per annum.

If we add the products of Europe and Asiatic Russia, of the East Indies and Africa, which some estimate at thirty-six tons of gold per annum, we perceive that a vast amount of the precious metal is unearthed and somewhere in use. The relative value of gold has certainly changed very much within a few hundred years, and it probably will change still more. But we do not think it is likely to depreciate one-half in our time, for many reasons, though some persons imagine it will.

The true secret of all this present excitement is this: the Anglo Saxon race, for the first time in their history, own and occupy gold mines of very great value. Hitherto Africans, Asiatic or Indians, have held them, and they have never shown that ardor combined with perseverance which belongs to us. England never had any mines of gold, or she would have worked them as diligently as she has those of coal. The Americans have now a golden chance, and they are the first of their blood that have ever had it. They will be sure to turn the opportunity to account.

At our leisure we will refer to some other interesting facts, in relation to the value of gold at different periods. We conclude with recalling one singular circumstance to the recollection of our readers, that when the Romans captured Jerusalem, they obtained so much gold, that the price of it in Syria fell one half.

* * * * *

LIEUTENANT L. LOESER, of the Third Artillery, a graduate of West Point, furnishes the following information respecting the gold region:

"We have been favored by Lieutenant Loeser, bearer of dispatches from Governor Mason to the government at Washington (who also brought on about $20,000 of gold dust, which he deposited at Washington,) with a general description of the gold region, the climate, &c., of California. He says the gold region is very large, and there is sufficient ore to profitably employ one hundred thousand persons for generations to come. So far as discovered, the gold is found in an extent of country four hundred miles long, by one hundred and fifty wide, and no particular portion seems more productive than another. In the river and on the flatlands the gold dust is found; but among the rocks and in the highlands it is found in lumps, from the size of a man's hand to the size of an ordinary duck-shot, all of which is solid, and presents the appearance of having been thrown up by a volcanic eruption. So plenty is the gold, that little care is paid to the washing of it by those engaged when he left; the consequence of which is great quantities are thrown away. In the highlands he was walking with a man who found a piece weighing about thirty-five pennyweights, worth $29, but which he purchased for $4. The piece is solid, and has the form of a perfect acorn on the top of it. He has had it, just as it was found, converted into a breastpin. A man, by ordinary labor, may procure from $50 to $200 per day. With regard to the climate, he says, it is salubrious, at no time being so cold as to require more than a light blanket to sleep under. When he left, the people were sleeping under the trees, without the fear of sickness from exposure. The rainy season begins about the first of November, and continues until March, though there are five clear days for every rainy one. Provisions are generally high, at least such as cannot be obtained in the country. Flour is worth $80 per barrel, though a fine bullock may be obtained for $3. Clothing is very high, and the demand is very great. The Indians, who have heretofore used no clothing whatever, now endeavor to imitate the whites, and will give any price for garments. The report relative to the Mormons requiring 30 per cent. of all the gold found, he says, is a mistake. When the gold was first discovered, one of the leaders of that people demanded that amount from all the Mormons, but they remonstrated, and refused to pay it, which remonstrance caused not the slightest difficulty among the people. He was in San Francisco when the gold was first discovered, about forty miles from that place.

The news was received one day, and the following morning, out of the whole company to which he was attached, every one deserted except two sergeants, and took with them all the horses belonging to the officers. In a few days the city was almost entirely deserted, and Col. Mason, the governor of the territory, was, and has ever since been, obliged to prepare and cook his own food. A servant cannot be had at any price; and the soldiers have not sufficient pay for a month to subsist on for a week. The salary of the governor is not sufficient to support him; and, like all others in the more wealthy circles of life, he is obliged to be his own servant. He speaks of the country as offering the greatest inducements to young men of enterprise, and thinks there is ample room and gold for hundreds of thousands.

* * * * *

ADVICE TO THOSE GOING TO CALIFORNIA BY THE CAPES.

The following article, condensed from correspondence in a daily paper of New York City, will be found to contain many valuable hints to the California bound traveler. It came to hand too late to appear in its proper place, where the four different routes are spoken of:

The first grand desideratum is, to secure comfort on the passage, by the most efficient and economical means, thereby, as far as possible insuring the arrival of the company at their destination in good health and condition.

To insure the most perfect health and comfort attainable on so long a voyage, a vessel should not be fitted up as our European passenger ships are, with bunks for the passengers to sleep in, but the berth deck should be free from bulkheads fore and aft. This arrangement would give plenty of room for the company to swing their hammocks or cots, which could be stowed on deck in pleasant weather, leaving the berth deck free from encumbrance, for the company to amuse themselves with conversation or exercise. Such an arrangement would secure a more perfect ventilation (a very important consideration) than bunks could possibly admit of, as bunks unavoidably harbor filth and vermin, besides leaving very little room for the exercise so absolutely necessary in preventing the diseases incident to a protracted voyage. Before the company proceeds on the voyage, each member should subscribe to a code of regulations, and officers be appointed to carry them into effect.

This arrangement should be made in order to obviate the vexation and annoyance which inevitably occur wherever a large number of persons are promiscuously on shipboard. A simple system, such as regularity of meals and cleansing the interior of the ship, similar to the Navy regulations in that particular, are indispensible and will contribute much to the pleasure, comfort, health, and good fellowship of all on board.

The company should be composed of ***practical persons***-- Agriculturists, Mechanics, and Artisans, as ***nearly equal in pecuniary condition and intelligence*** as circumstances will admit, and it would be very important for the most useful and necessary arts to be well represented. By such an organization, the company would be very efficient; for by taking on board cloth, leather, iron, lumber, brick, &c. their clothing, shoes, iron and wood work of a brick house might be made on board. And would employ the various mechanics connected with those arts, would tend to relieve the monotony of the ocean, and PRACTICALLY ***illustrate the benefits and many advantages*** of a true ***association*** of interests.

The agricultural implements of the most approved method, together with the choicest varieties of young fruit trees and garden seeds, should be provided. Instead of the usual ballast for the vessel, brick and lime, if necessary, could be taken for that purpose, which might be used by the company or disposed of to great advantage at San Francisco. The vessel might be profitably employed in transporting passengers to and from the Isthmus, with great profit to the company, of which the officers and ship's company should be members. A ***skillful surgeon*** should belong to the association. Every member of the company should contribute all the useful books he could, as a library on ship-board would be a constant source of amusement and instruction.

Persons about embarking on so long a voyage should be very particular and have their provisions carefully put up. The United States service rations will be found to be very economical. The following is the weekly allowance per man:--

Sunday   14 oz. bread, 1 1/4 lb. beef, 1/2 lb. flour. Monday   14 oz. bread, 1 lb. pork, 1/2 pint beans. Tuesday   14 oz. bread, 2 oz. cheese, 1 lb. beef. Wednesday 14 oz. bread, 1 lb. pork, 1/2 pint of rice. Thursday   14 oz. bread, 1 1/4 lbs. beef, 1/2 lb. flour. Friday   14 oz. bread, 4 oz. cheese, 2 oz. butter, 1/2 pint rice, 1/2 pint molasses, 1/2 pint vinegar. Saturday   14 oz, bread, 1 lb. pork, 1/2 pint beans, 1/2 lb. raisins.

The spirit ration is omitted.

This is sufficient for the hardest-working seaman. The flour should be kiln dried; any baker can do it. It is only necessary to evaporate all the moisture, and pack it in air-tight casks. Pine-apple cheese is the best and should be put up in water-tight boxes, saturated in alcohol. Sour crout, pickles, &c. are excellent antiscorbutics, and should be eaten freely. Be careful and lay in a good store of "salt water soap."

N. B. The flour should be packed in casks that have contained distilled spirits.

A vessel bound for California by the way of Cape Horn by touching at Rio Janeiro, Brazil and Callao, in Peru, would divide the voyage into three periods, increasing its interest without much addition to its length of time. Rio Janeiro has one of the most magnificent harbors on the globe, far surpassing in natural grandeur the bay of Naples. The approach to the stupendous mountain coast is inexpressibly grand. The entrance to the capacious roadstead is through a narrow strait of great depth of water unobstructed by rock or shoal, flanked on the North by the huge fortress of Santa Cruz; on the South the "Sugar Loaf" rock proudly rears its lofty cone near one thousand feet above the surface of the deep. The entire bay is nearly surrounded by numerous mountain peaks of every conceivable form.

Leaving Rio we prepare to encounter the terrors of the "Horn," having overcome its Westerly gales and "head-beat seas" debouching on the vast Pacific, we career onward before the "trades" to Callao, the port of Lima and capital of the Peruvian Republic. Here the refreshments peculiar to the Tropics are plenty and of excellent quality. We ride at anchor over the ancient City of Callao, (destroyed and sunk by an earthquake 1746,) in sight of the lofty Andes, the mighty cones of Pichnia and Cotopaxi blazing their volcanic fires far above the region of eternal snow, their ice- frosted summits glittering in the sun, forming a dazzling contrast with the clear deep azure of the tropical skies.

Waving adieu to Callao, our canvas spread to woo the "trades," we sweep onward to Alta-California, and entering the "Golden Gate" of the Cornucopia of the Pacific, drop our anchor in the bay of San Francisco.

www.bookjungle.com *email: sales@bookjungle.com fax: 630-214-0564 mail: Book Jungle PO Box 2226 Champaign, IL 61825*

The Codes Of Hammurabi And Moses
W. W. Davies

QTY

The discovery of the Hammurabi Code is one of the greatest achievements of archaeology, and is of paramount interest, not only to the student of the Bible, but also to all those interested in ancient history...

Religion   ISBN: *1-59462-338-4*   Pages:132
MSRP $12.95

The Theory of Moral Sentiments
Adam Smith

QTY

This work from 1749. contains original theories of conscience amd moral judgment and it is the foundation for systemof morals.

Philosophy   ISBN: *1-59462-777-0*   Pages:536
MSRP $19.95

Jessica's First Prayer
Hesba Stretton

QTY

In a screened and secluded corner of one of the many railway-bridges which span the streets of London there could be seen a few years ago, from five o'clock every morning until half past eight, a tidily set-out coffee-stall, consisting of a trestle and board, upon which stood two large tin cans, with a small fire of charcoal burning under each so as to keep the coffee boiling during the early hours of the morning when the work-people were thronging into the city on their way to their daily toil...

Pages:84

Childrens   ISBN: *1-59462-373-2*   *MSRP $9.95*

My Life and Work
Henry Ford

QTY

Henry Ford revolutionized the world with his implementation of mass production for the Model T automobile. Gain valuable business insight into his life and work with his own auto-biography... "We have only started on our development of our country we have not as yet, with all our talk of wonderful progress, done more than scratch the surface. The progress has been wonderful enough but..."

Pages:300

Biographies/   ISBN: *1-59462-198-5*   *MSRP $21.95*

www.bookjungle.com *email: sales@bookjungle.com fax: 630-214-0564 mail: Book Jungle PO Box 2226 Champaign, IL 61825*

The Art of Cross-Examination
Francis Wellman

QTY

I presume it is the experience of every author, after his first book is published upon an important subject, to be almost overwhelmed with a wealth of ideas and illustrations which could readily have been included in his book, and which to his own mind, at least, seem to make a second edition inevitable. Such certainly was the case with me; and when the first edition had reached its sixth impression in five months, I rejoiced to learn that it seemed to my publishers that the book had met with a sufficiently favorable reception to justify a second and considerably enlarged edition. ..

Reference ISBN: *1-59462-647-2* Pages:412 MSRP *$19.95*

On the Duty of Civil Disobedience
Henry David Thoreau

QTY

Thoreau wrote his famous essay, On the Duty of Civil Disobedience, as a protest against an unjust but popular war and the immoral but popular institution of slave-owning. He did more than write—he declined to pay his taxes, and was hauled off to gaol in consequence. Who can say how much this refusal of his hastened the end of the war and of slavery ?

Law   ISBN: *1-59462-747-9*   Pages:48   MSRP *$7.45*

Dream Psychology Psychoanalysis for Beginners
Sigmund Freud

QTY

Sigmund Freud, born Sigismund Schlomo Freud (May 6, 1856 - September 23, 1939), was a Jewish-Austrian neurologist and psychiatrist who co-founded the psychoanalytic school of psychology. Freud is best known for his theories of the unconscious mind, especially involving the mechanism of repression; his redefinition of sexual desire as mobile and directed towards a wide variety of objects; and his therapeutic techniques, especially his understanding of transference in the therapeutic relationship and the presumed value of dreams as sources of insight into unconscious desires.

Psychology   ISBN: *1-59462-905-6*   Pages:196   MSRP *$15.45*

The Miracle of Right Thought
Orison Swett Marden

QTY

Believe with all of your heart that you will do what you were made to do. When the mind has once formed the habit of holding cheerful, happy, prosperous pictures, it will not be easy to form the opposite habit. It does not matter how improbable or how far away this realization may see, or how dark the prospects may be, if we visualize them as best we can, as vividly as possible, hold tenaciously to them and vigorously struggle to attain them, they will gradually become actualized, realized in the life. But a desire, a longing without endeavor, a yearning abandoned or held indifferently will vanish without realization.

Self Help   ISBN: *1-59462-644-8*   Pages:360   MSRP *$25.45*

www.bookjungle.com email: sales@bookjungle.com fax: 630-214-0564 mail: Book Jungle PO Box 2226 Champaign, IL 61825

QTY

	Title	ISBN	Price
☐	**The Rosicrucian Cosmo-Conception Mystic Christianity** by *Max Heindel*	ISBN: 1-59462-188-8	$38.95
	The Rosicrucian Cosmo-conception is not dogmatic, neither does it appeal to any other authority than the reason of the student. It is: not controversial, but is: sent forth in the, hope that it may help to clear...		New Age/Religion Pages 646
☐	**Abandonment To Divine Providence** by *Jean-Pierre de Caussade*	ISBN: 1-59462-228-0	$25.95
	"The Rev. Jean Pierre de Caussade was one of the most remarkable spiritual writers of the Society of Jesus in France in the 18th Century. His death took place at Toulouse in 1751. His works have gone through many editions and have been republished...		Inspirational/Religion Pages 400
☐	**Mental Chemistry** by *Charles Haanel*	ISBN: 1-59462-192-6	$23.95
	Mental Chemistry allows the change of material conditions by combining and appropriately utilizing the power of the mind. Much like applied chemistry creates something new and unique out of careful combinations of chemicals the mastery of mental chemistry...		New Age Pages 354
☐	**The Letters of Robert Browning and Elizabeth Barret Barrett 1845-1846 vol II** by *Robert Browning and Elizabeth Barrett*	ISBN: 1-59462-193-4	$35.95
			Biographies Pages 596
☐	**Gleanings In Genesis (volume I)** by *Arthur W. Pink*	ISBN: 1-59462-130-6	$27.45
	Appropriately has Genesis been termed "the seed plot of the Bible" for in it we have, in germ form, almost all of the great doctrines which are afterwards fully developed in the books of Scripture which follow...		Religion/Inspirational Pages 420
☐	**The Master Key** by *L. W. de Laurence*	ISBN: 1-59462-001-6	$30.95
	In no branch of human knowledge has there been a more lively increase of the spirit of research during the past few years than in the study of Psychology, Concentration and Mental Discipline. The requests for authentic lessons in Thought Control, Mental Discipline and...		New Age/Business Pages 422
☐	**The Lesser Key Of Solomon Goetia** by *L. W. de Laurence*	ISBN: 1-59462-092-X	$9.95
	This translation of the first book of the "Lernegton" which is now for the first time made accessible to students of Talismanic Magic was done, after careful collation and edition, from numerous Ancient Manuscripts in Hebrew, Latin, and French...		New Age/Occult Pages 92
☐	**Rubaiyat Of Omar Khayyam** by *Edward Fitzgerald*	ISBN: 1-59462-332-5	$13.95
	Edward Fitzgerald, whom the world has already learned, in spite of his own efforts to remain within the shadow of anonymity, to look upon as one of the rarest poets of the century, was born at Bredfield, in Suffolk, on the 31st of March, 1809. He was the third son of John Purcell...		Music Pages 172
☐	**Ancient Law** by *Henry Maine*	ISBN: 1-59462-128-4	$29.95
	The chief object of the following pages is to indicate some of the earliest ideas of mankind, as they are reflected in Ancient Law, and to point out the relation of those ideas to modern thought.		Religion/History Pages 452
☐	**Far-Away Stories** by *William J. Locke*	ISBN: 1-59462-129-2	$19.45
	"Good wine needs no bush, but a collection of mixed vintages does. And this book is just such a collection. Some of the stories I do not want to remain buried for ever in the museum files of dead magazine-numbers an author's not unpardonable vanity..."		Fiction Pages 272
☐	**Life of David Crockett** by *David Crockett*	ISBN: 1-59462-250-7	$27.45
	"Colonel David Crockett was one of the most remarkable men of the times in which he lived. Born in humble life, but gifted with a strong will, an indomitable courage, and unremitting perseverance...		Biographies/New Age Pages 424
☐	**Lip-Reading** by *Edward Nitchie*	ISBN: 1-59462-206-X	$25.95
	Edward B. Nitchie, founder of the New York School for the Hard of Hearing, now the Nitchie School of Lip-Reading, Inc, wrote "LIP-READING Principles and Practice". The development and perfecting of this meritorious work on lip-reading was an undertaking...		How-to Pages 400
☐	**A Handbook of Suggestive Therapeutics, Applied Hypnotism, Psychic Science** by *Henry Munro*	ISBN: 1-59462-214-0	$24.95
			Health/New Age/Health/Self-help Pages 376
☐	**A Doll's House: and Two Other Plays** by *Henrik Ibsen*	ISBN: 1-59462-112-8	$19.95
	Henrik Ibsen created this classic when in revolutionary 1848 Rome. Introducing some striking concepts in playwriting for the realist genre, this play has been studied the world over.		Fiction/Classics/Plays 308
☐	**The Light of Asia** by *sir Edwin Arnold*	ISBN: 1-59462-204-3	$13.95
	In this poetic masterpiece, Edwin Arnold describes the life and teachings of Buddha. The man who was to become known as Buddha to the world was born as Prince Gautama of India but he rejected the worldly riches and abandoned the reigns of power when...		Religion/History/Biographies Pages 170
☐	**The Complete Works of Guy de Maupassant** by *Guy de Maupassant*	ISBN: 1-59462-157-8	$16.95
	"For days and days, nights and nights, I had dreamed of that first kiss which was to consecrate our engagement, and I knew not on what spot I should put my lips..."		Fiction/Classics Pages 240
☐	**The Art of Cross-Examination** by *Francis L. Wellman*	ISBN: 1-59462-309-0	$26.95
	Written by a renowned trial lawyer, Wellman imparts his experience and uses case studies to explain how to use psychology to extract desired information through questioning.		How-to/Science/Reference Pages 408
☐	**Answered or Unanswered?** by *Louisa Vaughan*	ISBN: 1-59462-248-5	$10.95
	Miracles of Faith in China		Religion Pages 112
☐	**The Edinburgh Lectures on Mental Science (1909)** by *Thomas*	ISBN: 1-59462-008-3	$11.95
	This book contains the substance of a course of lectures recently given by the writer in the Queen Street Hall, Edinburgh. Its purpose is to indicate the Natural Principles governing the relation between Mental Action and Material Conditions...		New Age/Psychology Pages 148
☐	**Ayesha** by *H. Rider Haggard*	ISBN: 1-59462-301-5	$24.95
	Verily and indeed it is the unexpected that happens! Probably if there was one person upon the earth from whom the Editor of this, and of a certain previous history, did not expect to hear again...		Classics Pages 380
☐	**Ayala's Angel** by *Anthony Trollope*	ISBN: 1-59462-352-X	$29.95
	The two girls were both pretty, but Lucy who was twenty-one who supposed to be simple and comparatively unattractive, whereas Ayala was credited, as her Bombwhat romantic name might show, with poetic charm and a taste for romance. Ayala when her father died was nineteen...		Fiction Pages 484
☐	**The American Commonwealth** by *James Bryce*	ISBN: 1-59462-286-8	$34.45
	An interpretation of American democratic political theory. It examines political mechanics and society from the perspective of Scotsman James Bryce		Politics Pages 572
☐	**Stories of the Pilgrims** by *Margaret P. Pumphrey*	ISBN: 1-59462-116-0	$17.95
	This book explores pilgrims religious oppression in England as well as their escape to Holland and eventual crossing to America on the Mayflower, and their early days in New England...		History Pages 268

www.bookjungle.com email: sales@bookjungle.com fax: 630-214-0564 mail: Book Jungle PO Box 2226 Champaign, IL 61825

			QTY
The Fasting Cure by *Sinclair Upton*	ISBN: *1-59462-222-1*	**$13.95**	
In the Cosmopolitan Magazine for May, 1910, and in the Contemporary Review (London) for April, 1910, I published an article dealing with my experiences in fasting. I have written a great many magazine articles, but never one which attracted so much attention...		*New Age/Self Help/Health Pages 164*	
Hebrew Astrology by *Sepharial*	ISBN: *1-59462-308-2*	**$13.45**	
In these days of advanced thinking it is a matter of common observation that we have left many of the old landmarks behind and that we are now pressing forward to greater heights and to a wider horizon than that which represented the mind-content of our progenitors...		*Astrology Pages 144*	
Thought Vibration or The Law of Attraction in the Thought World	ISBN: *1-59462-127-6*	**$12.95**	
by *William Walker Atkinson*		*Psychology/Religion Pages 144*	
Optimism by *Helen Keller*	ISBN: *1-59462-108-X*	**$15.95**	
Helen Keller was blind, deaf, and mute since 19 months old, yet famously learned how to overcome these handicaps, communicate with the world, and spread her lectures promoting optimism. An inspiring read for everyone...		*Biographies/Inspirational Pages 84*	
Sara Crewe by *Frances Burnett*	ISBN: *1-59462-360-0*	**$9.45**	
In the first place, Miss Minchin lived in London. Her home was a large, dull, tall one, in a large, dull square, where all the houses were alike, and all the sparrows were alike, and where all the door-knockers made the same heavy sound...		*Childrens/Classic Pages 88*	
The Autobiography of Benjamin Franklin by *Benjamin Franklin*	ISBN: *1-59462-135-7*	**$24.95**	
The Autobiography of Benjamin Franklin has probably been more extensively read than any other American historical work, and no other book of its kind has had such ups and downs of fortune. Franklin lived for many years in England, where he was agent...		*Biographies/History Pages 332*	

Name	
Email	
Telephone	
Address	
City, State ZIP	

☐ Credit Card   ☐ Check / Money Order

Credit Card Number	
Expiration Date	
Signature	

Please Mail to: Book Jungle
                    PO Box 2226
                    Champaign, IL 61825
or Fax to: 630-214-0564

ORDERING INFORMATION

web: *www.bookjungle.com*
email: *sales@bookjungle.com*
fax: *630-214-0564*
mail: *Book Jungle PO Box 2226 Champaign, IL 61825*
or PayPal *to sales@bookjungle.com*

Please contact us for bulk discounts

DIRECT-ORDER TERMS

20% Discount if You Order Two or More Books
Free Domestic Shipping!
Accepted: Master Card, Visa, Discover, American Express

www.ingramcontent.com/pod-product-compliance
Lightning Source LLC
Chambersburg PA
CBHW082104230426
43671CB00015B/2600